Designing Authenticity into Language Learning Materials

Freda Mishan

intellect™
Bristol, UK
Portland, OR, USA

First Published in the UK in 2005 by

Intellect Books, PO Box 862, Bristol BS99 1DE, UK

First Published in the USA in 2005 by

Intellect Books, ISBS, 920 NE 58th Ave. Suite 300, Portland, Oregon 97213-3786, USA

A catalogue record for this book is available from the British Library

ISBN 1-84150-080-1

Cover Design: David Lilburn, University of Limerick, Limerick, Ireland

Copy Editor: Holly Spradling

Printed and bound in Great Britain by Antony Rowe Ltd.

For Reuben and Bob

Table of Contents

viii   Acknowledgements
ix   Introduction
ix   Materials design
x   Authenticity
xi   Aims
xi   Outline
xii   Terminology

1   PART I: AUTHENTICITY IN LANGUAGE LEARNING:
THE THEORETICAL GROUNDING

1   Chapter 1:
Authenticity in language learning:
background and definition
1   1.1   Authenticity in language learning:
the historical background
10   1.2   Towards a definition of authenticity

21   Chapter 2:
Authentic texts for language learning:
the SLA rationale
21   2.1   Introduction
22   2.2   Input
25   2.3   Affect: motivation
27   2.4   Affect: the 'affective filter', engagement, empathy
and attitude
29   2.5   Learning style
32   2.6   Instructed SLA
36   2.7   Autonomous learning
37   2.8   Consciousness-raising
38   2.9   Language processing
41   2.10   Conclusion

44   Chapter 3:
Authentic texts for language learning:
the pedagogical rationale
45   3.1   Culture
55   3.2   Currency
60   3.3   Challenge
64   3.4   Conclusion

67   Chapter 4:
Authentic texts and authentic tasks

67 4.1   Introduction
67 4.2   Task
70 4.3   Towards a framework for task authenticity
83 4.4   Task typologies
92 4.5   Conclusion

95   **PART II: USING CULTURAL PRODUCTS FOR LANGUAGE LEARNING:** A TEACHING RESOURCE
95   The 3 c's: culture, currency and challenge
96   The tasks

97   **Chapter 5: Literature**
97 5.1   Defining literature
100 5.2   Literature and culture
104 5.3   Literature and currency
109 5.4   The 'challenge' of literature
112 5.5   Literature for language learning: summary and principles
113 5.6   The tasks

132   **Chapter 6 : The broadcast media**
132 6.1   Television: Using entertainment media for learning
135 6.2   Television and culture
136 6.3   Television and currency
137 6.4   The challenge of television
138 6.5   Radio
139 6.6   The broadcast media for language learning: summary and principles
140 6.7   The tasks

154   **Chapter 7: Newspapers**
154 7.1   Newspapers and culture
156 7.2   Newspapers and currency
162 7.3   The challenge of newspapers
163 7.4   Newspapers for language learning: summary and principles
164 7.5   The tasks

182   **Chapter 8: Advertising**
182 8.1   Advertising and currency
185 8.2   Advertising and culture
188 8.3   Advertisements for language learning: summary and principles
189 8.4   The tasks

196   **Chapter 9: Song and music**
196 9.1   Song and culture

197 9.2   Song and currency
204 9.3   The challenge of song
206 9.4   Songs for language learning: summary and
                 principles
207 9.5   The tasks

216 Chapter 10: Film
216 10.1   The challenge of film
225 10.2   Film and culture
227 10.3   Film for language learning: summary and principles
228 10.4   The tasks

241 Chapter 11: ICT
241 11.1   Introduction
242 11.2   The Web
250 11.3   E-mail
256 11.4   Corpora and concordancing
264 11.5   Conclusion
265 11.6   The tasks

283 Appendix I
285 Appendix II
287 Bibliography
315 Index

Acknowledgements

A great debt of gratitude goes to the supervisors of the research that underpinned this book, Professor Angela Chambers and Dr Jean E. Conacher, both of the Department of Languages and Cultural Studies, University of Limerick. I am immensely grateful to Professor Chambers who, as the book took form, gave so generously of her time and her academic expertise, and who was such a consistent motivating force. I would also like to thank the other members of the Department of Languages and Cultural Studies, the University of Limerick Language Centre and Mary Immaculate College, Limerick, who took part in initial trials of the tasks developed for the resource section of the book.

I must also acknowledge the generous financial support of the IRCHSS (the Irish Research Council for the Humanities and Social Sciences) whose post-Doctoral award to me over the period 2001-2003 made the writing of this book possible.

On a more personal level, heartfelt thanks to my husband Bob Strunz who gave me so much moral, practical and technical support. Also to my parents, E. J. Mishan and Ray, for setting me off on the academic track and for their continuing encouragement. And finally, one of my biggest debts to the smallest person, Reuben, whose own language learning over the course of my writing of this book has been such an unending source of inspiration and delight.

Introduction

Nobody who has witnessed language blossoming in a small child can be in any doubt that language learning is a natural - an *authentic* - activity. It is ironic, therefore, that the 20th century - a century which saw an unprecedented interest and growth in second language learning - initially brought forth some of history's most contrived methods for teaching it. This is not to say that such methods as the Audiolingual or Direct methods were necessarily the less effective because of this, but it was not until the late 1960s that the most 'natural' approach - the learning of language *as* communication and *through* communication - began to take root.

The Communicative ethos has by now become engrained in language teaching (in the West at least) and has been consolidated by the revolution in information and communications technologies (ICT). ICT effectively concretised the concept of communication at the same time as opening up unlimited access to authentic texts from the target language culture, thereby impelling the issue of authenticity of texts and interactions to the fore in language pedagogy.

This then is essentially the background to what is put forward in this book, a comprehensive approach to exploiting authentic texts in the language classroom. This 'authenticity-centred' approach directly informs the design of language learning materials -exemplifying the symbiotic relationship (pointed out by Nunan 1989: 15), between the *approach* to learning and the *content/materials* used in applying it. The central premises of the authenticity-centred approach are the use of authentic texts for language learning and the preserving of this authenticity throughout the procedures in which they are implicated. The rationale for this approach - essentially, the reasons *why* authenticity is important at all in language learning - draws, as Chapters 2 and 3 explain, on second language acquisition research on the one hand, and on pedagogical experience on the other.

The authenticity-centred approach deploys a pedagogical model that has become broadly accepted and applied in language learning, the *task*. Task in relation to language learning is generally described in such terms as 'a goal-oriented communicative activity with a specific outcome where the emphasis is on exchanging meanings, not producing specific language forms' (Willis 1996: 36). The marriage of the authentic text and the task model is a felicitous one, in that both derive from the 'real-world', with the notion of task in pedagogy today broadening to encompass personal and divergent tasks as well as more practical ones.

Materials Design

The authenticity approach is materials-centred and upholds the importance of materials design not only as a professional skill applied by coursebook writers, but as one used by individual teachers in individual teaching contexts. Materials design remains a fairly neglected area in English Language Teaching (ELT) research and publication; 'the professional literature on language pedagogy has, until this time, benignly overlooked the act of writing' (Dubin 1995: 13) (whether this is due to a reluctance on the part of ELT publishing houses to endorse materials writing as a non-professional skill that might eventually undercut their market, is a matter for speculation). Responding to this effective gap in the literature, the handful of recent books in the area, notably Byrd 1995, Tomlinson 1998 and McGrath 2002, are all geared towards redressing the lack of a systematic approach to materials design and evaluation, and to research in the field. All of these works also voice the need for recognition of materials development as a 'professional track' within the professional field of ELT (see, for example, Byrd 1995: 6). Significantly, a common thread in all of these recent publications is the one that is the major focus of this book, the use of authentic texts for language learning and teaching.

Another concern voiced in recent literature in this field comes out of today's heightened consciousness of cultural identities and differences. The endeavour to produce 'global' language learning coursebooks that are suited to a range of cultural audiences makes coursebook-writing today a frustrating activity that is fraught with compromises (see, for example, Pulverness 1999a, 1999c; Rinvolucri 1999; Bell and Gower 1998). The logical solution - for teachers to produce their own materials from within their own teaching contexts (possibly publishing them at national level) - is one being touted by growing numbers of practitioners (e.g. Jolly and Bolitho 1998: 110-1, McGrath 2002). One of the objectives of this book is to offer some direction for materials design for teachers in this predicament

Authenticity

It is perhaps incumbent to deal at the outset with the issue of adopting terms like *authentic* and *authenticity,* so weighted by the value judgements implicit in their gloss as *real, genuine, bona fida, pure*[1]. Such value judgements have meant that *authentic* materials and *authenticity* are a naturally appealing proposition for language practitioners and learners alike. Their opposite poles - *inauthenticity* and *artifice* - appear at first glance to offer mean and meagre pickings by comparison. Yet, as has eloquently been described in Cook (2000), artifice in language, 'language play', is at the heart of the learning of our first language and remains central to our socialisation throughout our lives. The 'artificiality' of the classroom (Hughes 1981: 7) and the suspension of reality in the pedagogical situation (Widdowson 1984) reveal learners as willing collaborators in the learning game. It is interesting to surmise, therefore, what, at the eve of the 20th century, made the appeal of authenticity so strong as to have become the predominant paradigm for the language teaching classroom. The theoretical 'authenticity debate' (covered in some detail in Chapter 1 of this book) has been all but sidelined in the rush to exploit authentic texts for pedagogical purposes. The authenticity 'explosion' is probably in part a consequence of the symbiotic relationship between two movements - the one sociological and the other pedagogical. The first is the aforementioned revolution in information and communications technologies (ICT), which has opened up access to authentic texts of all types in hundreds of world languages. The second is the shift towards self-direction in learning, the transferring of the responsibility for learning, and the paths to information and knowledge, from the teacher to the learner. All this means that today's language learner has high expectations of authenticity - of target language texts, of facts about the target culture and, not least, of the interactions used to obtain this information.

Aims

This book is intended to be of interest to linguists, language teachers, teacher trainers and trainees. The book's structure and content reflect an attempt to break out of the 'theoretical' versus 'practical' genre division in ELT publications, while at the same time broadening the scope of the latter by covering not one, but a cross-section of genres and media. While not attempting to supplant the comprehensive coverage of single genre resource books (to which the reader is referred in 'further reading' sections) this book is intended as a 'one-stop' publication for language teachers who are interested in sourcing authentic texts from a range of cultural products and in using classroom tasks that are correspondingly authentic. It is envisaged that the book might therefore serve either as a supplementary resource to the traditional syllabus, or, more optimistically, as a basis for the type of text-driven syllabus described in Chapter 3.

Outline

The book falls into two parts. The first is principally theoretical and consists of four chapters. The second part consists of seven chapters each focusing on one cultural product. Each of these chapters covers the pedagogical issues involved in using the cultural product for language learning and follows this up with a database of classroom tasks.

The content of the book, in affectionate homage to the author's teaching background, basically responds to the *who, what, why, where, how,* of authenticity and language learning.

Who used authentic texts in the past? (Chapter 1)
What are 'authenticity' and 'authentic texts'? (Chapter 1)
Why use authentic texts for language learning? (Chapters 2 and 3)
How do we use authentic texts in language learning materials? (Chapters 4 to 11)
Where do we source authentic texts (Chapters 5 to 11)

The first chapter of the book gives the historical background to the concept of authenticity in language teaching, then traces recent trends with the aim of offering a working definition of authenticity in the language learning context. In Chapter 2, findings of SLA research are presented to endorse the use of authentic texts in language learning. The third chapter establishes the pedagogical rationale for the use of authentic texts, crystallising these as 'the 3 c's' - *culture, currency* and *challenge*. Chapter 4 constitutes the transition between the theoretical part

(Part I) and the practical part (Part II) of the book, concretising the authenticity-centred approach into a practical framework for authentic task design.

Chapters 5 to 11 cover seven different 'cultural products' - literature, newspapers, the broadcast media, film, song, advertisements and ICT respectively. The strengths of each as potential language learning material are highlighted and the particular types of tasks suited to it are discussed. Each 'cultural product' chapter is backed up by a *summary of the main principles* of its use in language learning, a brief *guide for further reading* and a *task reference section* containing a set of step-by-step descriptions of classroom tasks for that cultural product.

Terminology

Most of the terminology and acronyms used in this book are fairly standard. Certain terms, however, need to be carefully delineated in the context of the subject matter. Notably, two of the core terms are distinguished in line with the conventions used in other publications in the field (Tomlinson 1998, McGrath 2002), *viz.*: *text* is used to refer to audio, visual and graphic as well as printed texts which are drawn from the target culture (*TC* - see below), while the term *material* is used to refer to the combination of the text and the language learning activity/ies based on it.

Activity: Action or exercise involving the target language, but not necessarily goal-oriented (see *Task* below). A *task* may constitute a number of *activities*.

Cultural Product: the concept of *cultural products* is used in Tomalin and Stempleski (1993: 6-7) and Carter (1998: 50) and is adopted in this book as the supernym for the materials drawn from a variety of media and genres from the target culture.

Discourse type: Discourse type is identified through *medium* (the physical way in which the linguistic message is transmitted to its receiver i.e. via phonic or graphic means) and on a cline of *modes* from spoken to written (distinctions based on McCarthy and Carter 1994: 4-9). There are an almost infinite number of discourse types which may vary from culture to culture. In English, samples of discourse types range from conversation to lecture, from newspaper article to novel, from advertising jingle to opera. The cultural products discussed in the book are sub-categorised by discourse type in the task databases.

ELT: English language teaching

FL: Foreign language

Genre: 'A genre comprises a class of communicative events, the members of which share some set of communicative purposes [...] exemplars of a genre exhibit various patterns of similarity in terms of structure, style, content and intended audience' (Swales 1990: 58).

ICT: Information and communications technologies

L1: First or native language

L2: Second language (the second or foreign language being learned)

LSP: Language for specific purposes

Language variety: 'a system of linguistic expression whose use is governed by situational factors' (Crystal 2001: 6). Varieties of written language are defined according to these five features: graphic, orthographic/graphological, grammatical, lexical and discourse. Features specific to spoken language are: phonetic and phonological features (Crystal 2001: 6-9).

Material: The combination of the *text* (see below) and the language learning task/s based on it.

Medium: the means of transmitting text (phonic, graphic) (McCarthy and Carter 1994: 4).

NS: Native speaker

NNS: Non-native speaker

Register: 'Functional language variation' (Swales 1990: 40), 'a variety of a language distinguished according to its use' (Bhatia 1993: 6). Register is characterised via a correlation of situational (functional) linguistic variables (Leckie-Tarry 1993: 30).

SLA: Second Language Acquisition

Task: Learner undertaking in which the target language is comprehended and used for a communicative purpose in order to achieve a particular outcome (goal). (The concept of task is elaborated in Chapter 4).

TC: Target Culture. The culture of the target language (*TL* - see below). For learners of an internationally-spoken language such as English, the TC may be variable (see Chapter 3 Section 3.1.2).

Text: Paper-based or electronic (audio or visual) data which can be in graphic, audio or print form and includes video, DVD, television, computer-generated or recorded data.

TL: Target Language. The language being learned.

Notes

1   Synonyms from the *Merriam-Webster online thesaurus* http://www.m-w.com./cgi-bin/thesaurus.

Part One
Authenticity in Language Learning
The Theoretical Grounding

Chapter One:
Authenticity in language Learning

Background and Definition

The elusive definitions of the terms 'authentic' and 'authenticity' and their application to language learning have been the subject of great controversy over the past three decades. The stimulus for this can be dated back to the inception of Communicative Language Teaching (CLT) in the 1970s. Giving precedence to communication over form, CLT rejected previous, strictly structural approaches to language learning and opened the way for the use of authentic texts, texts which had been created for a genuine communicative purpose. This prompted the so-called 'authenticity debate' in which the nature of authenticity has been applied to everything from the original appearance of a text to perception and validation by the text user, and which has been further complicated by the advent of texts and interactions occurring on information and communications technologies (ICT). Before getting on to the complexities of the current debate, however, this chapter starts by situating this contemporary 'search for authenticity' within its historical context, where it will emerge that the quest is not, after all, unique to the modern era.

1.1 Authenticity in Language Learning: The Historical background

The total corpus of ideas accessible to language teachers has not changed basically in 2000 years. What has been in constant change are the ways of building methods from them, and the part of the corpus that is accepted varies from generation to generation, as does the form in which the ideas present themselves. (Kelly 1969: 363)

With this in mind, sifting through the history books reveals many precedents for authenticity in language learning, and these can be seen to fall into three groups: 'communicative approaches' in which communication is both the objective of language learning and the means through which the language is taught, 'materials-focused' approaches, in which learning is centred principally round the text, and 'humanistic approaches'[1] which address the 'whole' learner and emphasise the value of individual development.

1.1.1 'Communicative' approaches

The cyclical nature of the evolution of language pedagogy is nowhere more apparent than in the communicative approaches used at both extremes of the five millennia covered here. This may be justification for arguing that this is after all the most natural approach, based as it is on the premise that a means of communication can only be learned by using it for this purpose. 'Communicative' approaches were used in the earliest colonial contexts. As early civilisations discovered and conquered other lands, the need to communicate with speakers of other languages arose. Historians have found evidence that second language teaching took place among the Sumerians from around 2700 BC (Titone 1968: 5), when they were conquered by the Akkadian Semites who then wanted to adopt the 'local' language. Much of this early language learning and teaching in colonial contexts then and later (for example, in the Egyptian and Roman Empires) may be said to have been authentic in spirit, in that the language was usually acquired in non-classroom situations and without specially prepared language materials. It was usually done via direct contact with native speakers, either through sojourns in foreign parts or, as was common among the Romans, through the employment of a Greek-speaking tutor or slave (Titone 1968: 6). Roman education was bilingual from infancy. The basis for foreign language teaching in Roman times can therefore be said to have been communicative in its purpose and authentic in execution, even though this may have been for reasons of convenience more than pedagogical principle.

Pedagogical principle was, on the other hand, certainly the impetus for one of the best-recorded instances in history of a genuinely communicative and authentic approach to language learning; that taken in the 16th century in the education of Michel de Montaigne:

> In my infancy, and before I began to speak, he [my father] committed me to the care of a German [...] totally ignorant of our language, but very fluent, and a great critic in Latin. This man [...] had me continually with him: to him there were also joined two others [...] who all of them spoke to me in no other language but Latin. As to the rest of his family, it was an inviolable rule, that neither himself, nor my mother, man nor maid, should speak anything in my company, but such Latin words as every one had learned only to gabble with me [...] I was above six years of age before I understood either French or Perigordin [...] and without art, book, grammar, or precept, whipping, or the expense of a tear, I had, by that time, learned to speak as pure Latin as my master himself. (Michel de Montaigne 1575[2]).

The present-day permutation of the notion of communicativeness emerged in the 1970s following a century of frenetic experimentation and development in language teaching methodology. The preceding hundred years had seen a transformation from academic approaches, to experimentation with so-called 'Natural' and 'Direct' methodologies, to the first attempts at harnessing technology for learning purposes. However, while all these approaches had some influence on the synthesis of CLT, its real roots may be traced to the advent of the new field of *linguistics* around the turn of the century. From this developed the branch of psycholinguistics, the study of the cognitive faculties involved in the acquisition of language. The publication of *Aspects of the Theory of Syntax* (Chomsky 1965) in which the distinction is drawn between speakers' *competence* (their knowledge of the language system) and their *performance* (their use of the language) is generally seen as the spark which ignited the Communicative philosophy that was to dominate the last three decades of the 20th century (Howatt 1984: 271). Chomsky's notion of competence was later transformed into one of 'communicative competence', which encompassed language use: 'There are rules of use without which the rules of grammar would be useless' (Hymes 1971; 1979: 15). Competence was now seen as 'the overall underlying knowledge and ability for language use which the speaker-listener possesses [...] this involves far more than knowledge of (and ability for) grammaticality' (Brumfit and Johnson 1979: 13-14). In other words, an individual's communicative competence involved what s/he needed to know about the language and its culture, and how well s/he was able to use the language in order to communicate successfully, that is, to get the desired outcome from the interaction. It is this notion of communicative competence that is the cornerstone of CLT.

The Communicative philosophy meant a reorientation of former teaching priorities; the teaching of communication via language, not the teaching of language via communication (Allwright 1979: 167). In other words, effective communication was the goal, the language merely the means; and it was through the attempt to communicate using the language that the language was acquired. The idea of using texts 'communicatively', that is, exploiting them for their content rather than for their linguistic structure, represented a key precept of CLT, *viz.*, the predominance of meaning over form. The pivot of Communicative methodology - and where it can and does so easily fall down - is the design of, and learner engagement in, genuinely communicative activities. Typical activities of the early years of CLT used the strategy of information gaps; in order to bridge the gap, learners had to communicate (Johnson 1979: 201). The gap was produced basically by providing information to one member of a pair and withholding it from the other, as in the now standard 'pair-work' exercise. By the 1980s, 'Communicative' was the buzzword in all ELT coursebooks, although, as is often the case with commercial permutations of pedagogical approaches, Communicative 'templates' were sometimes used without their *raison d'etre*. Nevertheless the realia creeping into the Communicative coursebook heralded the advent of the use of authentic texts which would eventually help return CLT to its 'meaningful' roots.

1.1.2 Materials-focused approaches

As with communicativeness, materials-focused approaches also have a long history, with instances of the use of authentic texts for language learning occurring as early as 9th-century England. At that time, Latin was the international (European) language of communication. However, there were attempts to improve the education of the common people by integrating the vernaculars - Old English, Anglo-Saxon - into the education system, through translation of books into the vernaculars (some translations were done by the famous King Alfred himself, according to Pugh 1996: 160). Both the texts and methods of learning may be defined as authentic; long stretches of text were read in what has been called a 'holistic, reading for meaning approach' (Pugh 1996: 163).

The teaching of Latin passed through different stages over the centuries during which it was an international language, but by Medieval times, the teaching method used (in England as elsewhere) was the 'scholastic method' which consisted of breaking down words into their constituent parts. Learning the alphabet was therefore the pre-requisite for reading, and finally memorising, sections of 'primers'. These were not specially written texts for children, but were authentic texts, basic prayer books. This highlights one of the controversial issues of the use of authentic texts for learning, one that will be touched on in Chapter 3, *viz.*, their potential for political, cultural or, in this case, religious indoctrination. As well as being identified with literacy (the Latin verb *legere* was used to mean specifically 'to read *Latin*'), Latin had crucial religio-political importance in the Middle Ages, and the objective of learning Latin as opposed to the vernacular 'was not to acquire a wide competence in reading [...] but to express the elements of Christian teaching' (Clanchy 1984 cited in Pugh 1996: 162).

A more liberal application of authentic texts in language learning can be seen in the method devised by Roger Ascham in the mid-16th century. Ascham developed a 'double translation' method, in which pupils translated the target language text into the mother tongue, and then re-translated their versions into the target language. Ascham used simple but authentic texts in this process - when applied to the teaching of Latin, for instance, he used texts by Cicero. Interestingly, this technique is currently being revived in the context of cultural awareness-raising, where double translation at discourse level (rather than simply word/sentence level) is seen as a means of raising consciousness of cultural implications of linguistic choices (Pulverness 1999a: 9). The 'inductive approach' (whereby readers infer grammar rules out of the texts) adopted by Ascham (and later by others) is also strikingly modern (Howatt 1984: 24, 35, Titone 1968: 12).

An 'inductive' approach is also the basis of the theory of language pedagogy put forward by Henry Sweet in his 1899 work *The Practical Study of Languages*. Sweet used the term 'inductively' slightly differently from the modern sense (which he called the 'inventional method' and dismissed as being slow and frustrating for the learner). By 'inductive', Sweet meant that teachers should illustrate grammar with appropriate paradigmatic texts, which learners could then examine for more examples. Sweet maintained that the foundation of language study should be what he called 'connected texts' (this was in part a reaction against the dominance of the detached sentence in language teaching); 'it is only in connected texts that the language itself can be given with each word in a natural and adequate context' (1899: 164). He argued that the connected text was the best context for learners to establish and strengthen the correct associations between words, their contexts and their meanings (1899: 164-73) and that only after it has been thoroughly studied and assimilated should the teacher draw out of it grammar points and vocabulary items (1899:192-3). The arguments that Sweet made for the use of authentic texts sound strikingly modern in that the practice persists to this day: 'If we try to make our texts embody certain definite grammatical categories, the texts cease to be natural: they become either trivial, tedious and long-winded, or else they become more or less monstrosities' (Sweet 1899: 192).

Like Ascham, Sweet also saw the need for maintaining authenticity with lower level learners by providing simpler language samples. He suggested that such levels be catered for by selecting certain genres which are simpler than others, such as descriptive pieces (Sweet 1899: 177). In this he anticipated by almost a century, present-day arguments for authentic texts: 'Texts need not be "grammatically sequenced" they need only to capture student attention and be comprehensible' (Krashen 1989: 19-20). Sweet also took pains to stress the positive advantage of using what he called 'natural' texts, because of their variety:

> *The great advantage of natural, idiomatic texts over artificial 'methods' or 'series' is that they do justice to every feature of the language [...] the artificial systems, on the other hand, tend to cause incessant repetition of certain grammatical constructions, certain elements of vocabulary, certain combinations of words to the almost total exclusion of others. (Sweet 1899: 178)*

On the other hand, he was not averse to textbook writers producing simpler 'natural' texts for more elementary learners, as long as each text was not dedicated to a single grammatical rule, but presented variety ('everything' as he put it). It is interesting that this point was, and has been, frequently ignored in textbook writing to the present day.

The 20th century was dominated by materials-focused approaches albeit embodying many different theories of language acquisition. First came the 'New Method' of the 1950s, which developed out of research into vocabulary frequency and the subsequent development of the 'lexical distribution principle' (Howatt's term, 1984: 247). This principle was reflected in a spate of publications of grammars, dictionaries and word-lists all containing limited and controlled lexical and grammatical material. The graded reader concept began at this time, in which new words were restricted in number and introduced progressively. The principles of the approach led, more critically, to the much-maligned practice of simplifying works of literature - 'simplifying great fiction is like reducing a stock when cooking - it rapidly becomes too concentrated and indigestible' (Prowse 1999 cited in Kershaw and Kershaw 2000; see also arguments in Vincent and Carter 1991 and Valdes 1986a, among others).

Other methods followed; the 'Oral Method', the 'Situational Approach', the 'Direct Method', and the 'Audiolingual Method', all of which relied on carefully structured materials and prescribed classroom practices. The culmination of such approaches was an effective 'cult of materials' (Howatt, 1984: 267), in which 'the authority of the approach resided in the materials themselves'[3] (Howatt *ibid.*). This may be seen as the start of a debilitating phenomenon in the ELT profession that still exists today; of dependency on, and subservience to the textbook, still the teaching material of choice for the majority of teachers (see Chapter 3). As the importance of foreign language learning increased with the progress of the century, it effectively developed into a modern industry accompanied by ever-evolving methodologies and production of pedagogical literature. This meant that, ironically, as the need for learning foreign languages for genuine communicative purposes increased, the authenticity of the languages in terms of materials tended to decline.

1.1.3 Humanistic approaches

Another thematically related group of approaches relevant to authenticity, can be termed 'humanistic' approaches, and these recurred periodically throughout history, frequently in reaction to more mechanistic teaching methods. Reaction to the practice of rote-learning which pervaded the learning of Latin and Greek during the 16th century, for instance, came most memorably from the great humanist educator, Comenius. In his work on language, the *Orbis Sensualium Pictus* (1658), Comenius gave a singularly modern emphasis on (to use modern terminology) 'language use' rather than 'language usage'[4]: 'Every language must be learned by practice rather than by rules, especially by reading, repeating, copying, and by written and oral attempts at imitation' (Comenius cited in Titone 1968: 14-15). Comenius also advocated an 'intuitive approach', which used sensory experience as the starting point for language learning. The main tenet of this approach was that learners respond to visual stimuli, objects and pictures, and not to abstracts, such as grammar rules.

These ideas reappear in a number of 20th-century approaches, all of which place emphasis on exploiting the whole sensory repertoire of the brain during the learning experience. Suggestopedia, (Lozanov 1978), Total Physical Response (TPR) (Asher 1977), The Silent Way (Gattegno 1972) and Neuro-Linguistic Programming (NLP) (Bandler and Grinder 1975) all draw on cognitive psychology, and are methods intended to exploit the potential of the human brain for learning more fully than conventional methods. Suggestopedia and TPR are based on the assertion that the human brain can most easily process large quantities of new information when in a state of relaxation. The contention is that conventional classroom language learning situations are stress-inducing for the learner, inhibiting the language acquisition process. For example, the pressure in the traditional classroom to perform, to produce language output, is unnatural, in the sense that it is the antithesis of first language learning, where production is preceded, for many months, by the silent processing of input ('the silent period'). Furthermore, conventional learning methods tend to promote left-brain activity, the left hemisphere being the centre for more abstract language processing (see 'Whole brain' processing, Chapter 2). If right-brain processes were stimulated (the right brain hemisphere being the locus of motor activity) instead of, or as well as, the left brain, as naturally occurs in L1 acquisition, L2 learning might be enhanced. Involvement of the 'whole brain' can therefore be seen as a realistic and authentic interaction with input, as reaction to language input is not always limited to the cognitive. These ideas are not alien to more mainstream ideas on language acquisition as will be demonstrated in Chapter 2.

The approach 'The Silent Way' incorporated two other trends in learning popularised in the 1960s and 70s, problem-solving and discovery learning. The method encouraged learners to take a problem-solving approach to deciphering language structures, a process of discovery and creativity rather than mere repetition of language. In that this entails a process of personal involvement with the language, it might be expected to promote language acquisition (see 'Affect' in Chapter 2).

Neuro-Linguistic Programming (NLP), developed by Richard Bandler and John Grinder in the mid 1970s (see Bandler and Grinder 1975), is an approach for expanding self-awareness, fulfilment and communication (relational) capacity in all spheres of life (including language learning). As its name suggests, Neuro-Linguistic Programming draws on the areas of neurology, linguistics, and, lastly, anthropology (in the sense that it looks to observable patterns ('programs') of behaviour). NLP is based on the process of modelling; observing both internal and external models of 'excellence' and applying or emulating them. Applied to learning, NLP involves enhancing learners' awareness of themselves and of others in order to fully exploit their learning potential. This awareness applies particularly to sense perception - visual, auditory, kinaesthetic, olfactory and gustatory. By incorporating multi-sensory awareness into the learning process, and alerting learners to their own personal preferences in their sensory experience of the world, the tenets of NLP maintain that learners can be empowered both as learners and in their lives in general. In resource books such as Revell and Norman (1999), advocates of NLP offer activities for language learners which incorporate the raising of sensory awareness with language learning. NLP may therefore be seen very much as part of the contemporary trend in language learning (and other fields) to implicate affect and self-awareness in learning, a trend that can be seen in Suggestopedia (see above), in the integration of culture and language learning (see Chapter 3), and in the move towards more independent modes of learning (see below).

The latest broad movement in language pedagogy, *learner autonomy* or *self-directed learning*, is also included here under the theme of 'humanistic' approaches because of its emphasis on, and respect for, the individualism of the learner. Over the past thirty-odd years there has been a gradual shift of preoccupation in the field from *teaching* to *learning* and thence to *the learner*. This shift can be traced through changes in the terminology we use to characterise our profession. We started with language *teaching* (as, for example, in the name Communicative Language Teaching), moved on, in the late 1980s, to 'language teaching and learning' and culminated in the 1990s with 'language learning'. These changes reflect the recognition that it is the learner who stands at the centre of - and ultimately controls - the learning process. No amount of pedagogical intervention or skill can induce learning in a student with flawed learning strategies or lack of motivation (see Chapter 2 Section 2.3). This factor of control, and the responsibility this brings with it, is central to learner autonomy: 'The main characteristic of autonomy [...] is that students take some significant responsibility for their own learning over and above responding to instruction' (Boud 1988: 23).

Learner autonomy is not *an approach* to learning but rather *a condition* involving 'the internal psychological capacity to self-direct one's own learning' (Benson

1997: 25) through detachment, critical reflection, decision-making and independent action (Little 1991: 4). Attaining this capacity is a developmental process, an 'internal transformation within the individual' (Benson 1997: 19), involving, most fundamentally, attaining an awareness and acceptance of responsibility for one's own learning (see also below). This capacity cannot really be learned or taught, but merely *fostered* through particular pedagogical practices which create the appropriate conditions (Benson 2001: 110). What these conditions are, and how feasible it is to provide them, depends on a variety of factors ranging from personal preferences to cultural contexts and practical constraints. The most indispensable in the context of language learning, is access to abundant language input (I will suggest below that this should be authentic texts: see also Chapter 2 Section 2.7 which deals with autonomous learning and language acquisition) plus a pedagogical environment that encourages interaction. Beyond this, a range of practices and frameworks are suggested by the research and practice in the field. These tend to fall into two broad strands: provision of self-access structures and learner-directed curricula. Self-access is probably the best-known approach to encouraging autonomy and refers to a learning environment which includes access to resources, materials and information technology (the self-access *centre*) in which learners and teachers co-operate to promote learning and autonomy. The success of self-access depends on learners being supported and trained in using the resources effectively (and on avoiding the trap of being erroneously identified with *isolation*, Esch 1997: 168). For this reason, the other broad strand of approaches to autonomy, in which learners go through awareness-raising processes which enable them to make informed input into their learning procedures and curriculum, is often a necessary element of the use of self-access.

The level at which awareness-raising needs to begin varies among individuals and cultural contexts (see also Nunan 1997: 194-201 for the concept of levels of implementing autonomy). Learners may initially need to be prompted to think about their own and their teacher's role in their learning, and their degree of dependency on the teacher/curriculum. From this, they can be encouraged to examine pedagogical goals (of the teacher/curriculum) and to think about, and compare these, with their personal ones. Since, as Little points out, 'in the development of learner autonomy, learning goes hand in hand with learning how to learn' (1997: 230), an essential step towards autonomy is for learners to think about how they learn, by analysing their preferred learning styles (see Chapter 2 Section 2.5). This type of awareness can help learners to manage their learning more effectively and even to circumvent an imposed learning style (such as one constrained by the more teacher-centred pedagogies of some cultural contexts). It can also help learners identify the types of learning tasks and ways of going about these that best suits them. At this level, learners are ready to make informed input into the curriculum as regards content (i.e. drawing on their personal goals) and procedures (drawing on their insight into their preferred learning styles and modes of studying). This might well involve the transition to a self-access set-up as individual differences in learning needs and strategies emerge. Not to be neglected are the most telling procedures: monitoring and evaluating progress in both autonomous modes of learning and in language acquisition.

It is important, finally, not to interpret learner-direction of curriculum and content as a form of ceding to the demands of the learner. The principles of autonomous learning are not meant to imply that the learner knows what is best, 'at the beginning of the learning process, learners do *not* know what is best' (Nunan 1997: 194), but that learners have within them the potential to *discover* what is best for them.

It is clear from even this brief description, that in autonomous learning environments, the role of the teacher shifts dramatically. The teacher is no longer the traditional purveyor of information, but rather, a counsellor, facilitator and resource (Little 1991: 44-5, Benson 2001: 171). These roles can demand broader knowledge, expertise and initiative than does the expository model of teaching, and contradictory though it may seem, require even greater confidence than does taking 'centre-stage' in the classroom. Confidence, first of all in the autonomous approach that s/he, the teacher, has adopted; the confidence, secondly, to 'stop talking' (countering the belief, to be inferred from some teacher practices, that if s/he is not talking, the learners cannot be learning; see Little 1991: 45); and thirdly, confidence in the learners - that they already know a great deal and possess the ability to exploit this knowledge productively (Wright 1987: 62).

The radical change in the power structure of pedagogy involved in autonomous learning is often seen as a European cultural construct (e.g. Benson 2001: 58) and inappropriate to certain other cultures: 'To encourage learner autonomy universally, without first becoming acutely aware of the social, cultural and political contexts in which one is working, may lead at best to inappropriate pedagogies and at worst, to cultural impositions' (Pennycook 1997: 44) (the issue of cultural differences in pedagogy is discussed further in Chapter 3). On the other hand, it can be argued that the potential for autonomy is a human universal (e.g. Little 1999: 15) and that, in common with the other humanistic approaches described in this section, the ethos of learner autonomy simply acknowledges the undeniable individuality of the learning process - that people learn things at different rates, in different orders, using different strategies and with different agendas.

In the language learning context, autonomy and authenticity are essentially symbiotic. The 'ideal', effective autonomous learner will utilise a wide variety of authentic sources in his/her learning and it is in an autonomous learning environment that such texts can best be explored. Case studies on learner-experiences in self-instruction, for example, have found that particularly at higher proficiency levels, learners benefit from interacting with authentic texts in autonomous modes (Fernández-Toro and Jones 1996: 200). Conversely, authenticity fosters autonomy:

> *Activities based around authentic texts [...] can play a key role in enhancing positive attitudes to learning, in promoting the development of a wide range of skills, and in enabling students to work independently of the teacher. In other words, they can play a key role in the promotion of learner autonomy (McGarry 1995: 3).*

Exposure to, and familiarity with authentic texts also help instil confidence in the face of the TL (Little 1997: 231), an important factor in autonomous language learning, as well as spurring learners towards authentic sources. Authentic sources, in turn, tend to stimulate learners to further independent discovery and learning[5]. In truly autonomous learning, the authentic source text itself may be left to direct the learner: 'These are uncharted waters; but a dip is all it takes to generate new energy for exploration' (Guillot 1996: 152).

Learner autonomy may be seen as a logical progression of the Communicative environment in which it developed, particularly in the context of the burgeoning use of information and communication technology (ICT) in education (as elsewhere). Today, learner autonomy means taking advantage of the technological resources now widely available, and extends the notion of communicativeness to encompass computer-mediated communication (see Chapter 11). On the sociological side, autonomy means a more egalitarian relationship ('communication') between the learner and the information provider.

1.1.4 Conclusion

Sifting through the history of language teaching for precedents for authenticity has clearly illustrated Kelly's observation of the cyclical movement of language pedagogy (Kelly 1969). Over a thousand years ago, England's King Alfred initiated educational use of authentic texts. In the 16th century, Roger Ascham and Michel de Montaigne described authentic approaches to the learning of Latin. Henry Sweet made arguments in favour of authentic texts that predate those of today's advocates by a hundred years. The concept of purposeful, authentic interaction is integral to the Communicative Approach conceived in the 1970s; and authentic texts may be said to be central to autonomous learning practices which are subtly displacing CLT. The aim of this section has been to give historical weight and perspective to the concept of authenticity in language learning. The following section examines the modern-day interpretations of the concept against this background.

1.2 Towards a Definition of Authenticity

1.2.1 Introduction

'Authenticity [...] is a term which creates confusion because of a basic ambiguity' (Widdowson 1983: 30). At the time this was written, it was probably not intended as the understatement that it appears twenty years on. Recurring periodically throughout the history of language teaching as the previous section has illustrated, the modern-day preoccupation with authenticity in language learning is born of prevailing currents from three areas. The first is from SLA research, the second is from language pedagogy itself - Communicative and approaches to language learning, and the third is sociological - the growing influence of information and communications technologies (ICT) on our work and learning practices.

The implications of the first influence, SLA research, are covered in detail in Chapter 2. Very briefly, there is substantial research evidence to support the use in language learning of the linguistically rich, culturally faithful and potentially emotive input supplied by authentic texts. What is more, there is little evidence of a fixed acquisition order, which is the rationale for the use of phased language instruction and which is often used to repudiate the use of authentic texts for language learning.

The notion of authenticity is, secondly, embedded in prevailing language pedagogies - communicative and autonomous modes of learning, as has been shown in the previous section. The emphasis in Communicative language teaching (CLT) on 'real' language use begs the question of what is real, authentic, while among the choices students face in more independent language learning, are the types of texts they work with and the resources they use. Increasingly today, these resources are electronic ones, ICT, the third 'current' implicating the notion of authenticity.

What makes the notion of authenticity such a crucial one to describe and define, therefore (its centrality to the premise of this book apart), is its embedding in, and its drawing together of, these three related areas, SLA research, language pedagogy and ICT. Through a review of the literature generated in the authenticity debate, this part of the chapter traces the permutations of the definitions of the term *authenticity* from its relatively simple beginnings, to a present complexified by the nature of text and language in IC technologies. The aim of this review is to establish, if not a definitive definition, then some workable *criteria* for authenticity which can be applied in the context of this book in particular, as well as in the design of language learning materials in general.

The core distinction made in Breen 1985, Taylor 1994 and elsewhere: 'some writers [...] think of authenticity as essentially residing in a text while others think of authenticity as being, in some sense, conferred on a text by virtue of the use to which it is put by particular people in particular situations' (Taylor 1994: 3), constitutes the framework for this part of the chapter. The first section covers the increasingly tortuous search for a finite definition of the *authentic text*, and the second looks at how authenticity has become applied to *language use*, in the sense of *learner interactions* with, and *interpretations* of the text. The two sections maintain the historical/thematic approach used in the first part of this chapter, since changes in the notion of authenticity have naturally tended to reflect pedagogical currents.

1.2.2 Authenticity of texts

Early definitions of the term 'authentic text' are typified by this one from Morrow: 'An authentic text is a stretch of real language, produced by a real speaker or writer for a real audience and designed to convey a real message of some sort' (Morrow 1977: 13). It is important that Morrow was here using *real* as an antonym of *imaginary*, in other words, an authentic text is one written for the purpose of communicating information (not of illustrating specific language points). Set in its historical context, coming in the mid 1970s, Morrow's definition turned on the concept of *purpose*, so central to the Communicative approach that was taking hold at that time. If interaction was to have purpose and be meaningful, it followed that the input and context had to be 'real' or 'authentic'.

Throughout the CLT era, definitions have naturally tended to reflect the primacy of communicativeness:

> *For the purposes of the FL classroom, an authentic text, oral or written, is one whose primary intent is to communicate meaning [...] such a text can be one which is written for native speakers of the language to be read by other native speakers [...] or it may be a text intended for a language learner group. The relevant consideration here is not for whom it is written, but that there has been an authentic communicative objective in mind.(Swaffar 1985: 17)*

> *The term authentic [...] refers to the way language is used in non-pedagogic, natural communication.' (Kramsch 1993: 177). 'A text is usually regarded as authentic if it is not written for teaching purposes but for a real-life communicative purpose, where the writer has a certain message to pass on to the reader. As such, an authentic text is one that possesses an intrinsically communicative quality (Lee 1995: 324).*

In the 1980s, reflecting the new sensitivity afforded the socio-cultural aspects of learning a language, the spotlight began to fall on the cultural community within which this communication took place: 'Essentially, an authentic text is a text that was created to fulfil some social purpose in the language community in which it was produced' (Little *et al.* 1989: 25). Authentic texts are those being used 'by native speakers in culturally authentic contexts of use' (Kramsch *et al* 2000: 78). The idea that to be authentic, a text has to be faithful to its original cultural context calls into question the inclusion of such texts in ELT coursebooks. Early Communicative coursebooks were notorious for being besprinkled with realia; broadcasting schedules, bus timetables, newspaper snippets and the like. This use of realia has been accused of making for a 'touristic' rather than a cultural approach (Shanahan 1997: 165), one in which 'culture is conveyed in an anecdotal non-reflective manner' (Kramsch 1998: 82) and which diminishes genuine cultural artefacts into token realia. Kramsch maintains that the cultural authenticity of a piece of realia, a menu, for instance, 'derives from [its] being embedded in a host of social and symbolic relations in the C2 - price of food, taxes and tips, restaurant-going habits of customers' (1998: 84), so that it is meaningless as a stand-alone artefact of the culture. This lack of socio-cultural context can even be misleading, according to Nostrand: 'Authentic texts from one culture may give a false impression to a student from another unless they are presented in an authentic context which makes it clear precisely what they exemplify' (Nostrand 1989: 49). The need, in general, for learners to achieve a rounded picture of the language-and-culture - *cultural awareness* - as an integral part of language learning, is elaborated in Chapter 3.

The issue of context has, meanwhile, continued to prove the most problematic recurring theme in the whole authenticity debate. From the outset, there was the preoccupation that texts are de-authenticated if their original context is tampered with. At one level, 'context' meant a stringent adherence to the original appearance of the text, a concern stemming from the aforementioned early trends in CLT of presenting semi-authentic snippets:

> *Authenticity means that nothing of the original text is changed and also that its presentation and layout are retained. A newspaper article, for instance, should be presented as it first appeared in the paper; with the same typeface, the same space devoted to the headlines, the same accompanying picture [...] The picture, the size of the headline, the use of bold-face type, all contribute to conveying the message to the reader (Grellet 1981: 8).*

On a deeper level, 'original context' came to be identified as a unique and therefore un-replicable occurrence: 'An authentic text is by definition a unique thing. It represents one speaker/writer's communication to one particular audience at a given moment' (Morrow 1977: 14). 'A text can only be truly authentic [...] in the context for which it was originally written' (Hutchinson and Waters 1987: 15). 'Instances of language use are by definition context-dependent and hence unique' (Bachmann 1990: 310). By equating 'authentic' with 'unique', then re-using such text makes it counterfeit: 'By using it in a classroom for teaching purposes, we are destroying this authenticity' (Morrow 1977: 14). The logical conclusion to this argument is that 'the concept of 'authentic' in language teaching terms [is] unattainable [...]. We cannot recreate absolute authenticity in the texts we use' (Morrow 1977: 14-15).

Morrow's stand here was less uncompromising than it may appear, since his was in fact a timely warning against the headlong rush to use authentic materials willy-nilly, in the early days of ESP (English for Specific Purposes). It was not enough, Morrow suggested, to simply give chemical engineers (for example) authentic texts about chemical engineering and expect this to be relevant for them, since factors such as topic, function, channel and audience (Morrow 1977: 14-15) all affect this appropriacy. Morrow was nevertheless highlighting what was to remain a key criterion for authenticity. That long-standing presence in the authenticity debate, H.G. Widdowson, has also consistently argued that the use of authentic texts in language learning is a contradiction, since the language forfeits its authenticity once taken out of its context: 'Reality [...] does not travel with the text [...] What makes the text real is that it has been produced as appropriate to a particular set of contextual conditions. But because these conditions cannot be replicated, the reality disappears' (Widdowson 1998: 711-12).

This brings us right up to the present, to an era when the concept of text authenticity has to encompass electronic data as well. Indeed, context is the main bone of contention in relation to the *corpus*, an electronically stored text collection, just one of the new sources of texts available to the teacher/learner (see Chapter 11 Section 11.6.3 'Corpora, concordancing and language learning'). Consisting of thousands of 'authentic' texts on a single platform, it would seem self-evident that corpus data is 'authentic'. Indeed, this is one of the main attractions of using a corpus for learning purposes. Yet it can be argued that because of the form a corpus takes, context is in effect lost in the transition from source to electronic data. Once it has been incorporated into the corpus, the language becomes part of this larger whole, losing the original context (at all levels, from discourse to situational and socio-cultural) on which its meaning and authenticity depended. The sheer amount of language in a language corpus (Widdowson refers to a corpus as 'text *en masse*' 2000: 6) may be said to obscure the authenticity of its component parts, the individual discourses and texts. The texts collected in a corpus are left, therefore, with only a 'reflected reality: they are only real because of the presupposed reality of the discourses of which they are a trace. This is decontextualised language, which is why it is only partially real' (Widdowson 2000: 7). The only way to authenticate such discourse is, paradoxically, to try to re-contextualise it by the inauthentic 'recreation' of the contextual conditions in which it occurred (Widdowson 1998: 711-2, 2000: 7). This is further problematised in the learning context because learners are, by definition 'outsiders' from the discourse community in which the language was originally produced (Widdowson 1998: 711). The only solution to this 'problem' of authenticating corpus data comes via the learner's *interaction* with it. This is suggested in the section 'Authenticity of language use', below.

The opposite may be said of the learner's 'relationship' with another new platform for language, the Internet. As users of its two most commonly used Internet technologies, the Web and e-mail, learners and other NNSs are members of these Internet communities on a par with native speakers, authoring texts and contributing to the evolution of the new varieties of language developing within them (see Chapter 11 and Crystal 2001 'Language and the Internet' for descriptions of these). 'People have more power to influence the language of the Web than any other medium', notes Crystal (2001: 208), 'because they operate on both sides of the communicative divide, reception and production. They not only read text, they can add to it. The distinction between creator and receiver thus becomes blurred' (*ibid.*). With the Internet, the authenticity wheel has in a sense come full circle, from cherishing the prerogative of the native speaker as sole 'producer' of the authentic text (see, for example, traditional definitions summarised in Kramsch 2000: 78) to conflating authenticity with *authorship* (Kramsch 2000: 96), which is the right of any Internet user regardless of his/her native language.

To glance back from this point, it can be seen that pedagogic trends, sociological preoccupations and technological advances have meant that the concept of an authentic text has become deeply complexified since that innocently straightforward definition of Morrow's in the 1970s. So far, it would appear that the abundance of definitions and provisos as to what authenticates text amounts to a batch of criteria rather than a honed definition. These criteria include:

-Provenance (which subsumes 'authorship', in the Internet community)

-Original communicative purpose
-Socio-cultural function and context
-Activity or interactivity

These last two in particular are taken up in the following section.

1.2.3 Authenticity of language use

The concept of 'authenticity of language use' has proved somewhat less difficult to pin down than that of authenticity of texts. Early on in the debate, Widdowson had made a seminal terminological distinction between the concept of authenticity and what he termed *genuineness*: 'Genuineness is a characteristic of the passage itself and is an absolute quality. Authenticity is a characteristic of the relationship between the passage and the reader and it has to do with appropriate response' (Widdowson 1978: 80). The crux of the term authenticity is, then, that it applies not to any characteristic of the material itself, but to the interaction between the user and the text.

The fact that this distinction was never universally adopted (despite having an enormous influence on the debate as will be shown below) has left us with a chronic terminological ambiguity:

> *[Authenticity] can, on the one hand, be used to refer to actually attested language produced by native speakers for a normal communicative purpose. But the term can also be used, quite legitimately, to refer to the communicative activity of the language user, to the engagement of interpretative procedures for making sense, even if these procedures are operated on and with textual data which are not authentic in the first sense. An authentic stimulus in the form of attested instances of language does not guarantee an authentic response in the form of appropriate language activity. (Widdowson 1983: 30)*

In other words, authenticity may be something that is realised in the act of interpretation, and may be judged in terms of the degree of participation of the learner. This concept has critical implications for the pedagogical context, where it implies that what is important is what we *do* with a text rather than its having occurred in a 'real' environment:

> *Authenticity is not brought into the classroom with the materials or the lesson plan, rather, it is a goal that teacher and students have to work towards, consciously and constantly[...] authenticity is the result of acts of authentication, by students and their teacher, of the learning process and the language used in it' [emphasis in the original] (Van Lier 1996: 128).*

Such definitions became broadly integrated into the concept of authenticity and were given more pragmatic application and direction by associating them with the concept of 'task': 'Use of authentic materials does not imply that tasks will be authentic [...] it is what trainees or students DO that counts [emphasis in the original] (Arnold 1991: 238).

As a pedagogical model, task achieved a raised profile in the field of language learning from the 1980s onwards. The task-based approach ranged from full-blown methodologies (e.g. Prabhu 1987), to inclusion of variously interpreted versions of 'tasks' in ELT textbooks of the time. The notion of task figures in a much-cited set of applications of the term authenticity by Breen:

1. Authenticity of the texts which we may use as input data for our students.
2. Authenticity of the learner's own interpretations of such texts.
3. Authenticity of tasks conducive to language learning.
4. Authenticity of the actual social situation of the language classroom. (Breen 1985: 61)

It can be seen that the notion of learner authentication embodied in Breen's number 2 is in line with the Widdowson and Van Lier concepts cited above, that is, with concepts of authenticity as the relationship between learner and text (Widdowson 1978: 80), as a process of personal engagement (Van Lier 1996: 128), or as a process of validation by the learner (*ibid*: 128). In a similar vein, Lee (1995) subsumes Breen's numbers 2 and 3 in her definition of learner authenticity as 'the learner's interaction with [materials], in terms of appropriate responses and positive psychological reaction' (Lee 1995: 323).

Authenticity, in brief, was now being associated less with the text that the learners use, than with their interactions with it, i.e. with the task. It would seem, then, that task might have emerged as the predominant pedagogical model to be associated with authenticity. This association is pursued in Chapter 4, where the notion of *task authenticity* is developed to form a practical framework for the authenticity-centred approach.

The centrality of the pedagogical task is consistent with the position that the pedagogical context itself as an authentic environment (see Breen's Criterion number 4 above). 'We must' writes Taylor, 'acknowledge that the classroom itself is a real place' (1994). It is unquestionably a reality, as Hughes points out, for millions of children who spend a large portion of their childhood within one (1981: 7). The pedagogical situation itself, it can be argued, is at least as authentic as that of the post office or bank so enamoured of communicative dialoguists: 'We must recognise that the classroom has its own reality and naturalness [...] participants in the language classroom create their own authenticity there as they do elsewhere' (Taylor 1994, see also Kramsch *et al.* 2000: 79). Or as Widdowson puts it: 'There is a widespread assumption that the classroom is of its nature an unreal place [...] but there seems no good reason why the classroom cannot be a place of created context, like a theatre, where the community of learners live and move and have their being in imagined worlds, purposeful and real for them' (Widdowson 2001: 8). This image is in many ways consistent with the impression - felt by some language learners - of assuming an alternative personality when speaking and interacting in a foreign language (see Chapter 2 Section 2.4 on the language learning advantages of having permeable language ego boundaries).

The 1990s saw a logical transition from this concern to authenticate the classroom to concern for *its occupants'* authentication of the pedagogical situation, of their place within it and of the activities enacted therein. Such writings as Lee's 1994 article *Text authenticity and learner authenticity*, which emphasises the importance of learner-response to texts, and Van Lier's concept of learner authentication as expounded in *Interaction in the Language Curriculum: Awareness, Autonomy and Authenticity* (1996), are in many ways typical of the era. As the decade progressed, foreign language teaching, and indeed, pedagogy in general, increasingly 'homed-in' on the learner. Approaches were *learner-centred*; the learner was at the centre of instruction and learning, with the curriculum, materials, teaching methods, and even evaluation systems, being derived from the needs and goals of the learners (see, for example, Tudor 1996). As Clarke points out: 'The notion of authenticity itself has become increasingly relative, being increasingly related to specific learner needs and less and less concerned with the 'authentic' nature of the input materials themselves' (1989: 73). This shift of focus is noticeable in Wilson's 1997 definition: 'Authenticity: texts and accompanying tasks [...] perceived by the teacher and the learner as having a real-life communicative purpose' (Wilson 1997: 3). Further on in the same paper, Wilson establishes a sort of middle ground between authenticity 'purists' and those who view it as the relationship between the user and the text: 'Authenticity lies not only in a text's mother-tongue purpose but also in its foreign-language purpose when used by teachers and learners' (Wilson 1997: 7).

Widdowson, meanwhile, had taken a harder line, metaphorically throwing water on the flames he himself had helped to kindle:

> *The central question is not what learners have to do to use language naturally, but what they have to learn to do to use language naturally. In my view the authenticity argument is invalid because it does not distinguish between the two questions: it confuses ends and means and assumes that teaching language for communication is the same as teaching language as communication. (Widdowson 1990: 46)*

From which he controversially concludes that: 'Inauthentic language-using behaviour might well be effective language-learning behaviour' (Widdowson 1990: 46-7).

All this can be usefully tied in to the 'language-learning behaviour' stimulated by the interactions and texts offered by the IC technologies discussed earlier, corpora and the Internet. Applying the term authenticity to *activity* (i.e. process) in accordance with Widdowson 1983: 30, authenticity becomes derived from the *learning activity*. This authenticates that supremely interactive medium, the Internet, as a learning medium (see below) and likewise the pedagogy most associated with corpora, data-driven learning (DDL). The centre-pin of DDL is research activity. The learner uses the corpus as a resource of attested instances of language which illustrate patterns of language use, a resource from which s/he can make inferences (e.g. induce rules, infer meanings) about language use. (See Chapter 11, Sections 11.4.1 and 11.4.3 for a fuller description of the methodology). This helps resolve the dilemma encountered earlier, of the questionable authenticity of text once amassed in a corpus, since the text is in a sense authenticated by the activity in which it is used.

As with corpora, the authenticity of the Internet technologies, the Web and e-mail, are most accurately defined in terms of the activity they engender rather than the language texts they proffer. It is something of a truism to define the Web is an inherently interactive medium. However, this does not apply only to the way the user seeks and/or inputs information, but also to the fact that the 'text' that any one user 'reads' or assimilates, is unique, actively 'created' by him/her in the process of collecting and sifting this information from various Web links (see also the subsection on 'Web language and Authenticity' in Chapter 11 Section 11.2.2). User-authorship is also at the heart of e-mail, where the language used is authenticated by reason of its communicative and interactive function, and where learner response is concretised and externalised as messages and replies in the correspondence (see Chapter 11, Section 11.3 'E-mail').

'Authenticity of language use' has, in sum, a rather more satisfactory and universally agreed application than that of what constitutes an authentic text. Authenticity of language use relates to the *response of the language user*. It is thus a factor of the activity or task the user-learner undertakes, and of his/her perception and conviction of the task.

1.2.4 Conclusions: authenticity defined

This overview of the past 30 years of debate on authenticity has illustrated the divisive nature of the issue and the inconclusiveness of many of the arguments surrounding it: 'One point of interest is the degree of contradiction which exists' (Clarke 1989: 84), 'even a cursory reading of the relevant literature will bring to light a confused and contradictory picture' (Taylor 1994: 1). Nevertheless, the stated purpose of this review was to extract from the debate, if not a definitive definition, then a set of criteria by which the authenticity of texts might be assessed in the context of language learning materials design.

The various positions and arguments discussed in this chapter may be synthesised in the following set of 'criteria for authenticity':

Authenticity is a factor of the:

1. *Provenance and authorship* of the text.
2. *Original communicative and socio-cultural purpose* of the text.
3. *Original context (e.g. its source, socio-cultural context)* of the text.
4. *Learning activity* engendered by the text.
5. *Learners' perceptions of and attitudes to*, the text and *the activity* pertaining to it.

The last two criteria in particular will emerge as crucial ones for the development of an empirical interpretation of the concept of task authenticity in Chapter 4. A more general application might be in the course of the development and evaluation of language learning materials based on authentic texts, either in individual or publishing contexts.

In seeking to refine a contemporary definition of authenticity here, the incipient influence of ICT has become plain. Our perceptions of authenticity are beginning to shift to accommodate the nascent linguistic varieties of electronic mail and the Web (not to mention the language of chat rooms and text-messaging which are omitted here for reasons of brevity), varieties in which the prerogative of the native speaker to authorship has been usurped, in a sense, due to the egalitarian effect of the technologies. Furthermore, as ICT becomes increasingly part of our daily reality, the dichotomy between 'real life' and 'the classroom' which theorists struggled to resolve during the authenticity debate (see previous references to Hughes 1981, Taylor 1994, Widdowson 2001), is becoming something of an anachronism. Given access to the technology, today's learners can reach out and touch 'real life' at the tap of the keyboard. 'The physical properties of the electronic medium and the students' engagement with it' (Kramsch *et al.* 2000: 78) are thus causing a paradigm shift in our conception of authenticity. It is above all ICT, it can be concluded, that has raised the profile of authenticity today, taking an abstract notion debated by theoreticians and placing it squarely at the centre of contemporary pedagogy.

In conclusion, our conceptions of what constitutes an authentic text have clearly come a long way across the milliennia, from the weighty sanctity of the Latin prayer book to the ephemeral, inconsequential e-mail text. Authenticity, on the other hand, has, from the first, been fundamentally identified with communication - whether between Michel de Montaigne and his Latin tutor in the 16th century or between the Web-user and the information s/he accesses, in the 21st. This historical and theoretical background to authenticity forms the backdrop to the following chapter, in which the research evidence on the use of authentic texts and interactions in second language learning is presented.

Notes

1   These terms are chosen for their descriptiveness in this context only. It is intended to suspend temporarily, the connotations which terms such as 'communicative' have acquired in the language teaching context. The term 'Communicative' is capitalised when it refers to the Communicative Approach to language teaching.

2   From Chapter 15 'Of the education of children', *The Essays of Montaigne*, Michel de Montaigne, Translated by C. Cotton, Edited by W. Hazlitt, 1877.

3   These comments were originally made about the American 'Army Specialised Training Program' or ASTP.

4   A distinction originally made by Widdowson (1978), between the learner's knowledge of the formal properties of the grammatical rule systems of a language (*language usage*) and the speaker's ability to apply these rules for effective communication (*language use*).

5   A nice example of this occurred during one of my 'project modules' in which learners had decided to produce a class newspaper. One Intermediate level Japanese student, having found a short newspaper item on the Armed Forces, was so intrigued by what he considered the tiny size of the Irish Defence Force, that he proceeded to investigate the sizes of armies in other countries. He went to various statistical resources within the University library, copied pages of data and other information, and distilled this into a concise 2-page article comparing the relative sizes of the armies in a number of countries.

Chapter Two:
Authentic Texts for Language Learning
The SLA Rationale

2.1 Introduction

The arguments for the use of authentic texts in language learning may all be reduced to one quintessential point: that their use enhances language acquisition. As second language acquisition (SLA) research becomes increasingly pedagogically focused (Lightbown 2000), no call for the use of authentic texts would be valid without justification by research evidence from this field. This chapter looks at a number of factors which are generally accepted as significant for language acquisition - among them, *input, affect* and ways of *language processing*. It examines the research evidence of the impact of authentic texts on these factors, when such texts are used as the basis for language teaching and learning.

One of the difficulties with attempting to justify teaching methodologies in terms of what is known about second language acquisition, is that there is no single SLA 'formula' against which these may be assessed. SLA theories are notoriously diverse and numerous. In a 1993 paper on the subject, Michael Long identified between 40 and 60 theories of SLA (Long 1993: 225). This 'theoretical ferment' is said to be a typical feature of a discipline in its early stages (Long 1993: 229); SLA has only been a field in its own right for about 30 years. In concluding his mammoth work on SLA, Ellis remains non-committal as to whether a 'single unifying account of L2 acquisition' is either necessary or forthcoming (Ellis 1994: 689-90). Meanwhile, the 'pluralist' view, which accepts that different models of SLA theory can coexist, would seem to be the only realistic one to take.

Another important preface to a chapter applying SLA theory to pedagogy is this. Linguists have traditionally advocated caution about applying linguistic theory directly to practice (see Lightbown 1985: 182 and 2000: 452-3, Krashen 1989: 44-5, Widdowson 1990: 66, Nunan 1991: 15 and Ellis 1994: 687). This scepticism was originally based on the fact that the young field of linguistics failed to deliver viable teaching methodologies - or rather, it delivered flawed ones such as the audiolingual method of the 1960s. By the 1980s, the 'backlash' against applying theory to practice seemed to be complete: 'second language acquisition research does not tell teachers what to teach, and what it says about how to teach they have already figured out' (Lightbown 1985: 182). In the introduction to their work on the subject, Larsen-Freeman and Long admitted that SLA research was still far from dictating teaching practices (1991: 3-4). Widdowson, meanwhile, argued that theory and research were not applicable to language pedagogy other than through teachers engaging in a 'process of pragmatic mediation', examining how their pedagogical problems could be solved through looking at theories (1990: 66). This insistence that principles should be inferred from practice, and not vice versa, was strongly endorsed by practitioners such as Nunan: methodology, materials, tasks and so on should not be based on dogma or ideology, but on evidence and insights into what constitutes effective language teaching (1991: 15). However, the tide was already beginning to turn at the start of the 1990s, as SLA research began to take on an increasingly applied orientation (as noted by Ellis 1993). By the end of the decade, the shift was complete, with Lightbown noting 'a huge increase in SLA research which is either carried out in the classroom or which has been designed to answer questions related to FL/SL pedagogy' (2000: 438). Today, there is a large enough body of research relating SLA theory to FL learning in the classroom, to inspire confidence in this relationship: 'I believe that there is now a sufficient consensus of opinion for SLA research to be used as an informative base for the formulation of criteria for the teaching of languages' (Tomlinson 1998: 7).

It is no coincidence, then, that much of the empirically based SLA research cited below is fairly recent. The concept with which we start, however, is a classic one, one of 'the most powerful ideas to have come out of SLA studies' (Ellis 1993: 8), comprehensible input.

2.2 Input

The primacy of *input* is part of the premise of this book and has recurrently been at the core of SLA theories. One of the most well-known permutations is the concept of 'comprehensible input' (Krashen 1981 etc.), a term famously configured as *i+1*, signifying that input should be just above the current level of the learner but comprehensible enough for him/her to grasp the meaning (1981: 102-3). Krashen maintained that it is in straining to fill the gap between his/her current language knowledge and such input, that the learner acquires[2] language. In a sense, then, it is the *incomprehensibility* in the input that spurs acquisition, not its comprehensibility (White 1987a: 95). While Krashen has remained strenuously loyal to his own terminology over the years, the inherent vagueness of the term has allowed him to embrace the use of authentic texts as written and aural input, for those learners advanced enough for these to be 'comprehensible' (Krashen 1989: 18-21), and the term by now appears to have lost the pseudo-scientific gloss given it by its original *i+1* formulation.

While not diminishing the importance of the concept of comprehensible input, an important - if obvious - proviso must be borne in mind here. Comprehensible input strictly 'facilitates' language acquisition but cannot guarantee it (Ellis 1994: 279). This is because input is not automatically converted into *intake* - useable learner knowledge. What is understood, in other words, is not automatically *acquired* (Terrell 1991: 46). Learners are not merely passive recipients of input, they 'control' the comprehensibility of the input by either negotiating with their interlocutor in the case of aural input, or by varying the pace of reading, re-reading and so on, in the case of written input (Larsen-Freeman and Long 1991: 142-3). Furthermore, the processes by which input is converted to intake remain little known. Leow (1993), for instance, addressing the issue of written intake, claims to be the first to do so (*ibid.*: 342). His study appears to support the findings of others (such as White 1984) that 'external manipulation of the input may not only be haphazard but also inadequate to address what may appropriately facilitate learners' intake' (Leow 1993: 342).

The principal way of 'externally manipulating' input in order to render it more comprehensible, is that traditional strategy used in ELT coursebooks and readers, *simplification*. Input is simplified in a number of ways. Morphological and syntactical adjustments in speaking and writing include shortened utterances/sentences, fewer clauses, adherence to canonical word order both in statements and questions, and clear marking of grammatical relations (Yano *et al*. 1994: 192). Semantic adjustments include reduced use of idiom, colloquialism, metaphor and allusion, preference for concrete over dummy verbs (such as *do*), repetition of nouns instead of pronouns and use of high-frequency vocabulary (Vincent and Carter 1991: 211; Yano *et al*. 1994: 192, Leow 1993: 337, Young 1999: 350). On the phonological side, NSs addressing NNSs tend to use slower speech rate, fewer contractions and more careful articulation, stress and pauses to emphasise key words (Yano *et al*. 1994: 192).

The most striking outcome of research on simplification is that of these, the only adjustment which has been shown to improve comprehension is *speech rate* (Ellis 1994: 276, Yano *et al*. 1994: 200). An increasing number of studies have revealed that not only do these types of simplification of input fail to increase comprehensibility, but, most significantly, they can actually *inhibit* language acquisition (for example Yano *et al*.1994, Larsen-Freeman and Long 1991: 142-4, Krashen 1989: 28, Swaffar 1985: 17, Nunan 1991: 216). Larsen-Freeman and Long, for instance, examining the results of 13 studies carried out between 1980 and 1987, conclude that: 'Input (linguistic) modifications are [not] necessary [...] the very process of removing unknown structures and lexical items from the input in order to achieve an improved level of understanding simultaneously renders the modified samples useless as a source of new acquirable language items' (1991: 143-4). Krashen reaches similar conclusions: 'Some research bears on the use of simplification as a means of making texts comprehensible, and, taken as a whole, it is not encouraging [...] Blau (1982) [...] actually found that simplification could impair comprehension by removing elements crucial to comprehension' (1989: 28).

There seems to be considerable agreement that the type of modifications that *can* improve comprehensibility and stimulate acquisition in conversational and written discourse, are *elaborative* changes (Larsen-Freeman and Long 1991: 134-9, Yano *et al*. 1994, Krashen 1989: 28, Ellis 1994: 276-7). Elaborative modification involves adding features to the text which resemble conversational adjustments, such as repetition, paraphrases, contextual and extralinguistic clues and greater topic-saliency. This can result in slightly increased linguistic complexity and might even lengthen the text. These elaborative adjustments may be interpreted in pedagogical terms as the 'negotiation of meaning' so central to Communicative language teaching. Texts with elaborative modifications, even when more linguistically complex, have been shown to be no more difficult for subjects to comprehend than simplified texts (Yano *et al*. 1994). Interactional modifications are said to provide learners with the linguistic complexity and novelty required to further their language acquisition while not affecting comprehension of meaning (Yano *et al.* 1994: 214). They are therefore felt to be preferable to simplified texts in that they provide richer, more naturalistic input (*ibid.*).

There is little further proven SLA rationale for altering linguistic structures in the interests of simplification: 'Research results on whether [linguistic simplification] actually increases comprehension are inconsistent' (Young 1999: 350). With sparse evidence of the acquisition order of linguistic features (see, for example, Ellis 1994: 612), substitution of one syntactic structure with another can be fairly arbitrary (see Leow 1993: 342, Young 1999: 359, 362). Furthermore, it has been theorised that one effect of pedagogical simplification may be to help learners understand individual words, but this does not necessarily help them make conceptual connections between them, and is therefore at the expense of the whole text (Young 1999: 361, Swaffar 1985: 17). Simplification may ultimately send the erroneous message that 'every word in a text is significant' (Young 1999: 361). The implications of all this for the convention of simplifying input texts in materials - and coursebook-writing are no less than staggering. Far from assisting our learners, by 'simplifying' and shortening texts, we risk not only eliminating elements crucial to comprehension but also generally impoverishing learners' input.

We are inevitably led to look instead to authentic texts which provide rich, varied and stimulating linguistic input as well as: 'the essential predications of language proficiency: linguistically authentic comprehensible input presented in a fashion which allows students to practice decoding message systems rather than individual words' (Swaffar 1985: 17). It is notable here that 'comprehensibility' still remains a central requisite for texts to promote language learning - 'a rich but comprehensible input of real spoken and written language in use' (Willis 1996: 11), but now glossed more generously than Krashen's original *i+1*, as 'understandable enough to achieve a purpose for responding to it' (Tomlinson 1998: 13). There is a crucial distinction, in other words, between *simplification* and *simplicity* which can make for such comprehensibility. Unlike simplification, which is reductive, simplicity is a positive attribute; think of the wealth of books written for children, or even some canonical literature (Hemingway's *The Old Man and the Sea*, Beckett's *Waiting for Godot*, for instance).

A final contribution to this discussion on input comes, fittingly, from Krashen. In a fascinating chapter entitled 'The Din in the head, input and the language acquisition device'[1] (1989: 37-45), Krashen describes the experience of himself and two other linguists, of what was termed 'the Din in the head' experienced during short intensive periods of immersion in a foreign language in the country whose language the protagonists spoke to varying levels of proficiency. 'the Din in the head' consisted of hearing 'snippets' of the language 'playing' in the head in the voices of people who had spoken to them. This included 'rehearsals' for their own utterances, but was not conscious or controllable. In the cases described it did help improve production enormously and very quickly. 'The Din' appears to be a common phenomenon in situations of foreign language immersion. Krashen hypothesises that:

> *The Din is a result of the stimulation of the LAD [language acquisition device] ...this hypothesis has two corollaries; 1. The Din is set off by comprehensible input. 2. This input needs to contain significant quantities of the i+1, structures that the acquirer has not yet acquired but is 'ready' for (note that i+1 is probably a set of structures and not just one). (Krashen 1989: 39-40).*

To get learners studying in non-target language countries to experience this 'din', Krashen maintains, the TL environment could be simulated by the use of quantities of authentic listening texts. This is consistent with ideas of researchers such as Little *et al.*, who talk of 'bombarding' learners with authentic texts to recreate the total immersion conditions - the 'language bath' - under which the first language is acquired (Little *et al.* 1989: 4-6, 26). Other research, (e.g. Terrell 1991: 54), also supports the idea that the *amount* of comprehensible input is a factor in successful language acquisition. Krashen notes that as it took one or two hours of 'good input' for the 'din' to be activated, such classes might be sustained over longer time periods than the normal 60-minute lesson (Krashen 1989: 40).

It would be misleading to emphasise the role of input in language acquisition disproportionately. There is still a distinct dearth of research, for example, in the role of reading as a source of input (Devitt 1997a: 462, 464). It is, furthermore, difficult to weight the role of input against other factors in language acquisition as a whole. While input is certainly central to Krashen's conception of the acquisition process, other linguists, such as Ellis and Sharwood Smith, are more cautious:

> *We are still a long way from explaining how input interacts with the learner's internal cognitive mechanisms to shape the course of language acquisition and even further from being able to assign any weighting to external as opposed to internal factors. In all likelihood, input combines with other factors such as the learner's L1, the learner's communicative need to express certain meanings and the learner's internal processing mechanisms. No explanation of L2 acquisition will be complete unless it includes an account of the role of input but...input should be seen as just one of a "conspiracy of factors" [Sharwood Smith 1985: 402]. (Ellis 1994: 287-8)*

As one of these factors, then, input would appear to be most valuable when it is in the form of authentic texts which contain a rich variety of unmediated elements from which the language learner can source his/her language acquisition.

2.3 Affect: Motivation

A key factor affecting successful language learning, and indeed learning in general, is largely agreed to be *motivation* (see for example Ellis 1985: 11, 119, Ellis 1994: 508, Oxford and Shearin 1994, Van Lier 1996: 98, Hopkins and Nettle 1994: 160). Indeed, S. Pit Corder famously went so far as to claim that it is the single biggest factor: 'Given motivation, it is inevitable that a human being will learn a second language if he is exposed to the language data' (1974: 22). While a detailed analysis of what constitutes motivation is beyond our scope here, the broadly accepted conception is that motivation concerns 'those factors that energise behaviour and give it direction' (Gardner 1985: 281). Motivation can, therefore, be seen as having a quantitative dimension, intensity, and a qualitative dimension, goal-directedness (Dörnyei 1994b: 516).

The motivation factor is one of the key justifications for the use of authentic texts for language learning (see Peacock 1997, Swaffar 1985, Bacon and Finneman 1990, Little *et al.* 1989). It is telling, first of all, that motivation itself has been defined in terms that are frequently used to describe learner interaction with authentic texts:

> *For this study 'motivation' is defined ... [as] interest in and enthusiasm for the materials used in class; persistence with the learning task, as indicated by levels of attention or action for an extended duration; and levels of concentration and enjoyment. (Peacock 1997: 145).*

If these are taken as referents for/components of motivation, as Peacock suggests (*ibid.*: 145-6), then authentic learning texts would appear to be the ideal motivators.

The type of motivation Peacock describes above is usually defined in today's literature as *intrinsic* (the motivation being the learner's own interest or curiosity), as distinct from *extrinsic* (the motivation coming from external forces) (Arnold and Brown 1999: 14). The more 'traditional' definitions of motivation for language learning are, however, perhaps more relevant to our context. Traditionally, motivation is distinguished as stemming from a desire either to integrate with the target language community (*integrative motivation*), or to achieve a practical goal (*instrumental motivation*) (Gardner and Lambert 1972). Of the two, integrative motivation has been found to be by far the most compelling, and is invariably related to second language achievement (Ellis 1994: 510). It is integrative motivation, furthermore, that authentic language texts appeal to most directly; real material from the target culture which learners can perceive as being 'a stepping stone' towards their own integration with, and understanding of that culture (see Bacon and Finnemann 1990: 460). Clearly, whether motivation is integrative or instrumental depends on both the language learning situation and on individual learner differences. Learners studying a language away from the target language country do not usually experience the yearning for integration into the TL culture that those studying within it might feel, nor do they have the same incentive (or opportunity) to emulate the native speaker. The language learning situation itself might thus be one factor influencing learners' attitudes to authentic language texts (see also Note 2).

All this shows that the successful use of authentic texts does not correlate directly with *type* of motivation. Authentic texts might appeal to the instrumentally motivated learner in situations where the target language is essential as a *lingua franca* (e.g. English in the Philippines) or for study purposes (e.g. English in

Israel). Similarly, in LSP situations, where learners need the specialised language for professional advancement, authentic texts might be more motivating because learners recognise them as pertaining to the professional community to which they aspire.

One of the chief elements of motivation is often claimed to be *interest*: 'Students' goals and interests must be the starting point if motivation is to be high and developmental progress to occur. Moreover, for motivation and progress to exist, instructional input to students must be challenging and relevant' (Oxford and Shearin 1994: 23, see also Ellis 1994: 514, Little *et al*. 1989: 26). Yet motivation as intrinsic interest is an as yet largely unexplored area of research (Ellis 1994: 517, 1993: 8-9), in spite of the fact that this is one aspect of motivation which practitioners are able to influence: 'Language teachers can't really do very much to influence learners' instrumental or integrative motivations, *but* they can do a tremendous amount to try to develop some kind of intrinsic interest in the performance of different kinds of activities' (Ellis 1993: 8-9). Authentic texts, selected by the teacher on the basis of their learners' interests, will inevitably be more interesting for them than inauthentic ones, so we might well presume that this element of motivation at least will be activated by their use[3].

It has been pointed out that while motivation clearly affects acquisition, the direction of the effect - whether it is motivation that stimulates acquisition or successful language learning that provides motivation - is not clear (Ellis 1985: 119). A similar two-way effect is perceived in relation to learner disposition towards the language. Positive attitudes towards the target language culture may either stimulate learning, or may develop as a *result* of successful learning (Little *et al*. 1989: 19). In reality, the two effects probably operate simultaneously. The motivational argument for using authentic learning texts that represent the target culture remains strong whatever the case. Motivation is only one of a set of affective factors influencing second language acquisition. Others are dealt with in the following section.

2.4 Affect: The 'Affective Filter', Engagement, Empathy & Attitude

Affect may usefully be defined in the context of language learning as 'aspects of emotion, feeling, mood or attitude which condition behaviour' (Arnold and Brown 1999: 1). The influence of affective factors on the language acquisition process has been conceived (notably by Krashen, e.g. 1981: 22) as an 'affective filter'. The term refers to the way in which affective and attitudinal factors alter learners' receptivity to the target language. One of the reasons why integratively motivated language learners have greater success than instrumentally motivated ones, may be explained in terms of a lowered affective filter due to their involvement with the TL. The strength of this filter depends on a host of variables, including the learner's socio-cultural background, personality and attitude to the target language and to the TL speaking community (see below and Ellis 1994: 198-200). For language acquisition to be promoted, the teacher has to consider how the learners' affective filters will react to the texts they interact with in class. Krashen identifies materials which tend to lower the affective filter as 'comprehensible input on topics of real interest' (Krashen 1989: 29), that is, authentic texts. This is asserted time and again by practitioners (for example, Shanahan 1997, Swaffar 1985). Appropriately selected, such texts lower the affective filter by engaging the learner affectively. This is particularly true of literature, as will be argued more fully in Chapter 5. Rather than struggling against affect as an obstacle to learning (as implied by the term 'affective filter'), literature exploits the positive side of affect, the ability of language to engage the emotions (Shanahan 1997: 167).

Engagement is another factor that has been claimed as essential to successful learning (see, for example, Harmer 1996: 11). Being involved or engaged in a text and/or activity distracts the learner from the basic objective (language acquisition), thereby reducing anxiety, lowering the affective filter and allowing acquisition to take place. Engagement in a text/learning activity also presupposes some degree of *empathy*, either with the topic under discussion, the interlocutor, or whatever the activity entails, and this has always proved a forceful argument in favour of using authentic materials: 'There are strong indications from psychological and psycholinguistic research that the quality of a given psychological interaction relates to the extent to which the interactant sees the material being processed as having personal significance' (Little *et al.* 1989: 5-6). Little *et al.* claim, in fact, that engagement and empathy with the learning text actually have a direct effect on the language learning process: 'The more texts are related to learners' personal concerns and interests the deeper and more rapid the processing will be' (Little *et al.* 1989: 71-2).

In a broader context, empathy means identifying with speakers of the TL and/or with the TL culture. Empathy of this sort has been identified as an influential affective factor in language acquisition (Ellis 1994: 517-8, Larsen-Freeman and Long 1991: 190-1, Krashen 1989: 29). Empathy is, of course, a factor of personality in general, and personality is a major factor in determining success in language learning (Ellis 1994: 517). Guiora *et al.* (1972) give an intriguing psychoanalytical explanation of why an empathic personality tends to succeed in language learning. They see empathy as part of the 'language ego' that individuals develop, originally in their first language, and later in a second language if one is acquired. Learners who are more empathic have more 'permeable' language ego boundaries, they are able to suspend their native language identities and are consequently better able to acquire language; particularly pronunciation and colloquialism in the L2. The sensation felt by some people that they are 'a different person' when they speak the L2 supports this analysis. However empathic a personality a learner has, though, empathy cannot operate in a vacuum, and only authentic socio-cultural texts can be expected to engage him or her sufficiently to help promote language acquisition.

Engagement and empathy with a text, a language and its native speakers are all part of the learner's *attitude*, another complex affective factor influencing language learning (Ellis 1994: 198-200, Larsen-Freeman and Long 191: 175, Bacon and Finneman 1990: 459). Attitude is, of course, in itself a factor of motivation. Attitude can be sub-divided into attitudes towards the language itself, attitudes to its native speakers, to the TL culture and so on. With respect to the use of authentic texts, it is socio-cultural attitudes which interest us most. Texts drawn from the culture of the target language tend to be more involving to the learner and can thus be more emotionally demanding. This requirement for involvement in a sense tests the learner's attitude towards the TC. A positive socio-cultural attitude is displayed by a willingness to become involved with the input, which helps promote language learning. Conversely, where the TC is not liked or respected or is mistrusted, learning is hampered. Negative socio-cultural attitudes help explain why some immigrants, particularly those driven from their country by war or economic necessity, never achieve great competence in the language of their adopted culture. On the other hand, a 'chicken and egg' situation might be hypothesised; in the same way that success in acquisition of the L2 has been shown to breed positive attitudes towards the TC (Larsen-Freeman and Long 1991: 177), involvement with the TC through authentic texts might stimulate interest in/affection for the target culture, thereby creating a positive socio-cultural attitude and predisposing the learner to language acquisition.

The influence on affect of using authentic texts can admittedly be negative as well as positive. It can increase anxiety because of the (perceived) level of difficulty (Peacock 1997: 144) or due to feelings of linguistic inadequacy (Bacon and Finneman 1990: 461). On the other hand, it can raise confidence and enhance learning where students consider they are being treated as 'native speakers'[4]. Furthermore, once a precedent for the use of authentic texts has been set, learners soon adapt to the higher level of affective engagement that is required by them, and reject purpose-written learning texts[5].

2.5 Learning Style

Learning style is a core learner variable to influence the second language acquisition process and one that is keenly relevant to learners' reactions to authentic texts and tasks. Learning style may be defined as 'a composite concept which englobes a number of poles of individual difference (psychosocial, cognitive, sensory) to produce a profile of learners' behavioural and interactional preferences with respect to language learning' (Tudor 1996: 126). As learning styles (both culture- and learner-specific) are alluded to throughout the book[6], we shall look at them in some detail here.

Learning styles have been classified according to different criteria by different researchers, with some of the most comprehensive work on the subject from Willing (1988) and Oxford (notably, the Style Analysis Survey, (SAS), 1993). The SAS identifies five learning style contrasts, based on five variables, each ranging between identified poles[7]:

1. The use of physical senses:
Visual - students learn via visual stimuli, the written word, films, pictures, etc.
Auditory - learners prefer to hear the language e.g. via audio-tapes, speaking activities, lectures, role-plays, discussion, conversation.

Kinaesthetic or hands-on - learners prefer movement and activity, including doing projects, active games etc.

2. Dealing with other people:
An individual's degree of sociability lies on a continuum from *extroversion* to *introversion* which has the following implications for learning style:
Extroversion, according to Skehan (1989: 100-1), consists of two components, sociability (which in a language learning context manifests itself in a willingness to participate in a range of social activities, debates, role plays and so on) and impulsivity. The latter subsumes willingness to take risks, such as to enter into social situations offering the opportunity for language learning.
Introversion - introverted-type learners have an independent and more systematic approach to learning, preferring to work autonomously or with a partner they know well.

3. Handling possibilities:
Intuitive-random - learners who are oriented towards the future, who are able to identify the global principles of topic, who value speculations about possibilities, enjoy abstract thinking and eschew step-by-step instruction.
Concrete-sequential - learners who are present-oriented, prefer step-by-step activity, and need clarity of direction.

4. Approach to tasks:
Closure oriented - learners who are organised, forward planners, who meet deadlines, prefer neatness and structure, and want instructions, rules etc. to be clearly spelled out (Tudor 1996: 104).
'Open-learners' (Tudor's term: 1996: 104) - learners preferring discovery learning, who have the ability to pick up information in an unstructured way, who prefer to learn without deadlines/rules and who tolerate confusing situations and ambiguity (Tudor 1996: 101, 103-6).

5. Dealing with ideas:
Global learners - holistic learners who are prepared to guess meanings, predict outcomes and to communicate even if lacking relevant vocabulary or concepts (i.e. by paraphrasing, gesturing); learners who are spontaneous. Global learners possess the 'risk-taking' trait (see Tudor 1996: 103-6, Skehan 1989: 106-9) attributed to 'extroverts' mentioned in (2) above.
Analytic learners - learners who have a preference for focusing on details, logical analysis of data, a systematic approach to problem-solving, autonomous modes of working, contrastive analysis, rule-learning, and dissecting words and phrases.
(Based on Oxford 1993 and drawing on Skehan 1989: 100 - 18, Tudor 1996: 101 - 17 and Tomlinson 1998: 17 - 18).
Turning to the other comprehensive work on learning styles mentioned above, that conducted by the Adult Migrant Education Service (AMES) in Australia and reported by Willing (1988), the AMES study yielded the four most commonly known learning style profiles, ones which subsume many of the distinctions made

in Oxford's works, and which have, as Tudor observes, 'a ring of intuitive plausibility that many teachers recognise' (Tudor 1996: 117).

These learning styles are profiled as follows:

Analytical - learners who are autonomously orientated and who prefer analysis of language in terms of rules.

Communicative - learners preferring to learn by participating in communicative situations and using materials from the TL culture.

Concrete - students who prefer learning-by-doing activities.

Authority-oriented - often visually oriented learners who show preference for the traditional teacher-focused classroom, rule learning etc.

(Tudor 1996: 114-7, attributed to Willing 1988).

Learning style analysis is not intended to imply that learners slot neatly into learning style categories, nor that any of the learning styles described are intrinsically 'better' than others. A particular learning style may result in successful language learning in one situation but not in another. The extrovert learner, for example, whose substantial contribution in a classroom setting can be monitored by a teacher, may be at a disadvantage in the TC where NSs do not correct errors and where his/her loquacity prevents him/her from observing NS use of language. The reticence of the introverted-type learner, on the other hand, may be of concern to the teacher in the classroom situation, but may prove a valuable trait in the target culture where it allows for close scrutiny of the native speaker language and behaviour.

It has frequently been pointed out in the context of today's heightened awareness of cultural differences in learning, that learning style is as much conditioned by the cultural and pedagogical background of the learner, as reflective of individual preference (Tudor 1996: 108; Skehan 1989: 118; Little and Singleton 1990: 14; Riley 1990: 43). For example, in one study, the learning style preferences of Irish students from Trinity College Dublin, are reported as being for oral interaction and group learning, styles which reflect the 'general tendency of pedagogical practice in western Europe' (Little and Singleton 1990: 14). In contrast, the sort of open, 'risk-taking' learning style identified in the Oxford classification above is less likely to be prevalent among learners from societies such as Japan, where maintenance of 'face' is a high priority (see, for example, Skehan 1989: 118).

Authentic texts probably hold the most obvious appeal to the 'open', 'global' or 'communicative'-type learner (to use the terminology defined above), in terms of their motivational aspects, their cultural content and their integrative potential. Meanwhile, the breadth of TC media, ranging from the audio (songs, radio) to the audio-visual (films, television), appeal to a range of learning types, from those who respond best to visual stimuli to those who prefer the auditory. The *task-based* model which this book proposes for the use of authentic texts (see Chapter 4) also caters to the kinaesthetic learner who prefers movement, activity, and creativity. The task-based framework might, nevertheless, be one that is better suited to some individual and culturally conditioned learning styles, but less so to others.

However, this is one area in which learning-style research can usefully be applied. Insights into learning style variation lend practitioners the wherewithal to enlighten learners as to the range of learning style options open to them, and to help them extend their 'stylistic comfort zone' (the term is Oxford and Ehrman's, 1993: 198); that is, to adopt learning styles other than their preferred style/s (see also Tomlinson 1998: 18). For one of the most valuable findings of learning style research is that a learner's preference is not necessarily fixed, but can be swayed through the development of learner self-awareness (see Little and Singleton 1990: 14-16). It may also vary according to what is being learned, the learning environment, other group members and the motivation for studying a particular language (Tomlinson 1998: 17-18). Hence, if the use of authentic TC texts are felt to be essential to a comprehensive experience of the language and culture (as is the contention in this book), it would seem that all learners might be encouraged to adapt to the learning styles that cope best with such texts and with the activity-types they involve.

2.6 Instructed SLA

(Unbiased) research to date [...] shows people learning despite instruction, without instruction, and in ways that differ from the goals of a particular instructional pro- gramme. The value of instruction is by no means undermined in principle. Its value has simply been called into question.' (Sharwood Smith 1994: 21)

Analysing the effects of instructed language teaching would seem to be the *raison d'être* for SLA research - why study how language is acquired if there is not an endeavour to find ways of accelerating and improving the process? In fact, the effect of formal, instructed, classroom learning on the process, rate and success of language acquisition has become a major focus of SLA research.

Let us look first of all at what is meant by 'instruction'. Krashen made the distinction in his early work between 'instructed environments' - those containing the features of rule isolation/presentation and feedback, and 'informal environments' where these features are lacking (Krashen 1981: 40). In more recent research, formal instruction is defined as 'explicit grammar instruction' ('EGI') (as in studies by Terrell 1991 and Vanpatten and Cadierno 1993). In others it is more loosely identified with 'grammar teaching' (as in Ellis 1994: 611 and in Larsen-Freeman and Long 1991: 304). The only overall constant is that 'instruction' applies to that which takes place within the classroom environment. Beyond that, it seems to range from explicit grammar instruction or form-focused work to communicative classroom activities. Because of this inconsistency in the definition of 'instruction', there is a problem with comparing research studies in this area.

Most pertinent to our present concern, would be research comparing the effects on language acquisition of EGI using authentic texts, versus grammar instruction in coursebook - or grammar-syllabus-based situations. Unfortunately, the bulk of research in this area focuses not on the learning materials, but on the effects on language acquisition of instructed versus non-structured, 'naturalistic', learning contexts. The criteria typically used in this type of research are: acquisition processes, rate of acquisition and acquisition order, structural accuracy, ultimate learner proficiency and retention of learning (Larsen-Freeman and Long 1991: 299, Terrell 1991: 54, Ellis 1994: 612). Of these, the criterion perhaps most relevant to the context of learning via authentic texts is the effect of instruction on acquisition order. It is relevant because one of the main reservations about using authentic texts with learners is that they might not be familiar with, or 'prepared for' some of the language the texts contain. The concept most associated with acquisition order is *interlanguage* (Selinker 1972). The interlanguage refers to the linguistic system of the TL that learners build up, and which is manifested by their 'observable output' (Selinker 1972: 214). The interlanguage is conceived as a continuum, which is continuously revised, recreated and restructured in the direction of the target language. Research has shown that the order of the interlanguage stages that learners pass through are, firstly, dependent on the target language rather than the first language and, secondly, relatively fixed (Little *et al.* 1989: 8-9). Such evidence is forthcoming because the interlanguage is the outward manifestation of the learner's internal and unobservable 'temporary' grammar of the FL, so it is amenable to observation.

The findings of interlanguage/acquisition order research have startling implications as regards formal grammar instruction. According to comprehensive overviews of acquisition order research, there is strong evidence that, regardless of the learning situation, the natural sequence of acquisition order is immutable (Little *et al.* 1989: 8-9, Larsen-Freeman and Long 1991: 307, Ellis 1994: 635, Lightbown 2000: 442)[8]. This rather dismal conclusion (at least as far as the language teaching profession is concerned), is somewhat moderated by Pienemann in his teachability hypothesis: 'The teachability hypothesis predicts that instruction can only promote language acquisition if the interlanguage is close to the point when the structure to be taught is acquired in the natural setting' (Pienemann 1985: 37). In other words, since there are processing and other prerequisites to the learning of any given structure, learners will only acquire those structures that their interlanguage is primed to acquire. The obvious question is, how can the teacher know when the learner is 'ready' for any given structure, how can he or she establish which stage of their interlanguage the learner has reached? While many attempts have been made in this regard (see research cited in Ellis 1994: 636 and Larsen-Freeman 1991: 307-9), identifying readiness for learning particular structures remains a fascinating area to be researched (Larsen-Freeman 1991: 309, Sharwood Smith 1994: 184-5, Ellis 1994: 636).

The research discussed above, does, on the other hand, constitute a powerful argument in favour of using authentic texts with language learners. Since there appears to be little evidence that the order in which syntax is acquired corresponds to the order in which it is taught, and since the stages in interlanguage progression are as yet poorly understood, then syntactically and lexically rich input - authentic, unmodified language - would surely offer the learner the greatest range of potentially acquirable language (Little *et al.* 1989: 13). This idea is supported by research and by evidence that 'even' elementary learners can handle authentic texts (see research cited in Bacon and Finnemann 1990: 460).

The teachability hypothesis also relates to another of the criteria by which formal and informal instruction are compared; grammatical accuracy. The conclusions regarding this criterion appear to be similar to those relating to acquisition rate. Improvements in accuracy in any given structure, depend on whether the learner's interlanguage is at the appropriate receptive stage when learning the form. This appears, once more, to be true regardless of the type of learning situation:

> *One important factor determining whether formal instruction results in improved accuracy is the learner's stage of development. Instruction may lead to more accurate use of grammatical structures in communication providing the learner is able to process them. In other words, there are constraints on learners' ability to acquire grammatical structures, and if formal instruction is to be successful, it has to work in accordance with the internal processes that govern why some structures are acquired before others. (Ellis 1994: 627).*

Ellis's conclusion, based on a considerable body of research, is supported by similarly comprehensive work by Larsen-Freeman and Long. Larsen-Freeman and Long also found that instruction does not appear to impact on accuracy and attribute this to 'the researchers' choice of items which were developmentally beyond the reach of the learners involved, i.e. to poor timing of instruction' (Larsen-Freeman and Long 1991: 308). Reaching a similar conclusion, that grammar instruction is not a major factor in improving the accuracy of learners' speech, Terrell adds that one factor which *does* appear to impact on accuracy is *the amount of comprehensible input* (Terrell 1991: 54).

The accumulated evidence that specific grammar instruction does not impact on learner accuracy goes to support the call for the use of authentic texts as plentiful, varied and comprehensible input. With or without dedicated grammar consciousness-raising activities (which may or may not result in acquisition, in accordance with the teachability hypothesis) authentic texts appropriate to the learners' proficiency level provide the rich and comprehensible input that they can draw on freely in the development of their grammatical competence.

Given the evidence as regards the relative immunity of developmental orders and accuracy to formal instruction, indications that the *rate* of acquisition is increased as a result of classroom instruction (this is among the conclusions of Ellis, 1994: 659, Larsen-Freeman and Long, 1991: 312, 321, and Terrell, 1991: 55) would appear to be contradictory. One explanation is that this is due to the augmented quantities of comprehensible input provided in the classroom as opposed to in naturalistic settings where the learner has to 'seek out' input (Krashen 1985; Terrell 1991: 55). Classroom input is more likely to be roughly tuned to the $i+1$ level of the learner and is thus more appropriate as intake than input received during natural exposure. If this is so, then similarly 'roughly tuned' quantities of authentic texts may be as useful a supply of comprehensible input for this purpose.

The final two criteria regarding the instructed versus naturalistic learning environment, the effects on the learner's *ultimate proficiency* and the *durability* of learning, are clearly linked. It is in these two areas, however, that sufficient convincing and consistent research evidence is least forthcoming. This is in part because of the previously mentioned ambiguity in the variables used in the studies, and partly because the last criterion, durability, can only be tested within fairly long-term longitudinal studies. As yet these have been too few for definitive conclusions to be drawn (Ellis 1994: 638).

This brief overview of the research into the effects of classroom instruction has revealed the uncertain state of SLA research in this area. What it has clearly shown is that there is a need for specific definition(s) of 'formal instruction' (Larsen-Freeman and Long 1991: 322) which in turn would promote investigation into which type of instruction might be most productive (Ellis 1994: 638-9). There are suggestions, for example, that grammar instruction might be effective if introduced at particular points during the learner's processing of input (Vanpatten and Cadierno 1993), that it might be given an expanded role in supporting the acquisition process (Terrell 1991) or that the very notion of grammar might be conceived in psycholinguistic terms, as the processing of rules (Garrett 1986), with consequent implications for our teaching of it.

What is also clear is that the traditional presentation and practice of grammar rules has no overwhelming empirical justification in terms of enhanced language acquisition. As Ellis concludes, summarizing his overview of research into the effect of formal instruction:

> *There is little, if any, support for the claim that classroom learners must have formal instruction in order to learn the L2 [...] there is general recognition that much of the language learning that takes place in the classroom takes place 'naturally', as a result of learners processing input to which they are exposed. (1994: 657).*

This leaves open the possibility that learners' acquisition processes might respond better to alternative modes of inputting language data. Alternative models for language learning range from *discovery learning* (broadly based on the works of John Dewey writing in the early years of the last century), through task-based methodologies (see Chapter 4) and latterly, to autonomous learning, which as we will now see, has a particular affinity for the use of authentic texts.

2.7 Autonomous Learning[9]

'We are born, self-directed learners' (Benson 2001: 59). The autonomous learning mode is in a sense a return to our earliest experiences of learning, for despite taking place at so early an age, L1 acquisition is essentially an autonomous process. It precedes formal education and is controlled and directed by the child-learner. The learning of a second language is, therefore, unlike the learning of any other subject in that it has a precedent, in every individual, in the learning of their first language. The L1 learning paradigm has a number of implications for autonomous L2 learning. Firstly, in spite of the fact that the 'unconscious' autonomy that characterizes our earliest learning experiences is often overlaid by our subsequent experiences in formal education where we are forced into conformity to curricula, teaching methods and learning expectations, it might be that this early ability for autonomous learning can be reactivated in the appropriate conditions. Most essential among these are opportunities for learners to metaphorically step outside these constraints and to critically analyse their own motivations and expectations for learning, the learning procedures that work for them, and their dependency on the pedagogical system. To come to an informed awareness, in other words, of their own centrality to their learning (see also the description of the pedagogy of autonomy in Chapter 1 Section 1.1.3). Other conditions which help reactivate this innate autonomy in language learning, are those that incite the young child to attempt to use the language as an instrument of communication and interaction: a genuine and compelling incentive to do so. These are the very conditions, of course, that are striven for in the Communicative classroom, and it is no coincidence that learner autonomy has emerged in the wake of CLT.

A second area where L1 learning and autonomy in L2 learning coincide, concerns pace and content. Although L1 development proceeds in (largely predictable) stages, the pace is dictated by the child and is not subject (to any significant degree) to the control of external forces (Little 1991: 20). The same is true of L2 learning, where, as famously formalized by Pienemann in his teachability hypothesis (see Section 2.6 above), it is recognized that learners only learn when and what they are ready to learn of a language: 'learner control over the cognitive processes involved in language learning is a crucial factor in what is learned' (Benson 2001: 67). The control the learner wields is among the arguments in favour of naturalistic language learning (made most notably by Krashen, e.g. 1981), in which acquisition is conceived as a gradual analysis and absorbing of an internal grammar through exposure to comprehensible but not necessarily systematised input. As we have seen above, these arguments are usually contrasted with the difficulty of gauging the effectiveness of formal instruction (see, for example Ellis 1994: 611 ff. and 659).

A third factor linking autonomy and language learning is the *process* of language learning. The processes of language learning and language use are, as Little notes, 'essentially inseparable' (1997: 227), 'language use is the indispensable channel of language learning' (Little 1991: 37). Efficient language use i.e. communication in the TL, depends in large part on independence, self-reliance, and adaptability in varying social contexts (*ibid*: 27); in other words, on the capacity to function autonomously. If language use is indistinguishable from language learning, it follows that the latter is predicated on the capacity for independent interaction, as well as on the capacity to learn from interaction with others.

The last constituent in this complex interplay between language learning, language use and autonomy, is the authentic text: 'If language learning depends on language use, we shall want to embed the language learning process from the very beginning in a framework of communicative language use, and one indispensable part of this framework will be an appropriate corpus of authentic texts' (Little 1997: 228). Authentic texts implicate autonomy partly because their use demands greater personal investment on the part of the learner, who has to rally his/her knowledge of the target language and culture, thus making the vital connection between the classroom and the 'real world'. They also, of course, create the language-rich environment within which the autonomous language learner-user can flourish (McGarry 1995: 3). Research evaluating the acquisition of vocabulary from authentic texts in an autonomous learning context, for example, has shown this approach to be at least as successful as textbook approaches, with the added benefit of steeping learners in the L2 and developing their overall L2 competence (Dam and Legenhausen 1996: 280 reported in Benson 2001: 214 - 18).

To sum up, it has been argued here that language learning is 'naturally' an autonomous process, almost wholly so in the case of the L1, and far more so than it is convenient for traditional pedagogy to acknowledge, in the case of the L2. Since the process and progress of L2 learning depends so keenly on internal factors such as readiness and willingness, which the learner alone controls, it would seem reasonable to accede to this control by adopting approaches which exploit this autonomy rather than ones that seek to coerce it into the pedagogical straitjacket of set curricula and methods, and teacher-direction.

2.8 Consciousness Raising

Evidence from both first and second language acquisition research suggests that acquisition is a result of inductive processing whereby people notice and infer linguistic rules from the input they receive. Nonetheless, as has been explained above, acquisition does not occur until the learner is 'ready' for it. If *noticing* or *awareness* of systemic features of the language is the first step towards learning, then it follows that language teaching methods should foster this by (a) exposing learners to as rich a variety as possible of (authentic) language input, and by (b) guiding them towards these inductive ways of learning from such input.

While SLA research has been slow to confirm the necessary jump from *awareness* of systemic features to *acquisition*, that is, the ability to *apply* this knowledge, what has become known as a 'consciousness-raising approach' to learning grammar has been receiving growing validation in recent years: 'consciousness-raising constitutes an approach to grammar teaching which is compatible with current thinking about how learners acquire L2 grammar' (Ellis 1991: 224, see also Ellis 1994: 643-5). Meanwhile, reports from practitioners applying consciousness-raising approaches (e.g. Tomlinson 1998: 13-14, Fox 1998: 42, Carter *et al.*1998: 79-80, Willis 1998: 45-6), suggest that learners do indeed eventually acquire features they have been encouraged to notice in this way, 'provided that the learners receive future relevant input' (Tomlinson 1998:14).

The rationale of the consciousness-raising approach is that given sufficient exposure and opportunity, learners will discover elements of L2 grammar and 'reach conclusions which make sense in terms of their own systems' (Willis 1998: 56). This involves reconciling their new findings with their current interlanguage, that is, 'noticing the gap' between their understanding of the use and usage of a particular feature, and examples of its use by native speakers. This leads to revision of the interlanguage towards more a native-like form and eventually towards acquisition of that form. In the natural and unforced aspect of this means of acquiring language, the consciousness-raising approach can be seen to draw on L1 acquisition (see Lightbown and Spada 1993: 7, de Villiers and de Villiers 1978: 53 on this aspect of first language learning). And like L1 acquisition (and unlike the PPP approach - Presentation, Production, Practice - with which it contrasts) it does not constrain the learners to immediate *production* of a particular grammatical form.

This naturalistic aspect is only one of the advantages of the consciousness-raising approach. Another is that in the longer term, it nurtures language awareness, sensitising learners to the structures of the target language in a way that passively receiving information about language rules does not. Applying this approach trains learners in techniques which they can then use to study independently. In the affective sphere, self-discovery nurtures curiosity and builds confidence (Tomlinson 1998: 88). One crucial benefit of using a consciousness-raising approach is that by linking the study of grammatical structure firmly to language encountered within texts, it checks the tendency to perceive grammatical forms as isolated phenomena. It encourages identification of structures with the discourse types in which they typically appear:

> *An examination of grammar in texts means that grammatical form is not an exclusive focus, for grammar is necessarily seen only as part of a more complex social and textual environment and as realising specific functions in a purposeful context. A study of grammar in texts is a study of grammar in use. (Carter 1997: 33-4)*

Even by its advocates, however (such as Ellis, see 1994: 645), the consciousness-raising approach can be seen to have some limitations: the main one is that it is not suited to all learning styles or to all learner levels. The approach is most suited to analytic-type learners (see Learning Styles above), while young and elementary learners may not have the necessary L2 basis to study language in this way.

2.9 Language Processing

One of the strongest justifications for learners to receive authentic rather than artificially structured language input comes from (what we understand of) how language input is processed. There is a basic distinction made in the literature on language learning between *bottom-up processing*, i.e. decoding the incoming message itself (Nunan 1989: 25; 1991: 4) and *top-down processing* (deployment of 'background' knowledge). *Bottom-up processing* involves the learner in:

- Segmenting the input into recognisable/comprehensible components.

- Selectivity/identifying redundancy: differentiating between elements having semantic content and those with low content.

- Detecting syntactic patterns which organise the input into semantic chunks/constituents.

- Detecting relationships between constituents: e.g. via lexical indicators such as discourse markers, conjunctions etc.

(drawn from Nunan 1989: 25, Grauberg 1997: 181, Underwood 1989: 2, Byrne 1986: 8)

Top-down processing involves imposing stored schematic information (contextual, situational, socio-cultural) to 'make sense of' the input, for example:

- To identify the participants, situation, discourse topic, type of communicative event.

To infer relationships, sequences of events, missing information.

- To anticipate outcomes.

(based on Nunan 1989: 26)

The absence of schematic information - situational clues - is actually one source of humour, where brief interchanges are heard or repeated out of their context. The utterance 'Oh dear, I've forgotten my banana!', for instance, is rather comical until put in its situational context (uttered by an athlete in the changing room; eating a banana within 15 minutes of exercising speeds recovery by replacing the potassium and carbohydrate lost during exercise). The importance of contextual information for comprehension illustrates, as Nunan points out, 'that meaning does not reside exclusively within the words on the tape recorder or on the page. It also exists in the head of the listener or reader' (Nunan 1991: 18).

The conceptualisation of these two 'opposing' types of processes is necessarily a theoretical rationalisation of the complex processes involved in comprehending input. In reality, the two processes probably 'work [...] together in parallel, feeding off each other, rather than a strict sequence of stages' (Harben 1999: 27). Nevertheless, if learners are made aware of these different ways of processing language input, and of their implications for comprehension and ultimately language acquisition, they may be able to achieve 'control' over them so that they become, in effect, learning skills.

The two processes tend to be balanced differently at different levels of language proficiency. Elementary level learners are particularly reliant on top-down processing. Having little syntactic or lexical knowledge of the TL, they deploy stored schematic knowledge, that is, they rely heavily on context and on their own knowledge of the subject matter, in their attempts at comprehension. The operation of such processes is particularly striking in low level students of LSP, whose expertise in their subject area enables them to cope with TL texts in their specialism which lay native speakers might have difficulty with[10]. It may be inferred that the best type of texts for the encouragement of top-down processing are – because they are related to a real cultural or topical context or subject area of which learners can be expected to have some knowledge – authentic texts. These should preferably be ones that are free of the typical 'comprehension' apparatus of discrete point questions, structural and/or lexical focusing and so on, since these interfere with a holistic approach to them and constrain learners to implement bottom-up processes (step-by-step decoding, and so on) (Swaffar 1985: 17). It has furthermore been suggested that texts have not only to be authentic, but reasonably long, to allow the students' background knowledge to be called into play (Krashen 1989: 20-1). It is now being recognised that learners can benefit more from practising language processing strategies such as these, than from focusing on correctness and correction of output (Van Patten and Cadierno 1993, Vogely 1995).

This conception of language processing as a holistic rather than a piecemeal process is central to another area of research relating to language acquisition. Work in the field of neurophysiology revealing where in the brain input is received and how it is processed have given rise to new perceptions about how language might be learned. Neurophysiology research has demonstrated that the two hemispheres of the brain process different types of information. The left hemisphere processes in logical and analytical modes, handling verbal processing and hence language. The right brain deals with the intuitive, affective modes and handles non-verbal processing (of musical and visual input, movement etc.) and is thought to house long-term memory (Hooper Hansen 1998: 311). The implications for language learning, and indeed, learning in general, are that conventional teaching practices engage the left hemisphere leaving the right-hemisphere under-exploited and, what is more, ignoring its potential for deep (durable) learning. Harnessing the potential of the 'whole brain' has been the rationale for a number of 'alternative' language learning approaches such as those described in Chapter 1 Section 1.1.3, Suggestopedia, Total Physical Response, Neuro Linguistic Processing as well as the humanistic approach (for example, Rinvolucri 1999a: 194-210).

These findings have by now impacted on the mainstream, however. Arnold and Brown talk of whole-brain learning as one of the 'mega-trends for learning in the twenty-first century' (Arnold and Brown 1999: 7-8, see also Tomlinson 1998: 20-1). Whole-brain learning may therefore be said to be the neurological rationale for the crucial place now given to affect in language learning (see Sections 2.3 and 2.4

above), since more of the brain's potential is said to be activated when the emotions are engaged. The concept also justifies the centrality of the *task* paradigm in learning (see Chapter 4), where language is used to achieve a goal, and is more likely to be linked to non-verbal activity (such as drawing, singing or physical movement). The stimulation of affective engagement through the use of authentic texts (particularly ones using audio or audio-visual media) and through the creative tasks that involve them, is in line with these findings on laterality, as these maximise the brain's potential and open the way to deep learning.

2.10 Conclusion

This chapter has examined some of the SLA research relevant to the use of input from authentic language texts. What has been revealed is that the results of current research on the whole appear to support the use of authentic texts for language learning. The validity of the pedagogical practice of 'simplifying' input is being called into question, while the richness of authentic input is shown to be beneficial in a number of ways. Increased understanding of inductive language processing has highlighted the importance of a having rich linguistic context in which to operate. Richness of content, it has been shown, creates a positive environment for affective factors essential to learning, most notably, motivation and engagement. Furthermore, conclusive evidence of the impact of structured language instruction on such factors as grammatical accuracy, acquisition order or durability of learning is conspicuously lacking. This undermines that major perceived barrier to the use of authentic texts, the perception that they do not 'fit into' the systematised language syllabus.

The implications of SLA research for the use of authentic texts as the basis for language learning materials may be synthesised as follows:

• Authentic texts provide the best source of rich and varied comprehensible input for language learners.

• Elaborative changes to a text enhance comprehensibility better than does simplification.

• Authentic texts impact on affective factors essential to learning, such as motivation, empathy and emotional involvement.

• Learning style (individual or culturally-conditioned) need not be an impediment to the efficacy of the use of authentic texts and tasks for learning.

• Authentic texts are suited to a naturalistic, consciousness-raising approach to learning TL grammar.

• Authentic texts are particularly suited to the deployment of the more holistic mode of language processing, top-down processing.

• Authentic texts (from the audio and audio-visual media in particular) stimulate 'whole brain processing' which can result in more durable learning.

As well as establishing the SLA research evidence for the use of authentic texts in language learning, the findings of this chapter inform the pedagogical rationale for the authenticity approach, presented in the next chapter, and the design of a practical framework for the approach in Chapter 4.

Notes

1   The concept of a Language Acquisition Device (LAD) was originated by Chomsky (1965: 25-37).

2   In this chapter, the terms 'learning' and 'acquisition', differentiated most notably by Krashen (for example, 1981: 1) to denote conscious and unconscious processes respectively, are used interchangeably. This is in line with the observation that the distinction, though striking at the time, has neither been adhered to consistently in the literature (Ellis 1994: 14), nor fully accepted by researchers (*ibid.*: 359-61).

3   Some intriguing 'preliminary' findings by Peacock (1997), however, indicated that although learners were more motivated by authentic texts, they found them 'significantly less interesting' than artificial ones. This finding may be accounted for by the fact that Peacock's subjects were learners whose motivation was instrumental rather than integrative: they were Koreans studying English in Korea for future study or work requirements.

4   In feedback on one project module I ran, one of the students commented that he had enjoyed the module and benefited from it because he had been given the opportunity to work in a native-like way: 'This class is real University of Limerick's class for Irish students!'

5   I became aware of this on an occasion when I attempted to follow a class in which learners had worked with a recording of the previous evening's news, by a class that used a textbook 'imitation' of the news. One learner's question 'and which day is this from?' brought home to me the importance of maintaining the levels of affective (and cognitive) involvement demanded by authentic texts.

6   Most notably in Chapter 3, where the Communicative Approach is said to assume particular learning styles and in Chapter 11, where certain learning styles are associated with the use of particular technologies.

7   The classification below is based on Oxford but glossed where relevant with criteria from other writers.

8   This supports anecdotal evidence from practitioners who have had the frustrating experience of teaching and practising a particular grammatical point only to hear learners subsequently revert to the 'incorrect' form.

9   See also Chapter 1 Section 1.1.3 for an outline of the principles and practices associated with autonomous learning.

10 In my experience teaching English to Ukranian pilots at the University of Limerick Language Centre (ULLC) in 1992, even those with low level proficiency in the language had few problems understanding the Boeing Aircraft manual, as they imposed their schematic knowledge of such manuals in their own language.

Chapter Three:
Authentic Texts for Language Learning
The Pedagogical Rationale

The last chapter put forward the arguments for using authentic texts in language learning based on evidence from SLA research. In this chapter we turn to the pedagogical arguments for the use of authentic texts for language learning. These are encapsulated here as *'the 3 c's'*, *culture, currency* and *challenge*. *Culture*, in that authentic texts incorporate and represent the culture/s of speakers of the target language; *currency*, in that authentic texts offer topics and language in current use, as well as those relevant to the learners; *challenge*, in that authentic texts are intrinsically more challenging yet can be used at all proficiency levels. In making arguments for the strengths of authentic texts under these three headings, the implicit contrasts are unavoidably with the materials traditionally used for language learning today, viz., the coursebook, and comparisons are drawn in each case.

It is argued, in the first section, that culture and language are indivisible, any and every linguistic product of a society from a newspaper headline to a food label embodying/representing the culture. This means that it is crucial to include consciousness-raising of this cultural element in language teaching, and the only vehicles suitable for this are these very linguistic products, authentic texts. It is argued that to neglect the cultural element, or seek to neutralise it - an accusation that has been levied towards the ELT coursebook as a genre - is to present only a partial picture of the language. This can actually inhibit language learning because it does not allow for the development of the *schemata* of the target language culture, i.e., culture-specific elements vital to a command of the language. The 'spanner in the works' of this argument is that, in the context of English as with other global languages, one language does not mean one culture. The solution to this quandary suggested here, in the context of teaching the English language-and-culture, is to locate it firmly in the local culture, using locally sourced authentic texts.

Section two makes the next argument for the use of authentic texts for language learning and this is summarised in the term *currency*. In this context, as well as 'up-to-date-ness' and topicality, the meaning of the term is expanded to encompass the advantages born of these, *relevance* and *interest* to the learner and the affective factors these imply. Authentic texts, it is argued, offer learners this sort of currency of both subject matter and language, that the ELT coursebook as a genre cannot, due to the breadth of its markets and the constraints of its medium. This section then addresses the issue of building a syllabus based on authentic texts to replace the traditional one (which these days is often the syllabus provided by the coursebook).

The last section, 'Challenge', makes the argument that the very feature of authentic texts that is often perceived as an impediment to their use with language learners, *difficulty*, is in fact an advantage. Firstly, it is argued that challenge is a positive impetus in learning and that students should not be denied interesting learning material on the basis of their proficiency level. Secondly, it is shown that 'difficulty' is a factor not of the text used but of the task set. Finally, it is argued that in any case, suitable authentic texts can be found for *all* levels of learner proficiency and the reader is referred to the subsequent chapters of this book for lengthier discussion and illustrations of this.

3.1 Culture

The core argument in favour of the use of authentic texts in language learning is that all linguistic products of a culture are representative of the culture within which they are produced; 'even the humblest material artefact which is the product and the symbol of a particular civilisation, is an emissary of the culture out of which it comes' (T. S. Eliot 1948: 92). In maintaining that culture and language are thus part of a symbiotic whole, an obvious first step is to seek a definition of what we mean by culture. Yet a 'definitive' definition of culture remains elusive- elusive enough for the poet T. S. Eliot to have felt the need to write an entire treatise on the subject in his *Notes towards the Definition of Culture* (1948). Among the definitions that Eliot draws out are the 'anthropological' definition of culture in which are included 'the characteristic activities and interests of a people'[1] (Eliot 1948: 31). Today this anthropological aspect is conventionally termed 'culture with a small 'c'', defined by more recent writers in terms such as the following: 'Culture means the total body of tradition borne by a society and transmitted from generation to generation. It thus refers to the norms, values, standards by which people act, and it includes the ways distinctive in each society of ordering the world and rendering it intelligible' (Murphy 1986: 14).

The anthropological aspect is one of two facets of culture that make up its contemporary definition. The second is the traditional concept of culture as the 'intellectual refinement' and artistic achievement of a society, its literature, art and music; 'culture with a capital 'C''. In fact, of course, the two facets are interdependent. The intellectual 'products' of a society *affect* but at the same time *reflect* the behaviours and values of its people and the frameworks within which they function.

The vital element common to both these facets of culture is language. The relationship between language and culture has been endlessly reconfigured over the centuries. Underlying the contemporary notion of the language-culture relationship are the writings of Sapir and Whorf. What became known as the Sapir-Whorf hypothesis suggests that the language we use determines the way in which we view and think about the world around us, 'language is a guide to 'social reality'. As Sapir expressed it: 'It is an illusion to think that we can understand the significant outlines of a culture through sheer observation and without the guide of the linguistic symbolism which makes these outlines significant and intelligible to society' (1958 [1929]: 68).

The symbiotic nature of the culture-language relationship means that neither can be understood if studied in isolation:

> *Language is not simply a reflector of an objective cultural reality. It is an integral part of that reality through which other parts are shaped and interpreted. It is both a symbol of the whole and a part of the whole which shapes and is in turn shaped by sociocultural actions, beliefs and values. In engaging in language, speakers are enacting sociocultural phenomena; in acquiring language, children acquire culture [...] Given this theoretical viewpoint, it follows that to teach culture without language is fundamentally flawed and to separate language and culture teaching is to imply that a foreign language can be treated in the early learning stages as if it were self-contained and independent of other sociocultural phenomena. (Byram 1991: 18)*

In our language teaching, then, we cannot 'tack on' a cultural element like 'an expendable fifth skill' (Kramsch (1993: 1), since culture so fundamentally underpins the language we teach. Furthermore, if the texts used for learning the language are to truthfully represent the culture of the target language, they must be ones that are products both *of* and *for* that culture, i.e. authentic texts.

The cultural element present in authentic texts is, of course, not necessarily explicit. As Tomalin and Stempleski point out: 'Little benefit will result from merely displaying a cultural document or artefact in class. Students need to be trained to extract appropriate information from the material' (1993: 8). Rather like a page written in invisible ink, the cultural message is there to be read, but only if one has learned how to make the invisible writing appear. Such a skill is known as *cultural awareness* and involves sensitivity to the impact of culturally-induced behaviour on language use and communication (Tomalin and Stempleski 1993: 5). The implication is that such awareness will lead to empathy - an important step in successful language learning being the capacity to identify with the target language culture (see Chapter 2 Sections 2.3 and 2.4 'Affect'). Such empathy can be difficult to achieve, however. In learning about another culture it is impossible to be entirely objective, since the native culture quite simply 'gets in the way'; 'the native cultural experience is bound to shape the perception of the new reality by relating and evaluating both fields of experience' (Buttjes and Byram 1991: 232-3) (the importance of the learner's native culture is also discussed in Section 3.1.2 below). Nevertheless, the fact that the native culture always serves as a reference point for the foreign one can actually be used to great advantage in the language learning classroom. Drawing comparisons and contrasts between cultures can serve as a useful exercise in itself or as a starting point for deeper explorations into them. It can also broaden understanding and ultimately improve the learner's ability to communicate with native speakers of his/her target language culture.

The 'treasure chests' of cultural exploration are of course, authentic texts which 'contain' the culture. Exposure to TC films, television programmes, newspaper/magazine articles, literature and so on, gives learners the opportunity to observe TC customs, behaviours and interactions, and thence to infer underlying values and attitudes. As 'keys for opening up the TL society' (Maley 1993: 3) then, authentic texts help the learner build a sort of 'cultural framework' for the language. This leads us to one of the most intriguing theories associated with the language-culture bond, and one of the most convincing pedagogical arguments for using authentic texts which incorporate a cultural element: the concept of *schema*.

3.1.1 Schema theory

The relevance of schema theory to language learning is, to put it briefly, that it offers a psycholinguistic explanation for what can be misconstrued as linguistic misunderstandings. The concept comes from the field of psychology, where *schemata* are defined as 'cognitive networks that encapsulate our expectations regarding more or less standardised situations and/or more or less standardised types of discourse' (Edmonson 1997: 51). Schemata may thus be conceived as structured groups of concepts which constitute generic knowledge about events, scenarios, actions, or objects that has been acquired from past experience. Schemata are culture-specific and to some extent idiosyncratic since these concepts are formed within an individual's mind influenced by his/her own cultural background and through his/her personal experience. They are, then, an individual's notional representation of social/behavioural norms and phenomena which s/he has constructed during the process of acculturation into his/her own culture. When processing language input, the reader/listener effectively 'maps' the input against an existing schemata that is compatible with the incoming information. The classic illustration of how schemata work comes from Collins and Quillian (1972):

> The policeman held up his hand and stopped the car.

Layer upon layer of implicit information comes into play in the comprehending of this sentence; a knowledge of the mechanics of a car (which has a braking system to stop it); an assumption that there was a driver inside the car who operated the system; acquaintance with conventions regarding traffic control and the role a policeman might play in it, and so on. The knowledge required to understand this sentence might be termed a 'traffic cop schema' (Carrell and Eisterhold 1988: 77-8). The sentence would be interpreted via an entirely different schemata, however, if the policeman were known to be Superman (*ibid.*). Comprehension thus emerges through an interactive and cyclical process occurring between the reader's background knowledge and the text (Carrell and Eisterhold 1988: 76). This process is far more vigorous in the case of the non-native speaker-reader who is in the process of creating new sets of schemata for his/her new linguistic culture. New schemata are built up through a process of continual revision as new input is compared to what has previously been conceived.

Schemata include abstract notions such as behavioural norms and so on, as well as more concrete ones such as lexical terms referring to administrative, political and social systems. The most accessible ones are obviously those having lexical representations. The cultural specificity of these is evidenced by the fact that they are often so difficult to translate that they are used in the original - an example being the Irish word *craic*[2], which has recently come into currency in British English. The complexities of its usage mean there is no single-word equivalent in English: 'When learners acquire an understanding of the connotations of lexical items in the foreign language and contrast them with the connotations of an apparently equivalent item in their own, they begin to gain insight into the schemata and perspectives of the foreign language' (Byram *et al*. 1994: 44). This experience is potentially 'disconcerting' (Byram *et al*. 1994: 26), since discovering new ways of conceptualising experience entails 'unpicking' and challenging one's own culture-specific schemata. A revealing description of such an experience is given by a Japanese student, in this account of learning English in Ireland:

> *When I joined the English course at UL[3], there was a student who had been there for months. When he spoke to teachers and staff, he just used their first names. I regarded him as extremely rude. I have never called my teachers, lecturers and professors just their first name during my life in Japan [...] When I was a college student in Japan, I took an English class which was taught by Americans. I remember that when they introduced themselves, they said 'Please call me John (or something).' But we never called them by their first name but surname. I thought they were just trying to be friendly and did not want to be called by their first name. So I called our lecturers and staff 'Mrs' or 'Mr.' in Ireland for a while. But one day a lecturer asked me why I called her 'Mrs'. According to her when someone is called by surname using 'Mr.' or 'Mrs' it is official situation. She told me that they do not usually call someone by their surname, and if someone addresses her as 'Mrs' she will feel strange. This truth is very shocking to me [...] After my lecturer mentioned about the way of calling people by their first name, I tried. I felt strange for a while but I coped with that way.*[4]

While what is being described here might appear superficially to be a simple case of inappropriate register, the degree of introspection and discomfiture involved, the difficulty the student had in first accepting, and then adapting to Irish mores, are symptomatic of culture-shock, that is, the experience of having one's core cultural concepts shaken.

The concept of schemata, therefore, helps rationalise pyscholinguistic sources of misunderstandings: 'Failures to access appropriate schemata (i.e. comprehend) are often interpreted solely as deficiencies in language processing skills' (Carrell and Eisterhold 1988: 82). Nunan, for instance, cites a study which found a lack of appropriate background knowledge to be a more significant factor in the ability of L2 learners to understand school texts than linguistic complexity (measured by various readability formulae) (Nunan 1991: 5). The importance of cultural background to comprehension helps explain why for example, one of my groups of advanced level Japanese students initially had difficulties comprehending a passage from the Roddy Doyle novel *Paddy Clarke Ha Ha Ha* where the young protagonist's father pretends to talk to Father Christmas by shouting up the chimney (in Doyle 1993: 33). The students were acquainted with the Father

Christmas tradition, as it has been adopted to some extent in Japan, but were apparently not familiar with the use of the chimney as Father Christmas's traditional mode of entry into houses. In the now-famous study by Steffensen and Joag-dev (1984), subjects from two ethnic groups, Indian and American, were found to make various errors when asked to recall two parallel reading texts describing Indian and American weddings, even though they were highly proficient readers. Comprehension, it was concluded, is a function of cultural background knowledge, i.e. schemata, as well as linguistic competence.

Schema theory, in brief, gives a psycholinguistic interpretation to the role of cultural knowledge in the learning and understanding of the target language. The emphasis it places on acquiring knowledge of the target language culture is one of the strongest arguments for the use of authentic texts which incorporate this cultural information. It also begs two further questions which will be dealt with in turn below. First of all, how can we talk about a 'target language culture' in the case where the language is used by many different societies and cultures, as is the case with English? And, secondly, how can such a disparate selection of English-speaking cultures be adequately represented through centrally-produced teaching materials, i.e. ELT coursebooks?

3.1.2 English as an international language

The relativism that is inherent in the concept of culture is nowhere more apparent - or more problematic - than in the context of an international language such as English. English is spoken worldwide in many diverse L1 and L2 cultures which inevitably embody many different sets of values, customs and life experiences. It is a first language for between 325 and 450 million people worldwide[5]; only Mandarin Chinese has more first-language speakers. English remains a first language in islands such as St. Helena and the Falklands and as far away as Pitcairn Island in the far eastern Pacific. English is a second language in most former British colonies; in India, Sri Lanka, and in most African countries (in South Africa, English is increasingly the *lingua franca* despite the country's officially multilingual status[6]). More people speak English as a second language than any other (between 150 and 350 million): in fact, if current population and language learning trends continue, within 10 years there will be more second language than first language speakers of English (Crystal 1997: 11). English has some kind of special administrative status in over 70 countries, including Nigeria, Singapore, Mauritius, the Seychelles, Hong Kong and the Philippines. It is used for official and/or educational purposes in the islands of the Pacific, such as Fiji and the Solomon Islands (Trudgill 1993: 14-15). As of time of writing, it is estimated that up to a billion people are learning English, this figure boosted by the great numbers of learners in China, Japan, Indonesia and Brazil (Crystal 1997: 10). It is estimated that the English language will eventually share global linguistic hegemony with the other two dominant languages, Spanish and Chinese (Graddol 1997: 3).

English is used as a *lingua franca,* or, more accurately, as an International

Language, in the fields of tourism, business, science, technology, education and entertainment - as Modiano points out, 'English is now a prerequisite for participation in a vast number of activities. The global village is being constructed in the English language as are the information highways[7]' (Modiano 2001:341). Modiano also notes the phenomenon of the use of English by non-native speaker artists to create cultural artefacts such as songs (as did the Swedish pop group ABBA, for instance) in order to access global markets (Modiano 2001: 342).

The status of the English language as described here reveals English culture to be fragmented, in fact, into a myriad of major and minor (or sub-) cultures. As the world market for English continues to grow, so the connection between the language and its original (British) culture becomes more and more tenuous. Many of the former colonies have retained English as a first or second language but long ago won their independence and integrated traces of the colonial culture with their own. The existence of multiple English language cultures might be represented via some version of the much-used Venn diagram, overlapping in some areas but separate in others:

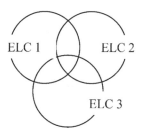

ELC = English Language Culture

Examples which spring to mind are the 'overlap' of sports such as cricket in the former British colonies, India and Pakistan, places where another element, religion, distinguishes the cultures. The Venn diagram motif is an essential one to be borne in mind when conceiving English language teaching materials for use by cultures where English has some status as L1, L2 or official language, because it is all too easy to make the assumption of an intrinsic commonality of English language cultural reference points. It might be hard for Britons and Americans, for instance, to conceive of English language cultures so remote that such (to them) 'core' cultural icons as *the Pope, the Beatles, Charlie Chaplin, Romeo and Juliet, Bob Dylan* and *Superman* are actually unheard of. This was a chastening lesson I learned when including such icons in draft materials being written for an International audience with a Hong Kong-based publisher[8], who pointed out that: 'We are dealing with world English and should therefore be wary about assuming a natural link to a British/Irish/American culture, or sense of culture and sense of humour [...] Europe is amazingly remote and unimportant to people in Hong Kong' (Stokes 1997[9]). Yet this is an assumption - we might even say a presumption - to which ELT coursebook writers remain typically prone - look, for example, at the way Western pop icons such as *George Harrison, Eric Clapton, Abba* and *Annie*

Lennox[10] are repeatedly trotted out. This is just one example of the cultural problems that the coursebook runs up against, and it is to the problematic issue of culture and the ELT coursebook that we now turn.

3.1.3 Culture and the ELT coursebook

The ELT coursebook as a genre has to deal with two culture-related problems: one regards the English language culture it presents; the second regards the culture/s of the learners who use it. The argument made below is that these two demands - and the interplay between them - give the centrally-produced ELT coursebook a close to impossible agenda and leave as the only alternative, the production of materials and coursebooks on local/national scales.

The ELT coursebook has become the customary whipping horse as far as the presentation of English language culture is concerned. From the 1980s, the ELT coursebook as a genre was faced with myriad accusations - of being Anglo-centric (Prodromou 1988: 76), 'relentlessly British' (Rossner 1988: 145), of projecting Western (and mainly white, middle class) Anglo-Saxon, values and educational attitudes (Rossner 1988: 160, Dendrinos 1992:153, Rinvolucri 1999b: 12-14) and much, much more, many of these being hurled by people who themselves write coursebooks, such as Rinvolucri (1999b), Bell and Gower (1998) Tomlinson (1999) and Pulverness (1999a, 1999b). ELT publishers responded manfully in the attempt to acknowledge English as the world language it has become, churning out new books with a determinedly pan-European and trans-global gloss. Today's coursebooks offer international stories and topics rather than the predominantly British-oriented ones of yesteryear. A Dutch girl survives a jungle plane crash (*Lifelines Intermediate*, Hutchinson 1997: 18), life in a Greek village (*Initiative*, Walton and Bartram 2000: 52), how to be a Carioca (person from Rio de Janeiro) (*Activate your English Intermediate*, Sinclair and Prowse 1996: 7). They look more towards other English-speaking countries - *Language to Go Pre-Intermediate* (Cunningham and Mohamed 2002) has texts about Australia (p54-5) India (p34-5) and a number about the USA (p 4-5, p32-3, p 40-1 and p48-9).

In representing Britain, the 'white middle class' aspect of the coursebook has begun to shift. The proportion of British people from ethnic groups figuring in coursebooks is now more reflective of British society; in a typical cross-section of books published since 1996[11], between 11.5% and 20% of photographs of people featured non-whites[12]. However, 'successful' people, such as sports and entertainment personalities figured conspicuously among these, and with such notable exceptions as a photograph of a homeless white man, and a group of shabby punk rockers (both in *English Panorama*, O'Dell 1996: 102 and 72), representation still remains insistently middle class, both in populace and the activities they pursue, giving the typical ELT book that clean, happy, smiley glow normally attributed to the advertisement.

It would seem, then, that the ELT coursebook is still caught in its attempt to serve two masters, due to the trans-global reach of its commercial agenda. By broadening the language and culture link to acknowledge English as a world language, the ELT coursebook serves the requirements of its non-Anglocentric global audience, who have little interest in British or other English L1 cultures. But in doing so, the coursebook risks denying its cultural roots and transmuting into an a-cultural entity (see, for example, Pulverness 1999a), one where the language-culture link is all but imperceptible. This is the risk run by books geared towards international business people using English as a *lingua franca*, such as the *International Express* series, whose Pre-Intermediate coursebook has only two sections about the UK, one about Harrods (pp10-12) and another on tourism in the UK (pp18-21), and one about Australia (pp26-31). Where coursebooks do retain a tighter language-and-culture link, this tends to remain largely that of the UK, with the behaviours, customs and values portrayed in them being too culture-specific for teachers and learners using them in non-UK settings (this was one of the findings in a survey of EFL teachers in Barcelona, reported in Gray 2000).

In general, while the changes wrought in the ELT book as a genre over the past two decades show that writers/publishers are far more culturally aware than they once were, the question remains as to how far these books actively go in fostering cross-cultural awareness in their *users*. In a survey of 15 coursebooks published between 1997 and 2002 (see Appendix I), less than two-thirds had any material aimed at raising cross-cultural awareness, and only *two* made serious attempts at this (and these had the same author and were part of the same series: *International Express Intermediate* and *Pre-Intermediate*). The latter has a whole seven-page unit on 'Communicating across cultures' (pages 98-105) but this is the only case in the 15 books reviewed where cross-cultural awareness-raising materials cover more than two consecutive pages. Materials on this subject in coursebooks are generally studiously neutral. They tend to take the form either of fairly bland texts giving examples of cross-cultural differences (e.g. the text 'Culture Clash' in *Lifelines* 1997: 51), or of 'culture quizzes' which test learners' superficial knowledge of the customs of other cultures (e.g. 'Around the world quiz' in *International Express Intermediate* 1997: 88-9) - and in using a genre more often identified with teenage magazines, there is, arguably, a risk of trivialising the subject matter. It is debatable how far using materials like these can genuinely foster inter-cultural awareness or tolerance. As Maley points out, for this we need materials that sharpen observation and encourage critical thinking about cultural stereotypes (1993: 3). What seems clear is that although the need for cross-cultural awareness is recognised by some coursebook-writers and editors, the commercial demand for cross-cultural *acceptability* takes priority and has a neutralising effect on the materials designed on this issue.

Let us now turn to the second aspect of the problem of culture and the ELT book, the culture of the learner market that the product serves. Most products that are produced for an international market are 'tweaked' for their different cultural markets - they might be given a different name (for instance, Honda's *Fitta*, launched in 2001, was renamed *Honda Jazz* for the Nordic market[13]), or they might have a different selling point (Volvo's advertising campaigns, for example, highlight the car's safety to UK audiences, its status to the French market and its performance to the Germans, Goddard 1998:80). So let us consider the handling of one key cultural factor by the centrally-produced ELT coursebook, the *pedagogical* cultures of its learner markets. Like other cultural factors - work ethos, eating habits, leisure activities – learning is a culturally-conditioned behaviour (Nelson 1995: 29). Such aspects as teacher-learner relationships, classroom practices, learning styles, degree of learner autonomy and so on, all vary between cultures. If the native learning culture is ignored and unsuitable teaching models enforced, this can be confusing, traumatic and unproductive to learning. Yet this has been the case if we look at the way the Western pedagogical ethos, the Communicative approach to language teaching, has been imposed on learners over the past 20-odd years via the global ELT coursebook. This in spite of the fact that the approach is manifestly unsuitable for certain cultures and pedagogical backgrounds. The task-based and problem-solving activities requiring pair and group work which are so characteristic of the Communicative Approach are distinctly student-orientated, and they represent Western modes of communication that are alien to those of the East (Alptekin 1993: 139, Nelson 1995: 28). Learners from the collectivist cultures of Japan, Korea and China find it hard to adapt to the Western concept of group work (despite this apparent paradox, to Western eyes). Their small-group dynamic, coming out of this collectivist orientation (rather than the Western, individualistic one) operates via different processes and protocols and has different priorities, such as the imperative of group consensus. These cultures also have very teacher-centred traditions, in which the information flow is traditionally from teacher to student or from textbook to student, but never from student to student. Students from such cultures cannot be expected to learn via activities which constrain them to behave 'in ways which are both alien to their educational culture and proscribed in their daily life' (Alptekin 1993: 139-40). It is hardly surprising that Eastern learners might perceive time spent talking with or listening to other students, as a waste of time[14]. Similarly, activities which encourage personal expression (a welcome feature of coursebooks according to Tomlinson *et al.* 2001: 96), might actually be seen as improper to learners from cultural contexts, such as China, in which self-expression is not suited to so 'public' an arena as the language classroom (Nelson 1995: 28). Some Communicative activities in textbooks are so alien as to ultimately confuse learners as to what they are expected to do, as was reported in the Kuwaiti context by Zeyand (1997: 271). All this means that many teachers in non-English speaking countries are understandably reluctant to embrace the Communicative Approach in their own teaching contexts, at least not without making some concessions to these contexts - see, for example, Prodromou (1988: 76) in relation to Greek teachers, Zeyand (1997: 298) in relation to Kuwaiti teachers and Alptekin (1993: 140) on Chinese teachers.

The predominance of the Communicative Approach might well be viewed, therefore, as effective pedagogical imperialism, the West using its commercial hegemony - in this case, in the form of the centralisation of the ELT publishing industry - to impose a blanket pedagogy over EFL and ESL-learning contexts worldwide. This is not only ethically dubious, but a fundamental pedagogical flaw:

In the design of methodologies, the cart is still before the horse. We are still paying insufficient attention to the social needs of all the people we expect to use them. Methodologies for teaching, for educating teachers, for designing curricula [...] continue to be refined, but without sufficient attention to, or knowledge of, the people who will be involved. (Holliday 1994: 2)

The lack of consideration apparent on a macro level is also true at the level of the individual learner and learning styles. As Tomlinson *et al.* note in their review of eight recently published EFL books (2001: 86-7), coursebooks tend to cater predominantly to the analytic type learner - that is, learners who have a preference for focusing on details, rule-learning and analysis, and for dissecting words and phrases; learners who have a systematic approach to problem-solving and a preference for autonomous modes of working (see Chapter 2 Section 2.5 'Learning styles'). This is evidenced by the insistence on spelling out the rules, in the ubiquitous 'grammar-focus' sections in ELT books. Few of them cater to the 'open' or 'experiential' learners who prefer discovery learning, i.e. learners who have the ability to pick up information in an unstructured way, who prefer to learn without rules and who can tolerate confusing situations and ambiguity. Activities for learners who are kinaesthetic, that is, who prefer movement and activity, doing projects, active games and so on, are to be found in children's language learning books but rarely in ones for adults.

In sum, considering the ELT coursebook's general disregard of the diversity of its audience in the area of pedagogy, it has shown over-zealous sensitivity in another sphere, that of the *subject matter*. Yet as will be demonstrated in the section below ('Currency'), censoring learning content can have as negative repercussions for learning as using inappropriate pedagogy. Bearing such fundamental problems in mind, what is being recognised by growing numbers of writers/practitioners (e.g. Tomlinson, Prodromou, Pulverness, Jolly and Bolitho), is that geographical and cultural differences are distancing factors which weaken the coursebook: 'The further away the author is from the learners, the less effective the material is likely to be' (Jolly and Bolitho 1998: 111). Practitioners such as those in Asian, Middle and Far Eastern and South American contexts (see, for example, Toh and Raja 1997; Prodromou 1988; Zeyand 1997; Gonzalez 1994) are realising that the only appropriate means of dealing with the cultural diversity of the language learner is to eschew materials produced for a global market and gear materials' production to a local level, publishing local/national or context-specific coursebooks, or using collections of materials or context-specific syllabi (see the section on text-driven syllabus, below). Such materials might be authentic texts drawn from the local English-speaking culture (if one exists, as in ESL and L2 contexts), ones that are relevant to the teaching context (texts set in, or related to, the teaching context) or ones that are simply of interest to a particular group of learners. The basic point is that texts and materials should be 'culturally and experientially appropriate for learners' (Prodromou 1988: 76); that is to say, that account should be taken of both the *native culture* of the language learners (and this includes pedagogy), and of the English language culture most relevant to them.

3.2 Currency

The second advantage of using authentic texts for language learning has been synthesised in the term *currency*. Currency has here been taken as a sort of key word, expanded to encompass as well as 'up-to-date-ness' and topicality, the advantages that stem from these, especially relevance and interest to the learner. All of these are interdependent to some extent, in the context of authentic texts that might be engaging and motivating to any given individual group of learners.

The advantages of this sort of currency in promoting language acquisition are discussed in Chapter 2, where the link between interest in subject matter and personal engagement in providing motivation is discussed (Chapter 2 Section 2.3). The crucial part that motivation plays in language acquisition is one area upon which SLA theorists agree (Arnold and Brown 1999: 13). Chomsky is among those to point out how essential to motivation is the factor of *interest*; 'the truth of the matter is that about 99% of teaching is making the students feel interested in the material' (1988: 181), or as Ellis puts it, motivation depends on 'engaging [students'] interest in classroom activities' (1994: 517). Ellis goes on to point out that an important part of that motivation is the desire for *communication* (*ibid*). Using texts which will provide incentives to communication is thus an important motivating factor, and this is where the authentic text selected on the basis of its relevance to, and immediacy for the learner group, comes into play. Such texts can spur *intrinsic* motivation (in which the learning experience is its own reward, Arnold and Brown 1999:14), in that they help to stimulate 'natural curiosity and interest' which 'energizes' the students' learning (*ibid*.). The motivational impulse that the authentic text can provide is particularly strong for *integratively* motivated learners, that is, learners interested in absorbing or integrating into the culture of the target language. Such learners view authentic texts as a way of getting under the skin of the target language society, with information gleaned from them perceived as 'cultural currency', use of which can help learners 'feel more confident and [...] sound more fluent in the target culture'[15] (Tomalin and Stempleski 1993: 39).

This sort of currency of both subject matter and language is where the authentic text has huge advantages over the traditional option, the ELT coursebook, whose content is restricted by the breadth of its markets and the constrictions of its (print-based) medium. The dilemma that traditionally taboo subjects in ELT are precisely those which are potentially the most engaging and stimulating to learners is one pointed out by many writers (e.g. Rinvolucri 1999: 14, Thornbury 1999: 15-16 and Bell and Gower 1998: 123, 128). In an article charting their experience of coursebook-writing titled *Writing course materials for the world: a great compromise*, Bell and Gower comment: 'We did not want to fight shy of sex, drugs, religion and death (still THE taboo subjects in EFL coursebooks), but found ourselves doing so and being expected to do so' (1998: 128). A recent review of 8 current coursebooks likewise laments the 'absence of controversial issues' and 'lack of adult content' (Tomlinson *et al.* 2001: 97).

Using authentic texts, on the other hand, a teacher can opt to cover issues that are more controversial or have more 'adult' content than those contained in the ELT book, in order to meets the interests of his/her learner group. The 'PG-rated' nature of the world of the ELT coursebook (to use Wajnryb's metaphor, 1996: 291) can be raised (at least to a 15 certificate!) where the teacher knows the cultural and age profile of his/her audience and their interests. S/he can include controversial or even taboo subjects for ELT books such those mentioned above - sex drugs, religion[16], death - plus others such as drugs, war, violence, politics, poverty, relationships and alcohol, all subjects customarily eschewed by the coursebook treading the minefield of cultural sensitivities laid by the trans-global reach of its market. My syllabus for NNS EFL teachers, in the teaching context of the Irish Republic, for instance, includes subjects such as illegitimacy (in the Roddy Doyle novel *The Snapper*) and the politics of Northern Ireland. The self-selected syllabus of a multi-cultural group of young adults in the same context (as represented by the class newspaper they produced) ranged from 'Bloody Sunday' (the event in which 13 human rights marchers were killed in Derry in 1972) to a recipe for fish curry[17], while the drinking habits of the Irish is a subject of seemingly endless fascination for foreigners (yet alcohol is a topic generally excluded from global coursebooks to make them saleable in Muslim countries, see Dingle 1999).

There can, in sum, be no predicting the interests of any given group of learners in a particular context. The ELT coursebook, with its restricted, censored range of topics - those which recur with monotonous regularity in today's coursebooks include; the weather, travel and tourism, health, sports and hobbies, fashion, food, money, ecology, history, the future, education and business - is no match, in terms of its potential for learner involvement and hence for language learning, for the syllabus that is custom-designed to cater to the particular range of interests of a specific learner group. The issue of custom-designing syllabi based on authentic texts is dealt with in Section 3.2.2 below.

3.2.1 Currency and language

The key word *currency* applies not only to subject matter but to language. Language is constantly changing and growing, and no more so than in the decades witnessing the growth in communications technologies: 'an area of huge potential enrichment for individual languages', as David Crystal puts it, writing on the language of the Internet (2001: 241). In preparing learners for their experience with the language, it is incumbent on teachers to keep learners 'at the cutting edge' of language change. Like a self-fulfilling prophecy, the Internet offers us ever-growing quantities of authentic texts disseminating and propagating the new varieties of language associated with its various applications (e.g. electronic mail, chat rooms and the Web) and the neologisms they have spawned. In the many corpora of the spoken language, thousands of film scripts and numerous chat rooms accessible on-line, the Internet offers us an unmatched resource of the spoken language in flux. The ease with which all this can be accessed and channelled into language learning by the enterprising language teacher contrasts markedly with the difficulties that the issue of language currency poses for the ELT coursebook. Because the print medium in which it appears effectively 'fossilises' the language as at time of publishing, writers tend to steer clear of 'new' language which might not stand the test of time. They also tend to eschew spoken and non-standard forms, though not necessarily for the same reason (see below). Thus, in a review of 15 coursebooks published between 1997 and 2002 (see Appendix I), the Internet had found its way into only half of them (and mention of the Internet does not entirely correlate with date of publication). In the same 15 coursebooks, the fastest-growing communication medium between young people in the UK and Ireland today, the linguistic phenomenon of text messaging[18], goes entirely unmentioned.

The breakdown of the language skills in many of today's coursebooks reveals that publishers recognise that the skills most in demand these days are those of speaking and listening (Tomlinson *et al.* 2001: 97). Yet there is a distinct lack of correspondence between the skills being practised, and the language the students are fed to wield them. This is because there is a long-standing tradition in language teaching to draw on written rather than spoken paradigms: 'The distinction between the literary and colloquial form of the same language has considerably complicated the problem of learning languages [...] most grammarians tacitly assume that the spoken is a mere corruption of the literary language' (Sweet 1899: 50).

The legacy of this situation - acceptable in the days before there was the technology to record and thence analyse the spoken language - is one in which many forms regularly used in speech by native speakers (according to the findings of corpus linguistics working with corpora of spoken data, see below) are classed as non-standard and ungrammatical by textbooks. A classic case of a 'non-standard' form is the contraction *ain't. Ain't* is classed as 'widely disapproved as non-standard and more common in the habitual speech of the less educated' by the Merriam Webster Dictionary[19] and receives scant mention in ELT coursebooks[20], grammars[21] or learners' dictionaries[22]. Yet the contraction dates from 1778, according to the same dictionary, and its use is 'flourishing in American English', the examples the dictionary gives indicating how entrenched in the English language it is, in sayings such as 'If it ain't broke don't fix it' and in songs like *It ain't necessarily so* (from the Gershwin musical *Porgy and Bess*).

The characterisation of the verb *want* in coursebooks is another example of mis-representation. Learners are generally taught that as a 'state verb', *want* is only used in the simple form[23], yet there are many examples in spoken corpora of continuous forms (e.g. 'I'm wanting to get a bus', 'I was wanting to take my guitar in'[24]). The verb is also commonly used 'ungrammatically' in the spoken language, with inanimate subjects; Carter (1998: 48) cites the sample: 'that one wants to go first class' (referring to a parcel being sent in a post office). To give yet another example, the passive is taught in most coursebooks and grammars with little or no mention of the *get* passive which is extremely common in spoken English (Carter and McCarthy 2000) to signal things that happen to us which are negative or adversarial: Carter and McCarthy cite examples from spoken corpora such as *get burned, get burgled, get ripped off. (ibid)*. The construction did not figure in the teaching of the passive in any of five coursebooks reviewed at random[25], and was given only a 5-line mention in one pedagogical grammar consulted[26]. Once again, this is because it is used chiefly in the spoken language with few representations in the written language upon which most pedagogical works still draw. Added to this, of course, are the many new forms evolving in the spoken language that have yet to find their way into coursebooks. These include the use of *like* and *go* as quotative verbs[27], as well as the use of *like* as a 'hedge', i.e. to take the edge of one's statement ('He's, like, really obsessed'). Non-inclusion might also have to do with the sort of restrictive criteria for topics mentioned above: the word *gay*, though no longer new, has yet to appear in a coursebook, despite figuring among the 2000 most common words in the language (according to Thornbury 1999:16). And while *gay* is now given the definition *homosexual* in learner dictionaries, its adjectival comparative forms 'gayer, gayest', somewhat anarchically, still appears in at least one case (Collins COBUILD 1997).

Particularly for learners studying in English-speaking cultures, the fact that this type of colloquial language is only accessible through casual, out-of-class conversation or through films, television and so on, leaves them in the rather ironic situation of getting most of their input on the authentic spoken language *outside* the classroom (Rinvolucri 1999:13). Yet knowing up-to-date language such as this is especially important for young integratively motivated learners, who want to be able to use their English in native speaking context. The absence of such language from pedagogical works can be a source of frustration and puzzlement as learners struggle with the subtleties of appropriacy of language registers.

Today, this effective 'gap' in the language that we are teaching our students is gradually being narrowed, as findings from the field of corpus linguistics begin to inform pedagogical works. Drawing on corpora of the spoken language[28], rules are being codified from the spoken, rather than the written language, redressing the written-spoken balance. Coursebooks, grammars and dictionaries which draw on authentic spoken samples are now on the market; these include *Exploring academic English: a workbook for student essay writing*, Thurstun and Candlin 1997, *Vocabulary in Use Upper-intermediate*, New Edition, McCarthy and O'Dell (2001), the *Longman Grammar of Spoken and Written English* (Biber *et al.* 1999) and the *Longman Dictionary of Contemporary English* (latest edition, 2003), the last two both based on the 100-million word British National Corpus, the BNC.

In the interim, the teacher/learner has access to authentic samples of spoken English from many sources. Conspicuously, of course, from the Internet (from on-line corpora, film-scripts, streaming TV and radio and so on), but also from audio and video TV and radio recordings, and from some contemporary literature. The importance and means of exploiting these various media is dealt with in the chapters on the cultural products (Chapters 5 to 11). First, however, a means of devising a learning curriculum based on authentic texts, and reconciling it with a traditional syllabus is suggested.

3.2.2 Text-driven syllabus

It has been emphasised so far in this section that in using authentic texts for language learning, currency and content are paramount. The framework for the set of authentic texts used in a given teaching context - the 'syllabus' - cannot therefore viably be parameters set by grammatical features. This leads us to consider how the alternative, a more *text-driven* framework, might work. Language teachers do not need to look too deeply into their hearts to admit that more often than not, it is the coursebook that provides the syllabus. Insofar, then, as the contents of the coursebook syllabus represent contemporary thinking on language pedagogy, it would appear that we are moving into a reactionary, post-Communicative era, with a return to the centralisation of grammar. This is one of the 'negative trends' identified in a review of recent EFL coursebooks (Tomlinson *et al.* 2001) where it is seen as a reaction to the perceived failure of the Communicative approach to produce accurate users of English as a foreign language (Tomlinson *et al.* 2001: 87). The grammar-driven language syllabus - as exemplified in today's coursebooks - is conceived basically as a checklist of grammatical points covered in the units of the book. The texts used in the units incorporate and illustrate the use of the given grammatical/functional features; texts may be authentic, semi-authentic or purpose-written. The approach inherent in the use of the grammar syllabus remains the classic PPP - Presentation, Production, Practice - and as such it is teacher- (or coursebook)-centred.

What is suggested here is a text-driven approach, one that is, by contrast with that above, learner-centred and works in a converse fashion, in that it starts with (authentic) texts, and derives the language features to be studied from these. Rather than presenting the learner with the 'pre-packaged formula' of a grammatical feature, samples of its use and explanation of its structure, it uses a *consciousness-raising* activity, defined by Ellis as: 'A pedagogic activity where the learners are provided with L2 data in some form and required to perform some operation on or with it, the purpose of which is to arrive at an explicit understanding of some linguistic property or properties of the target language' (1997: 160). Basically, a consciousness-raising approach allows the learner him/herself to discover and make hypotheses about structures/rules of use, based on how s/he perceives them operating in the input data. These hypotheses can then be checked by looking at further contexts in other texts and/or in language corpora (see Chapter 11 Section 11.4), and consolidated by consulting up-to-date reference grammars based on authentic texts (such as the *Longman Grammar of Spoken and Written English* mentioned above) and/or the teacher or native speakers. The reader is referred to Chapter 2 Section 2.8 for a more detailed explanation of the consciousness-raising approach.

The text-driven syllabus is (ideally) drawn up by the learners on an individual basis, with the teacher schematising a master-syllabus for his/her own records. The syllabus is built up based on the 'discoveries' of the learners, and thus arises organically from the texts studied. The text-driven syllabus may be concretised as follows. The sets of hypotheses or rules 'discovered' by the learners can be consolidated into a structure or layout akin to a traditional grammar book, consisting of sets of headings (either grammatical or functional), under which come explanations, examples and references. The syllabus can be stored either on file (electronic or paper) or on a database, so that items can be added and further examples of contexts or usages can be inserted as they are encountered. Even if the teacher has to meet the requirements of a prescriptive syllabus, this can be done by cross-referencing it to the 'organic' one to check that the required grammar points are being covered. What is important to bear in mind as a teacher when using such a syllabus, is not to neglect the pedagogic principle written into good coursebooks, the periodic reiteration of language points and vocabulary for consolidation.

This text-driven approach to syllabus development has a strong rationale in SLA research evidence. Its starting point is the teachability hypothesis (Pienemann 1985, quoted in Chapter 2 Section 2.6) which, put in simple terms, suggests that learners only learn when and what they are ready to acquire. The hypothesis has been validated by research findings over the years:

> *Of the scores of detailed studies of naturalistic and classroom language learning reported over the past 30 years, none suggest, for example, that presentation of discrete points of grammar one at a time [...] bears any resemblance except an accidental one to either the order or the manner in which naturalistic or classroom acquirers learn those items. (Long and Robinson 1998: 16)*

This is, of course, a conclusion which undercuts at a blow, the rationale for the prescriptive syllabus - and which also explains that continual source of frustration to teachers, why students persist in making errors in language structures that have already been 'covered' in the syllabus. A syllabus drawn from consciousness-raising activities thus provides 'a logical way of avoiding many of the pedagogical problems that arise from the teachability hypothesis' (Ellis 1994: 645).

3.3 Challenge

> *Learners [...] like to have glimpses of something that is just a little beyond them. We all dislike unnecessary triviality (Sweet 1899:180).*

Probably the most famous representation of the concept of challenge in second language acquisition can be seen in Krashen's formula $i+1$ (Krashen 1981 etc.) by which was indicated that input (i) is comprehensible to the learner even when somewhat above his/her current proficiency level. The degree of comprehensibility can logically be linked to that vital factor for learning, motivation, which is only fostered where learning materials and tasks 'pose a reasonable *challenge* to the students - neither too difficult nor too easy' (Ellis 1994: 516) [my emphasis]. Conversely, the fact of successfully rising to a challenge is in itself motivating, building confidence and instilling a sense of achievement; 'when students realise they can successfully deal with and understand authentic texts, confidence in their own TL abilities soars' (Leloup and Pontiero 1997). This has been particularly demonstrated in recent years in relation to language learners' use of the Internet, with the technological as well as linguistic challenges that this presents (see, for example, Warschauer 1996). Gaining the ability and confidence to rise to a challenge has repercussions for another affective factor which impacts on learning, the readiness to *take risks* in the TL. *Risk-taking* refers to things such as guessing meanings based on context or background knowledge, speaking even if risking making mistakes and so on. Risk-taking is vital to learning, as long as these risks are 'moderate but intelligent' (Oxford 1999: 63) i.e. calculated, rather than mere carelessness. Indeed, according to Oxford, lack of practice in risk-taking can 'seriously stunt' language development (*ibid.*). The extent to which learners are willing to take these sorts of risks is a factor of, among other things, their *self-esteem*, a part of which is a sense of personal confidence (de Andrés 1999: 88). Self-esteem is a factor which correlates with learning, particularly in childhood, but continues to have an impact on life-long learning (Arnold and Brown 1999: 12). All in all, materials such as authentic texts which offer a challenge to language learners, also give them the opportunity to rise to it, and to take calculated risks, thereby boosting these affective factors essential to learning, confidence, self-esteem and motivation.

While such theory may be accepted in principle, the difficulties that authentic texts pose to lower level learners is more often seen in terms of the problems they pose than the challenge they present: 'The adoption of the principle of authenticity [...] has posed a particular problem as far as grading is concerned' (McGrath 2002: 117). As a consequence, the importance of these affective factors is too often neglected in the case of learners at lower levels of TL proficiency: 'Despite their very limited proficiency in the language, students need the challenge and stimulation of addressing themes and topics that have adult appeal, and which encourage them to draw on their personal opinions and experiences' (Lazar 1994: 116). Challenge as a factor of the *subject matter* itself is thus also an important impetus for learning, one that correlates with affective factors of appeal and potential for engagement. It is a factor too often ignored when availing of the pre-prepared, coursebook texts, which are tuned to the proficiency level of the learners but not necessarily to their interests, needs or personal and cultural contexts. There is, after all, a limit to the interest that can be milked out of the describing of personal details, favourite things, daily routines, jobs, eating habits, tourism and the like.

Challenge is not only a factor of the input text, however, but of the task required of the learners. Yet this too is a factor often ignored by materials writers who assume that most adult learners 'do not want and would not gain from intellectually demanding activities whilst engaging in learning the target language' (Tomlinson *et al.* 2001: 97). Yet as will be argued in Chapter 4, it is the task, with its inbuilt element of challenge to the learner, which is central to using (authentic) texts for language learning, in that the task 'mediates' between the learner and the text. It follows that texts can be made accessible to learners not by simplifying these, but by adjusting the demands of the *task* involving them. As Grellet says (in the context of reading skills): 'The difficulty of a reading exercise depends on the activity which is required of the students rather than on the text itself, providing it remains within their general competence [...] In other words, one should grade exercises rather than texts' (Grellet 1981: 7-9). This is a principle crucial to the use of authentic texts with learners, and we will now look at how and why it works in this context.

3.3.1 'Grade the task not the text'

A core principle in 'grading' tasks is to make the task *appropriate* to the text. This is the basis of the concept of *task authenticity* which is elaborated in the following chapter (Chapter 4), where it is suggested that tasks should coincide with the communicative purpose of the text, and be a 'rehearsal' or 'approximation' of tasks performed with the text in real life.

There are many tasks to be used with authentic texts which are suitable for learners from elementary level upwards and which are also authentic in that they emulate native-speaker interactions (see Chapter 4 Section 4.3.3). A useful principle to bear in mind in designing tasks for lower level learners is that 'partial comprehension of text is no longer considered to be problematic since this occurs in real life' (Guariento and Morley 2001: 348). If there is no requirement for detailed, word-for-word decoding of the input text, then quite complex ones can be used, with the tasks set reflecting the learners' own level/s. Fairly simple but authentic tasks appropriate to newspaper and magazines articles, for example, include getting the gist of the text by reading headlines, subheadings, first sentences of paragraphs, scanning for key words and using existing knowledge of a news story to clarify meaning. Significantly, these are some of the most common strategies applied to newspaper reading by native speakers (Grundy 1993: 7). The skill of skimming - and particularly of ignoring what is not clear or interesting at first glance - is a NS strategy for newspaper reading of particular value to NNSs. It 'deprograms' them, if necessary, from the habit of word-for-word decoding and helps them realise that far from being 'lazy', such techniques are efficient and appropriate to the genre. A genre such as the television news bulletin is likewise accessible to even low level learners, partly because its format and presentation is today fairly universal and thus familiar to learners, and because of its use of visual images. Once learners are trained to make the most of the accompanying visuals, of proper nouns (names of people and places), and of 'international' words (e.g. *terrorism, airport*), and encouraged to contribute their own knowledge about the items in the news, they can be expected to get the gist of most news items. The advantages of using such techniques is not only of making authentic texts accessible to low level learners, but of helping them develop useful learning strategies.

The range of media from which authentic texts can be drawn makes for great versatility in task design, as is illustrated in the classroom tasks given for the various cultural products in Chapters 5 to 11. Texts from the audio and audio-visual media (radio, songs, TV and film) can be encountered on many planes other than the linguistic, and lend themselves to an interplay of media and sense perceptions. Learners can view visual material without sound, listen without viewing, read song lyrics without music and hear a melody without the lyrics. They can be asked to match music to visuals e.g. to suggest the backing music for advertisements, film episodes and so on. Some cinema and TV advertisements are principally musical and visual, using language only in their slogans[29]. Indeed, the film industry managed very well largely without language for its first thirty years. By exploiting the multi-media features of these types of authentic texts, and not limiting the focus to the linguistic, their potential application with language learners of all levels is greatly increased.

In addition, the topical and often provocative subject matter of texts from the audio-visual media tends to stimulate discussion, speculation and reaction. This aspect - the authentic text as a trigger for language production rather than just as input to be processed - can be the basis of many tasks, as is illustrated in Chapters 5 to 11, and is another reason why learners need not be limited to texts geared to their proficiency level.

One of the aspects of the authentic text that is most significant in making it appropriate for learners of all levels, is its richness of *context*. Today's TV news relates to yesterday's and last week's and to news accessed on other media; personalities and places are real and contextualisable, presentation formats are familiar. Background knowledge, in other words is a resource to be exploited in learning and one which is not the prerogative of learners at high proficiency levels. This is, of course, a point often made in relation to the learning of language for specific purposes (LSP), where the background knowledge of a subject (business, technology, engineering and so on), that learners bring to the FL classroom provides a 'window' into target language texts on that subject. Knowledge of the subject presupposes a knowledge of the discourse of that subject (Devitt 2002) and thus equipped learners can often cope with texts well above their estimated proficiency level (Crandall 1995: 87). The universality of the discourse types and formats of the mass media - those used on the radio, TV, in newspapers, in advertisements, and on Web pages, also eases the learner's encounter with the input. In short, then, the learner coming to the foreign language classroom is not a *tabula rasa*, and particularly at lower levels of proficiency, his/her own world knowledge can be exploited to 'subsidise' his/her knowledge of the target language.

All this means that there are myriad ways of maintaining text and task authenticity while providing a suitably gauged level of challenge at any proficiency level: 'In developing [...] strategic competencies, texts do not, therefore need to be simplified; it is what learners are expected to do with the texts that has to be controlled' (Guariento and Morley 2001: 348).

3.3.2 The 'naturally graded' authentic text
To the argument made above for grading the task not the text, has to be added the fairly obvious proviso that authentic texts are not, of course, uniform in their level of (linguistic) difficulty. The essential information in a foreign language menu, for example, can probably be understood even by someone with an elementary knowledge of the FL (especially in the real circumstances where this has

implications for what s/he is going to eat!), while a FL newspaper might prove too challenging. A point that has been well made *a propos* of using literature for language teaching (e.g. McRae 1996: 23-4, Bassnet and Grundy 1993), but which is true of other media/discourse types, is that texts are 'naturally graded' and can be found for the full range of learner proficiency levels. As will be more fully detailed in Chapters 5 onwards, certain songs, advertisements, TV programmes, films, Internet discourse, poetry and novels are intrinsically linguistically 'simpler' than others. Obvious examples include 'action' songs, dialogue-free TV advertisements, TV weather forecasts (because of their visual component), and poems such as limericks. In some literature, stylistic simplicity is adopted as the writer's trademark - one thinks of the British poet Roger McGough or of Becket's *Waiting for Godot* - or it is used for effect (as in Hemingway's *The Old Man and the Sea*). In addition to these, there is the huge range of discourse types and levels of linguistic difficulty to be found in texts accessed on the Web, while the user-led nature of technologies such as e-mail and chat rooms means that users can actually 'set' interactions at their level of proficiency in the language.

In short, cherry-picking authentic texts from the huge range of cultural products can prevent the teacher falling into the trap of correlating proficiency level with subject matter, the criticism so often levelled at the ELT coursebook: 'Low-level learners can be stimulated and helped to develop high-level skills and should not be restricted by special materials which focus on linguistic decoding and simple language practice' writes Tomlinson (1999: 4), adding that there is a need 'to respect, stimulate and challenge the lower levels' (*ibid.*).

3.4 Conclusion

This chapter has developed the notion of 'the 3 c's', 'culture', 'currency' and 'challenge', keywords encapsulating the advantages of authentic texts over purpose-written ones and which constitute the central pedagogical rationale for using authentic texts in language learning. In the Culture section, the indelible cultural overlay on language products is shown to have implications for learners' comprehension of the language they are learning and their image of the society where it is spoken. The second section expands the word *currency* to embrace not only the topical potential of authentic texts and of the language they contain, but the advantages that these bring in terms of interest to the learners and hence, most vitally, motivational force. The last section, Challenge, addresses among other things, that 'thorn in the side' of advocates of authentic texts in language learning, perceived level of difficulty. Coping strategies for this - for both teachers and learners - are suggested here, not least of which is the adjusting of *the task*, not the text, to the learner level. It is, in fact, to the task and the concept of *task authenticity* that we shall turn in Chapter 4.

Notes

1   The evolving nature of these and the fact that culture has not only geographical but chronological boundaries, is charmingly illustrated by the list Eliot gives of what British culture

means to his contemporaries: 'Derby Day, Henley Regatta, Cowes, the twelfth of August, a cup final, the dog races, the pin table, the dart board, Wensleydale cheese, boiled cabbage cut into sections, beetroot in vinegar, nineteenth century Gothic churches and Elgar' (Eliot 1948: 31).

2   *Craic* could be loosely translated as *fun, goings-on*.

3   The University of Limerick.

4   Written by a Japanese student on the University of Limerick Language Centre (ULLC) Year-Round programme (YRP) 1998.

5   Statistics in this section are from *The Sunday Times* (1993) Wordpower supplement: Part 3, the global language: 7, unless otherwise stated.

6   Information from Butler 1999: 35.

7   Although the dominance of English on the Internet is steadily falling - see Chapter 11, Section 11.2.3.

8   In an informal poll taken by the editor of three Chinese people working in the publishing house (two of whom had graduated from English medium universities) the only icon on this list that they had all heard of was *Superman*.

9   Andrew Stokes, editor, Clarity Language Consultants Ltd, private correspondence, July 1997.

10 All of whom figure in *English File*, published in 2001 by OUP.

11 Books looked at were: *Language to Go Elementary*, Longman 2002, *Cutting Edge (intermediate)*, Longman 1998, *International Express (Pre-Intermediate)* OUP 1996, *English Panorama (Advanced)*, Cambridge 1997.

12 The 2001 census of Britain and Wales revealed the population to be 91.3% white and 8.7% ethnic: Source *BBC News* Web page http://news.bbc.co.uk/1/hi/uk/2756041.stm accessed 24 March 2003.

13 *Fitta* is a vulgar term for a woman's genitals in Swedish, Norwegian and Danish. Source: *Marketing Translation Mistakes*, http://www.i18nguy.com/translations.html, accessed 30 April 2003.

14 A complaint received from a Japanese student in a University of Limerick Language Centre (ULLC) summer course, 1997.

15 One of my Japanese students, for instance, made an effort to keep up-to-date on what was happening on the football scene since he found this a fruitful subject of conversation ('cultural currency') to use with native speakers.

16 Sensitivity to this subject is such that, in my own experience in writing materials for a world-wide audience, a mere reference to a 'church' on a town map had to be taken out.

17 University of Limerick Language Centre (ULLC) Year Round Programme (YRP) class newspaper 1998; *Voice of University of Limerick*.

18 Information from http://www.mda-mobiledata.org, accessed 3 March 2003.

19 Online at http://www.m-w.com./netdict.htm, accessed 13 October 2002.

20 One exception is a mention and illustration in the context of a line from a song, in a section on non-standard English and prescriptivism in *English Panorama 1*, O'Dell 1997, CUP.

21 A note to the list of contractions given in Swan 1996: 134 states: 'In non-standard English, ain't is used as a contraction of...', and 5 examples are given.

22 *The Collins Cobuild Dictionary* 1997 edition: 16, has 2 lines on *ain't* reading 'ain't is used in some dialects of English instead of 'am not, 'aren't' or 'isn't; SPOKEN'.

23 See, for example, the rules given in *Landmark* by Haines and Stewart 2000: 124-5.

24 Among occurrences on a concordance generated from the *Collins Wordbanks Online English* corpus concordance sampler http://www.cobuild.collins.co.uk accessed 11 March 2003.

25 *English File*, Oxenden, C and C. Latham-Koenig 2001; *International Express: Intermediate*. Taylor, L., 1997; *Activate your English: Intermediate*. Sinclair, B. and P. Prowse, 1996; *Language in Use: Upper Intermediate*, Doff, A. and C. Jones, 1997; *True to Life*, Gairns, R and S. Redman, 1998.

26 Swan, M. *Practical English Usage* (1995 edition): 'We can [...] use the structure to talk about things that happen to us. In this case, get means 'experience'. *We got our roof blown off in the storm last week. I got my car stolen twice last year* (1995: 223). By contrast, there are seven pages dedicated to the 'to be' passive (407-14).

27 See the article 'He goes and I'm like: the new quotatives revisited', Buchstaller, 2001.

28 Such as the 5-million word CANCODE corpus of spoken English discourse, compiled by researchers at the University of Nottingham and Cambridge University Press.

29 E.g. a memorable advertisement for Murphy's stout in which a group of Samurai traverse a traditional Irish landscape to a dramatic musical soundtrack and where the single utterance is in Japanese, the only other language being in the (written) slogan: *Murphy's stout - instantly*.

Chapter Four:
Authentic Texts and Authentic Tasks

4.1 Introduction

The first three chapters of this book have so far presented the rationale for what I have called the *authenticity-centred approach* to language learning materials design. Chapter 1 gave the historical perspectives on authenticity in language learning and reviewed the contemporary debate on the issue. Chapters 2 and 3 then laid out the advantages of using authentic texts for learning language according to current SLA research evidence (Chapter 2) and to current pedagogy (Chapter 3). The function of this chapter is to construct a pedagogic framework which interprets the authenticity-centred approach and renders it a practical teaching method.

Construction of the framework involves drawing up a number of sets of parameters. The set most central to the approach are the parameters delimiting and defining the concept of *task* in an authentic context, i.e. *task authenticity*. The other main set is the *task typologies* concomitant with task authenticity. The framework is schematised below:

The task authenticity framework

Parameter set 1: *Guidelines for task authenticity*
Parameter set 2: *Communicative purposes* (a factor of set 1)
Parameter set 3: *Task typologies*

The structure of the chapter corresponds basically to that of the framework, with the addition of a preliminary section on the task as a pedagogic model, which prepares the ground for the discussion on task authenticity.

It will be remembered that a key outcome of the analysis of authenticity in Chapter 1 was the identification of a pedagogical paradigm that has been increasingly associated with it, the *task* (see Chapter 1 Section 1.2.3). The shift of the attribute of authenticity from *text* to *task* - as McGrath puts it 'the narrow concern with text authenticity that characterised the early years of the communicative movement has since given way to a concern for the nature of tasks' (2002: 114) - means that the new focus is on what makes tasks *authentic*. Let us start first of all, then, by defining the term *task* in the language learning context.

4.2 Task

The contemporary notion of *task* as a pedagogical model was engendered within the Communicative approach to language teaching. Task emerged around the mid 1980s as the model for full-blown methodologies as described in Prabhu (1987), Nunan (1989) and later in Willis (1996). The task model was in one sense the ultimate, logical extension of the Communicative approach, a representation of 'what happens when meaning-based language teaching is carried out systematically and as an alternative to instruction which focuses on form' (Bygate *et al.* 2001: 3). Although as with many concepts in language pedagogy, a definitive definition of the term *task* remains elusive (Ellis 1994: 595, Bygate *et al.* 2001: 9-12) because it tends to differ according to the purposes for which the task is used (Bygate *et al.* 2001: 11), it is nevertheless useful to consider a few well-known definitions.

To turn first to one of its originators, Prabhu defines *task* as follows: 'An activity which required learners to arrive at an outcome from given information through some process of thought and which allowed teachers to control and regulate that process' (Prabhu 1987: 24). Significantly, the teacher fades out of later definitions, reflecting the switch of focus in pedagogy from the teacher to the learner (as epitomised by the learner-centred approaches of the late 1980s, see Chapter 1 and below): 'A communicative task [is] a piece of classroom work which involves learners in comprehending, manipulating, producing and interacting in the target language while their attention is principally focused on meaning rather than form' (Nunan 1989: 10). More recently, the primacy of *outcome* is increasingly included in the definition, task being defined as:

- 'A goal-oriented communicative activity with a specific outcome where the emphasis is on exchanging meanings not producing specific language forms' (Willis 1996: 36).

- 'An activity in which: meaning is primary; there is some sort of relationship to the real-world; task completion has some priority; and the assessment of task performance is in terms of task outcome' (Skehan 1996: 38).

As a pedagogical model, therefore, the task is inherently authentic; the focus is on 'getting the job done', in line with its etymological and connotative associations with *work* (pointed out in Cook 2000: 156-7).

A distinctive feature of the task in language pedagogy is that in pursuit of its goal, it comprises a number of stages which vary both in their degree of focus on language form, and in their degree of autonomy from the teacher and (sometimes) from other learners. This implies that the relative roles that the teacher and learners play in the task are likewise variable. In one of the pioneering models for task-based learning, the Bangalore project reported by Prabhu 1987, the task had three stages, each with differing teacher/learners relationships:

• the pre-task (whole class activity, under teacher guidance and control, in which the goals of the task were clarified)

• the task (individual or voluntary collaborative work, with assistance sought from the teacher if necessary)

• assessment of the task outcome (teacher marking of individual student's written statement of the task outcome)

(paraphrased from Prabhu 1987: 24-5).

It is notable that explicit language analysis is absent from the task as thus conceived; this reflects the S-O-S (Structural-Oral-Situational) method prevailing at the time Prabhu was writing. The key premise of the S-O-S method was that meaningful communication was sufficient to develop proficiency in the language, it thus eschewed rule- or form-focused activities; 'project teaching aimed at meaning-focused activity' to the exclusion of other types (Prabhu 1987: 28). In time, as the ability of meaning-focused work alone to trigger acquisitional processes was called into doubt (e.g. Skehan 1996: 40-2), the study of form was readmitted to the Communicative fold, albeit often in more learner-led guises such as consciousness-raising (see Chapter 2 Section 2.8 and Chapter 3 Section 3.2.2). In the context of the task, it became necessary to 'devise methods of focusing on form without losing the values of tasks as realistic communicative motivators' (Skehan 1996: 42). In a more contemporary permutation of the task model then, the language focus constitutes an essential element. This is illustrated by Willis' (1996) breakdown of the stages of a task:

• Pre-task (introduction to the topic of the task)

• Task cycle (consisting of three parts, the task, planning and report)

• Language focus (analysis of language used, practice of new words/patterns)

(Willis 1996: 37)

An alternative way of analysing the task, complementary to such linear breakdowns, is as consisting of a number of components. Nunan, for instance, specifies four; the goals, the input, the activities derived from this input and the roles implied for the teacher and learners (Nunan 1989: 47). The most basic of these components, in that it orients the task, is, unfortunately, also the vaguest. Definition of a task's *goal* ranges from 'the vague general intentions behind any given learning task' (Nunan 1989: 48), i.e. the general communicative, cognitive or affective outcomes, to the tighter definition of a goal as a concrete (creative or observable) outcome (as implied in Willis 1996: 23-4, 28). These, of course, might *attest to* accomplishment of these 'vaguer' goals e.g. to successful communication or logical thought processes.

Turning to teacher/learner roles, even before the task became such a standard pedagogic model, a radical shift in teacher/learner roles and relationships had been precipitated by the Communicative approach (Nunan 1989: 86). CLT loosened the reins of teacher control, allowing learners to turn to each other in the quest for real communication. In the approaches developed subsequently under the broad Communicative umbrella (such as learner-centredness, learner autonomy and, of course, task-based learning) the initiative has been gradually transferred from the teacher to the learner. The teacher's role has changed to that of guide, facilitator and resource (Benson, 2001: 171; Willis, 1996: 40 - 41) and it is only in the last function, as resource, that the teacher retains the traditional role of serving as source of knowledge and expertise (Benson, 2001: 171-2).

As regards another component identified in Nunan, *input*, this is presupposed, in the context of this book, to be authentic texts, and the value of authentic texts for language learning has already been evidenced in Chapters 2 and 3. Let us therefore move on to Nunan's third element, *the activities* derived from the input, for this takes us directly to the main concern of this chapter, task authenticity.

4.3 Towards a Framework For Task Authenticy

The issue of authenticity of task has lurked in the shadows of the authenticity debate for many years (see, for example, Nunan 1979: 60), implicit in even the earliest literature on using authentic texts for language learning (e.g. in Morrow 1977). A point that has been frequently reiterated - above all by Widdowson (but also by such writers as Davies 1984 and Van Lier 1996) - is that it is the relationship between the learner and the input text, and the learner's response to it, that should be characterised as authentic, rather than the input text itself (Widdowson 1978: 80). Authenticity, in other words, is a factor of the learner's involvement with the task. Ultimately, the swing from text to task in the authenticity debate (McGrath 2002: 114) may be attributed to two factors. One is that the first 'battle' of the debate - for the use of authentic texts in language learning - has largely been won - if nothing else, globalisation and the Internet have seen to that. Today, authentic texts have an ever-greater profile in ELT coursebooks and are the subject of a growing number of resource books[1]. The second is that the focus of pedagogy has homed in on the learner. There is an increasing concern for *learner-centredness*, whereby the learner is involved in the curriculum development process at all levels, from choice and production of learning materials (e.g. Tudor 1996) to methodology and curriculum-planning (Nunan 1989: 19). Although it is such a 'live' issue, however, task authenticity has rarely been addressed in a systematic way (as Guariento and Morley point out, 2001: 347), a gap which this chapter endeavours to redress.

Our attempt to draw out a definition of task authenticity, might usefully start by looking at a much-quoted distinction made in Nunan (1979: 40-5) between what he terms 'real-world'[2] tasks and the more traditional 'pedagogic'[3] tasks. The former 'require learners to approximate, in class, the sorts of behaviour required of them in the world beyond the classroom' Nunan 1979: 40). 'Pedagogic tasks', on the other hand, engage learners in tasks they are unlikely to perform outside the classroom (*ibid.*). An example of a 'real world' task might be to read a newspaper article and write a letter to the newspaper editor about it. The corresponding 'pedagogic task' would be to read a newspaper article and answer comprehension questions on it. The rationale for 'real-world' tasks is, of course, that they constitute a rehearsal for real-world situations. Pedagogic tasks, on the other hand, traditionally have their justification as practice in specific skills, language forms and so on. Nunan's discussion here is useful not just as a starting point for our definition of an authentic task, but because of the conclusions he draws; that the distinction between the authentic task and the 'pedagogic' one, is ultimately, not hard and fast but a continuum (Nunan 1989: 41). Furthermore, this blurring occurs not only on practical grounds (the task of listening to a weather forecast and writing a note to a friend telling them about the weather[4] might be seen to have limited real-life validity); the continuum between the pedagogic and the authentic task runs through psychological terrain as well. Tasks may be more or less 'real' to different learners and thus induce greater or lesser involvement depending on individual needs, interests and motivations. For instance, the apparently inauthentic task of reading through and marking up a technical manual may be keenly authentic to certain learners[5]. This suggests that we have to be aware that task authenticity is in great measure a factor of *task authentication*, i.e. it depends on the learner's response to it (this idea characterises Widdowson's and Van Lier's concept of authenticity, see Chapter 1, Section 1.2.3). In this sense, therefore, task authenticity lies less in the hands of the person who devises the task, than in those of the learner who performs it. Bearing this rather humbling consideration in mind, let us review the spectrum of definitions found in the literature of what makes a task authentic, in order to draw up a set of criteria for task authenticity.

One recurrent concern has been for tasks to reflect the original communicative intent of the texts on which they are based. After all, from the learning perspective, as Grellet points out, 'it is impossible to understand a text if one is not aware of its function' (1981: 90). Indeed, this factor is often exploited by advertisers as a ploy to create suspense and hence interest[6].

Originating in Widdowson, as is so often the case on the issue of authenticity, the integrity of the writer's intent has become paramount: 'Authenticity [...] is a function of the interaction between the reader/hearer and the text *which incorporates the intentions of the writer/speaker*' [my emphasis] (Widdowson 1979a: 166). Transferred to the pedagogical context, this suggests that 'we should not ask a student to listen without identifying - or helping him identify - a purpose that relates to the communicative value of the text', (Geddes 1981: 81, referring to listening skills). This is echoed (in the context of reading skills) by such writers as Grellet and McGrath: 'Exercises must [...] correspond as often as possible to what one is expected to do with the text' (Grellet 1981: 9). 'The meaning that we ask students to extract should be related to the meanings the intended reader is expected to derive from the text - i.e. the writer's intention' (McGrath 2002: 110). The notion is neatly summed up by Clarke: 'Teaching materials should reflect the authentic communicative purpose of the text' (Clarke 1989: 75). If we are using, for instance, a TV advertisement whose text is designed with the purpose of creating suspense as to the product being advertised (i.e. as distinct from the basic purpose of the advertisement, to sell the product), then playing on this suspense, eliciting guesses as to the product on the basis of the images, music, dialogue or voice-over, can be said to respond to this communicative purpose much more than, say, the default 'listening as dictation' type task, which is really only authentic to those in the business of transcribing aural language to written.

The concern to respect the original communicative purpose of a text necessarily implicates *response* - all text is conceived with some reader/listener response in mind, be this internal and affective/cognitive (pleasure, engagement, curiosity) or external (an action). This makes *response* another defining criterion for task authenticity: 'Authenticity is a characteristic of the relationship between the passage and the reader and it has to do with appropriate response' (Widdowson 1978: 80). Within the idea of response is implicated some level of involvement or *engagement*: 'Authenticity is not brought into the classroom with the materials or the lesson plan, rather, it is a goal that teacher and students have to work towards, consciously and constantly [...] Authenticity is basically a personal process of engagement' (Van Lier 1996: 128). Authenticity in this context, then, is crucially, a subjective concept. What is an authentic and absorbing task to one learner may not be for the next. Van Lier, for instance, confesses that he felt the now-discredited grammar translation method to be authentic, in the above terms, for him (*ibid*.).

In the language learning context, *engagement* may be the most crucial feature of task authenticity (Guariento and Morley 2001: 350-1), from the point of view of both the task *per se* and of the language learning anticipated from doing it. Failure of engagement (affective or cognitive) in the task, spells failure of its *authentication* (to use Van Lier's criterion for authenticity, 1996:127). At the same time, it may be remembered from Chapter 2, that engagement is a crucial condition for language acquisition.

Connected to both of the above factors, is the notion of task *appropriacy*, since learners can only be expected to respond to the original communicative purpose of the text if given an appropriate task: 'Teaching materials should reflect the authentic communicative purpose of the text by ensuring appropriacy of task' (Clarke 1989: 75). This is a significant factor since it challenges that trusted staple of the language teaching tradition, the comprehension question: 'We rarely answer questions after reading a text, but we may have to write a letter, use the text to do something [...], compare the information to some previous knowledge' (Grellet 1981: 9). Answering questions, particularly when the questioner already knows the answer, is an inauthentic and mechanistic procedure, its rationale probably has more to do with classroom management than pedagogy (Long 1991: 45). For example, in one task in a current resource book, learners are asked to read an episode from Steinbeck's novel *The Pearl* in which a couple watch a scorpion drop onto their baby's cot (Eckstut and Lubelska, *Widely Read*, 1989). They then have to answer the question (among others) 'Why do you think Kino and Juana were so frightened?' (*ibid*.: 52). This is not to dismiss the importance of checking comprehension of texts, but to point out that this has to be done in ways that are respectful of learners' sensitivities and intelligence, via questions or tasks that are appropriate to the texts. With this excerpt from *The Pearl*, for instance, this might be done more subtly by asking students to redraft the ending of the episode, or to script a dialogue between Kino or Juana and a *confidente* which takes place years after the event (to take the edge off their grief). Such an activity can extend and deepen learners' involvement with a text, and at the same time their understanding of it can be inferred from their scripts. As this example shows, appropriacy is particularly important when dealing with literature or other texts with the potential to evoke emotion; this will be discussed in more depth in Chapter 5. The concept of task appropriacy also works at the level of language skills - learners need to develop strategies adapted to the true purpose of their interaction/s with a given text type - it would be artificial to require detailed comprehension of a page of classified advertisements, for example (Grellet 1981: 4).

The next criterion for task authenticity has already been alluded to above and conceives of tasks as a rehearsal or approximation of 'real world' behaviours (Nunan 1979: 40). The 'rehearsal approach' (Nunan 1986: 41) has both its supporters and its contestants. It became a frequently reiterated feature from the 1980s in relation to the area of LSP (languages for specific purposes) that was burgeoning in that era. In LSP there is a particular concern for classroom tasks to relate to specific learner needs (Clarke 1989: 73), to have a 'clear relationship with real-world needs' (Guariento and Morley 2001:350) and to have a *'closeness to the real world* and *daily life experience* of the learners' (Candlin 2001: 235). One of the experiences most often requested for practice by learners in the Business field, for example, is the (to the native speaker) relatively simple and non-field specific act of talking on the telephone[7]. Other elements inherent in real-life activities that merit incorporation into learning tasks intended to emulate them, are *suspense* (Arnold 1991: 239) and *risk-taking* (Nunan 1989: 140), that is, indeterminacy. The precise outcome/s of a task cannot be anticipated and do not necessarily correspond to its goals. For instance, e-mail is increasingly used in language learning as a way for learners to correspond with native speakers of their target language; but results for such a task as 'getting details about the TL culture' from the NS partner can vary enormously, from no response at all, to the NS sending the learner a long list of 'culture-related' Web sites. The task (and the teacher devising it) has to be versatile enough to absorb this variability.

Opposition to this notion of the 'rehearsal function' of task comes notably from Widdowson, who maintains that the learning task is by its nature contrived and does not need to 'replicate or even simulate what goes on in normal uses of language [...] the point of pedagogy is not to replicate experience in advance but to prepare learners to learn from it' (1998: 714-5). Widdowson's conclusion, however, that 'a lot of time is wasted in trying to teach things that can only be learned by experience' (*ibid.*: 715) is usefully ambiguous, since the well-designed task can, arguably, actually *constitute* this experience. All in all, then, the notion of 'approximating' real-world behaviours has to be given careful consideration and interpretation in the pedagogical context.

This notion of task authenticity carries with it other 'real world' features, most notably, perhaps, the parameters of *culture*. As has been discussed in Chapter 3, no text stands culture-free, nor does the reader/listener of the text come to it as a cultural *tabula rasa*. The cultural 'baggage' of the reader/listener includes his/her native cultural background plus his/her knowledge of the target culture, with the former necessarily acting as a filter for the latter (see Buttjes and Byram 1991: 232-3 cited in Chapter 3 Section 3.1). An example of this was a case where a group of Japanese learners, seeing a film clip in which children from the travelling community were playing on horses, were initially confused by the mismatch between their equating of horses with wealthy lifestyles in their own culture, and the poverty of the children's lifestyle which they saw in the film[8].

Culture works not only as a barrier, of course, but as an *aid* to comprehension when learners are familiar with concepts typical of the target culture. The same group of learners mentioned above were well *au fait* with concepts associated with (Western) festivals like Christmas and Valentine's day (partly because these have been adopted into their own culture). This facilitated their understanding of texts about these festivals, such as children writing letters to Santa Claus, described in a novel they were reading in class[9].

The effects of culture works not only at the level of the input, but at the level of pedagogic interaction. As was noted in Chapter 3 Section 3.1.3 above, group work has a rather different function and *modus operandi* in collectivist cultures such as Japan, Korea and China, so that although students from these cultures would seem to be culturally disposed to working in small groups, they appear to have difficulty translating this into a second language and culture setting (Melles 2003). Learning activities, in other words, are culturally conditioned behaviours (Nelson 1995: 29). All this means that 'authentication' of the task by the learners is in part a factor of the cultural baggage, both native and foreign, that they bring to it; it is essential that this be taken into account when devising the task.

Another 'real-world' aspect of the authentic task pinpointed in the literature and one which clearly reflects its Communicative heritage is a concern that *real communication* takes place between learners, i.e. that communication is meaningful in that it has *a genuine purpose*: 'The task-based approach aims at providing opportunities for learners to experiment with and explore [...] language through learning activities which are designed to engage learners in the authentic, practical and functional use of language for meaningful purposes' (Hong Kong SAR Government Target Oriented Curriculum (TOC) Framework 1999: 45, see also Guariento and Morley 2001: 349, Willis 1996: 13, Candlin 2001: 233).

The idea of genuine purpose is relative, of course, to the aims of the communicator. The purpose can range from getting a practical outcome - such as obtaining information or receiving a response to an e-mail message, to one that is specific to the context of the language classroom. 'Communication about how best to learn to communicate', or 'metacommunication' (Breen 1985: 67) often has, in the language learning context, a very genuine purpose. This means that the criterion 'communication for a genuine purpose' has a useful flexibility in the context of the language task, as will be illustrated in the range of tasks suggested in Chapters 5 to 11.

This array of factors said to pertain to task authenticity show that as with most pedagogical concepts, perceptions of the concept vary, bearing out Nunan's point about the blurred distinction between authentic and pedagogical tasks (Nunan 1989: 41). In line with the intention of this chapter, it is nevertheless possible to extrapolate some core aspects of task authenticity based on the features that have been identified. To recap, these include; retention of the original communicative purpose of the input text and appropriacy to it; the stimulation of some affective and/or cognitive response to and engagement with the text; rehearsal for real-world activity; activation of the learner's existing knowledge of the target language and culture as well as awareness of the influence of his/her native culture in implementing the task; and finally, genuine and purposeful communication between learners in striving for the task goal. These are reformulated as the following set of guidelines:

In order for tasks to be authentic, they should be designed to

1. Reflect the original communicative purpose of the text on which they are based.
2. Be appropriate to the text on which they are based.
3. Elicit response to/engagement with the text on which they are based.
4. Approximate real-life tasks.
5. Activate learners' existing knowledge of the target language and culture.
6. Involve purposeful communication between learners.

This set of guidelines is intended to operate as a sort of checklist to be applied selectively while conceiving and designing tasks. It can also work conversely, as a set of criteria for evaluating the authenticity of learning tasks produced by others, in coursebooks and so on. What can be inferred as a core governing principle is that *the task is engendered by the text* (and not vice versa):

> *'An exercise should never be imposed on a text. It is better to allow the text to suggest what exercises are most appropriate to it. In other words, the text should always be the starting point for determining why one would normally read it, how it would be read, how it might relate to other information before thinking of a particular exercise' (Grellet 1981:10).*

This idea is neatly summed up by Duff and Maley (1990: 6), who talk about tasks being 'text-responsive'.

The next step is to expand on these guidelines with their practical implementation in mind. I shall start with the most important one, the one containing the concept with which readers are possibly least familiar due to its absence from much of the literature on materials development, *communicative purpose*.

4.3.1 Guideline 1: Consistency with communicative purpose
In order to adhere to the guideline, we need first of all to understand what is meant

by the term *communicative purpose*. Communicative purpose is defined most simply as 'what we do through language' (Wilkins 1976: 41) - it refers to what people want to do or accomplish through speech (Finocchiaro and Brumfit 1983: 13). Communicative purpose is a defining factor of the *genre* of a text (other factors include structure, content, form, intended audience and medium), genre being 'primarily characterised by the communicative purpose(s) it is intended to fullfil' (Bhatia 1993: 13). It is, incidentally, because communicative purpose is a characterising feature of text that makes simplification of a text for language learning purposes so damaging to its authenticity, for this changes its communicative purpose, thus compromising its 'generic integrity' (Bhatia's term, 1993: 146).

Since communicative purpose is not the sole factor identifying genre (other factors being content, form and so on, see above), commonality of communicative purpose does not guarantee commonality of genre. Furthermore, some genres may have sets of communicative purposes, as Swales points out (1990: 47). For instance, the overt communicative purpose of a news broadcast may be *informative*, but there may be elements of *persuasive* intent (to influence public opinion, to retain viewer/listener-loyalty and so on; *ibid.*). In using such texts as the basis for tasks, therefore, the task-designer has to allow for the possible co-existence of a number of communicative purposes.

All this presupposes that there exists a set of communicative purposes on which to draw. Interestingly, however, in spite of the fact that communicative purpose is a familiar concept in the literature on genre analysis (e.g. Kress and Threadgold 1988, Bhatia 1993, Swales 1990), discourse analysis (e.g. Brown and Yule 1983) linguistic analysis (e.g. Biber 1988), and language pedagogy - the concept informed the Functional-notional approach (Wilkins 1976, Finocchiaro and Brumfit 1983) - no generally accepted or finite set of communicative purposes appears to have been taken on board in the field of materials development. In order to bridge this gap and construct a useable set of communicative purposes for use in the field, the above-mentioned fields of literature were trawled for relevant breakdowns and analyses of this feature.

A useful initial baseline was laid by looking to a much-cited distinction between two of the basic functions of oral language, *transactional* (conveying 'factual propositional information' with a view to obtaining goods, services etc.) and *interactional* (maintaining social relationships), developed by Brown and Yule (1983: 1-4). This was supplemented by a proposed third function of language, one which is particularly relevant to literature, *reactional* (Duff and Maley 1990: 10). The reactional function refers to the desire to make listeners/readers 'react personally to other people's ways of seeing things' (*ibid.*). The communicative purposes eventually identified, all fell into one of these three basic categories.

From the list proposed by Wilkins in *Notional Syllabuses* (1976: 42) came three of the communicative purposes to be included in the set being drawn up here. The first was termed *persuasive* and was based on Wilkins' category *suasion*, in which

Wilkins includes speech acts such as *advising, ordering, warning, threatening* and *permitting (ibid.)*. This communicative purpose had a transactional function according to the distinctions made above. The two other of Wilkins' categories to be adopted were *personal emotions* and *emotive relations*. The implicit distinction between these two categories is in terms of internalisation or externalisation of emotion, *personal emotions* referring to emotions such as pleasure and displeasure and *emotive relations* to externalisations of emotion, as in the expressing of sympathy or gratitude. This internal/external distinction was felt to be a useful and significant one to make in the context of analysing communicative purpose, so in building our set, the former distinction was adopted and termed *engaging* (engaging the emotions, imagination etc.) and the second termed *provocative* (causing an external manifestation of inner emotion, in the form of an oral response, physical action etc.). While the communicative purpose *provocative* was seen as *interactional*, the communicative purpose *engaging* had to be classed as *reactional*, in accordance with Duff and Maley's definition above.

These draft categories were consolidated and supplemented with reference to work on linguistic analysis by Biber (1988). Biber analysed the linguistic features of written and spoken texts which co-occur frequently, and used them to identify underlying textual dimensions, '[a] technique [...] based on the assumption that frequently co-occurring linguistic features have at least one shared communicative function' (Biber 1988: 63). Of the six textual dimensions distinguished in the Biber model, two had overt communicative functions which were integral to their identity: Dimension 1: 'Involved versus Informational Production', and Dimension 4 'Overt Expression of Persuasion'. (*ibid.*: 122). Dimension 1 ranged from 'high informational density and exact informational content' to 'affective interactional and generalised content', with its communicative purposes ranging from 'informational versus interactive, affective and involved' (*ibid.*: 107). This dimension was the source for a further three communicative purposes for our set, one transactional, *informative*, one interactional, *interactive* and the last reactive, *engaging*. Meanwhile, Dimension 4 'overt expression of persuasion' served to consolidate identification of the *persuasive* category initially sourced from Wilkins (see above).

Reference to the literature on genre, discourse and linguistic analysis had thus provided a provisional set of five communicative purposes, two with transactional functions; *informative,* and *persuasive,* two with interactional functions; *interactive* and *provocative,* and the last, *engaging,* having a reactional one. As the definitive set of communicative purposes required for the model had to subsume a broad range of discourse types, the appropriacy of these five provisional categorisations had to be verified, and any gaps identified and filled. This was done by devising a framework constituting a question-response process, represented by the flow chart (Table 1) below.

The preliminary question in each case was *'what is the text intended to provoke?'*, to which the four anticipated answers were:

- The performance of a physical action
- A productive reaction
- An emotive/intellectual response
- Passive reception of text

For each of these answers, there were two further questions. For example, to the above response *'the performance of a physical action'* were added the two questions;

- Does this entail following instructions?
- Does this entail purchase/use of goods/services?

If the answer to the question *'Does this entail following instructions?'* was *'yes'*, the communicative purpose was identified as *instructional* (communicative purpose nomenclatures are defined in Table 2 below). If the answer was *'no'*, the next question was used; *'Does this entail purchase/use of goods/services?'* and the communicative purpose identified as *persuasive*. The same procedure was followed with another three alternative responses as demonstrated in the flow chart below.

Table 1: Flow chart showing derivation of communicative purpose

Is the text intended to provoke:

The performance of a physical action?		**Does this entail:**		**Communicative purpose**
	→	following instructions?	→	*Instructional*
	→	purchase/use of goods/services?	→	*Persuasive*
A productive reaction?				
	→	producing oral/written information?	→	*Soliciting*
	→	oral/written reaction which advances interaction?	→	*Interactive*
An emotive/intellectual response?				
	→	anticipated oral/written follow-up?	→	*Provocative*
	→	no anticipated follow-up?	→	*Engaging*
Passive reception of text?				
	→	no anticipated follow-up?	→	*Informative*

By this means, a set of seven communicative purposes was consolidated, comprising the five provisional ones drawn from discourse/linguistic analysis plus another two, *Soliciting* and *Instructional*. These last two were seen as particularly relevant to some types of authentic texts used for language learning such as classified advertisements ('soliciting') and instructions (e.g. technical instructions in ICT). Verified against the baseline of transactional, interactional and reactional communicative functions, the finalised set of seven communicative purposes slotted into these three categories thus: *instructional, informative, persuasive* and *soliciting* under 'transactional', *interactive* and *provocative* under 'interactional' and *engaging* under 'reactional'. The table below summarises the definitions of the terms used for these seven communicative purposes and classifies them according to their basic communicative function.

Table 2: Description of communicative purposes

Nomenclature	Communicative purpose of text is to	Basic communicative function
Informative	transmit information	*Transactional*
Persuasive	persuade (re. purchase, opinion, action etc.)	*Transactional*
Soliciting	interact or transact (business or personal)	*Transactional*
Instructional	give instruction for implementing a process	*Transactional*
Provocative	provoke emotive / intellectual / kinaesthetic reaction	*Interactional*
Interactive	interact or transact (business or personal)	*Interactional*
Engaging	engage imagination/emotions (including humour)	*Reactional*

It should be emphasised that the set of seven communicative purposes generated as a result of the above-described process is not intended as an exhaustive classification, but as a utilitarian one. Its function is to offer sufficiently broad categories to enable the materials developer/task designer to assign a fairly accurate communicative purpose (or number of communicative purposes) to an authentic text s/he has selected for classroom use. The real, worked, examples in Chapters 5 to 11 are the best illustration of how the communicative purpose is inferred and applied to task design, but let us meanwhile take a brief look at some examples here.

In some texts, the communicative purpose is self-evident. The genre of classified advertisements could fairly safely be categorised as *soliciting*, i.e. to elicit information or action. Tasks devised to go with such texts might require learners to provide the requested information or fulfil the action (this might involve writing a letter or e-mail or role playing a phone call). Instructions, such as technical instructions in ICT are intended to assist in the implementation of a process and can be termed simply *instructional*. The obvious task here is simply to follow the instruction - to download and operate a piece of software and so on. Much dialogue, oral or electronic (e.g. e-mail) may be classed as *interactive* i.e. an oral/written utterance which prompts and advances interaction or transaction - this communicative purpose can be fulfilled by setting up and communicating with an e-mail pen-pal from the target language culture (see Chapter 11 Section 11.3.1).

Good examples of texts that are intrinsically *persuasive* ('designed to affect the behaviour of others', Wilkins 1976: 46) are advertisements - but in this endeavour other communicative intents are often deployed. These might be *provocative* - the causing of external manifestations of inner emotion, manifested in the form of a physical activity, and its internal counterpart, *engaging* (implicating emotions and desires). Where a text is clearly designed to provoke (e.g. a television advertisement, a feature article in a newspaper), the task assigned should involve responding to this provocation: e.g. writing a letter to the editor of the newspaper commenting on the article or complaining about the advertisement. With advertisements, what is often most tempting (and fruitful, in terms of language production) is to design a task where learners analyse *how* the communicative purpose/s of the advertisement is/are achieved. *Engaging* is of course the communicative purpose inherent in genres such as poetry and song, where the emotions and imagination are triggered, but not necessarily externally displayed. Texts with this communicative purpose need to be treated sensitively, the emotions or thoughts produced in the learners by them might have to be elicited subtly - via individual written or graphic work, for example - rather than open class discussions.

4.3.2 Guidelines 2 and 3: Appropriacy, response and engagement

As stated in the quotation from Clarke 1989 above, designing learning tasks to reflect the original communicative purpose of texts presupposes the factor of appropriacy. This factor can be said to have two perspectives, one looking to the text, the other to the interaction between the learner and the text. The first perspective looks to the medium, discourse type and communicative purpose of the authentic text and derives the task from this. The second looks to the learner and includes his/her anticipated reaction/response to, and level of engagement with the text. It thus leads us into the domain of guideline 3, which is why guidelines 2 and 3 are treated together here.

The first perspective is not easily served; for many discourse types it sweeps away that old stalwart of the language teacher, the comprehension question, which is, as has been previously noted (with reference to Grellet 1981), a convention unique to pedagogy with little application in real life. So-called comprehension is, in fact, vastly over-rated in language pedagogy because it blinkers us, focusing on linguistic comprehension alone. Even as native speakers we often do not hear all the words of discourse types such as songs or film-dialogues but this does not spoil our appreciation of them. We skim over others such as news articles and instructions but they still serve their function in transmitting information. This means that partial comprehension is authentic and appropriate to many discourse types and is a concept that can be applied in learning tasks based on them (see Clarke 1989: 75).

Maintaining appropriacy, then, requires the task designer to look at a text and envisage a way of handling it that reflects its treatment by native speakers. Does the NS reader skim it, scan it, study it word-for-word or simply refer back to it for guidance? Does the listener/viewer listen carefully to words being spoken, listen for the main points only or pay more attention to musical or visual elements (if present)? Furthermore, and perhaps more significant (and this leads us into the domain of the second perspective that considers learner response to the text), what is the reader/listener's relationship or attitude to the text? Is it a text which instils respect or emotion (e.g. a piece from a canonical novel, a poem, a classic pop song), is it one that produces a momentary emotive response (e.g. a joke, a photograph, an amusing/moving newspaper article), or is it of little consequence (e.g. a memo, a weather forecast). Out of such considerations, the basis for an appropriate task should emerge.

Inappropriate tasks - such as inserting comprehension questions between the paragraphs of a humorous anecdote[10], or asking learners to point out activities using phrasal verbs in a distressing press photograph of women grieving on learning of a child's death[11], can be avoided, and ones sensitive to the texts and their emotive potential can be devised. The anecdote might be read aloud in its entirety and learners' comprehension gauged by the amount of laughter, its humour analysed afterwards to whatever depth the students desire. The background to the photograph, for example the civil war in which the boy was killed, might be discussed. Poems can be heard - in their entirety without the unnecessary preamble that textbooks tend to insert[12] - allowing the listener-learner the satisfaction of initially drawing his/her own inferences, which can be discussed and verified at a later stage. Songs can likewise be enjoyed for their melody as well as their lyrics[13] - indeed, for the unique combination of music and words that makes a song - foregoing the language element until the initial emotive impact of the melody has been absorbed (see also Chapter 9, 'Song').

4.3.3 Guideline 4: Approximate real-life tasks

The idea of the task approximating a native speaker task may be conceived in terms of a continuum. At one end of this lie tasks which *replicate* commonplace native speaker activities (such as adjusting plans on the basis of a weather forecast or replying to an e-mail). At the other end of the continuum lie more specialised tasks which pertain to particular professional contexts (such as advertising or journalism) and which may involve analysis of linguistic, visual or audio aspects of a text. Analysis of how the impact of an advertisement or news piece is achieved would be typical here, or the generating of diagram (graph, chart etc.) to represent statistical information gleaned from a written source. In between the two ends of the continuum lie learning tasks that externalise what, for the native speaker, are (generally) internal experiences. A task that consists of a step-by-step breakdown of what a native speaker does unconsciously when listening to/reading a text can therefore also be said to be authentic. An example might be to watch/listen to a news broadcast and note down the topic of each news item, its main protagonists, where the reported event occurred, and such like. This activity externalises and rationalises what a native speaker does internally and subconsciously when listening to/viewing the news. Other examples include noting and analysing non-verbal behaviour by speakers in news or chat show interviews, dialogues in soaps and films and so on, since we as NSs take a surprising amount of information from non-verbal signs (it has been estimated that up to 80% of our communication is non-verbal (Tomalin and Stempleski 1990: 4). This middle area of the continuum gives enormous scope for learning tasks and simply requires the task designer to deconstruct the way/s in which s/he as a native speaker reacts to or deals with a given piece of text.

4.3.4 Guideline 5: Exploit learners' existing knowledge

This guideline refers to the exploiting of the learners' cultural and linguistic 'reference points' in language learning tasks. It points up the importance of custom-designing materials for individual learner groups having, to the teacher's knowledge, been exposed to particular language or cultural points which recur in the new text/task and which can form the launching point for it. While the language structures a group will have studied is linked more or less to proficiency level, the cultural reference points of any group of individual learners will vary widely, depending on whether they are studying in the TL country or have visited it, whether they have friends or correspondents there, and so on. Their knowledge of the TC might range from the more obvious factual things (currency, cuisine, daily and leisure habits, infrastructures) to the deeper levels of social structures, values, gender and ethnic equality, consumerism and wealth, freedom of expression, and other cultural indicators[14]. More often, learners will have a better awareness of the former, but with encouragement may be able to use this to make inferences as to the latter. People's daily and leisure habits, for example, reveal their attitudes to work and to their private lives, and how they prioritise these; looking into cooking and eating habits can reveal conventions as to *who* prepares and serves meals, and so on.

Whatever the case, learning tasks for any given group should ideally be 'on the cusp' between building on what the learners know, and bombarding them with a superfluity of new concepts. Many's the teacher who has been misled by the apparent simplicity of a lively magazine article, for instance, only to find it is saturated with cultural reference points and idiomatic language. In its initial stage/s, a task might involve 'milking' the learners for prior knowledge of the subject of the text/task. This can be done in any number of ways, either explicitly - whole-class, teacher-led activities such as drawing a mind-map on the board, or note-making in groups or individually - or implicitly, in activities which require the deployment of this prior knowledge. For example, if the text the learners are going to use is a film excerpt showing a pub scene, they might be asked first to script a scene in a pub to show their idea of a typical grouping in this situation, drinking habits, who pays and when, and so on[15]. The benefits of this are two-fold: on the linguistic level, learners are alerted to, and thus 'equipped with' some of the language/concepts within the new text/task. On the affective level, such pre-tasks prove to learners how much they already know, and this is encouraging, motivating and provides incentive for the new task.

4.3.5 Guideline 6: Promote purposeful communication

This guideline links the authenticity-centred approach to its Communicative roots. As has been detailed in Chapter 1 (Section 1.1.1) the precepts of CLT originated in Hymes' notion of communicative competence, which centred on the concept of 'language as communication, a view in which meaning and the uses to which it is put play a central role' (Brumfit and Johnson 1979: 3). The concept of 'purposeful' or 'meaningful' communication became central to the methodological implementation of CLT. Many of the by-now classic activities conceived to implement the approach, e.g. information-share, information-pooling, jig-saw listening, text or map completion, following directions or instructions and such like (see activities described in Littlewood 1981: 22-36, Johnson 1979: 201, Brumfit and Johnson 1979: 207-11), have to be critically reassessed, however, for our more authenticity-oriented era. This means keeping in mind the *other* factors regulating task authenticity, especially adherence to original communicative purpose, appropriacy and realism. Assessed in this light, many Communicative activities deflate into mere pedagogical tasks. This is the case with such typical Communicative activities as listening to an audio piece and rearranging a jumbled printed text[16], drawing something from someone else's description[17] and converting drawings into written instructions[18]. While the communication has a purpose in the narrowest sense of completing the set task, the other factors are absent. What can nevertheless be taken from such tasks is the aspect of *creativity* that is inherent in all of them. This can be channelled it into a real, concrete outcome, such as producing a report based on the results of a questionnaire polled inside or outside the classroom, or conceiving a product and advertisement for it, based on the results of market research (again, carried out within or outside the classroom). Communications technology has of course, hugely facilitated our pursuit of tasks involving real communication; today, e-mail 'key-pal' partnerships offer opportunities for genuine correspondence between learners of different languages and cultures (see Chapter 11 Section 11.3).

4.4 Task Typologies

So far, our creation of a framework to rationalise the authenticity-centred approach has seen (a) the drawing up of a set of guidelines for task authenticity and (b) a set of communicative purposes to assign to authentic texts and which constitute the starting point for tasks based on them. The concluding step in the development of the framework is to establish a set of task types in which the guidelines for task authenticity can be implemented. Two sources were drawn on for this. The first was external - established taxonomies drawn from the literature. The second was internal - the guidelines for task authenticity themselves.

The first of the established task taxonomies is from Prabhu's seminal work on task-based learning, *Second Language Pedagogy* (1987). Prabhu's tasks were specific to the experimental project for which they were developed, the Bangalore Project. The rationale for the project was that 'development of competence in a second language requires not systematisation of language inputs [...] but rather the creation of conditions in which learners engage in an effort to cope with communication' (Prabhu 1987: 1), i.e. a Communicative approach. Few of the early Communicative activities such as the ones described by Prabhu had the later preoccupation with fidelity to real-life, they were not designed to meet 'social demands for immediate usefulness' (Prabhu 1987: 93), but to promote 'constant effort by learners to deploy their language resources in the classroom' (*ibid*.), i.e. to create a need for students to use the language and practise language skills. The task types used on the Bangalore Project were categorised according to the materials/texts used (e.g. maps, timetables, itineraries) a list that runs to 18 classifications. In order to facilitate comparison between this taxonomy and later ones, which are mostly classified according to the cognitive processes or linguistic skills involved in the tasks, the Bangalore project tasks were analysed and re-categorised on this basis. This yielded a set of eight task types:

Table 3: Task types used in the Bangalore Project (extrapolated from Prabhu 1987: 138-43)

Task type – skill or process	Examples
1. Following and giving descriptions, instructions (in oral, written, graphic form)	Naming parts of a diagram Placing numbers, letters in given formats Drawing figures, formations Constructing/completing maps, plans, timetables Giving directions Writing a CV Form-filling
2. Extracting information	Drawing up teacher timetable on basis of class timetable Extracting relevant information from a CV

3. Drawing inferences	Drawing up programmes / itineraries / timetables / maps, making appointments based on:
	    Routines
	    Narrative accounts, descriptions
	    Statements of needs, intentions
	    Work, travel requirements
	    Descriptions of travel
	Identifying 'odd one out' in sets of objects, lists
	Inferring quantities bought from money spent
	Relating individual needs to age requirements e.g. school enrolment, voting rights, driving

4. Making calculations	Time (from clock-face) Durations (from calendar) Age from year of birth/vice versa Expenditure (from shopping lists, price lists) Checking calculations Comparing pricing, income, expenses Comparing distances (on route maps)

5. Interpreting and extrapolating	Interpreting/extrapolating
	Information from tables/timetables
	Rules / anomalies from sets of regulations
	Generalisations from tables
	Classifications
	Personal information from a CV
6. Analysis	Making decisions/plans on basis of information (e.g. best route, best form of transport, best siting for school, based on given factors (e.g. cost).
	Analysis of the postal system (based on post codes)
7. Extension	Completing stories/dialogues
8. Reformulation	Interpreting telegrams
	Composing telegrams
	Reorganising a CV for given audience

Bearing in mind the fact that in re-categorising this set of tasks according to newer criteria, there was a risk that similarities which might arise could be a case of a 'self-fulfilling prophesy', it is nevertheless significant that Prabhu's set as expressed here is comparable to lists of task types proposed in later publications such as those in Willis 1996:

Table 4: Typology for TBL Task Design (based on Willis 1996: 149-54)

Task	Process	Outcome	Samples
1. Listing	brainstorming fact-finding	List, Poster, Mind-map	Words, things, abstracts, activities, questions
2. Ordering, Sorting	Sequencing, ranking categorising	Ordered set of data	Instructions, strategies, generic lists
3. Comparing	matching, finding similarities/differences	Matched items, groups of similar/ different items	Descriptions, visuals, versions (of texts/ accounts), cultures
4. Problem-solving	Analysing real or hypothetical situations, reasoning, decision-making	Solution to problem and evaluation	Puzzles, real-life problems, case studies
5. Sharing personal experiences	Narrating, describing, exploring attitudes, reactions	Personal: expansion of socio-cultural knowledge	Anecdotes, opinions, personal reactions
6. Creative tasks	brainstorming, factfinding, ordering, problem-solving	Product, project	creative writing, model, experiment, magazine, recording, video

Both taxonomies include tasks that require such cognitive processes as extracting, ordering and sorting information, making comparisons/contrasts and problem-solving (see comparison Table 6 below).

Finally, the set proposed in Maley 1993 as 'twelve generalizable procedures' i.e. exercise types which can be applied to 'virtually any text', is particularly appropriate to the task authenticity framework, since it was specifically conceived for use with authentic texts. This set too can be seen to have task typologies in common with the previous two taxonomies:

Table 5: 'Twelve Generalizable Procedures' (based on Maley 1993: xi)

Task type	Process	Examples
1. Expansion	Add something to the text	Add clauses, sentences, paragraphs, comments, specified items (e.g. adjectives)
2. Reduction	Shorten the text	Remove specified items (e.g. adjectives), clauses or sentences, Combine sentences. Rewrite in a different format e.g. telegraphese. See also *# 3 Media Transfer* and *# 8 Reformulation*
3. Media Transfer	Transfer the text into a different medium, format or genre	Transfer: Prose into visual form (e.g. pictures, graphs, maps, tables), poem or screenplay. Letter into a newspaper article (or vice versa). Headline into a proverb (or vice versa). Poem into prose/an advertising slogan (or vice versa)
4. Matching	Find a correspondence between the text and something else	Match text with a visual representation, a title, another text, a voice, music
5. Selection/Ranking	Select or rank a text or texts according to some given criterion	Choose the text that is - most suitable for a given purpose (e.g. inclusion in a teenage magazine). - the most/least (difficult, formal, personal, complex ...) - most/least like the original version. Choose words from a text to act as an appropriate title
6. Comparison/Contrast	Identify points of similarity/difference between two or more texts	Identify words/expressions/ideas common to or paraphrased in both texts. Compare facts or grammatical/lexical complexity (See also *# 11 Analysis*)

7. Reconstruction	Restore coherence/completeness to an incomplete or defective text	Insert appropriate words/phrases into gapped texts. Reorder jumbled words, lines, sentences, paragraphs etc. Reconstruct sentences/texts from a word array. Reconstitute a written text from an oral presentation (various types of dictation) Remove sentences/lines which do not 'belong' in the text
8. Reformulation	Express the same meaning in a different form	Retell a story from notes/memory/keywords Rewrite in a different style, mood or format (e.g. prose as poem) (See also # 3 *Media Transfer*)
9. Interpretation	Engage with the text relating it to personal knowledge/experience	Relate text to own experience Associate text with ideas, images Formulate questions for the text's author Assess the truth, likelihood, possible omissions of the text
10. Creating Text	Use the text as a springboard for the creation of others	Write a parallel text on a different theme Use the same story outline/model/title to write a new text Quarry words from text A to create a new text B Reshape the text by adding lines/sentences. (See also # 1 *Expansion* and # 8 *Reformulation*) Combine these texts to create a new text
11. Analysis	Linguistic analysis of the text	Work out and list the number/ratio of: - One-word verbs/two-word verbs - Different tenses - Content/function words - Different ways in which the word X is referred to in the text (anaphoric reference) Put words into semantic groups e.g. the sea, movement, ecology etc.)

12. Project Work	Use text as springboard for a product	Use the text as the centrepiece of an advertising campaign: decide on product, design campaign posters, jingles etc., present the product as a TV commercial.
		Use a text about a specific problem: design & distribute a questionnaire on this problem (to other groups). Tabulate & present results
		Use text presenting a particular point of view: prepare and then display a short magazine article supporting/disagreeing with this point of view

In all three cases, the task types have to be seen as functioning within the model of the task cycle as specified by each of the authors (see also Section 4.2 'Task' above). In Prabhu's case, this consisted of a teacher-led pre-task introducing the task, the task activity done in groups or individually, and a teacher-assessment of the task outcome on an individual basis. Willis's task cycle includes a comparable pre-task and task activity (although with group/pair work as the norm), but follows this with a specific language focus session drawing on the language generated during the task. Maley's tasks had a basic two-phase pattern of task completion, followed by comparing outcomes.

While varying in procedure, the task sets show a number of task types in common as the following table reveals:

Table 6: Comparison of task typologies of Prabhu, Willis and Maley

Prabhu 1987	Willis 1996	Maley 1993
Extracting information	'Ordering, sorting, classifying'	'Selection/Ranking'
Making calculations	'Comparing, matching'	'Comparison/Contrast', 'Matching'
Drawing inferences Analysis (facts)	'Problem-solving'	-
-	'Creative tasks'	'Project work'
-	'Sharing personal experiences, anecdote telling'	'Interpretation'
Analysis (facts)	-	'Analysis' (linguistic)
Reformulation	-	'Reformulation'
Extension	-	'Expansion'

What is interesting is that despite their common, ultimate goal of promoting language learning, what the three task taxonomies have most in common is tasks which involve cognitive processing; extracting, comparing, classifying and reformulating information. This reveals the Communicative basis of these three taxonomies, the notion that language learning is induced through purposeful use of language. But while this was fundamental to the earliest of these three task-based methodologies - 'project teaching aimed at meaning-focused activity' to the exclusion of 'rule' or 'form'-focused types (Prabhu 1987:28) - the more recent permutation of the Communicative approach embraces language study, as has already been noted above, particularly in the form of consciousness-raising of linguistic structures (see Chapter 2 Section 2.8 and Chapter 3 Section 3.2.2). This is reflected by the inclusion in Maley's procedures of a task type dedicated to linguistic analysis (procedure number 11) and in a language focus stage being integrated into Willis's task cycle (see Section 4.2 'Task' above). A similar form-focused task type is included in the set of task typologies drawn up for the task authenticity framework to which we now turn.

The chief 'internal' parameters guiding the development of task types are the guidelines for task authenticity drawn up earlier in the chapter. Referring back to these, if a task is to respond to the communicative purpose of a text (guideline number one) it may be inferred that there are various types of tasks, suited to different communicative purposes. Suitability to the communicative purpose of a text, furthermore, implies a task that is 'realistic', approximating 'real-life' activity (guideline number four). One means of creating a set of task typologies is, therefore, to look at texts having the various communicative purposes proposed in Table 2 above and to ask what would be 'realistic' way/s of working with them.

To illustrate this procedure, let us think about a text whose communicative function might be interpreted as *engaging* in that it evokes an emotional response, for instance, a poem about a subject with universal resonance such as the death of a loved one. In 'real life' our response to an emotive piece might well be wholly internalised, but this response might be externalised (in accordance with task authenticity guideline Number four) by such activities as writing a short prose piece describing how the poem makes one feel, drawing a sketch, discussing responses to it with other people, and so on. This suggests a *response* task type associated with expressing emotions. Cross-checked against the taxonomies given above, this corresponds approximately to Maley's procedure Number 9, 'interpretation', which involves clarifying the text through connection to one's own experiences.

A text at the opposite end of the emotive spectrum in that it is intended principally to *inform* (although this does not preclude other communicative purposes), is a radio news bulletin. As with the emotive piece, in 'real life' we usually process information unconsciously, although there may be reasons in real life as well as the language classroom for externalising it. For instance, we tend to pay closer attention to information with personal implications - a real-life example from my own cultural context is the tightening up of the Irish laws applying to speeding - and we might listen for pertinent facts. This suggests an *extraction* task type similar to 'extracting information' tasks in Prabhu's taxonomy. It also illustrates how we draw *inferences* from information presented (see Prabhu's tasks based on drawing inferences, Number 3) - in this case, how the new laws will affect us personally. We might also follow up on an item heard in the news, by looking for more information in a newspaper, on the Internet etc. - this suggests an *extension* type task (Maley's procedure Number 1 'expansion' is a similar, though more delimited, task type). We may, of course, simply discuss the news with other people -suggesting a media transfer type task (see Maley's procedure Number 3) in which information is transferred from one medium to another (broadcast information might equally well be re-written as a newspaper article, for example).

To look next at a genre much-beloved of language teachers, the advertisement, whose communicative purpose is self-evidently *persuasive*; a realistic task would be to *react* to this persuasion in some way; most obviously, to buy the product advertised (!), or perhaps to tear out an application form included in it (if text-based). A *reaction* type task includes the possibility of physical activity and creativity, thereby corresponding to Willis' Number 4, 'creative tasks' - designing a rival to an advertised product, for example. An advertisement, might alternatively, lend itself to *inferring* implicit information (e.g. regarding the product, its image, its market), or *extracting* facts (e.g. price, availability). The advertisement might also, of course, be *analysed* to discover how (linguistically/visually etc.) this persuasion is achieved (this corresponds to Maley's procedure Number 11).

Via this method, then, of considering a sample of texts incorporating each of the communicative purposes listed in Table 2 above, and identifying realistic or pseudo-realistic task types to go with them (see task authenticity guideline number 4), a set of seven task typologies was generated. In accordance with the texts' anticipated effects on the learners and the interactions stimulated, these were termed *response, extraction, inferencing, extension, transference, reaction* and *analysis*. Definitions and examples are summarised in the following table:

Table 7: Task typologies

Designation	Description	Examples
Reaction	Reaction (including kinaesthetic) to written, audio or audio-visual input of non-emotive nature e.g. acting on written, audio or visual instructions in order to create something, accomplish a task or participate in activity	- Make/alter plans on the basis of weather forecast - Stage a 'phone-in' on a controversial topic
Response	Response (manifested orally or represented in writing/graphically) to audio, written, visual, or audio-visual input of emotive nature	- Listen to instrumental section of a song and write a prose piece, poem, or draw a picture to illustrate what it evokes
Inferencing	Inferring/extrapolating/interpreting information/concepts (including cultural) from audio, written, visual, or audio-visual input.	- Watch a series of film trailers and infer the genre, setting, basic story, intended audience etc. of each.
Transference	Transference, translation or paraphrase from one medium, genre or culture to another (includes awareness of significance of these transferences).	- Deconstruct a newspaper/magazine article reporting findings of a survey to infer and write the original survey questions.
Extraction	Extracting factual information (including factual cultural indicators) from audio, written, visual, or audio-visual input.	- Extract factual information (e.g. price, ingredients, 'unique' features of product, from advertisements (e.g. foods, electrical goods, cars)
Analysis	Awareness-raising of linguistic forms and functions and of emotive / figurative / subjective use of language.	- Analyse how newspaper headlines achieve impact - Analyse conversational strategies on basis of dialogues from interviews, films, soaps.
Extension	Extension/prediction of development/outcome of event, situation presented via audio, written, visual, or audio-visual input	- Identify with a character in novel/story or film and develop characterisation

It should be clear from the means of extrapolating task typologies described above that the implicit communicative purpose of a text does not limit or constrain authentic response to it to a single task typology. A text's communicative purpose may stimulate a number of potential responses, all equally authentic, as is illustrated by the above example of an advertisement which has an overt *persuasive* intent but which has a number of authentic ways of responding to it in the form of tasks. Each communicative purpose may therefore be cross-referenced to a set of potential, authentic task typologies as shown in the table below.

Table 8: Cross-referenced task typologies by communicative purpose

Communicative Purpose	Authentic task typologies
Informative:	Extraction, Reaction, Transference, Analysis, Inferencing
Persuasive:	Reaction, Response, Analysis, Inferencing
Interactive:	Extraction, Reaction, Response, Inferencing, Transference
Instructional:	Reaction
Provocative:	Reaction, Response, Inferencing, Analysis
Soliciting:	Response, Reaction
Engaging:	Analysis, Response, Inferencing, Extension, Transference

The versatility that this potential offers texts becomes apparent from looking at some of the worked examples of tasks in Chapters 5 to 11.

4.4.1 Tasks and skills

A number of final points need to be made as regards the task model proposed here. The task typologies are described above in terms of the broad linguistic, cognitive and/or physical activity/ies they entail. The skills involved in carrying out these activities are what Nunan calls 'enabling' skills (1989: 60-3), that is, they are those which are needed to *enact* the tasks, the tasks are not designed *in order to* practise specific skills.

Language skills are conventionally conceived in terms of the 3-levels below, and language learning activities are often identified correspondingly with particular skills:

Level 1. A basic breakdown into two sets, receptive and productive.

Level 2. Four macro-skills, referring to the skills required to deal with the different media of input and output (e.g. reading skills are those skills used in dealing with input from the written mode, and so on).

Level 3. Micro-skills: these are specific to the task, e.g. the micro-skills of skimming and scanning of written texts that is specific to 'extraction' tasks.

A critical feature that distinguishes the task model of language learning from other models, is that it requires learners to combine and integrate the use and practice of skills. This is what helps make the task model so authentic, for in real life, skills are not only deployed in isolation (as they are so often practised in the classroom). For instance, we might use scanning skills on classified advertisements columns to find a specific requirement (a suitable flat-share, a second-hand bicycle), then we might make a phone call or write an e-mail, deploying speaking or writing skills. These skills in turn, involve combinations of linguistic and cognitive processes: we might listen to a news report, draw inferences and reach conclusions, using a mixture of listening skills and inferencing processes. The authenticity of the task model used here thus lies in the fact that it replicates these sorts of authentic combinations (see Nunan's criteria for communicative tasks, 1989: 140, and also McGarry, 1995: 17). Furthermore, the interactivity at the heart of the task model implicates essential collaborative and communication skills, such as negotiating meaning, exchanging instructional and explanatory input, agreeing and disagreeing, reaching consensus and so on.

Finally, any experienced teacher knows that no amount of theorising can predict what happens in the classroom. The distinctions between the task typologies classified here can often become blurred in operation. In particular, the inclusion of an *Analysis* type task, which specifically provides for language analysis, is not intended to imply that language analysis work be excluded from other task types. It is assumed that language points will arise naturally in any of the tasks, and that these will either be dealt with as they arise, or postponed until a dedicated language focus session (e.g. at the conclusion of the task - see Willis's task model outlined in Section 4.2 'Task', above).

4.5 Conclusion

The business of this chapter has been the development of a framework which actualises the concept of task authenticity. The framework consists of three sets of parameters which guide and rationalise the design of tasks for use with authentic texts. The sets of parameters draw on a wide range of influences, from genre and discourse analysis, to work on task-based learning. The framework is thus intended to give the concept of task authenticity a sound theoretical and pedagogical basis, and a means of practical implementation. The functioning of this framework 'in action' is demonstrated in the tasks described in Part II, the resource section of the book, which consists of Chapters 5 to 11.

Notes

1   Oxford University Press, for example, currently has at least seven resource books on using authentic texts including film, drama and the Internet. Cambridge University Press has at least six, including newspapers, literature and authentic video.

2   Nunan emphasizes that the term 'real-world' is used as a form of shorthand and is not intended to suggest that the classroom is not 'real' (Nunan 1986: 40).

3   Nunan uses the term 'pedagogic'; elsewhere in this book, the adjective used is *pedagogical*, in line with most common current usage.

4   Nunan's example, 1989: 41.

5   Based on my experience in 1992 of using the Boeing manual with Ukranian pilots who were being trained to fly Boeing aircraft at nearby Shannon airport.

6   For example, the seductive language used by a young man apparently flirting with his male flat-mate across the breakfast table is abruptly recontextualised in our minds, as we are given to realise that the young man is actually speaking to his girlfriend on a hands-free phone (a TV advertisement for Irish telecom company Eircom, screened in 2002-3).

7   From my experience teaching Business English at the University of Limerick Language Centre in 1993-7.

8   From my experience teaching Japanese learners at the University of Limerick Language Centre, 1995.

9   The novel being used with the students in question was *Paddy Clarke Ha Ha Ha*, by Roddy Doyle.

10 As done to an excerpt from Bill Bryson's *Notes from a Big Country* in the coursebook *English File* (Oxenden and Latham-Koenig 2001:18)

11 An activity from the EFL learners' newspaper *Arrow* 1998: 17, based on an EPA photograph taken in an Algerian village.

12 The W. H. Auden poem 'Stop all the Clocks' used in *New Headway* Intermediate (Soars and Soars 1996) is given the introduction 'it is a love poem' (*ibid*. 123), with another set of instructions beginning: 'a loved one has died...' (*ibid*.).

13 The lyrics are the entire focus in most textbooks: e.g. the only songs used in two books sampled at random are all given as gapped texts with no reference to their musical element: 'The Winner takes it all' (Abba), 'American Pie' (Don McLean) in *English File* (Oxenden and Latham-Koenig 2001: 15, 111), 'Everything Stops for Tea' in *Headway Elementary Video Activity Book*, Falla 1993: 44).

14 A comprehensive source for these is *The IONESCO World Culture Report 1998, Part 5: Building cultural indicators*. http://www.unesco.org/culture/worldreport/html_eng/wcr5.shtml, accessed 1 May 2003.

15 Designed for use with students at the University of Limerick Language Centre (ULLC) 1997, as pre-task prior to viewing of pub scene from the film *The Snapper* (Frears 1993).

16 E.g. listening to a radio advertisement and sorting a jumbled text, *Breakthrough*, Cleasby and Gallagher, 1995: 17.

17 This is pointed out by Rossner 1988: 149.

Part Two
Using Cultural Products For Language Learning
A Teaching Resource

Having 'set the scene' for the authenticity-centred approach in the first four chapters, this part of the book turns finally to its practical implementation. Part II consists of seven chapters, each covering a separate cultural product: *Literature, The broadcast media, Newspapers, Advertising, Music and song, Film and ICT.* Each chapter falls into two sections. The first section discusses how to use the cultural product in language teaching in ways that exploit the advantages of *culture, currency* and *challenge*, identified as the pedagogical rationale for using authentic texts for language learning in Chapter 3. This section concludes with a *quick reference* guide consisting of (a) a *set of principles* for the use of the cultural product for language teaching which summarises the preceding discussions, and (b) references for *further reading*, listing resource or other books offering fuller treatment of the cultural product for language learning. The second section of each chapter is a practical teaching resource. It contains sets of classroom tasks described in step-by-step format and designed within the task authenticity framework provided in Chapter 4.

The 3 c's: Culture, Currency and Challenge

The discussion section on each cultural product falls under the three headings introduced in Chapter 3 as 'keywords' to summarise the many advantages of using authentic texts for language learning: 'culture' 'currency' and 'challenge', 'the three c's'. The first one, 'culture', is fairly self-explanatory, referring to the interconnection between a culture and its (linguistic) products. It will be recalled that the keyword 'currency' was expanded to encompass not only the idea of authentic texts being up-to-date in both topic and language, but the advantages that this brings for their relevance and interest to the learner and thus the potential for affective involvement. The third term, challenge, was chosen to put across the positive rather than negative aspects of the (perceived) difficulties of authentic texts, and looked at basic task design principles which enable teachers to use authentic texts with learners of all levels of proficiency.

For each of the cultural products discussed, the balance, pertinence and relative strength of 'the 3 c's' obviously varies. Certain product-specific issues also arise, such as the definition of literature (in Chapter 5), the problems of channelling entertainment media for language learning (in Chapter 6, 'The broadcast media', and Chapter 10, 'Film') and the ideal length of audio-visual excerpts (relating to the same two chapters).

The Tasks

The layout of the classroom tasks given in the second part of each of the chapters is as follows:

Discourse type: each cultural product falls into a number of discourse types characteristic to it. For example, for the broadcast media discourse types include *news interviews* and *weather forecasts*; for newspapers they include *news item reporting an event* and *letters to the editor*, and so on.

Communicative purpose: the presumed communicative purpose of the text, identified and chosen from the set developed in Chapter 4, i.e. *Informative, Persuasive, Interactive, Instructional, Provocative, Engaging, Soliciting.*

Authentic task type: the authentic task type suited to a discourse type having the previously identified communicative purpose, chosen from the task typology set developed in Chapter 4, i.e. *Reaction, Response, Inferencing, Transference, Extraction, Analysis, Extension*

Learner level: ranging from level 2 (post-elementary) to level 6 (advanced) of *The English-Speaking Union Framework* yardstick of performance scales for English language learners (see Appendix II).

Aim: the intended learning outcomes of the task (including the skills/strategies the task involves and practises).

Preparation: the preparation required by the teacher.

The task: described in a step-by-step format.

Chapter Five:
Literature

5.1 Defining Literature

Like the term 'culture' discussed in Chapter 3, the term 'literature' is a dual-faceted notion. It is often distinguished in contemporary writings as 'literature with a capital L' and 'literature with a small 'l'. The definition typically given in the dictionary is as 'literature with a capital L', that is, 'writings that are valued for their beauty of form, especially novels and poetry and plays etc.' (*Oxford Paperback Dictionary*, 1983 edition), or 'writings in prose or verse; especially: writings having excellence of form or expression and expressing ideas of permanent or universal interest' (*The Merriam-Webster Dictionary*, on-line edition). This is probably the sense in which the term is most widely used in the lay context. While adopting this as a baseline definition in this chapter, the implications of such a definition will be analysed and eventually challenged below.

The use of literature in language learning has to be seen, first of all, in the context of evolving attitudes and approaches to the study of literature in the native speaker community. The evolution of ELT into a field in its own right from the mid-20th century onwards occurred at a time when the approach adopted in school and university curricula towards literature could be characterised as 'Leavisite'; that is to say, influenced by the works of the renowned literary critic F.R. Leavis. Put in simple terms, the Leavisite position was that literature is an established, elite *canon* with intrinsic textual and moral value, the study of which could hone intelligence and sensitivity. EFL teaching approaches of the mid-20th century onwards (the structural/functional approaches of the 1950s followed by CLT) saw no place for this conception of literature, and mainly eschewed literature in their efforts to represent language in an exclusively up-to-date, living societal context. By the 1970s, however, a paradigm shift in attitudes to literary criticism was taking place in the L1 context. Various reader-oriented theories such as *reader-response* theory, one of the most famous proponents of which is Wolfgang Iser (see, for example, 1980) were redirecting attention from the author to the reader. In reader-response theory, 'reading is not a direct 'internalisation', because it is not a one-way process', but 'a dynamic *interaction* between text and reader' (emphasis in the original) (Iser 1980: 107). Reading could thus be conceived as a *negotiation* or *transaction* between the reader and the text. In synthesis, reader-response theory held that 'text has no real existence until it is read. By completing meaning, thus actualising or reading it, the reader does not take a passive role, as was traditionally thought, but is an active agent in the creation of meaning' (Gilroy and Parkinson 1997: 215).

This bold, interactive approach to literature coincided fortuitously with Communicative principles of language learning, giving literature a conceptual framework within which it could operate in foreign language teaching. The type of methodology that this more interactive approach to working with literature has engendered has been termed *language-based* and *process-oriented* (Carter 1991: 3), as opposed to the *product-based* approach of the former school.

The espousal of literature into the foreign language curriculum came for another reason as well. Working within the structural/functional and early CLT approaches, practitioners had perceived a cultural void in language teaching, the broader cultural context of which could best be filled by historical and contemporary literature (see, for example, Kramsch 1993, Collie and Slater 1987).

The use of a language-based approach to literature in the field of language learning has not been without its controversies, however. The effective dereverentialising of literature implied by the approach led to keener analysis of so-called 'literary language'… and thence to the controversial position that ultimately, no linguistic or semantic criteria differentiate literary texts from other types of discourse: 'The distinction between standard and poetic language [...] has been challenged by many writers in the field of linguistics and language teaching [who] argue that it is not possible to isolate features which are exclusive to literary language' (Gilroy and Parkinson 1997: 214). Among such writers are numbered Cook (1990, 1992, 1996), Lazar (1993), Carter (1991), Brumfit and Carter (1991) and Short and Candlin (1991), and their standpoint on this issue is remarkably consistent. Short and Candlin, for instance, maintain that; 'we know of no particular linguistic feature or set of linguistic features which are found in literature but not in other kinds of texts' (1991: 107), a view echoed in Cook's assertion that 'whatever criteria are used [to define literature] - whether linguistic, semantic, functional, social or psychological - there are too many exceptions' (1992: xvi). Lazar notes the peculiar non-specificity of literary language as compared to its 'functional' counterparts: 'There is no specialised literary language which can be isolated and analysed in the same way as the language of specific fields, such as law; or specific media, such as newspapers' (Lazar 1993: 6). Carter, finally, is among those to reach the conclusion that 'in terms of actual words employed, there can certainly be no quantitative distinction between literary and non-literary texts' (Carter 1991: 124). A poem, for instance, 'only becomes a poem by being called a poem and by being set out typographically in a certain way'[1] (Duff and Maley 1990: 14). This is particularly true of much modern poetry, which does not necessarily use special, 'literary' linguistic features, but rather, 'foreground[s] ideas by putting them in a poetic frame' (*ibid*.). For example, one such feature, metaphor, is often held to be a distinguishing feature of literature, yet 'is pervasive in our daily discourse and, as a property of language, is not in any way unique' (Brumfit and Carter 1991: 6). In today's language and society, in other words, an irreversible blurring of genres has occurred in which the 'literary use' of language is not restricted to literature but can occur in many other genres ranging from everyday speech to jokes, graffiti, television soap opera and 'supremely [...] in the contemporary world, the language of literature is usurped by advertisements. In fact, we should not underestimate their role in bringing to an end a characterisation of literature as a particular use of language' (Cook 1990: 130). This issue is pursued in Chapter 7 'Advertising'.

Argued from another standpoint, literature cannot be regarded as exclusive for the very reason that 'one of the hallmarks of literature is that it feeds creatively on every possible style and register' (Lazar 1993: 6), or as McCarthy and Carter see it: 'Literary texts show a remarkable freedom of mixing of modes', citing as examples the range of features typical to conversation represented in literary texts (McCarthy and Carter 1994: 12). Colloquial speech patterns and idiom are, indeed, reproduced so naturalistically in some contemporary literature that dialogue from them transfers to another medium - film - almost unchanged. This goes for such Roddy Doyle novels as *The Commitments* (1987) and *The Snapper* (1990) (made into films in 1991 and 1993 respectively) and Irvine Welsh's *Trainspotting* (1993) filmed in 1996. New varieties, such as those from communications technologies have by now found themselves incorporated into literary genres such as the novel (e.g. *E-Mail: A Love Story*, Fletcher 1996).

If the concept of a distinct literary language appears therefore to be untenable, what may be more useful is the concept of a cline of 'literariness', as suggested by Brumfit and Carter: 'What is literary is a matter of relative degree, with some textual features of language signalling greater literariness than others. The category is one best identified along a gradient or cline, rather than as a yes/no distinction' (Brumfit and Carter 1991: 10).

Applying this concept, discourse types might be thought of as ranging from at one end, those consisting of 'neutral' objective language that merely conveys information (such as works of reference, information directories and so on), to 'discourse in which how the message is conveyed is as important, if not more, than the message itself' (Butler 1999: 34); works such as Joyce's *Finnegan's Wake* or the poetry of e. e. cummings representing this extreme. Adopting this concept might suggest a 'way into' literary texts in the language teaching context.

Ultimately, because the meaning and classification of literature has shifted so much during the history of the English language (Carter 1997: 123), what in scientific terms is the 'fuzziest' definition may ultimately be the most valid one; a definition in socio-cultural and sociolinguistic terms: 'The question of what is specifically literary about certain texts is a complex and problematic one. The answer may be a primarily sociological one and lie with the disposition adopted by the reader towards the text' (Carter 1991: 124). In the most reductivist terms, then, literature may simply be 'what people say is literature' (Cook 1992: xvi), something that is 'accorded considerable acclaim and value by individuals or by a society as a whole' (*ibid.*) in any given era. The 'evaluative function' of the term, therefore, may be 'more secure than the attempts of stylistics to define literature' (Cook 1990: 129).

This 'definition' is particularly validated in the light of the view which holds that the literature of the next generation is the lowly vernacular prose of the last (Cook 1996: 156-7), a process known as 'the canonisation of the junior branch' (*ibid.*). This is the process that saw the canonisation of Shakespeare, Chaucer and Dickens, elevating them from their original status of vernacular prose, rhyme and journalism into the realms of the literary canon; the process that might yet see the canonisation of the scripts of *Coronation Street*, of the songs of the Beatles, or of the journalism of Robert Fisk. Viewing them as the 'junior branch' acknowledges that non-literary discourse types also contain linguistic creativity of varying degrees of 'literariness' and recognises 'the co-existence of literature with a capital 'L' (canonical literature) and of literature with a small 'l' in texts ranging from proverbs to jokes to advertisements, all of which display literariness' (Carter 1997: 169).

The argument for the non-exclusivity of literature put forward here is not intended to devalue canonical literature, but on the contrary, to strengthen the argument for its use, together with works of 'literature with a small 'l'', as a valuable resource of creative language use. The position has two important corollaries for the context of language learning. Firstly, it implies that through literature, learners can become familiar with a broad range of discourse types. Secondly, it implies that learners can benefit as much from 'non-literary' genres, since these also contain creative, 'literary' uses of language. The non-exclusivist argument is, all in all, a compelling one in favour of the complementary use of all types of discourse in a reciprocal relationship with the teaching of language and culture.

5.2 Literature and Culture

Literature as conceived by the romantic or 'Leavisite' school, was traditionally part of 'high culture', 'culture with a capital 'C'', and thus embodied the 'best' of the culture in terms of language, ideas and principles. This concept of literature is by now largely outmoded, but remains so insidious (in the culture of the English language at least) that despite new approaches such as reader-response theory mentioned above, it continues to have an influence on the use of literature in the language classroom and beyond. As has already been noted, there has been a resurgence of the use of literature in the classroom in the past two decades. In the same period, consciousness of 'culture' in the sociological sense has grown, and the role of literature and culture is today seen as a reciprocal one. In fact, the perceptual divisions discussed above between 'canonical' literature, contemporary literature on the brink of canonisation and popular culture may be conceived as the three dimensions projecting a three-dimensional picture of contemporary society. Use in the language classroom of material from all three dimensions can help portray a fully rounded picture of the TC to language learners.

Although foreign learners come to TL literature without the prior knowledge and 'cultural baggage' that NSs have, their approach is often influenced by stereotyped notions of TL literature. Asked to name figures from English literature, for example, most learners do not get much beyond the names of Shakespeare, James Joyce and Dickens. From contact with a broader range of more contemporary TC literature - although never without a certain subjectivity resulting from the choices and attitudes of the native speaker teacher (see also below) - learners can receive insights into the behaviours, principles and values of the TL society. Works of literature can provide extended contemplations on a society's current concerns, complementing information from the media which might be less in-depth if more up-to-date and factual. Roddy Doyle's *The Woman Who Walked into Doors* (1996), for example, deals with the problem of wife-battering in depth, giving this abuse an (albeit twisted) rationale, by describing the motivations and explanations of both the batterer and the victim, to a depth that a newspaper item or article on the subject cannot do. Media coverage of the drugs problem in British society can likewise reveal the scale of the problem, but not the sordidness and amorality at its heart, in the way that Irvine Welsh does in the novel *Trainspotting* (1993). The preoccupations and habits of urban life of the archetypal English male or female are no better exposed than in such satires as Sue Townsend's *Adrian Mole: The Cappuccino Years* (1999), or Helen Fielding's *Bridget Jones's Diary* (1996), though the mass media, of course, can also offer colourful multi-media portraits of the everyday habits of people in the target language society. An informed analysis of the menus of the restaurant in which Mole works, 'Hoi Poloi', can reveal as much as any newspaper article about the British and their food, and can provoke comparisons with attitudes to food in learners' own cultures:

'*Fried eggs (two)* *
[...]
HP sauce or Heinz Ketchup
[...]
   * Please be assured: all our eggs are laid by battery hens.'
(Townsend 1999: 92).

This can be as informative as any newspaper article on the subject and can provoke comparisons with attitudes to food in learners' own cultures.

Contemporary literature can also provide a more accessible window into the society's past than more classic literature, because it is drawn from a present-day perspective: Frank McCourt's *Angela's Ashes* (1996) and John B. Keane's *The Field* (1965) describing, respectively, urban and rural Ireland of the mid-1900s, are good examples of this. Because - in the words of JP Hartely - 'the past is a foreign country, they do things differently there' (1953: 1), the literature of earlier generations can be more impenetrable (even to a NS audience) than contemporary literature. This is not to deny the value of looking to the past for the foundations of the culture of the present, for the rationale for contemporary preoccupations, attitudes, values and so on. It is only by reading Irish literature of the early 1900s, for example, so deeply permeated with the theme of religion (see, for instance, the early works of James Joyce), that the novelty of the religious-secular threshold at which present-day Irish society stands can begin to be understood. The same might be said of English literature, where the evolution of Britain into the multi-cultural society it has become today may be traced through the works of E. M. Forster, Graham Greene and thence to contemporary literature represented by writers such as Julian Barnes, Ian McEwan and Martin Amis.

The issue of multi-culturalism is impossible to avoid in the context of the English language, as has been noted in Chapter 3 Section 3.1.2. The books mentioned above, drawn from the British and Irish cultures relevant to my personal and teaching context, are only two of the many cultures represented through the medium of the English language. The multi-cultural status of English means that the choice of 'which' literature to use with learners has socio-cultural, attitudinal or even political implications. It is significant that much English literature with which foreigners still tend to come in contact, embodies value systems that are largely reflective of British, American or European society, rather than those of other English-speaking societies, notably the former British colonies. Indeed, in former times, this factor was often deliberately exploited for politico-cultural ends. The teaching of English in India during the period of the British *Raj*, for instance, was aimed at the creation of a literate population who would establish the language as that of the elite, and thus ensure cultural dominance of the colonial power (Pugh 1996: 174). The language and culture were deliberately taught as a means of creating 'a class of persons Indian in blood and colour but English in taste, in opinions, in morals and in intellect' (from Lord Macaulay's dictum of 1834 quoted in Phillipson 1992: 110). Linguistic imperialism was even justified, in the minds of some, on grounds of Godliness. Winchester (1998) parodies the views of the ruling classes in the late 19th century: 'God - who in this part of London society was held to be an Englishman - naturally approved of the spread of the language as an essential imperial device' (Winchester 1998: 68-9). The relationship portrayed between Robinson Crusoe and Man Friday in Defoe's 1719 classic has likewise been branded an example of linguistic imperialism, as well as 'reflecting the racial structure of western society at the heyday of slavery' (Phillipson 1992: 109). What is significant is that first of all, it is Man Friday who must learn Crusoe's language; secondly, the reason for this is so that he can serve him; and thirdly, in Defoe's fantasy, Man Friday is only too eager to assume this role: 'I was greatly delighted with my new companion, and made it my business to teach him everything that was proper to make him useful, handy and helpful; but especially to make him speak, and to understand me when I spake, and he was the aptest schollar that ever was' (Defoe 1719; 1965: 213). The imperialist stance of the book did not go unrecognised and, indeed, it was actually deployed in the latter days of the British Empire to imperialist ends. *Robinson Crusoe* was the first simplified reader to be produced by a British publisher (Longman in 1926) for colonial consumption (Phillipson 1992: 109).

The issue persists even as the empire fades. The Kenyan author Ngugi wa Thiong'o has pointed out the powerful implications of teaching literature that might be identified with particular imperialistic views:

> *The teaching of only European Literature, and mostly British imperialist literature, in our schools means that our students are daily being confronted with the European reflection of itself, the European image, in history. Our children are made to look, analyse and evaluate the world as made and seen by Europeans. Worse still, these children are confronted with a distorted image of themselves and of their history as reflected and interpreted in European imperialist literature. They see how Prospero sees Caliban and not how Caliban sees Prospero; how Crusoe discovers and remakes Man Friday in Crusoe's image, not how Friday views himself and his heroic struggles against centuries of Crusoe's exploitation and oppression. (Ngugi wa Thiong'o 1991: 225)*

The moral is that teachers need to be aware of the cultural implications of the literature they are using with their students and encourage critical analysis and questioning of cultural ideologies as well as linguistic conventions. Useful activities for revealing attitudes (to people of other class, gender and culture) are 'transference' tasks. For example, in *A Passage to India* (E. M. Forster 1924), which is set in the India of the *Raj*, how would the scene in which Dr Aziz first meets Mr Fielding differ if it occurred between two Englishmen rather than between an Indian and an Englishman? The scene begins when Fielding is dressing; Dr Aziz is announced and Fielding calls out,

> *"Please make yourself at home." The remark was unpremeditated [...]. To Aziz it had a definite meaning. "May I really, Mr. Fielding? It's very good of you," he called back; "I like unconventional behaviour so extremely." His spirits flared up. (Forster A Passage to India 1924; 1978: 57)*

(For a generic culture transference task of this kind see Task 7).

In the end, the representation of culture through literature will always be subjective simply because subjectivity is integral to the genre. Because reading is an interdependent process, a 'joint construction of a social reality between the reader and the text' (Kramsch 1985: 357), each reader's conceptualisation will in any case differ as s/he accommodates what is being read, into his/her own *schemata*- the sets of concepts which constitute our generic knowledge about commonplace scenarios, actions, etc. which are based on our past experience from within our culture and on our knowledge of the world in general (see Chapter 3 Section 3.1.1 for an account of Schema theory). These schemata have a restrictive effect - the native culture in particular is a filter through which we perceive others. Language teachers need to take account of this effect on both comprehension and appreciation, in the case of discourse types which are as culture-bound as literary ones. For instance, the typical British summer holiday scenario of soggy chips, cold sea, mottled legs and a pier with slot machines and dodgems described in the Lindsay Macrae poem *Can we go home now please?*[2] is very alien to cultures from warmer climes and may be less humorous than problematic and puzzling. Again, comparisons between this scenario and the equivalent one in the learner culture - for Italians, maybe *gelati*, warm sea, afternoon *passegiata* on the broadwalk - can help make learners aware just how culture-bound our schemata are.

Another way to deal with these differences is to *exploit* the concept of schemata, since a number of genres contain schemata which are 'trans-cultural'. The most obvious ones are universal literary genres, such as fairy tales and legends: 'Fairy tales, unlike modern short stories, cast foreign language readers into a role that is known to them despite some cultural differences. It is therefore easier for them to develop the appropriate schema' Kramsch (1985: 359). This trans-cultural referentiality makes for obvious comparisons between the same fairy tale/legend in different cultures. Little Red Riding Hood, for instance, wears a red coat in one culture but a red cape or a fur-trimmed hood in others. It has also been shown that in the recounting of a story containing universal schemata (a wedding, a meal etc.)

that has been heard or read in the TL, learners naturally tend to fall back on their own cultural schemata, thus the basic provisions which Little Red Riding Hood is carrying to her sick grandmother might include bread, cheese and milk in one culture, but bread and sausage in another (see Chapter 3 Section 3.1.1, with regard to the study carried out by Steffensen and Joag-dev). Discovery and analysis of these sorts of differences can lead to new understanding and perceptions of learners' own cultures, as well as that of the TL.

5.2.1 Culture, schemata and poetry

Certain genres may also be said to be 'trans-cultural' or universal, in that they exist in all cultures, one such being poetry. Poetry is universally characterised by its representational use of language. It is one that is generally governed by certain constraints of phonology; assonance, alliteration, structure and, of course, rhyme and rhythm. It has been suggested, with reference to the role of nursery rhymes in L1 development, that our response to rhythmic language may be instinctive and innate and may be a natural path to language acquisition: 'Rhythms map on to linguistic structures in ways which, while they do not entirely explain how the child moves from one to the other, do show how verse may facilitate this process' (Cook 2000: 23). Rhythm is, of course, a characteristic not only of poetry, but is a universal feature of song, music and dance and this reflects the fact that it is elemental to our existence. Rhythm is detectable in the womb as our mother's heartbeat, echoed in the rocking of the newborn, and carried on through our lives in our own heartbeat and breathing. Rhythm, in essence, is identified with life (Cook 2000: 22). (The importance of rhythm and music is pursued in Chapter 9 'Song and Music'.)

Another constraint governing poetry can be that of structure, as in the Japanese haiku, or in poems in which the words are arranged to form pictures of their subject, such as Apollinaire's 'Calligrammes' which give 'silhouettes' of such objects as the Eiffel Tower, a train etc. At the other extreme, poetry is a genre in which lexical, syntactic, cohesive and semantic conventions can be flouted in creative and original ways. The poems of e. e. cummings, for instance, include that triumph of psuedo-phonetic transcription *ygUDuh*[3] ('you godda').

Poetry typically deals with universal themes: love, life, death, age, feelings and the natural world, themes which make it a genre with strong affective power. Poetry is also a genre that, conversely, can show us trivial, everyday things in a new light - the Japanese haiku is perhaps an archetypal example of this, but many examples exist in English poetry (for example, Keats' sonnets such as *Ode to Autumn* and *Ode to a Nightingale*). Poetry may thus lead as familiar a path into another language as the genre with which it overlaps, song (see Chapter 9).

5.3 Literature and Currency

Like all authentic discourse types, contemporary literature can be used to breach the lengthy time lag between the evolution of colloquial uses, and their appearance (if ever) in textbooks and grammars (see Chapter 3 'Currency'). Some salient examples of these - such as the inexplicable absence of the common non-standard contraction *ain't* from most textbooks - have already been given in Chapter 3. The use of the interrogative to give *orders* - 'Will ye get out of my way?'[4] 'Goddamit, will you leave me alone!'[5] - is another example of a usage that is fairly neglected in pedagogical works, which typically assign this function to the imperative. In fact, the imperative is rarely used in speech to give orders; it is far more commonly used for invitations ('Take a look for yourself') and suggestions ('Slow down a bit...you'll wear yourself out'[6]). This is why it is so commonly used in advertisements (see Chapter 8). One way of alerting learners to such discrepancies is to select a text illustrating one of these neglected usages (the passage from *Angela's Ashes* from which the first of the above quotes was taken, has a number of further examples on pages 58-9). Students can be asked to put forward their own ideas on the use and meaning of the structure (or to research it in grammars, textbooks) before receiving the text, and then to compare these with what emerges on analysis of the text (see Task 3).

Literary dialogue can thus be extremely useful in illustrating colloquial functions of linguistic forms, despite the fact that it tends to be distilled and stylised rather than copied from the real world. The works of many recent and contemporary authors manage to 'capture the cadences of everyday discourse' (Pulverness 1999a: 9) and provide stretches of up-to-date colloquial usage. Authors with this capacity include Samuel Beckett and Harold Pinter (both providing dialogue that is at the same time naturalistic and poeticised), Roddy Doyle, Frank McCourt, Graham Swift and Magnus Mills.

5.3.1 Literature and affect

'We have to recognise that literature is always more than language' (Carter and McRae 1996: xxi). It is essential to bear in mind those elements other than the linguistic which make literature ideal for language learning; the potential interest and relevance of authentic texts to learners and the ability of such texts to arouse emotive responses. An attribute peculiar to works of literature (as distinct, perhaps, from other cultural products such as newspapers, television or film) is that because they involve such a personal interaction between the reader and the text, they retain a freshness that these others do not. The work 'comes alive' anew, as it were, for each new reader: 'Literature is a form of art with two creators, one being the author, who, with his linguistic competence and his subtle, creative power of words, sparks the imagination, the creative power of the other, the reader' (Bouman 1996: 29). Literature therefore has a 'currency' that has not necessarily to do with being contemporary, but to do with the eternal relevance and appeal of the issues it touches on and the relationships and feelings it describes. This personal, affective response to literature is central to the way it is used for language learning.

Affective responses to literature may range from anything from mild amusement or interest to deep engagement, pleasure, outrage or tears. Whatever form it takes, response to literature is essential for learning; 'the development of a personalised reaction to texts - i.e. one which engages not only the intellect but also the feelings, is, we feel, a very important part of the language learning process' (Duff and Maley 1990: 10). The very purpose of literature is, of course, to elicit response, or as Duff and Maley point out (speaking of poetry), to make the reader 'react personally to other people's ways of seeing things' (*ibid.*). Certainly, 'the teaching of literature is an arid business unless there is a response' (Long 1991: 42) as was memorably illustrated in scenes from Peter Weir's 1989 film *Dead Poets Society* in which pupils in a 'prep' school, jaded by having had literature rammed dry down their throats, are provoked to awaken and respond to poetry, by a new English teacher.

Since response is self-evidently personal and not necessarily an experience to be shared or communicated, however, there is a conspicuous clash between a personal-response approach and the rationale of many traditional Communicative techniques which are designed to force interaction between learners. The external manifestation of a genuine response to a moving piece of literature, for example, may well be silence: 'There are [...] silences which it is not appropriate for anyone, teacher or learner, to fill' (Bassnet and Grundy 1993: 6). The teacher's attempts to elicit vocalised response/discussion at such points may feel intrusive and artificial, and may reduce the impact of a piece. An example of such a work is the almost unbearably poignant Seamus Heaney poem *Mid-term Break* about the death of the poet's brother, which ends:

'Wearing a poppy bruise on his left temple,
He lay in the four foot box as in his cot.
No gaudy scars, the bumper knocked him clear.

A four foot box, a foot for every year.'
(From *Mid-term Break*[7], Seamus Heaney).

If learners' emotional responses are to be channelled into language learning, then, this has to be done with sensitivity and respect.

Even more alien to traditional language classroom conventions is the fact that a response does not necessarily require *comprehension* of a text. Once again, this is exemplified by the pleasure and reaction from very young children to nursery rhymes and stories, the meanings of which can hardly be understood (see, for example, Cook 2000: 14). This capacity for attaining enjoyment out of what is only partially understood can be regained, in adult life, from a genre such as poetry. Poetry is frequently not fully 'understood' at first encounter even by native speakers, which is probably why this genre in particular makes for repeated re-reading (in contrast to a discourse type such as a newspaper article, for example). Rather than being encountered solely at the cognitive level, poetry is *experienced*, through its imagery, sound (if it is heard), the pattern of text on the page, striking images or ideas and so on. Language learners can also be encouraged to experience poetry on these multiple levels and only later, if appropriate, to respond with interpretations, reactions and analysis of the language.

An excellent example of the primacy of response over comprehension is Edwin

Morgan's disturbing poem *The first men on Mercury*[8], which actually places the native speaker in the position of partial comprehension of the language learner (or young child), being composed in part of nonsense words, some of which are recognisable corruptions of words such as *yuleeda* ('your leader') and other non-words, such as *BAWR*. The poem takes the form of a dialogue between Earthmen and beings from Mercury, and begins:

- We come in peace from the third planet.
Would you take us to your leader?
- BAWR STRETTER! BAWR. BAWR. STRETTERHAWL?
Over the course of the poem, the beings from Mercury insidiously take over the Earthmen's language, and it ends:
- Stretterworra gawl, gawl ...
- OF COURSE, BUT NOTHING IS EVER THE SAME,
 NOW IS IT? YOU'LL REMEMBER MERCURY.
 (From The first men on Mercury, Edwin Morgan)

The poem relies less on the meanings conveyed by that part of the language that can be understood by the reader, than on the impact of the gradual deterioration of the earthmen's language. This is brought out particularly well in the classroom, if the learners divide into two groups to read out the two 'speakers' (the Earthmen and the Mercury men) in chorus. In chorus, the human voice carries a strength and packs an emotive punch that depends as much on the sound as meaning, as was classically exploited in the Greek plays. What is created in an exercise such as this is an aesthetic/emotive response that is only partly related to comprehension of meaning. Such a response distracts learners from the pressures of trying to understand 'the words' and helps create the positive affective climate so conducive to learning.

On the other hand, comprehension and the classroom techniques which try to probe it, can actually *deter* learning in some situations, by forfeiting response to mere linguistic decoding; 'immediate comprehension checks can kill the affective response gained during the experience of the text' (Tomlinson 1999: 4). Such questioning can distance the learner from the text and obstruct his/her imaginative engagement with it (Collie and Slater 1987: 7-8). When students answer a teacher's questions, 'these are a response to the teacher's questioning, they are scarcely a *response to the text* at all' [emphasis in the original] (Long 1991: 45). This is partly because comprehension questions tend to be discrete point questions which focus on detail 'at the expense of the whole' (Collie and Slater 1987: 7-8): 'The practice of insisting on detailed comprehension questions only ensures that students will focus on small points and will be prevented from reading for overall meaning and thus for pleasure' (Krashen 1989: 19-20, see also Tomlinson 1999: 4). Discrete point comprehension questions are intrinsically unsuitable to literature also because they tend to focus on information that is not essential to a deeper understanding of the text (McKay 1991: 191-8) but on often unimportant detail (such as - from the simplified, Longman edition of Daphne du Maurier's *Rebecca* - 'Where does the owner of Manderley meet his new wife?',

Ronaldson 1996: 102). As far as literature is concerned, then, discrete point questions can effectively stifle genuine learner response to the text. As Long (1991) queries cynically; 'it seems [...] legitimate to ask why the teacher asks questions (about literary works) at all, apart from following a general classroom procedure in which the teacher asks questions (to keep the students awake?)' (Long 1991: 45). In the end, the only appropriate place for the 'comprehension question' on literature is when it comes from *the learner* trying to check his/her understanding of the text.

The rationale for *teachers'* questions on literary texts should not, therefore, be to maintain attention or check comprehension of facts, but to guide learners towards a better understanding and thence (hopefully) appreciation of the text. Rather than direct verbal response to the teacher's questions, then, the most useful types of response to literature for the teacher to cultivate are, as Long goes on to point out (1991: 53-9), the *creative responses* to come out of interaction (individual or group) with and about the text. In this way, the ability of a literary work to engage the emotions can have the useful corollary of its potential for exploitation at the interpersonal level: 'Literature is one of the forms of language that most calculatingly plays upon affect as an inducement to *communication*' [my emphasis] (Shanahan 1997: 168). Once the material has engaged the learners, class or group discussions can ensue, either spontaneous or controlled/directed by the teacher, in which learners deploy their communicative skills. At the most pragmatic level, then, however tangential arguments may become as regards interpretation of the content, the text has served a purpose at the level of stimulating language use.

To conclude this section on how the emotive responses aroused by literature can be used in language learning, one obvious yet often neglected aspect is *enjoyment* - of the material *per se*, of the interaction with it, and of the learning experience itself: 'We have to recognise that literature is always more than language and that appreciation and enjoyment of literature transcend the development of linguistic capacities' (Carter and McRae 1996: xxi). The importance of enjoyment to language learning is particularly evident in the context of L1 acquisition where 'language play' has a crucial role (see Cook 2000), and its potential in L2 contexts too has often been flagged: 'There is good evidence that pleasure reading has a powerful effect on language acquisition' (Krashen 1989: 19-20): 'As enjoyment plays an important factor in any learning process, literature is a potentially useful aid to the language teacher' (Short and Candlin 1991: 91).

Enjoyment is just one factor of another affective aspect of using literature for language learning, motivation. Other motivating factors include the cultural content of literature, which makes it intrinsically appealing to integratively motivated learners in particular, as it represents, embodies and contains elements of the target culture to which they aspire. On another level, the very sense of achievement at being able to deal with authentic texts of the calibre of TC literature can itself be highly motivating; 'students may feel a very satisfying sense of achievement at having successfully read and discussed a text which is not only authentic, but is also considered worthwhile by native speakers of English' (Lazar 1990: 204-5).

5.4 The 'Challenge' of Llterature

'At first they [learners] can advance only slowly, and hence even a moderate amount of variety can only be secured by keeping the texts short [...] On the other hand, it is possible to make too great concessions to variety: an unbroken succession of very short texts is more wearisome than restriction to a single long one.' (Sweet 1899: 170)

Over a hundred years ago, Sweet put forward the idea that literature is an excellent source of naturally graded language material (1899: 164-93). Ironically it has taken a century for this idea to be taken up by practitioners. Now, there is an identifiable trend away from exclusivity in the level of learners with whom teachers are willing to use literature. This is apparent in much of the literature and resource books on using literature for language learning to have come out over the past decade (examples include Collie and Slater, 1987, Bassnet and Grundy, 1993, McRae 1996): 'Where Literature [*sic*] was considered appropriate only for upper-intermediate learners and above, it is now recognised that language awareness and text awareness have to be encouraged and developed from the earliest stages of language learning' (McRae 1996: 23-4). 'We believe that everyone, even - no, especially, early-stage second language learners, can read literature and write creatively' (Bassnet and Grundy 1993: 10).

The greatest 'challenge' that literature poses is thus to the *teacher*, who has to activate a sort of 'intuitive grading system' in sifting through the immense resource that is literature. For the lower level learner, an obvious genre to use is poetry. This is not, one might hasten to add, because poetry is 'simple', quite the reverse in many cases, as poetry tends to be denser and require more 'unpacking' than everyday language. Furthermore, editing and paraphrasing is even less feasible - or acceptable - in poetry than in other literary genres. But poetry appeals to (even - or especially) elementary learners on two levels. Firstly, at a fundamental level, the harmonies of poetic language appeal to natural acquisition processes, as in L1 acquisition. L1 acquisition, in its initial stages, is essentially 'poetic' and rhythm-based, both in its input (lullabies, nursery rhymes, songs, even stories[9]) and in its output. Output at the earliest stages consists of repetition of phonemes (*ma-ma, da-da*), then progresses to harmonious simplifications (*tacta* for tractor, *nana* for banana) and to poetic playing with language, as any parent of a young child will delight to recount[10]. The new learner of a second language is also particularly sensitive to the harmonies or 'music' of the language and this makes him/her very receptive at this stage to poetry and literature (as well as to songs, of course). This receptivity can be exploited in the L2 classroom, as it is with young children, in the learning of language as much (or indeed more) for its sound, its harmonies, rhythms and rhymes, as for its meaning. A child's delight in a nursery rhyme such as 'Ring a ring o' roses' or the poetic repetition in fairy tales ('What big eyes you have grandma!' 'All the better to SEE you with!' 'What a big nose you have grandma!' 'All the better to SMELL you with!'[11]) can be paralleled in that of elementary learners listening to or joining in (by beating out the rhythm or chanting) simple limericks, poems[12] or even prose (such as passages from fairy tales).

At a more pragmatic level, poems are quite simply shorter than other literary genres, and modern poems at least, can be excellent sources of contemporary colloquial forms: 'there is no harm in giving at an early period pieces of simple poetry. For there are many poems whose language is so simple and free of archaisms that it diverges but slightly from colloquial speech as regards vocabulary and grammatical structure' (Sweet 1899: 177). An example of a modern British poet who does this very successfully is Roger McGough whose whimsical style combines an ear for the common language and for the offbeat, with a tongue-in-cheek poeticism. Lines from the first stanza of the poem *Balloon Fight*[13], inspired by a newsreader's slip of the tongue[14], for example, go

You can't go around the world
attacking people with balloons
and expect to get away with it.
    (From Balloon Fight, Roger McGough)

Other poets popular with language teachers includes Brian Patten (e.g. *Little Johnny's Final Letter*[15] and *Little Johnny's Confession*), e. e. cummings (e.g. *may i feel said he*[16]) and Roald Dahl (e.g. *Revolting Rhymes*, 1984, Dahl's reworking of popular nursery tales). With their catchy rhyme scheme and intrinsic humour, limericks are also much-loved by language teachers and can be a good 'introduction' to more serious poetry.

The comparison to L1 acquisition and the suggested use of children's poetry is emphatically not intended to equate low level of target language proficiency with immaturity. The ability to draw inferences, connect ideas, visualise, act, and so on, is not limited by proficiency in the language, and learning activities which activate these skills can be as suitable for lower as for higher levels (Tomlinson 1999: 3-4). Neither does low proficiency level correlate with age, and adult learners should not be left hungry for material on themes and subjects with which they can engage, on the basis of their command of the language (Lazar 1994: 116). Giving learners an early taste for TC literature can ultimately impact on all the affective factors associated with learners, helping to build confidence, encourage curiosity and spur motivation (see, for example, Tomlinson 1998: 88, Freeman 1999: 29).

Other genres - novels, short stories and plays, can all be used with lower level learners, either using selected excerpts, or, stretched over a suitable time period, in their entirety. The plays of Harold Pinter are famed for their faithful replication of speech patterns (see Carter 1998: 53-4) while Samuel Beckett's *Waiting for Godot* (1953) is a wonderful example of very simple language that can be interpreted at many levels. Short stories useable with lower level learners include those by Graham Swift *Learning to Swim* (1985[17]) and the many collections by Roald Dahl. The simplicity of literary style that characterises certain novels or novelists makes them suitable for lower level learners. These might include such novels as *Paddy Clarke Ha Ha Ha* (Doyle 1993) which is written from the perspective of a 10-year-old child, Toni Morrison's *The Bluest Eye* (1970) also partially narrated by an eleven-year-old protagonist, and even the opening section of James Joyce's *A Portrait of the Artist as a Young Man* (1916) which uses simply structured, childlike sentences. The style of *The Old Man and the Sea* (Hemingway 1952) is famously as simple as it is moving, and finally, there are those works ubiquitous to secondary level syllabi, *Animal Farm* (Orwell 1951) and *The Lord of the Flies* (Golding 1958).

While literature does therefore offer texts that are simple enough for lower level learners, the basic principle pointed out in Chapter 3 (Section 3.3 'Challenge'), that texts are made accessible through the *task*, goes for literature as well as for other discourse types. Adjusting the task to the learner level can provide learners with a vital 'way into' a work of literature. This means that material is only as difficult as the task the learners are required to undertake with it: 'Difficulty is a function of the tasks we create as well as of the language of the text itself' (Durant 1996: 72). It is possible to carry out very simple tasks 'on passages which are scarcely understood at all' (*ibid.*). It is essential however, to exploit and make a positive start from what *has* been understood (Tomlinson 1999: 4), even if the task required of the learner is no more than a physical, written or monosyllabic response (see Tomlinson 1998: 13). A simple and non-threatening way to get even elementary learners to get to grips with literature is to have them read texts in chorus, as a whole class/in small groups, or alternately, act out a text as a whole class/in groups as it is read aloud (by the teacher or a fellow learner) (see Task 30). Dialogues and conversations lend themselves particularly well to both types of group activity as do dialogues or dramatic poems. Both choral reading and group acting have similar advantages. They allow the insecure learner to 'be led by the crowd' while still gaining a sense of enjoyment and achievement. They allow the confident learner, on the other hand, the gratification of 'leading the pack'. At the level of language learning, this type of activity can help stimulate learning, particularly in the kinaesthetic learner (see Chapter 2 Section 2.5 'Learning style'). Whatever the task addressed, at this level, successful accomplishment of the task is probably as important as whatever obvious language learning comes out of it, as success can spur motivation for learning and excite interest in the literature of the target language.

A final way to introduce literature to lower level learners is to present it through other media - on film or audio-tape. As is dealt with in greater detail in Chapter 10 'Film', literature has long provided ripe pickings for the big screen. Enacted on film, text loses its density (often so daunting for learners), and is punctuated with true-to-life spaces and silences which provide 'breathing space' for the learner - as well as opportunities for the resourceful language teacher. An archetypal example of a pregnant silence exploitable in the classroom is the scene in the BBC's 1996 serialisation of Jane Austen's *Pride and Prejudice*, where Darcy proposes to Elisabeth, a scene which begins with an agonising 50 seconds of awkward silence as Darcy summons the courage to begin. Even an audio introduction to works of literature via audio-tapes - more and more books are now being published with accompanying 'audio-books' - can be far easier on the learner than confronting the 'raw' text, since the intonation and stress patternings of the person reading it help to penetrate, interpret and, of course, enliven it (see Task 1).

5.5 Literature for Language Learning: Summary and Principles

One of the strongest arguments for using literature in the language classroom is the enormous scope it offers. Literature can range from being deeply culture-specific to being universal. Discerningly selected, it can be used with students of all proficiency levels, to reveal links between cultures, to enhance learners' knowledge of the target language and its culture, or as in the case of English, raise awareness of its plural cultural identities. Literature can create deeper involvement and closer interaction than almost any other cultural product. Literature is, after all, the most intense and intrinsically the most dense representation of the culture and the people who comprise it. It is the most exhibitionistic and most personal form of culture, the form in which members of societies have exposed ideas, thoughts and desires so strongly felt by some that they have been prepared to suffer or die for them. Literature is, all in all, the ideal linguistic form to explore for those wishing to 'get under the skin' of a culture.

Principles for the use of literature for language learning

• Use a combination of 'canonical' and contemporary literature and everyday genres (newspapers, television etc.) to project a fully rounded, three-dimensional picture of the contemporary TC.

• Use literature to stimulate *awareness* of language use and the *potential* of language on the continuum from the everyday and colloquial to the deliberately literary.

• Exploit *response*. Make use of non-verbal responses (especially at lower levels): e.g. visualisation (drawing, describing imagined images), acting/miming.

• *Respect* the learner. The learner's right to silence, cognitive ability and intellectual demands.

• Approach literature via the *task* (especially at lower levels). Set non-threatening and kinaesthetic tasks e.g. choral reading, (group) acting, actions, single word responses.

• Exploit the 'natural grading' of literature to suit different proficiency levels.

• Remember that difficulty can be a factor of text length, lexical choice or density, cultural-specificity and ... perception!

• Combine literary works with the other media in which they are available: films (see Chapter 10), audio-books.

Further reading

Collie, J. and S. Slater, 1987. *Literature in the Language Classroom*. Cambridge: Cambridge University Press.

Bassnet, S., and P. Grundy, 1993. *Language through Literature*. Harlow: Longman.

Duff, A. and A. Maley, 1990. *Literature*. Oxford: Oxford University Press.

Maley, A. and S. Moulding, 1985. *Poem into Poem*. Oxford: Oxford University Press.

Morgan, J. and M. Rinvolucri, 1983. *Once Upon a Time: Using stories in the Language Classroom*. Cambridge: Cambridge University Press.

Wessels, C., 1987. *Drama*. Oxford: Oxford University Press.

5.6 The Tasks

Task 1

Discourse type	Novel/story - section/s
Communicative purpose	Engaging
Authentic task type	Response
Level 5 up	
Aim: Visualisation of audio input. Aural introduction to a new novel or story.	

Preparation: Use an audio-book or read aloud a 2 to 3 minute section of the book/story.
- Ask learners to identify and visualise the:
-Narrative voice/voice of protagonist (first/third person, age, gender)
-Characters introduced and their relationships
-Setting (cultural, rural/urban etc.)
- According to their preference, learners can either draw pictures the text has evoked *or* make notes on key images.
Suggested novels: *The Graduate* (Charles Webb), *A Portrait of the Artist as a Young Man* (James Joyce), *Paddy Clarke Ha Ha Ha* (Roddy Doyle).

Task 2

Discourse type	Novel/story - section/s
Communicative purpose	Engaging
Authentic task type	Analysis
Level 6 up	

Aim: To raise awareness of language style.

Preparation: Select and copy a short extract or extracts from a novel, which are representative of the novel's style. (The novel can be familiar to the learners). Brainstorm to establish writing style variables e.g.
- sentence length and complexity
- vocabulary; choices, variety (use of synonyms or repetition)
- colloquial language
- language variety (e.g. Irish, British, American)
- language register, varieties of types of discourse (e.g. narrative, dialogue, internal monologue)
- viewpoint (authorial, first person etc.)
- style-switches
- use of punctuation.
Learners:
- Read text and analyse style according to variables.
- Discuss rationale for, and impact of, the author's style.
- Identify unfamiliar vocabulary/structures that impede comprehension, guess meanings in context, consulting peers, teacher, dictionaries or corpora if necessary.
Suggested authors: Roddy Doyle, Frank McCourt, Samuel Beckett, Sue Townsend, Graham Swift.

Task 3

Discourse type	Novel/story - section/s
Communicative purpose	Engaging
Authentic task type	Analysis
Level 5 up	
Aim: To explore linguistic structures and functions.	

Preparation: Find a few short excerpts from novels/stories which figure particular language structures e.g. imperative, interrogative, 'will' future, use of modal 'would'.
- Before giving the texts, tell the learners the structures they are going to focus on.
Each learner group:
Chooses, discusses and notes the functions of ONE of the structures from their own knowledge.
- Then receives the relevant text and scans it for 'their' structure.
- Analyses the function/s of their structure within the texts and compares/contrasts this with their prior assumptions about it.
- Shares findings with other groups.

Task 4

Discourse type	Novel/story - section/s
Communicative purpose	Engaging
Authentic task type	Analysis

Aim: To explore the versatility of delexical words e.g. go, get/got, make.

Preparation: Find a short passage from novel/story where at least one delexical word is used with a number of different meanings (e.g. *get/got* might appear in the same passage as: *got lost, got a letter, got to go*).

Learners work individually or in pairs to:

- Find all occurrences of the target word/s, analyse the meanings in context and note the different ways the word/s can be used.
- Think about how each use in context represents a particular language register and has implications for meaning[18].
- Compare findings in groups.

It is possible to extend this activity by looking at further passages from the novel/story for the same delexical word (to confirm meanings analysed and find further uses), *or* by looking at a concordance or concordances of the word/s, for examples of the same uses or further uses and meanings.

Task 5

Discourse type	Novel/story - section/s
Communicative purpose	Engaging
Authentic task type	Inferencing
Level 6 up	

Aim: To extrapolate socio-cultural information from novels of a particular period or social setting (including the present).

- Use an excerpt from a novel/story where particular socio-cultural mores of the TC are illustrated.
- Brainstorm socio-cultural indicators e.g. attitudes to family, authority (institutions, religion), wealth, class and status in the community (based on wealth, profession, gender, education, accent etc.)
- Learners read selected section/s (or possibly a whole novel set as homework).
- Identify presence of above indicators and rate importance within the society portrayed.
- Compare to those in own culture in equivalent historical period.

Suggested novelists: Somerset Maughan, Oscar Wilde, David Lodge, Graham Greene, Graham Swift, Daphne du Maurier (*Rebecca*), Kazuo Ishiguro (e.g. *The Remains of the Day*).

Task 6

Discourse type	Novel/story - section/s
Communicative purpose	Engaging
Authentic task type	Transference
Level 5 up	

Aim: To visualise a written text and transfer it to a visual medium.

Preparation: Teacher/learners select a (section of) novel or story to adapt for the screen.

Learners:

- Read the selected novel/extract or story in their own time, noting sections that will be difficult to transfer to screen (e.g. thoughts, interior monologue, author's comments)
- Identify unfamiliar vocabulary/structures that impede comprehension, guess meanings in context consulting peers, teacher, dictionaries or corpora as necessary. Before starting, ask what difficulties have been foreseen in text-to-screen transfer, then brainstorm repercussions of the differences between narrative and the visual medium e.g.
- emotions described in narrative can be shown on facial expressions
- thoughts can be given in voice-over
- author's comments can be put into the mouth of one of the characters
- Elicit from learners (or point out) that the screenplay consists of 3 different layers (a) what the narrative says (b) what the camera shows (c) what words are spoken.
- Divide the novel extract/story into sections, each group to work on a different section.
- Learners write a '3-layered' screenplay for their section, coping with identified difficulties using strategies such as those brainstormed previously.
- When finished, the groups team up appropriately to join the sections, comparing and ironing out any differences (in approach, setting etc) that may have been taken.
- Once the full screenplay has been finalised, learners may like to act out the 'film', which may be videoed if facilities are available[19].

Task 7

Discourse type	Novel/story - section/s
Communicative purpose	Engaging
Authentic task type	Transference
Level 6 up	
Aim: Cross-cultural transference of a literary text.	

Preparation: Use episode from a novel or short story that is fairly culture-bound (i.e. in TC).

- Before starting, discuss/brainstorm implications of transferring a story from one culture to another, in terms of differences in: gender roles and social hierarchies; values/attitudes; behaviour and reactions to events; settings and environment; daily routines and so on.
- Working in mono-cultural groups if possible, learners rewrite text, transferring events of the episode to their own culture, making alterations as noted previously, and changing the outcome of the episode if these alterations would seem to require it.
- Groups read the new versions to other groups for comment.
- Suggested novelists/novels: E. M. Forster's *Passage to India*, Graham Greene, David Lodge, Sue Townsend, Graham Swift, Roddy Doyle.

Task 8

Discourse type	Novel/story - section/s
Communicative purpose	Engaging
Authentic task type	Analysis
Level 6 up	

Aim: To raise insight into the versatility and meaning of delexical words (e.g. go, get/got, make) through double translation.

Preparation: Find a short passage from novel/ story where at least one delexical word is used with a number of different meanings (e.g. *get/got* might appear in the same passage as: *got lost, got a letter, got to go*).
- Learners work in same language groups.
- Groups find all occurrences of target word/s, analyse the meanings in context and note the different ways the word/s can be used.
- Encourage learners to think about how each use in context represents a particular language register and has implications for meaning.
- Groups translate the expressions containing the target word/s into their first language, bearing in mind the meaning in context, register etc.
- Groups then re-translate their translated items back into English staying as close as possible to the foreign language word/s. Thus, for example, the English expression *'I get it'* may have been translated into Italian as *'ho capito'* which re-translates into English as *'I have understood'*.
- Groups share insights with other groups.

Task 9

Discourse type	Novel/story section/s - gender roles
Communicative purpose	Engaging
Authentic task type	Analysis
Level 5 up	

Aim: To raise awareness of issues of gender and language.

Preparation: Select and copy an extract from a text in which gender pronouns are frequently used.
 - Distribute copies to learners, who (working individually) reverse all the gender pronouns ('he' to 'she', 'him' to 'her' etc. and vice versa).
 - Learners get into groups and one group member reads the 'revised' text aloud.
- Groups discuss the differences that these changes have made (e.g. a suggestion to meet made by a man may sound like a plea coming from a woman, and so on), including places where the change makes no difference (why?).
- Learners can infer attitudes to gender roles, gender-appropriate language and behaviour and so on (and whether these are their attitudes, society's or the author's).
- This may lead to discussion on changes in the English language over the past 30 years e.g. use of *s/he*, *Ms*, replacement of *he* with *she* as 'neutral' pronoun,

neutralising of gender-specific nouns (e.g. *chairman* with *chair* etc.) etc., as well as comparable changes in the learners' own languages.

Task 10

Discourse type	Whole novel
Communicative purpose	Engaging
Authentic task type	Extension
Level 5 up	
Aim: To engage with the text by empathising with characters within it.	

Preparation: Learners read the novel in short sections either in class or for homework. Ask them to guess unfamiliar vocabulary/structures that impede comprehension from the context, discuss them with peers/teacher, or consult dictionaries or corpora.
- As they read, they adopt roles of characters in a novel and
- Draw a portrait of the character.
- Develop the description of 'their' character to account for their behaviour: e.g. background - family and relationships, past events; likes/dislikes.
- Build on this to invent episodes centring on their character.
- Show the characters interacting by writing and enacting dialogues together with other 'characters' (learners).
Suggested novels: Golding's *Lord of the Flies*, Doyle's *Paddy Clarke Ha Ha Ha*, Orwell's *Animal Farm*.

Task 11

Discourse type	Whole novel/short story
Communicative purpose	Engaging
Authentic task type	Extension
Level 5 up	
Aim: To relate a novel/story to 'real life'.	

Preparation: Use a novel/story which the learners have read as a class, or integrate this activity with others.
- Learners draw up a list of the characters in the novel/ story, with short physical descriptions and character sketches if possible. (If there are a number of characters, learners can divide up this task).
- Tell learners that they are to draw up a cast list for the film version of this novel/short story. They can use cast any actors they think suitable (any nationality etc.). They may suggest adjustments to the character to suit the actor they want, if they wish!
- Learners do this in groups.
- Groups come together and compare their ideas, arguing their cases for the actors they want, in order to reach a class consensus if possible[20].

Task 12

Discourse type:	Whole novel
Communicative purpose:	Engaging
Authentic task type:	Transference
Level 6 up	
Aim: To synthesise information and transfer to a summative medium/discourse type.	

Preparation: Use with a novel that has already been read by the learners, either in or outside class. The novel may have been read in the TL or the L1.
- Discuss the (different?) aims of a book's *'blurb'*, an *advertisement* for a book and a *book review*.
- Consult samples of each discourse type to analyse and note typical content, stylistic features, length etc., checking unfamiliar vocabulary/structures by guessing meanings in context, or by consulting peers, teacher, dictionaries or corpora.
- Learners work in pairs if possible; decide on which discourse type they want to produce for the novel they have read.
- Use their knowledge and interpretation of the novel's characters and plot to prepare book's 'blurb', advertisement or review, according to the parameters decided previously.
Learner groups swap texts and
-   Assess adherence to style of discourse type.
- Discuss agreement with each others' interpretations/summaries.
This can also be done with novels read personally by the learners, in which case, the others can read the various blurbs/advertisements/reviews produced by their peers, and say which novel they would most like to read.

Task 13

Discourse type:	Film adaptations
Communicative purpose:	Provocative
Authentic task type:	Reaction
Level 5 up	
Aim: To visualise written text.	

Preparation: Choose a book that has a film version.
- Read short section/scene from the text (at home/in class).
Working in groups, learners:
- Check any unfamiliar vocabulary/structures which impede comprehension.
- Discuss how they imagine the characters and the settings.
- Prepare storyboards and dialogues for the scene.
- Enact the scenes for the other groups and discuss differences in interpretations.
- Watch screen version of the scene.
Compare to the imagined:
- appearance and depiction of characters (including behaviour, voice, manner)

- settings
- atmosphere
- effect (cheery, amusing, depressing, scary etc)
- Comment on any omissions/additions etc.
- Learners discuss how close the film comes to their visualisation of it.
- Infer the rationale for any changes made.
Suggested film-book adaptations:
Films of Jane Austen novels, *Pride and Prejudice, Sense and Sensibility, Emma*; Films of *The End of the Affair; Circle of Friends; The Dead; The Snapper; The Commitments; Remains of the Day*; Cartoon version of *Animal Farm*.

Task 14

Discourse type:	Poem - general
Communicative purpose:	Engaging
Authentic task type:	Analysis
Level 5 up	
Aim: To analyse lexical features of a poem and their imaginative effect.	

Preparation: Choose a poem (or ask learners to choose one).
- Learners work in pairs, each pair chooses one part of speech (adjectives, adverbs, verbs, pronouns etc.). Pairs:
- Change (by substituting others) each of their chosen parts of speech within the poem (e.g. all the adjectives, adverbs, verbs, pronouns etc.).
- Swap partners and read their revised version of the poem to new partner.
- The new pairs discuss and comment on the effect of changes; e.g. in what respect do they change the poem (its mood, how visual, evocative, moving, funny it is, etc.); are any changes improvements?
This activity draws attention to how the poem's original effect is created[21].
Suggested poem: W. H. Auden's *Stop all the clocks*[22].

Task 15

Discourse type	Poem - general
Communicative purpose	Engaging
Authentic task type	Analysis
Level 5 up	
Aim: To consider implications of lexical choices.	

Preparation: Produce a 'strategically-gapped' version of your chosen poem. Number each gap, and for each gap produce 2 feasible alternatives (e.g. if the original phrase is *fair hair*, the word 'fair' might be omitted and the 3 choices *fair, beautiful* and *short* offered). Cut into separate stanzas/sections, attaching the lists of alternatives relevant to each stanza/section.

- Each learner group gets gapped version of one verse/ section of the poem plus the list of alternatives.
- Learners opt for one word to fill each gap discussing implications of each alternative and reasons for choice.
- Each learner group speculate as to the position of its verse/section in the whole poem.
- Groups read their verses/sections to the others, and whole class decides on order of verses/sections.
- Read the completed poem in order (one member of each group read 'their' verse/section).
- Encourage learners to challenge lexical choices if they do not seem to fit.
- Read the original poem aloud or play a recording of it.
- Groups compare their choices to the original and where they had made different choices, comment on the difference this made to the meaning/effect of the poem[23].
Suggested poems: Jenny Joseph's *Warning*[24], Jorge Luis Borges' *Moments* (English translation), Carol Ann Duffy's *Stealing*[25].

Task 16

Discourse type	Poem - general
Communicative purpose	Engaging
Authentic task type	Analysis
Level 5 up	
Aim: To use linguistic/cultural knowledge to fill gaps.	

Preparation: Produce a 'strategically-gapped' version of a suitable poem. Cut into separate verses/sections.
Learners work in groups. Each group:
- Receives a gapped version of one verse/ section of the poem.
- Fills the gaps using their own linguistic/cultural knowledge and imagination.
- Speculates as to the position of its verse/ section in the whole poem.
- Splits up and pairs up with one member of another group.
- Pairs read verses to each other, giving/receiving feedback.
- Teacher puts up a slide containing all the missing words.
- Learners return to original groups and replace 'guessed' words with those from the slide thought to belong to 'their' verse.
- Revise ideas as to order of poem if necessary.
- The completed poem is then read in order (one member of each group read 'their' verse).
- Teacher reads or (if available) plays a recording of the poem.

Task 17

Discourse type	Poem - general
Communicative purpose	Engaging
Authentic task type	Analysis

Level 3 up

Aim: Use knowledge of linguistic structure to fill gaps.

Preparation: Choose 2 poems of similar length (copy enough of each for all students).
- Learners pair up; each partner is given a different text.
- Working individually, learners go through the poem and (a) note every word they do not know, then (b) white out/black out each of these words.
- Partners then exchange poems and complete their partner's gapped poem with words that might fit into the gaps.
- Alternately, learners can give their partners a list of the words they extracted from the poem, which the partner can then insert into the poem where they think appropriate.
- Learners read out their versions, which can be compared to the original.

Task 18

Discourse type	Poem - general
Communicative purpose	Engaging
Authentic task type	Transference
Level 5 up	
Aim: To engage with a poem by interacting with it	

Preparation: Give learners a selection of poems (on paper/recorded).
- Ask learners to choose and justify which one poem they would like to:
(i) translate
(ii) illustrate
(iii) set to music
(iv) meet the writer of [26]
- Learners do (i) - (iii) for chosen poem.
- Learners share their 'products' with others for comment.

Task 19

Discourse type	Poem - general
Communicative purpose	Engaging
Authentic task type	Transference
Level 5 up	
Aim: To engage with a poem on linguistic and cultural levels via 'double translation'.	

Preparation: Choose a poem that is fairly simple linguistically.
- Tell learners they are going to do a 'double translation' - translation from target language into their first language and then working only from this first language translation, back into TL.

- General discussion on (a) linguistic and (b) cultural implications this might have e.g. retaining rhythm, rhyme or sound of the original, structure (numbers of lines etc.) numbers of words, translation of slang, colloquialisms, culture-specific words or concepts etc.
-Working individually, learners
- check any unfamiliar lexis/structures by guessing in context or consulting peers/teacher, dictionaries or corpora.
- translate the poem into their L1.
- If there are learners with same L1, compare translations and discuss any differences.
- Learners with the same L1 swap their translations (so that their re-translation into the TL is from another learner's interpretation).
- Working ONLY from the L1 translation, translate back into the TL.
- Compare (read aloud) re-translations from (a) same 1st language and (b) from other languages.
- Discuss and account for changes that have occurred e.g:
- Change in/loss of rhyme, rhythm and other sound patternings etc.
- Structure: numbers of words and lines
- Effect on culture-specific concepts
- Effect on slang, colloquialisms
- Overall impact of the poem
- Discuss cultural implications of linguistic choices.
- If learners are interested, this can lead to a debate on translating of poetry - possibility / impossibility of doing so, literary and ethical implications etc.

Task 20

Discourse type	Poem - suspense
Communicative purpose	Engaging
Authentic task type	Inferencing
Level 5 up	
Aim: To infer core themes of poems.	

Preparation: Choose a poem where the title plays a key explanatory role.
- Withholding the title of the poem, read it aloud (or play recording if available).
- Give the learners the text of the poem (still without the title) and ask to interpret its main theme.
-Learners supply title according to their understanding of its theme/s.
- Supply title and include it in a re-reading of the poem.
- Ask learners to assess how the title alters (enhances?) the effect/impact of the poem[27].
Suggested poems: *Heaven-haven: a nun takes the veil*, Gerald Manley Hopkins; *A Martian sends a postcard home*, Craig Raine[28].

Task 21

Discourse type	Poem - suspense
Communicative purpose	Engaging
Authentic task type	Inferencing
Level 5 up	
Aim: Reaction to a poem.	

Preparation: Select a poem in which there is an element of suspense.
- Reveal your selected poem bit by bit (first title, then line by line as appropriate) by reading/or by gradually uncovering a slide.
- Encourage learners to make inferences / interpretations at each stage (re. unfamiliar lexis as well as content) and to revise interpretations as poem revealed.
- At end, analyse how the poet builds up the atmosphere/emotion.
- Suggested poems: Seamus Heaney's *Mid-term break, Heaven-haven: a nun takes the veil*, Gerald Manley Hopkins.

Task 22

Discourse type	Poem - personal
Communicative purpose	Engaging
Authentic task type	Inferencing
Level 6 up	
Aim: To infer poetic 'voices'.	

Preparation: Choose a poem in which there are particular 'voice/s' speaking in the poem and/or the poem is written *to* someone in particular.
- Give the text of the poem to the learners in pairs/groups.
- Ask learners to infer *who* is speaking, or to mark the words of each speaker.
- Change partner/groups and discuss interpretations.
Suggested poem: *A day in the life of...*' beginning 'It was Sunday I met your father' Maley (1985). Christina Rossetti's *Uphill*, Stevie Smith's *Not waving but drowning*.

Task 23

Discourse type	Poem - evocative
Communicative purpose	Engaging
Authentic task type	Analysis
Level 6 up	
Aim: Raise awareness of how sound conveys effect.	

Preparation: Choose a poem which plays on effects of rhyme, assonance, alliteration, phonology etc.
Read the poem (or use a recording of it).
- Ask learners to:

- Close their eyes and visualise the images in the poem, as they hear it.
- Draw their visualisations (or describe in words if preferred).
- Share ideas.
- Look at the text of the poem. Analyse how the sounds of words contribute to effects.

Suggested poem: *Jabberwocky*, Lewis Carroll.

Task 24

Discourse type	Poem - evocative
Communicative purpose	Engaging
Authentic task type	Analysis
Level 6 up	
Aim: To interpret figurative/metaphoric language.	

Preparation: Choose a poem that includes figurative language/metaphor.
Read poem aloud to class (or play recording).
- Ask learners to note (or sketch) any striking images.
- Re-read or re-play, then ask learners to exchange their impressions of images from the poem.
- Give learners the text and ask them to find and mark the images they had noted, adding any others they might notice from reading the text.
- Allow them to check any unfamiliar lexis/structures which hinders comprehension by consulting peers, teacher or dictionary.
- Ask them to think about whether the images they have marked are 'real' or metaphorical (and if so, what do they represent?).
- Ask them to think about and discuss (in small groups) the meaning/interpretation of these images.
Suggested poems: W. B. Yeats' *He wishes for the cloths of heaven.*

Task 25

Discourse type	Poem - evocative
Communicative purpose	Engaging
Authentic task type	Transference
Level 5 up	
Aim: To engage with a poem by interacting with it.	

Preparation: Choose a fairly simple but evocative poem with a variety of images.
- Read/play a recording of the poem.
Learners *choose* how to respond e.g.
- Draw a picture
- Draw a cartoon (series of pictures)
- Write+record a sequel (prose/poetry/dialogue)
- Write+record a 'prequel' (prose/poetry/dialogue)
- Write+record a response (prose/poetry/dialogue)

- Learn it by heart
- Learners prepare their chosen response (individually/in pairs).
- Learners share their 'products' with others for comment.

Task 26

Discourse type	Poem - unusual view
Communicative purpose	Engaging
Authentic task type	Analysis
Level 6 up	
Aim: To interpret unusual references/images in poem.	

Preparation: Choose a poem that looks at the world from a peculiar viewpoint (see suggestions below).
- Learners work in groups to prepare own interpretation/'translation' of unusual references/images in poem.
- Learner groups prepare comprehension/multiple choice questions incorporating their interpretations of the unusual images.
- Groups exchange question sheets.
- Groups respond to the questions, and re-group to 'mark' questions and discuss answers.
Suggested poems: *A Martian Sends a Postcard Home* by Craig Raine[29], poems by Roger McGough and e. e. cummings.

Task 27

Discourse type	Poem - representative of TC
Communicative purpose	Engaging
Authentic task type	Analysis
Level 5 up	
Aim: Raise awareness of cultural expectations and differences in common experiences.	

Preparation: Choose a poem describing a common experience e.g. a funeral, a holiday, a festival, a ritual (Christmas stocking-hanging etc.)
- Introduce learners to the theme of the poem (funeral, holiday etc.)
- Working in mono-cultural groups, learners brainstorm images/feelings /experiences connected to this theme in their C1.
- As whole class, brainstorm images/feelings/experiences connected to this theme in TC.
- Compare/contrast imagery/feelings/experiences re. this theme across cultures.
- Present poem - read aloud and/or give text.
Learners compare images/feelings/experiences arising in poem to:
- their own cultural expectations re. this theme as brainstormed above and
- their expectations re. this theme based on their knowledge of target culture as brainstormed above.

- Working in mono-cultural groups or alone, learners first check comprehension of any unfamiliar lexis/structures in the poem if necessary and then write their own (culture-specific) poem on same or comparable theme.
- Share poems with others, with explanations where necessary.
Suggested poems: Lindsay Macrae's *Can we go home now please?* (about English summer holiday, see discussion section above). Seamus Heaney's *Mid-term break* (Irish funeral rituals, see also above).

Task 28

Discourse type	Poem - universal theme
Communicative purpose	Engaging
Authentic task type	Extension
Level 6 up	
Aim: To engage with poetry through its themes.	

Preparation: Choose poems with universal theme e.g. love, ageing, death, war, regret, memory, nostalgia, childhood, *or* themes relevant/of interest to learners.
- Introduce poem via *other* suggested activities (see other tasks). Then:
Give a choice of various extension activities e.g.
- Assess attitude to this 'universal' theme in the TC as represented in this poem.
- Think of a poem in L1 on same theme, paraphrase it (or find a copy of it - library/Internet, and translate into English.
- Write and record a dialogue illustrating the theme of the poem.
- Write a poem / piece of prose on the theme of the poem.
- Describe how you relate to the poem.
- Write a 'literary review' of the poem.
  Suggested poems: Brian Patten's *Little Johnny's Final Letter*, Carol Ann Duffy's *Stealing*, Seamus Heaney's *Mid-term break*, W. B. Yeats' *When you are old* and *An Irish Airman foresees his death*, Dylan Thomas' *Do not go gentle into that good night*, Jorge Luis Borges' *Moments* (English translation).

Task 29

Discourse type	Narrative poem
Communicative purpose	Engaging
Authentic task type	Reaction
Level 5 up	
Aim: To engage and interact with a poem.	

Preparation: Choose a fairly long, narrative poem (e.g. a ballad).
- Read the poem aloud (teacher/student) with tape-recorder running. Possibly provide the text of the poem for learners to follow.
- Pause after each stanza or other suitable section.

- Elicit learners' spontaneous reactions (e.g. comments, questions, in-role improvisations, predictions, summaries).
- Give some time for reflection if required.
- Replay tape to discuss and analyse reactions after end of poem[30].

Task 30

Discourse type	Narrative poem
Communicative purpose	Engaging
Authentic task type	Reaction
Level 4 up	
Aim: To react to linguistic input.	

Preparation: Choose a poem with a number of characters and which describes events, action.
- Distribute roles of characters in poem among learners (for large classes: a group* can all play the same character. For small classes: one learner can play multiple roles).
- Teacher reads the poem and learners act out as it is read[31].
  Suggested poetry: Roald Dahl's collection *Revolting Rhymes* (1982) (poem adaptations of fairy tales); poems by A. A. Milne.
*Group acting recommended for lower level learners as better students can 'lead' those who are slower to understand.

Task 31

Discourse type	Rhyming poem
Communicative purpose	Engaging
Authentic task type	Response
Level 4 up	
Aim: To interact with poem via its rhyme/structure.	

Preparation: Introduce idea of poem with a particular rhyme scheme or structure; elicit examples from learner's own cultures (e.g. haiku).
- Tell learners they are going to interact with a poem with a specific rhyme scheme or structure (e.g. limericks, sonnets).
- Present the first line/s of the poem to end with a word that has a subsequent rhyme. E.g. with limericks, present the first line and tell learners the second and fifth lines rhyme with the first.
- Elicit words that rhyme with the rhyme word, and note on the board. Ask learners to choose the most feasible in the context of the poem so far.
- Point out the rhythm of the lines and ask learners to draft a possible line.
- Present the actual line - learners compare their suggestions.
- Repeat this pattern until the end of the poem.

- Once learners have grasped the rhyme/rhythm system of the poem, they may like to write one of their own.
Suggestions: limericks (Level 3 up) Edward Lear's *The Owl and the Pussy Cat*, Roald Dahl's collection *Revolting Rhymes* (1982).

Task 32

Discourse type	'Shape' poem
Communicative purpose	Engaging
Authentic task type	Transference
Level 5 up	
Aim: To engage with a poem on linguistic and visual level.	

Preparation: Use a shape poem such as Lewis Carroll's *The Mouse's Tail*, the words of which are arranged in the form of a tail.
- Give the poem to the learners, and ask them to translate it into their first language maintaining the shape of the poem or altering it to make another relevant, recognisable outline (e.g. in the case of this poem, a mouse or cat).
- When they are finished, learners read the poems in their own languages, then offer a rough 'double translation' back into the TL, explaining what changes had to be made and why.
Further suggestions: (for use with students whose L1 is French) shape poems, by Apollinaire - for translation into English as in stage one above.

Notes

1   An interesting classroom exercise, indeed, can be to re-write a poem as prose then ask learners to 'turn it back into a poem' by re-arranging it into lines of poetry.

2   From the collection *Ye canny shove yer granny off a bus - unexpected new poems by Linsay Macrae*, Puffin.

3   From e. e. cummings *Selected poems 1923 - 1958*.

4   From *Angela's Ashes* (McCourt 1997: 58).

5   From the novel *The Graduate* (Webb 1963: 4); this example was pointed out by Tomlinson (1995, ACELS seminar, Dublin).

6   The last two samples are from *The Restraint of Beasts* (Mills, 1998: 18, 35).

7   From the collection *Death of a Naturalist* published in 1966.

8   First published in 1973 in the collection *From Glasgow to Saturn*, Cheadle: Carcanet Press.

9   For example, the classic children's bed-time story, *Good night moon*, functions by using such

rhymes and repetition; 'good night kittens! Good night mittens! Good night moon! Good night cow jumping over the moon!'

10 My son of 22-months, for example, accustomed to seeing off the next door neighbour's puppy with 'Bye bye puppy!', one day while sitting on his potty, spontaneously came out with 'Bye Bye pee pee, bye bye Puppy!'.

11 From the fairy tale *Little Red Riding Hood*.

12 A suitable poem for this might be e. e. cummings' *may i feel said he* which gets its rhythm and rhyme from its line endings - alternately 'said he'/'said she'.

13 From the collection: Roger McGough, 1999. *The Way Things Are*.

14 'This morning, the American, Steve Fossett, ended his round-the-World balloon fight...I'm sorry, balloon "flight"...in northern India.' *The Today Programme*, Radio 4, 20 January 1997.

15 From the collection *Little Johnny's Confession* by Brian Patten, 1967. This poem is suggested by Tomlinson and Masuhara 1984.

16 *Selected poems 1923-1958*, 1969: 28-9.

17 Used in Duff and Maley 1990: 109-10.

18 Based on Duff and Maley 1990: 142-3.

19 Based on Duff and Maley 1990: 93-4.

20 From Chandler and Stone 1999: 28.

21 Strategy suggested by Sihui 1996: 181-2; Bassnet and Grundy 93: 74-5.

22 First published as 'Song IX' from Twelve Songs, 1936, reprinted in 1994 as 'Funeral Blues' in *Tell me the Truth about Love*, published by Faber.

23 Based on Duff and Maley 1990: 132-3.

24 First published in the collection *Rose in the Afternoon*, published by Dent, 1974.

25 From the collection *Selling Manhattan*, published by Anvil Press Poetry, 1987.

26 Activity suggested by Duff and Maley 1990: 35-8.

27 Based on Sihui 1996: 181-2; Bassnett and Grundy's treatment of Gerard Manley Hopkins' poem 'Heaven-haven: a nun takes the veil', Bassnet and Grundy 1993: 76-7.

28 In the collection of the same name, published by Oxford University Press, 1979.

29 Adapted from Bassnett and Grundy 1993: 64-6.

30 Activity suggested by Bassnett and Grundy 1993: 75.

31 Activity suggested by Tomlinson at ACELS workshop, Dublin 1995.

Chapter Six:
The Broadcast Media

The broadcast media offer the most diversified set of genres of all those discussed in this book. The broadcast media - radio and television - have many genres in common; news, current affairs, arts reviews and entertainment programmes such as quiz shows, soaps and plays. However, today's radio and television are very different media. This is probably due to the fact that over the past forty years or so, television has usurped the central role of radio as the principal news and entertainment medium for the population (in the UK, Ireland and North America at least). This has forced radio to reassess its role, and to transform itself into a more intimate medium which intermingles with our lives as background, distraction and even interaction (via the growing phenomenon of phone-in programmes). For these reasons, and because, as with all the media used for language learning, foreign learners' own attitudes to and experiences of the medium/a inevitably impinge on their attitudes to them as learning media, television and radio are for the most part treated separately here.

6.1 Television: Using Entertainment Media for Learning

The teacher needs to be aware that in using television for language learning, s/he is hijacking the medium with which today's learners are probably the most familiar. This has advantages and disadvantages. Learners are cognisant of the universal conventions of the medium; the continuity voice-over, the commercial break, the structure of a news bulletin. They are familiar with the range of genres; news bulletins, soaps, chat-shows and so on. Familiarity with the schemata of such genres eases the linguistic encounter; learners know the formats of such programmes, the sort of topics to expect, the language register and so on. On the other hand, this very familiarity can breed contempt. Learners may associate television strongly with the domestic not the pedagogical setting. More problematic still, they identify television with passivity and entertainment. This is a problem with all screen-focused media being used for learning. But the computer, at least, is interactive to a greater or lesser degree; the choice to see a movie, whether this involves going to the cinema or renting a video/DVD, presupposes a willingness to engage cognitively and affectively with the material. Television, however, is probably the medium into which people are used to putting the least 'effort', in cognitive terms. Unlike the radio, television, with its myriad sensory distractions of fast-moving colourful images, sound and music, does not force the viewer to concentrate on the spoken language in order to follow what is happening. And at its worst, television can act as virtual wallpaper, not penetrating our consciousness at all. This, then, is the type of behavioural norm that has to be combated in harnessing television as a learning medium. This is why a core principle reiterated time and again in the literature (e.g. Tomalin 1986: 30, Allan 1985: 37, Tomalin and Stempleski 1990: 6) is that successful exploitation of television for learning requires the teacher to create scenarios in which learners watch *actively*, and this means with a purpose.

Bearing in mind that the definition of an authentic task turns on maintaining consistency with its communicative purpose (see Chapter 4), it could, strictly, be argued that to attempt to counter the passivity which is part of the communicative purpose of the medium (most television programmes are, after all, intended to be uni-directional) makes for inauthentic tasks. What is argued here is that 'viewing with a purpose' can be given an authentic gloss. With items/programmes that are inherently functional and informative, this is not difficult to do. For example, no one watches the weather forecast for its entertainment value; they do so to find out what the weather will be like in a particular region in the coming days. This authentic purpose, then, can be configured into a pedagogical framework; learners can be asked to plan or cancel weather-dependent outings in different parts of the country and so on (see Task 20). The news is likewise functional, watched not only to find out what is happening in the wider world, but to keep in touch with what might affect us personally; rising crime rates, changing rates of tax, a strike, an election, a crisis in public services. On-going stories also induce us to watch - trials, political scandals, natural disasters. All of these reasons for listening/viewing can be reassigned to the learner. In ESL contexts, learners might be asked to look out for news items that pertain to them personally, or in EFL contexts, they can watch for items about, or relevant to, their own countries. They might also be interested to follow an on-going news story over a period of days. Authentic purpose is created by authentic interest and this is not hard to tap into with the broadcast news, a programme with relatively high ratings.

Counteracting passivity is also done, of course, by demanding *activity*. In the case of audio and audio-visual media like radio and television, this encompasses *interactivity*. Television (and radio too) is more interactive than one might assume; people often talk among themselves about what they are viewing as they are watching it, even talking directly to the television when really roused. This authentic activity can be replicated in the language classroom, and is an instance of generative language input (that is, using input not to *teach* language but to *release* it, Tomalin 2000: see more on this in Chapter 10 'Film').

Another way of countering passivity is to create that classic CLT technique, the information gap. The most obvious way to do this with videoed material is to block one of the modes; to cover the screen and listen to just the audio track, or alternatively, to turn the sound down and watch just the pictures. The latter in particular is an authentic enough activity; everyone at some time has had the experience of watching a television screen without the sound, through a shop window or in a noisy bar, for instance. While this situation can be replicated to constitute an information gap that can produce discussion ('what is she saying to make him so angry?' 'what are they laughing about?'), the interest in the missing mode can also wane quickly (in the real-life situations, we walk away from the shop window, we look away from the television in the bar). This is useful as a short activity, therefore (see Task 4), but teachers can expect diminishing returns on prolonging it in the classroom, as frustration progressively replaces curiosity.

A final point on the issue of television as an entertainment medium is this. Its role as entertainment should not blinker us to the fact that television is at the same time one of the prime affective media of our age, one with a corresponding capacity to upset, disturb and outrage. Its power stems in large part from its use of images, and although today's generation of viewers is arguably more immune to the live image having been weaned on it, care still needs to be exercised in the selection of texts for learning purposes. While engagement is in the main conducive to language learning, where this extends to emotional upset, this will tend to block the paths to learning[1].

6.1.1 Snippet length

The use of television and radio in the language classroom both present the same dilemma though for opposite reasons, and this is the problem of excerpt-length. With television, this problem is due to the fact that as an audio-visual medium, it is very dense. With radio, it is due to the isolation of the audio medium and its lack of support from any other. In both cases, the usual solution in the language classroom is to restrict snippet length. However, this can create as many problems as it solves because it removes *context*. Conveniently, this issue is becoming increasingly obsolete because of changes in styles of programme-making. These days, the twin influences of the 'sound bite' (a short, self-contained piece of information) and our reputedly shortening concentration span (a result of increasing visual overload and bombardment with fast-moving images), pervade the structure of radio and television programmes. Interviews are routinely abridged or ended abruptly (see also below) and brief slices of news action shown. Interviewees' remarks are edited and strung together to make audio or audio-visual collages, and even serious subjects such as health and social issues are presented in a magazine-style format. Instead of segmenting the material artificially, therefore, today teachers can avail themselves of the original editing cuts that abound in this style of broadcasting.

Some television genres are characterised by the way in which they end episodes at suspenseful points - soaps and made-for-television dramas, for instance. These natural cut off points can be appropriated for language learning purposes, for they generate language by prompting speculation. Teachers might find other scenes edited to create suspense and pause the programme there (see Task 13). A sort of reverse prediction exercise might also be done at any of these moments of suspense, with learners being shown the moment of suspense or short section preceding it and being asked to speculate how this situation might have come about. This type of activity simulates the 'real-life' circumstances in which we switch on in the middle of a programme/film and have to 'catch on' as to what has happened. The main proviso for using such techniques is not to overdo them, partly because this interferes with the genuine involvement that is part of the rational for using this potentially emotive material for learning, and partly because constant interruptions can simply be annoying and hence counter-productive to learning.

6.2 Television and Culture

What makes television such a valuable resource for learning about culture is that it is a universal medium with a recognisable set of genres whose familiarity belies the subtle - or not so subtle - differences between cultures. Presentation of the television news and weather, the characters and settings of soap operas, chat show presenters and production styles in a culture other than our own, appear at the same time familiar, yet alien. While the universal generic framework is, of course, very useful for NNS viewers since it gives them familiar schema to hang on to, there are perceptible cultural differences at many levels. At the level of content in any identified genre, for example, there might be differences in settings, styles of social interaction, cross-gender relationships and language register. There might be differences, too, at the holistic level; the attitudes of broadcasting companies to their audiences, for example, as disclosed by their styles of presentation, degree of commercialisation and so on.

To look first at content, television's value for language and culture learning is its representation of linguistic and visual aspects of the TC. In this, television is more comprehensive than its fellow audio-visual medium, film, since film is for the most part constrained within the dramatic template, while television extends over numerous genres. This means that such important indicators as cultural differences in non-verbal communication can be seen in the real-life situations shown on the news or current affairs programmes; the body language of the accused going into court, of victims of crimes, of people interviewed casually on the street or in the rehearsed interviews of celebrities or subject-experts. What is often of most interest in the context of language and culture learning is the deliberate or learned gesture, signalling such words as 'yes' and 'no', 'wait', 'come here', 'over there' or those replacing (or accompanying) verbal abuse, as such gestures can vary from culture to culture, and indeed, can be misleading and misunderstood[2]. These learned signals include ones used in social situations - the position of the knife and fork to indicate one has finished eating, putting one's hand over a glass, summoning a waiter in a restaurant (Allan 1985: 70-1). Unconscious body language that is culturally determined includes facial expression, the smile and 'eyebrow flash' (raising the eyebrows) that accompanies greeting in many cultures (Allan 1985: 68), the degree of eye contact, the distance we stand from one another, and whether - and when, how often and whom - we touch and kiss. Many of these also vary within a culture depending on the level of formality of the situation. Deliberate gestures such as shaking hands and kissing, are obviously the easiest to learn - it is harder to shake off the more unconscious body language of the native language culture and acquire that of another. Paradoxically, however, it is quite easy to teach (or at least make learners conscious of) this most complex and often subtle form of communication, using video/DVD. Turning the sound off reduces distraction, focusing attention on the visual, and learners enjoy speculating on the meanings of gestures and expressions, imitating them and discussing their varying interpretations in their own cultures (see Task 16).

To turn from a focus on content to the holistic level, one way that television reveals the values and attitudes of its culture is via the style of its broadcasting companies. Whether these are commercial, for instance, and if they are, how intrusive advertising is; the way they balance content, since this reflects (and/or determines?) the interests of their audiences; the relative proportions of air time dedicated to social problems, personal relations, politics, sport, game-shows, drama, the arts; the proportion of news to entertainment, and especially, the proclivity for presenting news *as* entertainment. All of this reveals the sort of society television is serving (or creating?). Even something as mundane as a television schedule, then, is valuable starting point for analysis of most modern societies (Tomalin and Stempleski 1993: 53-4, see also Task 25); the mere timing of programmes tells us about people's habits[3].

6.3 Television and Currency

6.3.1 The language of television

The variety of genres and registers in the language of television and radio has been pointed out above. The range goes from the relative formality of the news broadcast and the near-written register of the documentary voice-over, to the scripted colloquial dialogue of the soap opera and the spontaneous speech of protagonists in 'fly on the wall' programmes such as *Big Brother* - not to mention that fascinating discourse type, advertising (see Chapter 8). What is interesting about some of these genres and discourse types is that they are unique to broadcasting, and hence (in relative terms) startlingly new in the language, although they certainly have predecessors. The soap opera, for example, 'continued the tradition of women's domestic fiction of the nineteenth century, which had also been sustained in magazine stories of the 1920s and 1930s'(Allen 2002). Today as then, the characters in soap operas are ostensibly ordinary people, but the lives they live are far more eventful and tumultuous than our own and their language tends to be more direct and forceful. Another discourse type to have metamorphosed within broadcasting, is the news interview; this is examined in some detail here to illustrate how such discourse types can diversify from the everyday ones that they emulate.

News interviewing is superficially a dialogue. However, it is a dialogue that differs crucially from a spontaneous, naturally-occurring dialogue in terms of intent and of audience. In spontaneous dialogues, intent can range across the communication spectrum from informing to simply making contact, or from arguing to reassuring; however, the dialogue is usually self-restricting in terms of audience. The broadcast interview, on the other hand, is an exhibitionistic form of dialogue, ostensibly confined to two people, but destined for a wide audience. This gives it many differentiating features, notably the frequent omission of introductory exchanges, and of routinised responses (such as 'oh?', 'really?') (partly because the interviewer often knows the interviewee's answers in advance). This gives the interview a two-part, question-answer structure, rather than the more natural three-part dialogue structure (question - answer - response) with the interviewee's answers often followed directly with another question. Questions are, furthermore, as often intended to provoke a reaction as to elicit information, and there is often a calculated disregard for the feelings of the respondent. This accounts for the typical 'How disappointed are you that Manchester United have failed to qualify for the European Cup?'-type question. While learners gain much linguistic (as well as current affairs) information from exploring this discourse type, then, it is essential that this includes awareness of its peculiarities of structure, socio-cultural and interactive function. In order to achieve this, the press interview might be contrasted with the structure and language in other types of interviews (chat show interviews, job interviews) or with more naturally-occurring dialogue from film, television soaps or texts from a language corpus (see Task 9).

Similar points may be made about many of the genres present on television and radio; the semi-colloquial soliloquy that is the weather-forecast, the quick-fire repartee of the chat-show or panel game, the semi-literary style of the documentary and so on. Learners fed on a reasonable diet of TC television and radio will come to be familiar with these genres. What is important in the context of language learning is that learners be made aware of the socio-cultural, and often media-specific, contexts for which they are appropriate.

6.4 The Challenge of Television

A point emphasised throughout this book is that linguistic complexity is not necessarily the main criterion for the selection of texts for language learning. This is particularly true of television material (and of course, film) where the message is 'doubly' supported, coming via both linguistic and visual channels. As has been noted above, viewing of television is also aided by the universality of the schema of many programme types. Most trans-cultural of all, perhaps, is the television news bulletin (see also Chapter 3 Section 3.3 'Challenge'). The news is presented by one, or a pair of anchor people, who read a summary of each story, sometimes then handing over to an on-the-spot reporter. The format has an iterative structure, with headline stories being developed later in the programme and headlines repeated at the end. Domestic and international stories are interspersed but prioritised according to importance. News is usually followed by sport, after which there is a return to the anchor, often for a light, 'human interest' story, and, finally, comes the weather forecast, usually given by a meteorologist. At lower levels, learners can be asked to simply enumerate the news items, identifying their topics and the people, places and/or events in each item. This is quite a feasible task once learners have honed essential coping strategies for this genre, such as utilising the information gained from images accompanying the piece, from proper nouns (names of people, places, companies, organisations etc.) and from 'international' words (words which are similar across languages, such as *politics, president, taxi, computer*), as well as making use of their own existing knowledge of the stories in the news (see Tasks 1 to 3). Exploiting students' familiarity with the schemata and their prior knowledge in this way impacts strongly on motivation, boosting self-confidence and encouraging them to contribute to the class.

As well as the news, other genres peculiar to television, such as the soap opera, the chat show, made-for-television drama and short films can all offer input that is suitable for lower level learners. Selection criteria for material for such learners might include: dialogue with natural pauses (which give the learner time to process the language); plenty of visual signals, gesture, facial expression etc.; action sequences; samples of the written word, e.g. on street name plaques, pub signs, shop notices[4], and any other features which take the pressure off the learner to rely solely on decoding of audio input for comprehension.

With young learners at lower proficiency levels, some different principles apply. Children, especially young children, are far more tolerant of non-comprehension than adults (after all, up to a certain age, they do not fully understand a lot of what they hear in their native language). They also have more vivid imaginations and are less inhibited about giving them free rein. These factors give the teacher of children greater scope even at lower proficiency levels than teachers of adults have. They can use longer excerpts (as long as the substance is appealing to children), since children are happy to use the visual to support the audio message for the reason given above. Indeed, since, as Tomalin points out (1986: 65), children perceive all audio and audio-visual input as 'stories', they prefer to hear/see the chosen piece in its entirety, content to make the most of what they see and hear. Once they 'know' the story, as they see it, children are then happy for the teacher to go back over material to check comprehension or to do extension activities; children love nothing better than repetition, as any parent knows.

6.5 Radio

As has been pointed out at the start of this chapter, radio is today a very different medium from television. It is hard to believe that it was only a generation ago that television usurped radio's role as the medium for news and entertainment and in doing so, its very place in the home as the latter-day 'hearth'. As with its usurper, the role of radio in learners' everyday lives affects its use in the language learning classroom. Today, this role has drifted towards the background in the home, or distraction (in the car). 'Listening' to the radio, in other words, is usually done in tandem with another activity, so that it is rarely 'listened to' for a sustained period of time, it is 'heard'. In fact, the only medium where many of today's learners actually practise listening skills in isolation is on the telephone - and even this is being made redundant by text messaging and, soon, by picture messaging. It may therefore be unrealistic to expect learners to achieve a skill in a foreign language that they scarcely possess in their native one. This is not to say that teachers might as well eschew radio as a learning medium, but to get them to bear in mind, in developing materials, the ways in which people 'receive' radio broadcasts in their daily lives.

These days, much of our listening to the radio is for gist - the news headlines, the weather, the name of a singer of a particular song, the issues being tackled in a current affairs or phone-in programme. What we garner from this gist-listening is usually supplemented by/in addition to news and information from a variety of other sources. In the language classroom, practice in the authentic skill of gist-listening should likewise be linked to learners' knowledge of the input from other sources. If, on probing, learners have little prior knowledge of particular items of the radio input, they might fill this out by looking for more information from the Internet, newspapers, or television (see Task 21). Another authentic application of the skill of listening for gist is actually searching the airways and tuning into a radio station. This can easily be done in the classroom, with the teacher (or a student) pausing long enough on each station found, to determine the type of programme being broadcast, the topic being discussed (if applicable), and, finally, whether the learners would be interested in listening further[5] (see Task 24). This sort of 'surfing' can also be done on television using a remote control; a routine, authentic activity which all learners will have done on their own NS channels. A similar type of activity can also be done with programme trailers[6] (see Task 23).

A trend in programme style that has implications for the use of radio with language learners is the modern 'magazine' style of presentation. Programmes are made up of short self-contained units of information. While this trend is in one sense a sad reflection of our abbreviated concentration spans, it is fortuitous from the language teaching point of view; the short information 'bite' can be a juicy morsel in language study terms. Problems of context are reduced where the item is practically self-contained - as, for example, in items within arts, cookery or women's 'magazines' such as BBC Radio 4's *Front Row*, *The Food Programme*, and *Woman's Hour*, or music and prose miscellanies such as RTE Radio 1's *Sunday Miscellany*. Because of their relative brevity, items from such programmes can be listened to in detail if learners so wish. Today there is also valuable support from broadcasting company Web sites where programmes can be listened to again, or their information accessed in written form. The existence of radio and television station Web sites is, of course, indicative of an attempt to encourage interaction between broadcaster and audience. Indeed, interaction, in the form of programmes that elicit listener input via phone or e-mail, has become a growing trend in radio broadcasting as radio seeks to re-create a niche for itself (see above). Once again, this is auspicious from the language learning point of view. Phone-ins in particular give us a lot of authentic spontaneous, colloquial speech, a discourse type often missing from other forms of input. From the cultural point of view, they can also give us unique insight into the reactions, opinions and moral standpoint of TC members (see Task 22).

6.6 The Broadcast Media for Language Learning: Summary and Principles

The broadcast media, in conclusion, have huge potential for language and culture learning. As part of the so-called 'mass media', broadcasting is wholly familiar to learners from all cultures, and this very familiarity can be usefully exploited in the learning environment through the comparisons and contrasts that it invokes. As a primarily visual medium, television is comprehensible, on some level at least, to all learners, from *ab initio* upwards. The fact that radio and television are intrinsically emotive media means that they provide naturally the affective factor so crucial to language acquisition. Finally, the broadcasting of increasing numbers of radio and television programmes live on the Internet means that these media are now more easily accessible to teachers and learners in places hitherto beyond transmission range. The potential for interactivity offered by broadcasting station Web sites will hopefully help alter the perception of television (and radio) as uni-directional media and thus combat the passivity associated with them.

Principles for the use of the broadcast media for language learning

• Counter passivity by listening/viewing with a purpose, requiring interactivity or creating an information gap.

• Exploit original programme editing to determine excerpt length.

• Exploit the universality of broadcast genres: build on learners' knowledge of them for the study of both language and culture.

• View/listen in ways that are authentic to the medium and its genres: e.g. for gist, for specific information.

• (With television) exploit the visual component of television e.g. non-verbal communication, action and wordless sequences, the printed word on screen.

• Exploit all the multimedia features of television - audio, visual and Web site.

Further reading

Allan, M 1985. *Teaching English with Video*. Harlow: Longman Group Ltd.

Cooper, R., M. Lavery and M. Rinvolucri, 1991. *Video*. OUP.

Stempleski and B. Tomalin 1990. *Video in Action*. Hemel Hemstead: Prentice Hall Group International.

Tomalin, B. 1986. *Video, Television and Radio in the English Class: An introductory guide*. London: Macmillan.

6.7 The Tasks

Task 1

Discourse type	News bulletin
Communicative purpose	Informative
Authentic task type	Transference

Level 5 up
Aim: To reproduce input information in a different medium.

Preparation: Record/video a radio/television news bulletin.
- Play news bulletin to the class.
- Individuals/pairs select ONE item of interest to them.
- Re-play to allow learners to catch most important points via key words/expressions, names/titles, places, figures etc.
- Encourage learners to use own knowledge of event (if possible) to assist comprehension.
- Learners reproduce their chosen item as written article for a newspaper (on paper or electronically if PCs are available).
- Class assemble page(s) of newspaper (on paper, or if using PCs, as a file or class Web page if available).

Task 2

Discourse type	News bulletin
Communicative purpose	Informative
Authentic task type	Extraction
Level 3 up	
Aim: To extract main points from audio/audio-visual input.	

Preparation: A blank 6-column table, with the headings *number, names, key words, images, subject area, own knowledge.*
Record/video a radio/television news bulletin.
- Play news bulletin to the class. Ask learners to *number* the news items (in column 1) and note in appropriate columns:
- *names* (people, places, institutions, companies etc.)
- *key words* (e.g. 'international' words such as *terrorist, president, airport*).
- (If using television) *images.*
- deduced *subject area* of each.
- *own knowledge* of event
- After (2/3) listenings, learners work in pairs/threes to pool their information
- Groups crosscheck their findings with other groups.

Task 3

Discourse type	News bulletin
Communicative purpose	Informative
Authentic task type	Inferencing
Level 5 up	
Aim: To relate media information to self.	

Preparation: Record/video a radio/television news bulletin.

- Play news bulletin to the class. Ask each learner to
- identify at least one news item which relates to personal concerns /interests, or to those of own country.
- make notes on identified news item (listening to the broadcast a few more times as necessary).
- add coda, explaining how/why this item relates to self or own country.
- In groups, learners reveal news item selected and why/how it has personal/national/cultural significance.

Task 4

Discourse type	News bulletin
Communicative purpose	Informative
Authentic task type	Inferencing
Level 4 up	
Aim: To infer news stories from visuals only.	

Preparation: A blank 4-column table, with the headings *number, story type, key words, own knowledge*.
- Video a short television news bulletin.
- Play news bulletin to the class *with sound turned down*. Ask learners to use the visuals to:
- Count and *number* the different news stories (in column 1), and then to infer and note in appropriate columns:
- For each item, the *type of story*- e.g. political, terrorism, natural disaster, social problem, personal tragedy, sports
- Note *key words* they would expect to occur in each story.
- Their *own knowledge* of the event (if any).
- After 2/3 viewings, learners work in pairs/threes to pool their information.
- Groups cross-check their findings with other groups.
- If the learner level is appropriate, learners may check their ideas by viewing the news broadcast with audio.

Task 5

Discourse type	News bulletin
Communicative purpose	Provocative
Authentic task type	Analysis
Level 6 up	
Aim: To form and express personal perceptions about the news.	

Preparation: Record/video a radio/television news bulletin.
- Play news bulletin to the class. Ask learners to:
- Classify (note) each news story as 'good news' and 'bad news'.
- Compare notes with others and justify opinions[7].

Task 6

Discourse type	News bulletin
Communicative purpose	Provocative
Authentic task type	Analysis
Level 6 up	
Aim: To challenge 'objectivity' of news reporting.	

Preparation: Record/video a news bulletin.
- Play news bulletin.
- Ask learners to identify at least one story that they think might not being reported objectively and reach consensus (for logistical reasons).
- Replay selected story for learners to identify and note: emotive language; language betraying bias (political/gender/social/racial); value-judgements being made etc.
- (in groups) learners re-create story more 'objectively'.
- Compare re-created versions and vote for most objective!

Task 7

Discourse type	News item
Communicative purpose	Informative
Authentic task type	Inferencing
Level 5 up	
Aim: To infer semantic connections and reconstruct a piece of written discourse.	

Preparation: Choose a shortish, interesting news item. Extract from it words from (4) parts of speech e.g. nouns, verbs, adjectives, adverbs, and write on (4) transparencies according to POS.
- Tell learners they are to reconstruct a news item.
- Present transparency 1: nouns.
- Learners work in groups, write first draft of story inferred from these nouns.
- Present transparency 2: verbs
- learners revise story to include new words.
- Repeat as above, giving adjectives then adverbs.
- After final draft, compare groups' stories, vote for most feasible one, then compare with original news item (played on video/audio-tape)[8].

Task 8

Discourse type	TC news item
Communicative purpose	Provocative
Authentic task type	Analysis/Response
Level 5 up	
Aim: To raise awareness of relativity of cultural priorities/interests.	

Preparation: Select an item from recorded radio/television news relating to event of national (TC) relevance, as controversial as possible (e.g. crime, drug/alcohol abuse, taxes, ages of consent, social legislation on these etc.).
- Learners listen to/view item as many times as they require to proceed (see below), consulting peers/teacher/dictionaries/corpora, re: any unfamiliar vocabulary or expressions that hinder comprehension.
- Working in mono-cultural groups if possible, or else individually, ask learners to:
- Prepare to re-tell the story as radio/television news item from their own culture. Remind them to consider differences in cultural priorities and values i.e. how important would this issue be in their culture? How would it be interpreted? What would be their own cultural attitudes to the issue? etc.
- Each group/individual reads their prepared news item.
- Discuss differences; prioritisation of facts reported (any facts omitted or added?) attitudes to the issue etc.[9].

Task 9

Discourse type	News interview
Communicative purpose	Provocative
Authentic task type	Analysis
Level 6 up	
Aim: To analyse the discourse of news interviewing.	

Preparation: Record a news interview on a subject of interest to your students.
- Pre-listening; learners work in groups and pool ideas on principles for interviewing: if necessary, offer guidelines e.g.
- How begin/end an interview?
- What sort of questions should be asked (yes/no/wh- questions, neutral/revealing opinion).
- Paralinguistic rules: voice tone, pauses etc.
- Response to interviewee's answers?
- Turn-taking?
- Pool ideas to draw up set of 'principles for interviewing'.
- First listening; ask learners to form general impression of how well 'their' rules were observed.
- Re-listen as necessary, checking if their rules were observed/flouted and collecting evidence of how this is done (linguistic/paralinguistic).
- Pool ideas in class, citing evidence.
- In groups, re-script interview as necessary following own code of practice.
- Record/enact for class.

Task 10

Discourse type	Documentary
Communicative purpose	Informative
Authentic task type	Transference

Level 6 up

Aim: To transfer information from one media and genre to another.

Preparation: Record a documentary on subject of interest to your learners and suitable for this task.
- Assign (or let learners choose) professional roles (e.g. sociologist, historian, economist) to give focus for listening and production.
- Learners watch (excerpt from) documentary taking notes relevant to 'their' professional interests (according to assigned roles).
Ask learners to:
- Reproduce noted information as written article for newspaper (paper/electronic) *or* as lecture /presentation.
- Exchange articles with other students, or make presentations to class.

Task 11

Discourse type	Documentary
Communicative purpose	Informative
Authentic task type	Transference
Level 4 up	

Aim: To interpret schematically presented information in words.

Preparation: Find 2 different graphs, tables or other graphic representations within a documentary.
- Split the class into 2 groups and set one group (Group A) a task in another room!
- To the second group (Group B), play the first graph and as much of the video preceding it as is necessary to make it comprehensible (or take it from a documentary with which learners are already familiar).
- Pause on the graphic and ask learners to prepare to explain its content and significance. They can make notes, but their explanations should be in the spoken mode.
- Switch off the video when the learners are ready.
- Invite Group A back into the room and ask each person to pair up with a member of Group B.
- Learners from Group B explain the content and significance of the graphic they have seen; their partners ask questions to clarify if necessary, then represent the information graphically (this does not have to be in the same form as the original graphic).
- Repeat the procedure with Group A seeing the second graphical representation.

Task 12

Discourse type	Documentary
Communicative purpose	Informative
Authentic task type	Extraction
Level 3 up	

Aim: To extract data from discourse and reproduce graphically.

Preparation: Video a documentary containing figures, dates and/or statistics e.g. one on sociological trends or a biographical documentary.
- Show (excerpt from) documentary.
Ask learners to:
- Extract factual information (e.g. statistics, dates, stage developments).
- Working alone, reproduce this information graphically (e.g. table/ graph/flow chart).
- Exchange graphics with a partner.
- To test the accuracy of the graph, each learner works from his PARTNER'S graph and presents the information to a third student.

Task 13

Discourse type	television/radio fiction - dramatic
Communicative purpose	Engaging
Authentic task type	Extension
Level 3 up	
Aim: To predict behaviour/events.	

Preparation: Make a video/audio-tape of an excerpt from soap, serial, sitcom etc. which culminates in a dramatic event (argument, accident etc.)
- Show video/hear audio and PAUSE *before* the dramatic event.
- In groups, learners:
 - characterise protagonists, assess situation and predict event.
- write dialogue/screenplay showing their predicted event.
- record or video their scenes (if possible) and show to class *or* read as dialogue/act out.
- Watch/hear event as happens in actual soap/sitcom - compare own versions!

Task 14

Discourse type	television/radio fiction - dialogue/s
Communicative purpose	Engaging
Authentic task type	Analysis
Level 4 up	
Aim: To raise awareness of linguistic/paralinguistic conversational strategies.	

Preparation: Compile a number of video/radio conversations from soaps, sitcoms etc.
- Pre-viewing: Brainstorm outline of structure of a normal conversation and linguistic functions needed for it to ensue.
- Agree function outline on board e.g. *'beginning a conversation, sustaining a conversation, clarifying meaning, commenting, responding, ending a conversation'*

then draw up a 5-column table with the headings *1. function 2. suggestions: linguistic 3. suggestions: paralinguistic 4. authentic examples: linguistic 5. authentic examples: paralinguistic.*
- Learners add some of their own suggestions in columns 2 and 3.
- Watch/hear first conversation and in columns 4 and 5 note down how their outlined functions are effected by the speakers (e.g. commenting: *'Oh?'*, clarifying meaning - leaning forward etc.)
- Compare findings in groups.
- Listen to second/third conversation and add more examples in columns 4 and 5.
- Compare how well linguistic expressions/paralinguistic cues used, effect their functions.
- Discuss any cross-cultural contrasts that arise[10].

Task 15

Discourse type	television/radio fiction - dialogue
Communicative purpose	Engaging
Authentic task type	Response
Level 5 up	
Aim: Recall and reformulation of dialogue.	

Preparation: Find a short section of fictional dialogue from a soap, sitcom, radio/television drama etc. The dialogue should be intelligible and fairly free-standing. Mark short sections of the dialogue that you think the learners may be able to recall from memory.
- Play the whole dialogue and then ask the learners to recall as much as they can about the situation: who/where the speakers were, what they talked about and if they said anything striking.
- Re-play the dialogue stopping *before* the first short section you have assigned for recall. Ask the learners to recall as accurately as they can, the words following the pause. Encourage correct reformulation as well as accurate recall and write the closest suggestions on the board.
- Continue playing dialogue until the next assigned stopping point and repeat.
- Repeat procedure filling out the notes on the board.
- At the end, replay the whole dialogue to help learners consolidate their comprehension of it[11].

Task 16

Discourse type	television fiction (soap, drama etc.)
Communicative purpose	Engaging
Authentic task type	Inferencing
Level 3 up	
Aim: To examine and analyse non-verbal cues.	

Preparation: Choose a short section of a television drama (soap, thriller etc.) from the TC in which there is a lot of non-verbal communication (via gestures, facial expressions etc.)
- Play the section *with the sound down* a number of times as required.
- Tell learners they are to infer the meanings of these non-verbal interactions.
- Working in pairs/groups, learners 'deconstruct' the scene, itemising each significant gesture/facial expression and giving it an interpretation e.g. 'she's frowning = she's confused/angry' etc.
- Ask learners to note which gestures/expressions they have noticed are specific to the TC.
- Learners discuss any differences in their own cultures re. the meanings of these gestures/expressions.
- Mix groups in order to compare ideas.
- Play dialogue *with the sound up* to help confirm ideas.
- In groups or whole class, open general comparative discussion on cultural differences in gestures and expressions.

Task 17

Discourse type	'Star' interview
Communicative purpose	Provocative
Authentic task type	Reaction
Level 5 up	
Aim: To express strong opinions (orally).	

Preparation: Use (whole or section of) of television/radio chat-show interview with a famous personality, known to learners if possible - musician, model, sportsperson, politician etc.
- Show/play interview to learners, warning them they will be asked to 'phone-in' to the chat show to comment on it e.g. to voice opinions, disagreement, complaints, acclaim, sympathy, shock etc.
Ask learners to:
- Identify unfamiliar expressions that require replaying and/or explaining, and discuss these in pairs/groups, consulting teacher/dictionary if necessary.
- Discuss and prepare their comments on the chat show in groups/pairs.
- Stage post-viewing/listening 'phone-in': one learner volunteer to play chat show 'host'.
- 'Callers' phone in with their comments and 'host' fields the calls.
Note: It is useful to have done Task 22 prior to this to prepare for language and convention of phone-ins.

Task 18

Discourse type	'Star' interview
Communicative purpose	Provocative
Authentic task type	Reaction

Level 5 up
Aim: To express strong opinions (written).

Preparation: Use (whole or section of) of television/radio chat-show interview with a famous personality, known to learners if possible - musician, model, sportsperson, politician etc.
- Show/play interview to learners, telling them they will be asked to write an e-mail to the chat-show host to comment on it e.g. to voice opinions, disagreement, complaints, acclaim, sympathy, shock etc.
 - After first/second viewing, give learners time to discuss their reactions and comments in groups.
- Learners write their e-mails (on paper if no computers available) and send to one learner who has volunteered to play chat show 'host' to respond to messages.
- 'Host' replies to e-mails (out of class time may be more practical).
- Correspondence may be continued privately if desired.

Task 19

Discourse type	'Star' interview
Communicative purpose	Provocative
Authentic task type	Inferencing
Level 5 up	
Aim: To interpret non-verbal cues.	

Preparation: Select television interview with a famous personality (known to learners if possible - musician, model, sportsperson, politician etc.)
- Play interviewer's first question (skip greetings etc.). Ask learners to speculate on what the interviewee's response will be. e.g. happy/reluctant to answer, elusive, embarrassed, expansive, manipulative (of the listener's opinions etc).
- Play interviewee's response *with the sound down*. Learners note non-verbal cues and interpret their meanings to support their speculations (e.g. the interviewee smiled = relaxed or embarrassed?) etc. Remind learners that non-verbal cues may differ in different cultures.
- Play interviewee's response *with sound*. Learners confirm/refute their speculations.
- Continue sound down/sound up until reasonable repertoire of non-verbal cues has been built up.
- If desired, extend this to a discussion on cultural similarities and differences in non-verbal signs/cues.

Task 20

Discourse type	Weather forecast
Communicative purpose	Informative
Authentic task type	Reaction
Levels: 2 to 4	

Aim: To infer practical implications of input information for given situations.

Preparation: A set of roles/situations in duplicate. Roles relate to weather-dependent leisure/work activity situations e.g. *You are planning a cycling trip to the West of Ireland, leaving tomorrow. Listen to the weather forecast and think about; gear to take? alter plans (region /day /cancel)?*
- Give pairs of roles to 2 learners sitting separately.
Learners:
- Listen to/view weather forecast.
- Plan/alter plans for activity accordingly.
- Team up with partners and compare any adjustments to their plans.

Task 21

Discourse type	Radio - Current affairs
Communicative purpose	Engaging
Authentic task type	Extension
Level 5 up	
Aim: To practise gist-listening and research into topics in the news.	

Preparation: Choose a short item from a current affairs programme on a topic of interest to your students e.g. social issues in TC, drug/alcohol abuse, youth culture *or* on a TC festival (e.g. In Ireland, St. Patrick's Day) or sport.
- Tell students they are listening for gist only and the aim is to expand what they garner from gist-listening via research on other sources/media.
- Play the item *twice only*.
- Learners combine in groups/pairs to pool what they've heard plus any input from their own knowledge - the subject, the main thrust of the information on this subject etc. (if the majority draw a blank at this stage, replay the excerpt).
- In their groups, learners look at other sources (e.g. the Internet, newspapers), making notes, to fill out information on the subject.
- Learners mix with other groups to compare and pool findings.

Task 22

Discourse type	Radio phone-in
Communicative purpose	Provocative
Authentic task type	Analysis
Level 5 up	
Aim: Analysis of colloquial language. Insight into TC views, values and priorities	

Preparation: Record a free-standing section of a phone-in programme on a provocative topical subject e.g. a social issue - proposed smoking bans, drug-taking in sport, limitations on alcohol advertising etc.

- Tell learners their interest is both in the language used *and* the TC views being voiced.
- Listen once to whole section for gist.
- Learners note *the subject* under discussion.
- Second listening: Learners note *the number of speakers* (including the host), and the *sex, possible age, job* etc. of each.
- Learners pool what they have garnered as a whole class or in groups.
- Learners divide into groups. Assign one section of the dialogue to each group.
- Play sections of the phone-in repeatedly as required to allow learners to note the language used (i.e. semi-dictation).
- Learners discuss and explore language noted (colloquialisms, slang etc.), researching on Internet or in grammars if necessary.
- Each group contribute to a 'language digest' for the programme, noted on the board, on a circulated sheet, or on class Web page bulletin board if available.
- Following this language analysis, turn to content:
- One or more learners focus on each caller (+the host)
- Characterise the views of each speaker towards the subject under discussion e.g. 'he is anti-smoking', consider their level of bias etc.
- Discuss (as whole class/in groups) how typical of the TC, the views expressed by these speakers are.
- Compare with views of people from own culture on the subject under discussion.

Task 23

Discourse type	Radio trailers
Communicative purpose	Provocative
Authentic task type	Inferencing
Level 5 up	
Aim: To infer programme type and speculate on content.	

Preparation: Record a number of trailers for radio programmes on a single tape. Duplicate the tape for the number of groups in the class.
- Give each learner group a tape and ask them to:
- Decide what sort of program each trailer is advertising.
- Speculate what it might be about.
- Decide (on the basis of the above and of their own interests) which programme they would want to listen to, reaching a democratic decision and giving reasons for their choice.
- Each group then announces their choice, with reasons and the class tries to reach a unanimous decision on the basis of this discussion[12].
(This activity can be done with television trailers if there are a number of video players available.)

Task 24

Discourse type	Radio/television station-surfing

Communicative purpose	Provocative
Authentic task type	Inferencing
Level 3 up	
Aim: To contextualise input.	

Preparation: This activity can be done with either a radio or a television.

Pre-listening/viewing, tell the learners what the activity involves; ask them to brainstorm and note as many different types of programme as possible (news, sports, films, documentaries, current affairs, soaps, serials, advertisements and so on).

- Tell the learners they are going to 'surf' to find something they would want to listen to/view.

- (Slowly) tune the radio or surf television stations, allowing learners to hear/view short snippets, long enough for them to contextualise the snippet. This may be approx. 30 seconds, or the time it takes the teacher to do so plus an extra 10 seconds or so. It will also be easier to do with television than with radio.

- After each snippet, pause and ask the learners to speculate about what sort of programme it was - news, sport etc[13]. If necessary (this applies more to radio) ask them to justify their classification.

- If possible, learners might also try to identify different accents (American, British, Irish etc).

- After listening to/viewing a number of stations, ask the learners which one they would now tune to if they had their choice, and why (e.g. because they like this type of programme, because something in the action/discussion caught their interest etc.).

Task 25

Discourse type	Radio/television programme schedule
Communicative purpose	Informative
Authentic task type	Extraction
Level 6 up	
Aim: To extract/analyse cultural indicators from factual information.	

Preparation: Radio/television schedule from newspaper - either photocopied or a selection from different days.

- Brainstorm criteria for cross-cultural comparisons of television/radio schedules e.g. number of channels/stations, commercial or not, hours of broadcasting, classification of programmes (sport, news, current affairs, entertainment etc.), times at which different types of programmes are broadcast, programme length, programmes in different languages or about countries other than the TC, etc.

- Learners draw up a 4-column table (*criterion, TL culture, my culture, peer's culture*).

- Learner pairs/groups:

- Look through television/radio schedule for identified criteria and discuss and note findings.

- Note and compare criteria from own culture then interview other-culture peer for third set of findings.
- Analyse findings as cultural indicators; what do findings reveal about society's priorities, interests, expectations, age/class of audiences, routines, degree of government/commercial control of broadcasting etc[14].

Notes

1   This was demonstrated to me in a memorable instance where I was forced to abandon my attempt to use the videoed news broadcast covering the death of Princess Diana (in August 1997) in class the day after the event, because the learners found it too upsetting.

2   A classic case of this was Winston Churchill's famous 'V' (for victory) sign which embarrassed his hosts on a visit to Greece where the sign has a rather more vulgar significance.

3   For example, Italian television broadcasts its main news programme at 8pm at the time when most Italians have their evening meal, which is frequently taken in front of the television.

4   This idea is from Tomalin 1986: 5.

5   This activity draws on Chandler and Stone 1999: 80.

6   The last two activities based on Chandler and Stone 1999: 84 and 81 respectively.

7   Adapted from Little *et al*. 1989: 42.

8   Adapted from activity suggested by Sean Devitt, ELT Author's conference June 1997.

9   Adapted from Tomalin and Stempleski 1993: 50-1.

10   Based on Tomalin and Stempleski 1993: 106-7.

11   From Duff and Maley 1991: 147-8.

12   Based on Chandler and Stone 1999: 81.

13   Adapted from Chandler and Stone 1999: 80 and 84.

14   Adapted from Tomalin and Stempleski 1993: 53-4.

Chapter Seven:
Newspapers

Newspapers are the most easily available and accessible of the news media - anyone, anywhere can buy a newspaper (foreign language newspapers are today generally available internationally) - and they are less ephemeral than their broadcast counterparts. The informative value of the newspaper, in terms of the quantities of topical and cultural information provided in a single issue, is unparalleled by any other medium. This gives it the potential for *'multiple foci'*; a single newspaper can offer, on the one hand, a 'panoramic view' of the culture, and on the other, it can be used in 'close-up' (e.g. for language study). Such advantages have long been recognised by language teachers for whom newspapers have, until recently (that is, until the advent of the Internet), been basically the default authentic text. Yet newspaper language is also perceived as 'difficult' and this has often been an obstacle to the use of newspapers with lower level learners (this is countered in Section 7.3 'The challenge of newspapers' below).

7.1 Newspapers and Culture

Newspapers are probably the best single source of information about the contemporary culture of a country. Their currency, the breadth of their coverage (from politics to personal problems, from international terrorism to domestic trivia) and the intricacy and cultural-specificity of their terms of reference, all give them enormous potential for exploitation in the language classroom. As with other cultural products that are universal, one productive avenue of exploitation is comparison; in this case, with the Press of the learners' own countries.

The cultural specificity of newspapers is such that they are, in general, instantly identifiable. This is due to a whole range of cues, from the visual - the size of the newspaper, the relative proportions of headlines, text and photographs, use of colour - to other sensory clues such as the texture of the paper and the smell of the newsprint. It is not unreasonable to claim that some of these characteristics betray Press attitudes to its readership which are themselves culture-specific. Compare, for example, the typeset of the French broadsheet *Le Monde*, so tightly-packed and uncompromising, with that of one with an equivalent British readership, *The Times*, which is more accessible and 'reader-friendly'. Contrasts such as this can provoke discussions about the differences between the attitude and relationship of the Press of each country to its audience, differences between the expectations different cultures have of the Press, and so on (see Task 28). This may be linked to discussions about the comparative degree of autonomy the individual newspapers have in various countries. In Britain, for example, seven companies own the 21 national newspapers, down from 11 companies who owned the then 19 papers in 1965 (figures from Reah 1998: 8). Other criteria for comparison might include what is considered headline news on any given day; this will be seen to vary not only from country to country but also, of course, from newspaper to newspaper within one country. These variations might be seen to reflect priorities based on societal values as well as geographical differences. They also reflect different newspapers' attitudes to and interdependency with their readership. Newspapers tend to feed readers what they think they want to read. This is arguably a self-fulfilling exercise, since the newspapers themselves seek to impose their standards and attitudes onto those of their readers through their content and language as well as via graphology and photographic images. The high circulation, in some cultures, of tabloid newspapers which blatantly manipulate their readership (see Section 7.2.1 'Currency and newspaper language' below) suggests that many readers may actually like or need such direction and the feeling of solidarity that it imparts. The popularity of such newspapers, some of which do not even purport to objective reporting, or indeed, to much factual basis at all (e.g. *The Sun, The Sunday Sport, Bild-Zeitung*) may thus be attributed to this type of insecurity. It may also suggest the perception by some sections of these cultures, of news as entertainment, in which case titillation and scandal are clearly far more entertaining than the realities of current affairs.

As with television programming, the content, balance, location and presentation of information in newspapers have some universal features and other, culture-specific features. The amount of advertising in British newspapers, for example, is fairly high, ranging from 31% of *The Guardian*, to 43% of *The Sun* (figures from Reah 1998: 3). In both Britain and Ireland, the proportion of the newspaper that is dedicated to sport is indicative of its readership and hence, arguably, its 'quality'. Yet in Italy, there is at least one major newspaper dedicated entirely to sport, *La Gazzetta dello Sport*. The only Irish equivalents are the two (minor) newspapers covering horse-racing, *The Irish Field* and the *Racing Post*. An emphasis in a country's newspapers on a particular activity or interest (sport, motoring, property, health, gardening, leisure activities and so on) can be very revealing of a culture's priorities, preferences and preoccupations (see Task 29).

Finally, *how* people in different cultures read their newspapers is suggested by their layout. For instance, the front/back summaries of the stories found inside the newspaper - a fairly recent addition in some Irish newspapers (e.g. *The Examiner*) - might suggest that their editors consider their readers too busy or too impatient to scan the newspaper themselves. This might contrast with a less hurried society whose newspapers have front and back pages completely devoid of news and dedicated instead to advertising. This feature, the traces of which can still be seen in at least one Irish newspaper, *The Irish Times*, whose back pages still display only advertisements, might characterise the newspapers of some of the learners' cultures and might provide useful food for discussion.

The foreign newspaper can, finally, provide both a fascinating slant on news from learners' own countries and an exposure of TC attitudes to the learner's culture. Looking at how news from their native countries is reported in the foreign press gives learners both a different perspective on the news itself, and reveals something of the image their native country has abroad. This can broaden learners' perceptions of their own countries, giving them a less subjective view of themselves, as if they were 'looking at themselves in a foreign mirror' (see Task

30). Such an examination of the British Press, and the tabloids in particular, would also expose what may be a peculiarly British representation of, and attitude to foreigners in general. A range of cultural awareness-raising activities can be devised based on such observations. These might involve learners in

- Searching TL newspapers for items about their own countries, comparing them to native language reports and analysing/comparing the images projected;

- Analysing attitudes to their culture displayed in the British/TL press and suggesting possible historical, political or economic reasons for them;

- Tracing how racism becomes increasingly blatant during wars, international economic crises (such as the French blockade of British beef during the BSE crisis of the 1990s) and international sports events such as the World Cup.

To sum up, newspapers, these most traditional of the cultural products to be used in language learning, might be seen as having the most potential in terms of the sheer amounts of language materials they offer. As with other cultural products discussed here, the universality of the genre is helpful to learners as they are familiar with dealing with it in their native context and is also a useful launching pad for analysing subtle differences in the genre from culture to culture.

7.2 Newspapers and Currency

As far as language learning is concerned, currency is at the same time one of the newspaper's greatest assets but also its greatest shortcoming. Newspapers are 'the freshest foods in the language classroom and at the same time those with the shortest shelf-life' (Grundy 1993: 8). While we open today's newspaper with a sense of anticipation, there is nothing so uninspiring as 'yesterday's news'. In the classroom, this can be overcome to some measure by using so-called 'soft' news stories, the items - often human-interest stories - used as fillers by editors. Soft news items are fairly free-standing, they are usually unconnected to topics currently in the news and are thus hard to put a date on - however, they can be of limited interest for this very reason.

Another solution to the problem of providing up-to-date news items, is, of course, the Internet. As with so many other cultural products, today, the newspaper has a parallel existence on the Web. Online newspapers are, however, arguably a distinct genre. Most of them use very different public interfaces than their printed counterparts; as they are no longer competing at the newsstand, the tabloids have abandoned the classic front page blaring headline and full page photo[1]. Online newspapers use a standard hypertext type interface which requires users to click to access the section/article they require. Since space and layout are no longer an issue, articles tend to be longer, and the short news item and human-interest filler story so useful to the language teacher, are redundant. Online newspapers also contain breaking news sections, which means that they have overcome the principle shortcoming of the printed newspaper, i.e. dating. In this respect they now actually overlap with television and radio, making the competition between the two media of the press closer than ever. All of this, of course, gives the online newspaper quite literally a different 'look and feel' from the printed newspaper, one which arguably has affective and sociological implications. The unique texture and smell of the news-printed page, its physical proximity and immediacy, the identifying of reading the newspaper with relaxation - it is an activity often associated with having a cup of tea, coffee or a cigarette, and with domestic settings (the kitchen, living room and so on), all of these are altered when we read the newspaper online. We will in time doubtless condition ourselves to online newspaper reading as we have now to that other form of communication that technology has revolutionised, letter-writing.

All in all, the relationship between the online newspaper, its printed counterpart, and the broadcasting medium it is beginning to approach, is a fascinating one and one which offers great scope in the language classroom as well as elsewhere (e.g. linguistics, sociological and cultural studies). Comparison might range from the micro level, comparing the on- and offline versions of a single news story, to more macro levels, which could compare the focus, bias, balance (both of topics covered and of news reporting), breadth of scope and so on (see Task 7). On the sociological/affective side, some analysis and research into on- and offline newspaper reading habits of different cultures, might well reward learners with insights into their contrasting effects on emotional impact, sociological patterns and so on (see Task 32).

7.2.1 Currency and newspaper language

We now turn to another aspect of the keyword 'currency', the distinctive and ever-evolving *language* peculiar to the newspapers. Learners are, not unreasonably, frequently introduced to newspaper language via the most striking feature of the medium, the news headline. The headline is arguably a discourse type in its own right, indeed, it has been given the label *tabloidese* or *journalese* (Sanderson 1999: 29). Headlines summarise, simplify, dramatise, express and influence opinion with impressive and sometimes inspired concision (think of the tabloid coinage *Gotcha!* for example, which is used for everything from victories in war and sport to the capture of criminals). This feature of headlines is probably a trans-cultural feature known to learners from most cultures, but *how* this is done in each language differs. The study of the newspaper headline might usefully start with graphology - the visual aspect of headlines, their size, layout and their association with images (if any). The potential for analysis of this aspect alone shows that the complexity of the discourse type does not preclude its use with lower level learners (see Section 7.3 'The challenge of newspapers' below).

The headline uses a variety of linguistic, syntactic and stylistic devices to realise the two basic principles by which it is constrained, concision and impact. At higher levels of language proficiency, research into how these are achieved can be very rewarding (see Task 2). The following summary of the main devices used in headlines may serve as a checklist for student research as well as a guide for the teacher.

The headline - summary of linguistic, syntactic and stylistic devices

The use of the present continuous (-ing) and infinitive forms of the verb to refer to future events ('Women facing poverty in old age'[2] 'Irishman to assess Danube pollution'[3]);

The passive represented by the past participle only ('15 killed in boat accident'[4]);

The predilection for the simple present tense to give immediacy ('Sniper kills again at petrol station'[5]);

The eschewing of phrasal/polysyllabic verbs in favour of short, and if possible monosyllabic ones (e.g. *rap* in preference to *tell off* or *reprimand*);

The use of emotively weighted nouns (e.g. *sleaze, slump*) which integrate an adjectival function;

The use of linguistic devices such as alliteration, assonance, rhyme, polysemy (e.g. 'Butter battle spreads') and puns using homophones *('Dr. Spuhler will maintain Swiss role')* and homonyms ('Women who smoke have lighter children'[6]);

The exclusion of grammatical words (e.g. determiners, auxiliary verbs) e.g. 'Whites stripped of citizenship'[7];

The use of words that class-shift (most commonly, in headlines, words that can operate as verbs and nouns, e.g. *chase, split, spill, axe*);

The use of 'top-heavy' noun phrases as a form of shorthand ('Railtrack chiefs' booze bash'[8]);

The exploitation of phonological features to achieve impact (as, for example, in the headline above);

Intertextuality (the basing of a new text on one that is culturally familiar). E.g. 'Explorer comes in from the cold'[9], which makes reference to the Le Carré novel/film *The Spy who came in from the cold*[10].

What learners might also become aware of in studying the language of newspaper headlines is that such features are entirely peculiar to this discourse type, they bear little resemblance to the language people use in real life (Sanderson 1999: 30). 'Tabloidese' is a discourse type that has developed not only out of the need of headline writers for concision and effect, but also out of the more insidious intent to pass value judgements, to influence, to prejudice, and even to mislead, as a list of lexis typical of one of these features - verb-noun class-shifting - reveals: rap,

Designing Authenticity into Language Learning Materials

snub, slam, probe, dash, blast, hit, dump, crack, spiral, vow, grass, rat, butcher, axe (drawn from Reah 1998: 16-17 and Sanderson 1993: 29-30). While this list is instantly identifiable to the native speaker as tabloidese, the significance of the loaded nature of this type of language might elude NNSs unless carefully analysed both linguistically and within its socio-cultural context. For example, in a headline such as 'TSB to axe 440 jobs'[11], the use of the verb axe, with its connotations of violence and suddenness, acts as an implicit criticism of the company's policy. One way to help learners deal with this feature of the headline might be to point out that the short, weighted and often unusual word used in the headline is usually given a more common and often more neutral synonym or paraphrase in the body of the article12 (see Task 4).

One of the linguistic devices to cause most confusion to NNSs is probably the exclusion of grammatical words. Indeed, this is a device which sometimes creates ambiguity for NSs (Reah quotes a famous Second World War headline '8th Army push bottles up Germans', 1998: 19). Speakers of languages that do not have articles (e.g. Japanese, Hebrew) may need to have attention drawn to this feature, perhaps by way of an activity in which they are asked to replace the omitted articles. The strategy of weighting noun-phrases, which can result in very convoluted phrases, might likewise be dealt with by asking learners to unpack and expand them. The five-word noun phrase in the headline 'Bandit car chase police instructor fined $750 after death of nurse' (from Reah 1998: 20), for example, might prove an interesting challenge.

To turn from the discourse type of the news headline to that of the news story itself, in their structure at least, news stories can be seen to follow a fairly classic narrative structure. The parallel between the narrative structure identified by William Labov in his study of the language of the young New York black community (1997) and that of the typical news story is noted by Reah (1998: 106-7). The format is fairly universal - narratives and news stories both start with a summary or abstract, then give orientation details (when, where, who, what) and only then detail the sequence of events. The narrative concludes with a 'coda' (in newspaper articles, often a comment from one of the participants in the events or from the journalist). There are a number of strategies which are used to 'punctuate' the news story narrative, to add comment and emotional weight, and to encourage the reader to keep reading. One is the use (mainly by the tabloids) of single-word subheadings known as *crossheads* (e.g. 'Amazed', 'Immediately', 'Surreal'[13]). Another is the breaking up of the text with brief quotes, in large bold type, from the protagonists of the story (e.g. 'Carrying the pain and scars'[14]). The familiarity of this format/features, from newspaper reading in their own languages, should ease the learners into the foreign language news story. The narrative structure lends itself to authentic tasks such as practising the typical NS strategy of reading only the abstract/summary in detail, then skimming over the body of the article for a few additional details and finally 'homing in' on the summary or coda at the end. The use of crossheads and inserted quotes can also be exploited by getting students to emulate the way in which native speakers tend to use them; to find the reference of the crosshead (in the article mentioned above, for example, *who* was 'amazed', and *by what*?), or the speaker and reference of the quote (*who* was 'Carrying the pain and scars' in the article mentioned above, and *from what?*) (see Task 13).

While familiarity with an objective feature like the structure of news articles will make newspapers more accessible to learners on one level, the problem of the subjectivity of the language of newspapers remains. British tabloids ('the always hysterical British press' as the American journalist Randy Shilts calls them (1993)) are notorious for their repertoire of sensational and subjective language and their manipulating strategies. The choice of exaggerated vocabulary is, of course, a trademark of the tabloids; no one is ever upset, they are *distraught*; no one is ever surprised but *stunned* or *shocked*, bad luck becomes labelled a *curse*, and the power of words like *horror* ('Crash horror') and *terror* (which has now become shorthand for 'terrorism' or 'terrorist') has become diluted through overuse. In the West at least, an accepted characteristic of (especially tabloid) newspapers is manipulation of the opinions of the readers they purport to represent. They do this not only via the traditional editorial which addresses the reader directly ('The Sun says', 'The Express - Opinion') but by taking sides - a classic example in Britain is the reporting of the breakdown of the Prince and Princess of Wales' marriage by the British press in the mid-1990s. Tabloid newspapers also influence opinion by 'coercing' readers into artificially created readership groups (Reah 1998: 35-40) with headlines like 'Queen snubs 102,625 Daily Mirror readers'[15]. This is classically done through the use of the first-person plural possessive in headlines such as 'Shameful snub to our war heroes'[16] and references to *our lads* (usually footballers or soldiers).

One slightly less complicated feature of the discourse of newspapers (and of the broadcast media) and which can be useful to learners, is the existence of a large group of fairly stable collocations, pairings, clichés and idiomatic expressions that commonly reoccur in news reporting. Some examples of such collocations might include the choice of verb to describe confrontations between *police, protesters* and *demonstrators*, which is invariably *clash*[17]; clichéd expressions such as *tragic accident*; pairings such as *safe and well* and often-repeated expressions such as 'There are no reports of any injuries'. Familiarisation with such collocations can speed up comprehension, for they then come to be treated as a single unit.

7.2.2 Newspapers and affect

As with the other cultural products covered here, a key benefit of using authentic newspaper texts with language learners is the potential of affective involvement with these texts, dealing as they do with real people and real situations in the world we share. Admittedly, newspapers are a less obviously emotive medium than their broadcasting counterparts, since they do not have the advantage of moving images, musical accompaniment or the sound of the human voice. But affect is, of course, an internal factor that does not necessarily correlate with external influences and the use of newspaper texts for language learning can be seen to involve affect in a number of main ways.

First of all, in an era in which, thanks to communications technologies, we feel personal involvement with events even in distant parts, the news can often be of intense interest to us even if it is not of immediate personal relevance (as the boosts in newspaper sales after natural disasters, terrorist attacks and so on, reveal). Information might well, on the other hand, be of strong personal relevance and interest to learners. This might apply particularly to ESL learners living in the TL society, but can also apply to EFL learners reading material about their own countries seen from the TC perspective (see Task 30). Alternatively, a news item might be on a subject of universal interest (e.g. death, violence, sex, health, birth, children). In the classroom situation, personal response to news items can be stimulated via a range of activities. These might include reading (especially reading aloud), responding to and discussing what has been read, adding one's own knowledge of the events, relating the events or repercussions of them to oneself, and so on. These are notably strategies which are associated with authentic (native speaker) ways of interacting with newspapers (Grundy 1993: 8) (see also Section 7.3 'The challenge of newspapers' below).

The second affective factor relevant to newspaper reading is motivation. Particularly for the integratively motivated learner, TC newspapers can offer 'a short-cut to acculturation' (Grundy 1993: 9). Acculturation implies familiarisation and empathy with what people from the TC like and what they fear, with what they hold cheap and what they hold dear, with what makes them angry and with what makes them laugh. As was pointed out earlier (Section 7.1), an enormous range of cultural information can be garnered from newspapers, ranging from the obvious practical information (political and educational systems, crime, health, sports, leisure activities, television programs) to the subtlety of the cultural values, priorities and attitudes underpinning the society, which can be revealed through analysis of the practical aspects. Carefully analysed, the TC newspaper in a sense represents the TC in microcosm and integratively inclined learners can be guided to treat it as such (see Tasks 28 and 29).

Using newspapers in the classroom can be a source of another sort of motivation, the 'chicken and egg' motivation that stems from a sense of achievement at successfully confronting a challenge. Newspaper texts are perceived as being linguistically complex and culture-specific, as being one of the 'last hurdles' to proficiency in the language. If strategies for coping with them are successfully acquired, this can be highly motivating and particularly encouraging for lower level learners (see Section 7.3 'The challenge of newspapers' below).

An aspect probably more important to the use of newspapers than of other printed authentic texts in the classroom, and one that tends to be ignored by language teachers, is the physical quality of the materials learners are being asked to react to. As has been noted above, newspapers rely heavily for their impact on appearance - on the size of their headlines, the quality of their photographs (which have only recently graduated from black and white to colour in most newspapers), the layout of pages, and so on. When these are compromised, as they tend to be through repeated photocopying and by cutting and pasting, the impact of the news item/s is weakened, losing much of the *raison d'être* of using news material in the classroom. Working with tired photocopies that are hard to read (and that possibly suggest that the teacher has reused the material many times!) can be uninspiring and demotivating, forfeiting two key affective aspects of using these authentic materials for learning - enjoyment and motivation.

7.3 The Challenge of Newspapers

The above section has drawn attention to the unique qualities of the language of newspapers, and has pointed out the often dense and enigmatic nature of the language of headlines in particular. Yet to eschew the use of newspapers with lower level learners because the language is not 'straightforward' is to deprive them of material that can be of the most genuine relevance and interest to, and motivation for them (see above). As with other cultural products, converting perceived difficulty into a positive challenge, is largely a matter of the tasks devised. What is more, in dealing with newspaper articles, some of the simplest tasks are also the most authentic. Using an article as a stimulus for thought and discussion, for example, is a natural and real-life activity, far more authentic than the traditional language teaching practice of using it as a text for detailed decoding and comprehension. It does not require total word-by-word comprehension since in an open (or group) discussion, people pool their understanding of the text and their own prior knowledge of the event, and the discussion develops according to the level, pace and interest of the learner group (see, for example, Task 9). Other tasks feasible for lower level learners involve transferring the strategies they will have devised for reading newspapers in their L1. These might include getting gist from headlines, reading only the first sentences of paragraphs, scanning for key words, using crossheads and so on to get the gist of an article, and using one's prior knowledge of the news to help comprehension. As was pointed out in Chapter 3 Section 3.3 'Challenge', the practice of skimming for items that catch our interest (and the ability to happily ignore what is not immediately interesting or is unclear), is an L1 strategy which learners should be encouraged to transfer to the L2.

Scanning on a macro level, i.e. of the whole newspaper, is likewise a very useful NS strategy that learners of all levels can practise. Everyone at sometime has found themselves looking rapidly through a newspaper for a particular news items - for example for a follow-up story to a previous day's, for an article previously read or started, or for a news snippet heard on the radio, television or from an acquaintance, and about which they want to know more (see Task 31).

Another authentic approach to making news material accessible to learners is to use the pedagogical equivalent of 'blanket coverage' of a particular news story. This might start with a brainstorming session to elicit what the learners already know about the story. This could be followed up by looking at a number of different versions of the same story taken from different newspapers (possibly including online newspapers) and might include coverage of the story on the radio or television news (see Task 15). In this way, learners build up, use and become familiar with a set of vocabulary for a particular story, just as NSs do with a major ongoing news event in which new vocabulary emerges and then becomes part of the language (examples from the 2001 bombing of New York's Twin Towers, for example, would include such terms as *Ground Zero* and *9/11*).

Some of the classic, simple, pedagogical activities done with newspapers are also very authentic. One such is looking at headlines alone and speculating on their meaning and on the content of the article they precede. Headlines (particularly those of the tabloids) are created to be eye-catching and intriguing; at the most basic level, they are intended to sell the newspaper. This sets up a sense of anticipation and curiosity in the mind of the NS reader (for instance, a headline such as 'Beer Ad Rap'[18] would raise questions of *what* was done to *which* beer ad, *who* did it and *why*). This 'suspense' can be exploited and simulated in the pedagogical task of guessing meanings of headlines and the stories they might encapsulate (see Task 2). Another simple, authentic way of approaching a news story - available to items that include pictures - is via this accompanying photo. Without undue stress on the old maxim of a picture telling a thousand words, proof of the strength of the news photo is that, particularly in the tabloids, it is often left to speak for itself or is accompanied by a single word headline (that above-mentioned favourite of the tabloids *Gotcha!* is often used in this way[19]). In the language classroom, pictures can be used as prompts for learner knowledge ('what do you know about the story behind this photo?'), for reaction ('how does this photo make you feel?') and/or as a trigger for discussion ('should the press publish photos of vehicle crashes, tragedies, terror attacks, bereaved people?'). The authenticity of such activities is, once again, that they emulate genuine NS reactions to photos in the press and that in their authenticity, they can invoke real, emotive reactions which can be channelled towards language acquisition (see Task 5).

7.4 Newspapers for Language Learning: Summary and Principles

What has been stressed here is, first of all, that the sheer quantity and variety of TC information available in newspapers means that newspapers constitute a 'microcosm' of the target culture. It has been pointed out that newspaper language is an ever-evolving variety of language, language which is in many cases specific to the genre. It has its own neologisms spawned by new phenomena (e.g. *9/11*), its own priorities (such as concision and impact) and even its own grammar (as in the language of newspaper headlines). Finally, it has been shown that newspapers can be used to challenge even lower level learners via activities which are authentic and which help develop and hone valuable and transferable strategies for dealing with 'difficult' texts.

Principles for the use of newspapers for language learning

• Use *'multiple foci'* with newspapers: use close-ups (e.g. for language and for culture study) and panoramic views (e.g. for culture study/cross-cultural comparison).

• Exploit the cultural specificity of newspapers e.g. their *physical features* (e.g.

typography, use of images, colour), their range and balance of *content*, their (attitudes to) *readership* etc.

• Respect *the headline* as a unique and dense discourse type and exploit as such.

• Exploit the universality of the genre, e.g. the tabloid-broadsheet divide, the breakdown of content (news, sport, human interest, letters etc.), and the *narrative structure* of the news story.

• Beware *dating*! Refresh news article stock very regularly / use soft news stories / source material from online newspapers.

• Make use of the parallel medium, the *online newspaper*; as a resource for texts, and to compare and contrast the two media

• Practise and exploit strategies for newspaper-reading from the L1 - scanning, skimming, gist-reading and so on.

Further reading
Grundy, P. 1993. Newspapers, Oxford: Oxford University Press.

Reah, D. 1998. The Language of Newspapers, London: Routledge.

Sanderson, P. 1999. *Using Newspapers in the Classroom*, Cambridge: Cambridge University Press.

7.5 The Tasks

Task 1

Discourse type	Mastheads (names of newspapers)
Communicative purpose	Persuasive
Authentic task typology	Reaction
Level 3 up	
Aim: To infer newspaper type from its masthead.	

Preparation: Trim mastheads from a wide selection of newspapers, national, local, regional, daily and weekly.
- Put mastheads on a large table so learners can sift through them.
- Ask learners to analyse the meanings of mastheads e.g. *The Examiner, the Inpedendent.*
- Ask learners to speculate about each newspaper. Is it;
- A national, local, regional, daily or weekly paper.
- A broadsheet or tabloid

- What type of information might each newspaper contain (e.g. local information, TV schedules, entertainment listings, sports, business etc.)
- Ask learners to say which of the newspapers they would prefer to read and why.
- Provide newspapers from which mastheads has been cut and ask learners to match them up in order to confirm their ideas[20].

Task 2

Discourse type	Headlines (paper/electronic)
Communicative purpose	Provocative
Authentic task typology	Analysis
Level 6 up	
Aim: To analyse how headlines achieve impact.	

Preparation: *Stage 1*: Trim some headlines from news stories and mount the headlines on a poster.
- In groups, learners examine headlines, analyse and draw up some generalisations on how impact of headline is achieved (linguistic and typographical) e.g. via
- Word-play/puns
- Emotive or neutral language
- Register (level of formality, ranging from slang to specialised language - legal, technical etc.)
-Word-length
- Tenses used (e.g. present tense for immediacy)
- Font size and layout
Preparation: *Stage 2*: Trim the headlines from some (other) news stories.
- Give the headline-less stories to learners, who work in pairs/groups and
- Use strategies identified in *Stage 1* above to write headlines for these stories (write headlines on a separate sheet).
- Each group then gives this sheet of headlines and the stories to the other groups in turn who try to match them up.

Task 3

Discourse type	Headlines (paper/electronic)
Communicative purpose	Provocative
Authentic task typology	Inferencing
Level 6 up	
Aim: To interpret news headlines, make inferences and deploy own knowledge.	

Preparation: Trim the headlines from some news stories.
- In pairs/small groups, learners look at the headlines alone and infer what the story it heads may be about, by interpreting language and by linking to own knowledge of current affairs.
- Each group/pair:

- Chooses ONE headline whose story they feel they can prepare.
- Prepares mind-map of language/concepts to go with the chosen headline.
- Uses these prompts to write a short news story to go with the chosen headline.
- Exchanges headline and invented news story with another group.
- Each group assess the feasibility of other group's invented story.
- Give actual stories, without headlines so learners have to identify the story matching 'their' headline.
- Learners then compare 'their' story to the real one.

Task 4

Discourse type	Headlines
Communicative purpose	Provocative
Authentic task typology	Analysis
Level 4 up	
Aim: To analyse and familiarise learners with *tabloidese* (see below).	

Preparation: Select and copy a number of articles which use tabloidese in the *headline* and a more common *synonym* in the body of article.
- With whole class, introduce the concept of tabloidese - use of short, sensational words in headlines to grab interest, save space etc.
- Ask learners to look at each headline and article in turn. For each, underline the tabloidese word in the headline and its matching synonym in the article.
- Replace the synonym in the headline and see if helps comprehension of headline.
- Consider the change in impact/meaning of the headline.
- Consider whether the headline is an exaggeration and possibly a distortion of the facts.
- Discuss reasons for tabloidese words - brevity, sensationalism, impact.
- Compare the phenomenon in own cultures[21].

Task 5

Discourse type	Newspaper photographs
Communicative purpose	Engaging/provocative
Authentic task typology	Inferencing
Level 2 up	
Aim: To draw inferences and stimulate discussion based on newspaper photographs.	

Preparation: Cut out one or a number of striking photographs from newspapers.
- Present each photo in turn to the class (use the originals if a single copy will be visible to the whole class - if not, duplicate the photo as closely as possible). For each photo:
- Elicit what the learners know about the story behind the photo (use - Who...? What...? Where...? etc.)

- (If applicable) ask learners to interpret the emotions of the *people* figuring in the photo - distressed, happy, embarrassed etc.
- Elicit learners' own emotive reactions to the photo ('how does this photo make you feel?')
- Lead on to discussion of ethics - should the press publish controversial photos (is it fair on the people/events they show or on the newspaper readers?)
- Learners compare the ethics of the Press in this regard in their own cultures.

Task 6

Discourse type	News item/s - events
Communicative purpose	Informative
Authentic task typology	Transference
Level 5 up	
Aim: To extract factual information and transfer to another discourse type.	

Preparation: Select a number of newspaper/magazine items featuring factual information e.g. sequence of events, process, statistics.
Learners work in pairs/groups. Give each (or allow to choose) a different article and ask them to;
- Identify the type of factual information (e.g. sequence of events, process, statistics).
- Decide appropriate graphical representation (e.g. flow chart, graph, table).
- Extract the factual information and represent in selected graphical form.
- Team up with member of another group and synthesise and present the information in their article working from their graphical representation alone.

Task 7

Discourse type	News item - events
Communicative purpose	Informative
Authentic task typology	Transference
Level 5 up	
Aim: To compare versions of news item in a printed newspaper and its online counterpart.	

Preparation: Select a news item which occurs in a newspaper's printed and online counterpart. Copy the printed version and if possible allow learners to access the online version. If there is no computer access, print and copy the online version. Working individually or in pairs, learners;
- Compare the two items using criteria such as the headline (same?), length, information contained, language, level of sensationalism, overall impact.
- Combine in groups and compare findings.
- Consider the effect of the two media on the overall impact of the story; which have more impact, printed newspapers or their online versions?

- Discuss personal preferences for newspaper reading (print or online).

Task 8

Discourse type	News item - events
Communicative purpose	Informative
Authentic task typology	Inferencing
Level 4 up	
Aim: To infer semantic connections and reconstruct a piece of written discourse.	

Preparation: Extract words/phrases from a news item and put on (4) transparencies according to POS, e.g. *nouns, verbs, adjectives, adverbs*.
- Tell learners they are to work individually or in pairs/groups to reconstruct a news story.
- Present Transparency 1: *nouns*.
- Learners write a first draft of the story inferred from and using these words.
- Present Transparency 2: *verbs*.
- Learners revise and add to the story to include these new words.
- Repeat with all transparencies.
- After they have seen all the transparencies and completed their final drafts, groups compare their stories and vote for most feasible one.
- Show the learners the real story for comparison with their invented ones[22].

Task 9

Discourse type	News item - events
Communicative purpose	Informative
Authentic task typology	Inferencing
Level 3 up	
Aim: Personal interpretation of news events.	

- Individually, learners scan selection of page/s *or* full newspaper, classifying stories as 'good news' and 'bad news'.
- Pair up and compare to partner's choice: discuss similarities/differences[23].

Task 10

Discourse type	News item/s - human interest
Communicative purpose	Engaging
Authentic task typology	Extension
Level 5 up	
Aim: To engage with items in the news by interacting with them.	

Preparation: Select and annotate a number of news articles with 'editor's comments' e.g. 'add something here!' 'rewrite for more/less educated readers' 'add human interest!' 'too long - cut!' 'sensationalize!' , possibly supply tape/video news recording to write up as newspaper article[24].

- Give these to learners (alone/in pairs) at random for requisite editing, or allow them to choose.
- On completion, they return them to teacher-'editor' (or elect student-'editor') for comment *or*
- Hold a meeting at which the edited items are circulated for comment.

Task 11

Discourse type	News item/s - human interest
Communicative purpose	Engaging
Authentic task typology	Extension
Level 6 up	
Aim: To establish, encourage and involve learners in newspaper-reading habit.	

Preparation: This activity is initially prepared by the learners themselves out of class time. Ask them to work individually or in pairs/groups to:
- Select one ongoing theme/story/issue in the news and trace it over period of time, by collecting cuttings (paper/electronic) or taking notes.
- (In class time) analyse and synthesise their collection/notes and prepare to present them linked with their own comments / interpretations / predictions.
- Make their presentations to the rest of the class[25].

Task 12

Discourse type	News item/s - human interest
Communicative purpose	Engaging
Authentic task typology	Extension
Level 5 up	
Aim: To engage with news stories from the TC.	

Preparation: Find a number of human interest stories (and/or ask learners to find and bring in). Mount each of these at the top of a large sheet of paper and lay them out on desks around the classroom.
- Ask learners to circulate and look at the each of the stories, and to write questions, comments, predictions, continuations of the stories on the sheet[26]. Learners may also check and add notes on any unfamiliar or difficult expressions/vocabulary in the stories.
- At the end, discuss which story/ies was/were most 'productive' and why.

Task 13

Discourse type	News item/s - human interest

Communicative purpose	Engaging
Authentic task typology	Analysis
Level 5 up	
Aim: To analyse narrative structure of news stories.	

Preparation: Choose and copy one or a selection of human interest stories from the tabloids (articles should use *crossheads* - see below).
- Brainstorm concept of narrative structure - what is a typical structure of a news article? (Learners may not come up with all of these initially but will probably recognise them as they do their analysis of the article):
- Summary at beginning
- Summary of details: when, where, who, what
- Sequence of events in detail
- Ending - summary, or personal 'last word' from one of protagonists of story or from the journalist.
- Use of short, sensational, often single-word subheadings (crossheads).
In groups, learners;
- Examine one article in detail, identifying and marking its narrative structure as analysed in the brainstorming session.
- Look at the crossheads used: note how they are sensationalised summaries of the sections they head.
- Look for strategy of breaking up the text with quotes (in large bold type) from protagonists of the story or from the journalist.
- Consider how this typical narrative structure speeds up newspaper reading (for a short summary, we read only the first paragraph, we can trace the progress of the story via the crossheads etc.).

Task 14

Discourse type	News item - report
Communicative purpose	Informative
Authentic task typology	Transference
Level 6 up	
Aim: To infer questions and switch discourse types.	

Preparation: Choose a newspaper/magazine article that reports the findings of a survey.
With whole class, brainstorm principles of writing questionnaires e.g. question types (yes/no questions, multiple choice questions, open questions), writing non-leading questions etc. and give examples.
Learners:
- Deconstruct article to infer and write the original survey questions.
- Carry out 'their' survey and write up their own results as a news article, using the original article as a model if required[27].

Task 15

Discourse type	News items - selection
Communicative purpose	Informative
Authentic task typology	Analysis
Level 5 up	

Aim: Language development through 'blanket coverage' of a news story.

Preparation: Find a news story of interest to your students that is covered in a number of newspapers (including online newspapers). Cut out and copy the articles.
- Introduce the story via a (descriptive) headline selected from the articles.
- Brainstorm what the students already know about the story.
- Give learners the set of articles and ask them to work in pairs/groups to:
 - Compare the facts in the articles and extrapolate and write (in note form) their own 'best-guessed' version of the facts/events.
- Underline words, terms, expressions or syntax that the articles use in common, and identify any terms that are central to the story.
- Underline and link synonyms used in the articles.
- Compile a vocabulary list for the story (words, terms, syntax), listing items on the board, or on class Web page bulletin board if available.
- Groups/pairs compare and justify their own versions of the events.
Explain the pedagogical rationale for this type of 'blanket coverage' - familiarisation with (new), topical vocabulary and language use.

Task 16

Discourse type	News item/s - opinion
Communicative purpose	Provocative
Authentic task typology	Analysis
Level 6 up	

Aim: To identify subjective/emotive language.

Preparation: Make 2/3 photocopied montages of articles that betray bias, on broadsheet-sized pages.
- Give one page to each learner and ask them to cross out the most 'biased' (a) word (b) headline (c) story on the page and to write no. 1 next to each.
- Exchange with another learner for another montage and repeat (write no. 2), and so on.
- Group learners with the same page and compare what has been crossed out, in what order, and why.
Possible extension: Re-write the stories to make them less offensive[28].

Task 17

Discourse type	News item/s - opinion
Communicative purpose	Provocative

Authentic task typology	Inferencing
Level 5 up	
Aim: To extract 'core' of message and transfer to another medium.	

Preparation: Select a number of article/s that have an overt message.
- Learners work in pairs/groups, each on a different article.
- Infer 'core' of message and think in terms of reproducing it as a *cartoon*.
- Draw the cartoon.
- Show the cartoon to other groups/class, clarifying the message and (if appropriate) the serious point behind it.

Task 18

Discourse type	News item - TC
Communicative purpose	Engaging
Authentic task typology	Transference
Level 6 up	
Aim: To raise awareness of (relativity of) culture-specific issues.	

Preparation: Select (or ask learners to select) an article describing a situation specific to, or common in the culture (e.g. for Ireland, these might include alcohol abuse, gender-related conflicts, educational issues, religious issues, the environment, weather-related situations e.g. flooding).
- Learners:
- Read article quickly for gist and main points.
- Discuss in multi-cultural groups; each learner relate the situation to own culture: is this situation relevant to own culture? Would it be an issue in own culture? What degree of importance would be attributed to it? Would participants in situation react/act in same way? What different reactions might there be? What would be a comparable situation in own culture?

Task 19

Discourse type	Multiple reportings
Communicative purpose	Informative
Authentic task typology	Analysis
Level 6 up	
Aim: To identify subjective/emotive language, to challenge objectivity of news reporting; to raise awareness of interpretability of facts.	

Preparation: Find the same story reported in different newspapers/media (printed/online newspaper, radio, television). Prepare and copy an 8-column table for noting key details of news story e.g. *who? when? where? why? what? how many? how much?* + column for *associated subjective language*
- Learners work in groups:

- Read/listen to/view/ ONE version of the news story, noting key details on the table.
- Discuss /compare their version of the story with that of other groups and
- Identify subjective language that has contributed to differences in the stories.
- Relate these differences to the news medium and the intended reader-/listener-ship.
- Hypothesise as to which media's version is the most accurate.

Task 20

Discourse type	Feature article/s
Communicative purpose	Provocative
Authentic task typology	Analysis
Level 6 up	
Aim: To identify subjective/emotive language.	

Preparation: Use a news article presenting opinion e.g. editorial, feature article, journalist's column.
- Learners:
- Underline expressions or specific lexical choices which reveals the writer's attitude to the subject[29].
- Rewrite using more neutral alternatives.

Task 21

Discourse type	Letters to editor
Communicative purpose	Provocative
Authentic task typology	Analysis
Level 6 up	
Aim: To raise awareness of subjective use of language in the journalistic genre.	

Preparation: A number of 'letters to the editor' pages from a selection of current newspapers *or* a selection of current letters compiled from a number of newspapers and mounted on one page
- Learners scan pages and identify the most opinionated/biased letters.
Working in pairs/groups on these selected letters only, learners analyse:
- Expressions used to state opinions e.g. *'In my view, as far as I am concerned'*
-Use of language that is:
Emotive (e.g. *'tragic' 'heart-warming'*)
Subjective (e.g. *'brave' 'heroic')*
Biased
Working from ALL the letters, learners note:
- Usual openings/closings of letters
- Possible to refer to this 'corpus' for other letter-writing tasks (see Tasks 22 and 23).

Task 22

Discourse type	Letters to editor
Communicative purpose	Provocative
Authentic task typology	Response
Level 5 up	
Aim: To produce a response consistent with discourse type.	

Preparation: A number of 'letters to the editor' pages from a selection of current newspapers *or* a selection of current letters compiled from a number of newspapers and mounted on one page
- Working in groups or individually, learners scan the 'letters to the editor' page and identify a letter they would like to respond to (because they are interested in the topic, incensed by the letter etc).
- Working in groups or individually, and using the original as a model for letter-writing conventions, learners write a response to their chosen letter.
- Exchange letters with other groups/individuals for proof-reading (grammar, lexis, register, greeting/closing, politeness etc).
- Encourage learners to actually send their letters (e.g. via e-mail) if the issue is still current.
Note: it is useful to have done Task 21 prior to this.

Task 23

Discourse type	News item/s - opinion
Communicative purpose	Provocative
Authentic task typology	Response
Level 6 up	
Aim: To express written, personal/professional response to article.	

Preparation: Select (or ask learners to select) a number of 'provocative' feature articles/columns. Cut out and copy some samples of 'letters to the editor' for guidelines re. length, structure, register etc.
- Working individually/in pairs, learners:
- Choose an article they would like to respond to.
- Identify (underline /note) the points requiring response (e.g. because they are factually incorrect, use subjective, biased language etc.)
- Looking at the samples of letters to the editor for guidelines, write a letter to the editor (on paper/e-mail) giving responses and drawing attention to the identified points in the article.
- Learners circulate showing others the article and their letter for feedback.
- If the article commented on is from a recent newspaper, learners can actually send their letters/e-mails if they wish!
Note: it is useful to have done Task 21 prior to this.

Task 24

Discourse type	Letters to editor
Communicative purpose	Provocative
Authentic task typology	Inferencing
Level 6 up	
Aim: To raise awareness of 'personal' concerns of target society.	

Preparation: A selection of 'letters to the editor' pages from a cross-section of current newspapers.
- Learners scan letters to (a) infer a set of current concerns of target society (b) classify letters accordingly. Concerns identified (for Ireland/Britain) might include:
- The environment (ecology, transport, pollution, smoking)
- The economy (employment, incomes, prices, taxes)
- Crime (violence, abuse)
- Entrenched political problems (e.g. Northern Ireland)
- Racism
- Religious issues
- Education
- Entertainment
- Sports
- Learners work in multi-cultural groups or individually and decide how relevant these concerns are to their own culture, adding any own-culture concerns.
- As a whole class, compare the concerns identified in the TC list with those of learners' own societies and draw up a comparative ranking of importance.

Task 25

Discourse type	'Agony' column
Communicative purpose	Engaging
Authentic task typology	Analysis
Level 5 up	
Aim: To raise awareness of language used to offer advice etc.(written mode).	

Preparation: A number of 'agony column' letters pages from a selection of newspapers/ magazines.
- Working individually or in pairs, learners scan letters to identify *functions of language* characteristic to the genre.
- List these functions in Column 1 of a 2-columned table. Functions of language identified might include:
- Seeking advice
- Offering advice
- Criticising
- Reprimanding
- Expressing opinion

- Encouraging
- Working in pairs, learners identify and classify language expressions serving these functions and note these in the appropriate row in the table.
Note: This 'corpus' might be used for other letter-writing tasks, Tasks 22, 23, 27.

Task 26

Discourse type	'Agony' column
Communicative purpose	Engaging
Authentic task typology	Response
Level 5 up	

Aim: Raise awareness of 'personal' values/ priorities of target society as represented in 'agony columns'.

Preparation: A number of agony column letter pages from a selection of newspapers/ magazines.
- Allocate the letters/replies among the learners (or allow them to choose).
- Working in multi-cultural pairs/groups, learners read their selection of letters and assess the replies to them. Ask them to:
- Say whether they agree/disagree with the reply/advice given.
- Consider what the response implies about the values/priorities of the society (e.g. the family unit, social equality, image/ 'face').
- Speculate on the reply to such a letter in their own society.
- As a whole class, discuss inter-cultural variations in learners' assessments of 'agony' letter replies.

Task 27

Discourse type	'Agony' column
Communicative purpose	Engaging
Authentic task typology	Response
Level 5 up	

Aim: Raise awareness of cross-cultural differences in value-judgements and composition of reply to an 'agony column' letter.

Preparation: Compile and copy a selection of 'agony column' letters and remove the replies.
- Learners get into multi-cultural pairs (if possible); each pair chooses ONE letter.
- Learners work individually to analyse their letter in detail (checking any unfamiliar expressions with peers/teacher/dictionary or corpus) and compose a reply to it.
- Pairs compare their replies to the letter and identify any cross-cultural differences.
- Pairs team up with others to compare cross-cultural differences in replies to problem letters.

- Groups discuss cross-cultural variations in values and attitudes that these differences might indicate.
Note: It is useful to have done Task 25 prior to this one.

Task 28

Discourse type	Whole newspaper/s
Communicative purpose	Informative
Authentic task typology	Extraction
Level 5 up	
Aim: To compare general, cultural characteristics of newspapers and draw inferences about priorities, perceptions etc.	

Preparation: A selection of TC newspapers, plus newspapers from other cultures (especially the learners' cultures) if possible.
Brainstorm (whole class or in groups) criteria of comparison of newspapers ranging from physical features to content and organisation, e.g.
- Size of the newspaper
- Quality of newsprint (including smell!)
- Typography - fonts/size
- Use of pictures (size, colour/black and white, subjects)
- Organisation of contents, relative proportion of subjects (news, domestic /international, sport, leisure etc.)
- Advertising (proportion to other content, prominence).
- Prepare the criteria thus drawn up as Column 1 of multi-columned table.
- Working in multi-cultural groups if possible, learners look through TC newspaper/s and those from other/learners' cultures to fill in table.
- Draw inferences from findings, comparing priorities, values and perceptions of cultures, e.g. consumptionism, concern with social issues or leisure, insular or outward-looking etc.[30]

Task 29

Discourse type	Whole newspaper/s
Communicative purpose	Informative
Authentic task typology	Extraction
Level 5 up	
Aim: To identify characteristics of different types of newspapers within TC.	

Preparation: A selection of TC newspapers including broadsheets and tabloids.
- Brainstorm (whole class or in groups) criteria of comparison of newspapers ranging from physical features to content and organisation, e.g.
- Size of the newspaper
- Quality of newsprint
- Typography - fonts/size

- Use of pictures (size, colour/black and white, subjects)
- Organisation of contents, relative proportion of subjects (news, domestic /international, sport, leisure etc.)
- Advertising (proportion to other content, prominence)
- Prepare the criteria thus drawn up as Column 1 of multi-columned table.
- Working in multi-cultural groups if possible, learners look through sample of newspaper-types (e.g. 2 broadsheets, 2 tabloids) to fill in table.
- Draw inferences from findings re. *readerships* of each newspaper type e.g. the typical readers' priorities, values, interests, concern with social issues/leisure, insular or outward-looking, attitudes to other cultures, attitudes to gender, social, class, racial equality.
- Groups compare their readership profiles for each type of newspaper.
- Learners make comparisons to equivalent newspapers in their own culture (if possible)[31].

Task 30

Discourse type	Whole newspaper/s
Communicative purpose	Informative
Authentic task typology	Inferencing
Level 4 up	
Aim: To relate media information to self.	

Preparation: A selection of the day's (or recent) newspapers.
- Each learner:
- Scans newspaper/s to identify at least one news item which relates to personal concerns /interests, or to those of own country.
- Makes notes on identified news item.
- Notes accuracy of information about own country (if relevant).
- Adds coda, explaining how/why this item relates to self or own country and predicting how it may affect him/her professionally/personally in short, medium or long term.
- In groups, learners reveal news item selected and why/how it has personal/ national significance[32].

Task 31

Discourse type	Whole newspaper/s
Communicative purpose	Informative
Authentic task typology	Extraction
Level 5 up	
Aim: Macro level scanning of whole newspaper.	

Preparation: From the radio or television, compile a selection of intriguing/sensational news headlines and record them onto audio/video tape (it may be more convenient to record television headlines onto audio tape). Find the matching news stories in a selection of newspapers and buy a few copies of each (these will need to be collected over a period of time). Place all the newspapers on a large desk.

- Tell learners this is a race to see who can find a particular news story in a newspaper quickest!
- Explain the rationale for this type of fast scanning - desire or need to find information on specific story quickly.
- Emphasise that the radio/television headline will not be exactly the same as the newspaper headline
- Play the first headline.
- Working in pairs/groups, learners take a 'likely' newspaper and sift through it to find the news story which matches the headline. First group to find it wins a point!
- Repeat with each headline.
- Once the race is finished, learners may be interested in reading particular items in more detail - Tasks 12 or 13 might be used for this.

Task 32

Discourse type	Whole newspaper, printed and online
Communicative purpose	Informative
Authentic task typology	Analysis
Level 5 up	
Aim: To compare printed newspapers with their online versions.	

Preparation: Buy a selection of the day's printed newspapers (tabloids and broadsheets) which have online versions.
- Tell learners they are to compare the two media. Brainstorm for comparison criteria and list on board for learners to copy e.g.
• Visual appearance: does the newspaper *look* similar on the two media?
• News items (are they the same in the two media? Length of items?)
• Number of news items?
• Depth of coverage?
• Range of subjects and topics covered (current affairs, business, sport etc.)?
• Advertising?
- In groups, learners select one printed newspaper of their choice and then access the online version.
- Compare the two media according to criteria above (others will probably occur to learners in the course of the analysis).
- Meet with other groups to compare findings re. different newspapers.
- Following these discussions, as a whole class, rank the newspapers according to similarity with their online versions.
- Conclude with general discussion: which medium do the learners prefer? What are the newspaper reading trends in their own countries? What are the differences between reading a newspaper online and in print, in terms of emotional impact, our daily habits etc? What is the future of the newspaper?

Notes

1 The home page of *The Sun* online (http://www.thesun.co.uk/) has an online version of its front and back pages but includes a link to a full size version of the pages exactly as they appear in print.

2 From Sanderson 1999: 262.

3 From *The Irish Times* online (http://www.ireland.com), 26 February 2000.

4 *The Irish Times* 19 January 2000: 13.

5 *The Irish Daily Mirror*, 11 October 2002: 1.

6 The last 3 examples taken from Reah 1998: 17-18.

7 *Electronic Daily Telegraph* 13 May 2000.

8 From *The Sun* (online) 15 May 2000.

9 From Reah 1998: 17.

10 A favourite of headline writers; even a headline such as 'The baby who came out of the freezer' (*The Irish Daily Mirror*, 11 October 2002) can be seen to echo the Le Carré title, in its structure and lexis (substitution of the word 'cold' with 'freezer').

11 From the newspaper *Today*, 1992.

12 This is pointed out by Sanderson 1999: 28-9.

13 Crossheads in the article headlined 'Martin's quick Xit in spoof interview' *The Evening Herald*, 10 October 2002: 3.

14 From an article headlined 'Shameful snub to our war heroes' *The Daily Mail* 11 October 2002: 18-9.

15 Cited in Reah 1998: 38.

16 *The Daily Mail*, 11 October 2002: 18-9.

17 Samples from *The Irish Times* 1 April 2000 (online) include 'Protesters clash with Mugabe supporters' and 'Indonesian police clash with students'.

18 Headline from *The Daily Mirror*, 1992.

19 It was used in *The Daily Mirror* (25 July 2002), for instance, under the photos of the men being brought to trial for the 1993 murder of the black British teenager Stephen Lawrence.

20 Adapted from Tomalin and Stempleski 1993: 48-9.

21 Based on Sanderson 1999: 28-9.

22 Adapted from activity suggested by Sean Devitt, ELT Author's conference June 1997.

23 Based on Little *et al*. 1989: 42.

24 Adapted from Grundy 1993: 94-5.

25 Adapted from Grundy 1993: 105.

26 Adapted from Grundy 1993: 39-40.

27 Adapted from Grundy 1993: 102.

28 Adapted from Grundy 1993: 127.

29 Adapted from Grundy 1993: 8-9.

30 Based on Tomalin and Stempleski 1993: 44-5.

31 Based on Chandler and Stone 1999: 10.

32 Activity suggested by Grundy 1993: 37.

Chapter Eight:
Advertising

'Advertising is a prominent discourse type in virtually all contemporary societies' (Cook 1992: 5). In British society it is estimated that by the age of 35, the average person will have seen 150,000 television advertisements, equivalent to 75,000 minutes or two months[1]. The fact that advertising is such a recognisable, universal discourse type is only one reason why it is such an obvious recruit for language learning. Designed specifically to appeal, the linguistic density and multi-sensory impact of (television) advertisements, and the fact that they succinctly embody and demonstrate cultural values and behaviours make them ideal, ready-made teaching units. This deft integration of language and culture arises partly from the parasitic nature of advertising, the fact that it feeds on other types of discourse (Cook 1990: 130). Advertising also, however feeds *into* the culture, contributing to how we perceive ourselves and to the construction of our value system; this is discussed in Section 8.2 'Advertising and Culture'. Advertising, finally, also invigorates our language, as we will see in the following section.

8.1 Advertising and Currency

8.1.1 Advertising and language
Because of the need to send multiple messages as rapidly as possible, the linguistic density of advertising copy is among the highest of any discourse type (poetry being probably the most comparable). This density means that the impact of advertisements traditionally turns on the 'code', i.e. on the language itself (Picken 1999: 250) (although today, a shift of emphasis may be observed from the linguistic to the visual, see Section 8.1.2 'Advertising and affect' below). This linguistic density is created through the use of various linguistic techniques. Those most characteristic of advertising include

Rhyme: 'Don't be vague, ask for Haig' (Haig Scotch);

Puns: 'First relationships last' (First National Bank of Chicago);

Intertextuality (the basing of one text on another, in order to appropriate by inference, some of the message of the first); 'Once driven, forever smitten' (Vauxhall), echoing the saying *once bitten twice shy*. (See more examples below);

Assonance and alliteration; 'Don't dream it, drive it' (Jaguar[2]).

Repetition and substitution; 'Have a break - have a Kitkat!'

As such slogans illustrate, their (superficial) simplicity is often belied by semantic complexity. This linguistic 'simplicity' makes them accessible to learners even from lower levels of proficiency, giving such learners the opportunity to exercise sophisticated cognitive skills that they are often denied because of their language level (see the argument in Chapter 3 Section 3.3 'Challenge'). The Egg Marketing Board's *'Go to work on an egg'* (1957), for example, evokes an amusing visual image, but the ambiguity of the slogan may not be clear to learners unaware of the range of meanings of the preposition *on*. In the language classroom, all this language play offers great potential for language analysis and development. Obvious first steps might be to analyse the linguistic device or devices used (pun, alliteration etc.), to elicit the meaning or meanings of the slogan and to assess its impact and effectiveness. Learners might go on to look at slogans of a selection of advertisements to analyse the devices that they use[3], then build on this information to invent slogans for other existing (or invented) products. Learner might even be asked to recall slogans for the same products in their L1 and compare the word-play used. This works well for internationally advertised products such as Coca Cola, some beers (Carlsberg, Heineken) and cars (Volvo, Fiat) (see Task 1).

As with other cultural products discussed here, advertising has its own 'set' of characteristic language forms. Perhaps the most traditional of these is the imperative. By analysing the function of the imperative in advertising contexts, learners will notice that the function of the imperative includes to encourage ('Make a snack decision - today!'[4]), to intrigue ('Give us a second of your time and that's all you'll pay for'[5]) and to tempt ('Let the train take the strain'[6]). These functions, interestingly, belie the function most commonly attributed to the imperative in textbooks, that of ordering or directing[7] (see Task 2).

Language use in advertising may challenge conventional grammar and semantics partly because it is so keenly up-to-date. Advertising copywriters are at the leading edge of colloquial language. Not only do they reflect trends in current language use, they also actually contribute to and direct them. Many of the most memorable advertising slogans over the years can be seen as having had this dual effect of entering - or reflecting? - common parlance. This is another reason, of course, why they can be of such interest to language learners. This ability to insinuate themselves into the vernacular is exemplified by slogans from the famous campaigns by the Milk Marketing Board, who played on the rhyme and rhythmic potential of their original slogan 'Drink a pint of milk day' (1959) to give 'Milk's gotta lotta bottle' (1983). This sort of memorability and potential for paraphrase is also true of slogans like Carlsberg's *'probably the best beer in the world'* (dating from 1973) and Heineken's 'Heineken refreshes the parts other beers cannot reach' (1974) both of which were widely used and paraphrased by people for years afterwards. As for more contemporary ones, there is Nike's 'Just do it' (1988) or the slogan for the Lotto 'It could be you', which was ingeniously changed in 2003 (for the Irish Lotto) to 'Play lotto - or it could be him' ('him' being an obnoxious character, a self-important golfer or manic car-park developer). In addition to the usefulness to language learners of the currency of advertising language, there are, of course, the socio-cultural moods that are encoded in advertisements. We can sense the drive and optimism of the late 1980s represented in the Nike slogan, or the gradual equalising of social and economic opportunity at the turn of the century (the Lotto slogan). We shall see more of this later, in the 'Advertising and culture' section. Ironically, the latest trend in advertising slogans, minimalism (epitomised by Budweiser's slogan 'True' and Kellogg's 'Shine', see Fraser 1999) looks set - temporarily at least - to reduce the usefulness of advertisements as far as the language input is concerned.

Another fascinating aspect of advertising language is the extent to which it borrows from other discourse types, and in particular, from literature (see Cook 1990: 130 and Chapter 5, 'Literature'). Advertising copywriters delight in intertextuality and this makes advertisements a useful and non-threatening 'way into' other discourse types. Those commonly scavenged in this way include poetry (which advertising resembles, according to Cook 1990: 133), songs, proverbs and even other advertising slogans. The slogan 'Naughty but nice', originally used to advertise cream cakes was transmuted to 'Nautical but nice', for instance, in a car advertisement featuring a car on a cliff-top (Goddard 1998: 69). The proverb *there's no time like the present*, was appropriated by Guinness, who replaced the last two words with *Guinness time,* to give the slogan 'There's no time like Guinness time'. The semantics of the word 'time' here are an interesting subject of analysis for language learners, particularly for those whose L1s distinguish between two concepts, as with the French distinction between *le temps* and *l'heure*. Similarly, the simple poeticism of such classics as the Mars advertisement - 'A Mars a day helps you work rest and play', and the proverb it echoes - *An apple a day keeps the doctor away*, is very appealing, yet on analysis is a fairly cynical use of intertextual reference.

8.1.2 Advertising and affect

Much advertising today works through a rapid and powerful appeal to affect. Yet the affective factor in advertising involves a fine balance. Since the aim of advertising is basically to sell, if advertisements stimulate emotion, this has to be geared towards creating a positive disposition towards their product. Lowering the 'affective filter' might be said to be as important to advertising copywriters as to language teachers. Hence advertisements can be serious, funny, exciting, enigmatic, sexy and so on, but, with the notable exception of health and safety campaigns (such as those intended to discourage drink-driving), they are rarely unpleasant. The appeal of television advertisements comes through an interplay of images, language and music. The deployment of all these aspects in advertisements are tactics familiar to foreign learners, and, in the language learning context, can be appreciated, deconstructed and analysed (see Tasks 3 and 9).

The balance of these elements has been changing over the years, however. Mirroring larger sociological changes in modes of communication, advertising is moving steadily away from written modes towards audio-visual communication. According to Cook (1992: 37), language is the dominant means of communication in only in a minority of advertisements today; sound, music and pictures play as large parts in creating mood and imparting information (*ibid.*). Nor is it coincidence that these elements have been so keenly embraced by advertisers, for they have more direct sensory impact than the written word. Hence the conception of that insidiously memorable association of music and words, the advertising jingle. Some spoken (voiced-over) advertising catch-phrases have similar effects as jingles because of the calculated musical quality of their language. Many of the most enduring and memorable advertising campaigns, such as the *Bulmers cider* or *Hamlet* advertisements, are a result of a successful combination of music overlaid with musical language.

The importance of the music in television advertisements arises too from the fact that the message/s from its other components - the language and visuals - can be 'unreliable'. In advertisements, the convention that the visual message reflects the linguistic one is frequently deliberately flouted. A typical advertising tactic is to make the visuals depend on the language to rationalise them; scenes cannot be understood until the linguistic message appears (Picken 1999: 250). In one memorable campaign on Irish television in the 1990s, a group of Japanese Samurai warriors are seen riding purposefully through typical Irish countryside, then striding threateningly into a traditional Irish pub ... to order bottles of *Murphy's* stout. The protagonists as well as the dramatic accompanying music were deliberately at total cultural-odds with the product they were advertising. This strategy of leaving viewers guessing is obviously a 'quick and dirty' way of involving them. Rather than inhibiting the use of advertisements for language learning, this often obscure schema of reference can constitute a 'ready-made' information gap which can itself be exploited in learning activities. Why, for instance, are the two young boys industriously dirtying dishes to stack in the dishwasher? So their father will take them to Macdonald's, of course! (Rather than face cleaning dishes in order to prepare dinner at home[8]) (see Task 9).

In some advertisements, the visuals can evoke linguistic word play (as in the advertisement where the comment 'I see you have a good grasp of figures' prompts the image of a man in a disco grasping a girl round the waist). Images can even eliminate the need for language altogether, and be used representationally, like hieroglyphics, as in the long-running *Silk Cut* newspaper and poster advertisement showing silk cloth with a cut in it. As Cook points out, there *is* language in the *Silk Cut* advertisement - the statutory health warning imposed by the government, which appears in cheekily large print - but 'nothing could testify more strikingly to the advertiser's faith in the superior power of pictures over words than their evident belief that it is still worth advertising in these conditions' (Cook 1992: 55). The visual and the musical components of television advertisements are, in conclusion, at least as important as their linguistic ones, and particularly since they have such affective impact, should be exploited in language learning by using them to *produce* language via discussion, analysis and creativity.

8.2 Advertising and Culture
'You can tell the ideals of a nation by its advertisements' (Norman Douglas 1917).

Perhaps the most fruitful dimension of advertising in the context of language learning is its cultural dimension: 'Although advertisements are ephemeral in that each one is short-lived, their effects are longstanding and cumulative: they leave traces of themselves behind which combine to form a body of messages about the culture that produced them. These messages can then function both to reflect and to construct cultural values' (Goddard 1998: 3).

The cultural specificity built into many of our advertisements makes them invaluable sources of information on social/cultural habits, behaviours and priorities. The proportion of advertisements dedicated to confectionary and convenience foods on British/Irish television says much about our eating and snacking habits, for example. While alcohol advertising remains legal on Irish television[9], the proportion of advertising for beer and cider and the frequency of the pub setting is a fair reflection of the role alcohol plays in this society. Advertisements for alcohol, the places in which it is consumed and the people who consume it, the British/Irish breakfast table - replete with cereals, bacon, sausages etc. - all make advertisements a useful 'cultural shorthand' for exploration in the language classroom (see Tasks 4 and 5). One basic advertising ploy which advertisers use might also provide useful insights into the TL society, and this is the strategy of problematising aspects of life that can be 'solved' by means of a product (Goddard 1998: 91). The Americans, for example, were among the first to be made aware of the condition known as 'body odour' which, needless to say, had to be combated using a new product (Bryson 1994: 285). Advertisers on American television continue to cash in on (and aggravate?) the hypochondriac tendencies of the population. In Britain and Ireland, we have seen the phenomenal rise of anti-bacterial cleaning agents to combat germs of which we were hitherto unaware, breeding unchecked on every household surface. In Ireland, advertisers regularly exploit the context of the Irish diaspora. We see Irish emigrants in far-flung countries wistfully indulging in Irish products; typically in the USA (*Barry's* tea) but also as far away as Russia (*Galtee* bacon). References such as these may, of course, be missed by non-natives but can prove useful introductions to this aspect of Irish culture for learners studying within the country.

Advertising is in many ways the litmus paper of society. It has its finger on the pulse of societal change, which it perceives and exploits, thus, arguably, helping to perpetuate it. This is another aspect that makes the advertisement an invaluable part of the language teaching repertoire if learners are to tune into the contemporary target language society.

One such change in British/Irish society which is reflected in advertising trends, is our attitudes to gender roles. The kitchen was once the sole domain of the woman (see the classic *Bisto* gravy advertisements of the 1950s, for instance, in which the wife's chief aim in life was to appeal to her husband's palette). Today, as reflected in advertisements, men have a place in the kitchen more and more. Roles have not shifted too radically, however. It is significant that the presence of a man alone in the kitchen usually heralds a convenience food (oven chips, microwaveable pizza) - so easy, even someone with the culinary ineptitude of a man can prepare it. While women in advertisements are sometimes permitted to wield power in traditionally male domains (women are portrayed in executive roles, as, for example, in the *Kenco* instant coffee advertisements), any threat this might pose is usually undermined by their sexiness and femininity (see Task 7).

Sex, of course, has classically been used to sell products, from the curvaceous model on the car bonnet at motor shows to the sexual innuendos used in advertisements for things like *Cadbury's* Chocolate Flake and *Häagen-Dazs* ice cream. While advertisers still show an ingenuity in making everything - from gravy to butter and cleaning products - suggestive and sexy, what is much more recent, and arguably reflective of the economic well-being of turn-of-the-century Britain and Ireland, is a new-found self-confidence and self-sufficiency, which makes us now (apparently) prioritise food over sex. There is the girl who would rather eat her *Dolmio* pasta than go out on a date, the man who drops the 'perfect date' because she eats 'virtual' butter, the women who regularly rebuff handsome suitors in favour of a night in eating *Philadelphia* cream cheese, and the man whose sizzling stir fry drowns out the phone call from his girlfriend making a last ditch attempt to save their relationship[10]. Also born of a new self-confidence, is a brash selfishness, characterised in advertisements for luxury foods such as chocolate and desserts. 'It's not Terry's, it's mine', declares the plump lady of the classic *Terry's* Chocolate Orange; a mother devours *Jaffa cakes* in front of her son, while another filches the *Müller rice* dessert from her son's lunchbox and replaces it with an apple. The attitudes and behaviours that contemporary advertisements like these portray can precipitate stimulating discussion in the multi-cultural classroom, as learners draw comparisons between advertisements from their societies and the characteristics implicit in them.

Perhaps the greatest social change in recent times, precipitated in large by economic and political expediency, is the rapprochement of British and Irish societies with those of continental Europe. A review of advertisements of even the recent past reveals how our attitudes to other Europeans are changing. The famous sun-bed advertisement (where a British man beats a group of Germans to the sun-bed by throwing a large Union Jack towel onto it) appears by now very dated. A new internationalism has crept into advertising, symbolising new attitudes to, and acceptance of, our fellow Europeans. The French are now not only allowed into our homes, but even to seduce our men and women (the 2000 *Kerrygold* butter campaign). The *Kerrygold* advertisement also demonstrates how foreigners are seconded to promote some of the most culture-specific products. In the *Murphy's* stout advertisement described in the previous section, this very Irish beverage was - by some obscure quirk of advertising genius - recommended to its native-drinking audience by Japanese Samurai warriors. Even though, at the moment, British/Irish representation of people from foreign cultures remains fairly stereotypical[11], the new schema of international reference in advertisements makes them useful in the language classroom as it contributes a ready-made cross-cultural element from which to launch discussion (see Task 6).

While the growing transnationality of advertisements may facilitate schematic access to the learner, variations in advertisements for many internationally marketed products (such as soft drinks, beers, cars) may also be very revealing of differing cultural priorities. A pan-European campaign by *Volvo* in 1990, for example, promoted 'the car's safety to Swiss and UK audiences; its status to French audiences [...] and for Germans, its performance' (Goddard 1998: 80), variations which are very revelatory of cultural differences. From the language learning aspect, familiarity with an advertisement in the native language eases comprehension of target language items in the TC one. Subtle changes made in translation (especially of the slogan) may also be noticed by learners, alerting them to the flexibility and potential for ambiguity of different languages. Changes can even occur within advertisements used in the same language but for different cultures. The slogan in an otherwise identical advertisement for *Guinness* some years ago, was 'There's no time like Guinness time' on Irish television, but 'Guinness - pure genius' on British stations. The mobile phone operator, *Orange*, had, for obvious reasons, to rethink its slogan 'The future's bright, the future's Orange', for marketing in Northern Ireland (Goddard 1998: 83). Such considerations reveal the differing terms of reference even within two cultures that speak the same language and which are fairly close. Variation within cultures sharing a common language is probably best epitomised by the contrasting hard-sell/soft-sell approaches of American as distinct from British/Irish advertising. Such types of comparisons serve to raise awareness of both cultural differences in values, attitudes and reactions to commercial pressure, as well as increasing cultural similarities in today's 'shrinking world'.

8.3 Advertisements for Language Learning: Summary and Principles

To summarise, the popularity of advertisements with language teachers is based on both sociological and pragmatic factors. The prominence of advertising in most societies gives it trans-cultural accessibility. The visual, audio or audio-visual appeal of the advertisement, targeted at the consumer, is easily re-directed at the language learner. The combination of linguistic simplicity and semantic complexity of much advertising copy and slogans make them ideal subjects for language study by learners of all levels. The condensed cultural content of advertisements and their function as reflectors of society also make them attractive sources of information about the target culture. Finally, in terms of using them in language learning, the potential of advertisements for linguistic and cultural exploitation is unmarred by any real scruples about doing so. Unlike similar exploitation of a literary work, for instance, which may be distasteful to the teacher (or learner) who holds the canon of literature in high regard, interfering with a genre whose *raison d'être* is exploitation of the consumer can be done with a fairly clear conscience.

Principles for the use of advertisements for language learning

• Exploit the inbuilt appeal of advertisements.

• Exploit the linguistic density of advertisements.

- Exploit intertextuality as a 'way into' other discourse types.

- Exploit the affective appeal of advertisements e.g. visual, audio and musical components.

- Exploit the advertisers' strategies for eliciting interest: enigma, 'information gap' etc.

- Analyse cultural behaviours and values implicit in advertisements.

- 'Advertising is the litmus paper of society'; analyse societal changes and trends portrayed in advertisements.

Further reading
Goddard, A., 1998. *The Language of Advertising*, London: Routledge.

Cook, G., 1992. *The Discourse of Advertising*, London: Routledge.

Kelly-Holmes, H., 2004 forthcoming. *Advertising as Multilingual Communication*. Basingstoke: Palgrave Macmillan.

8.4 The Tasks

Task 1

Discourse type	Advertisement with high language content
Communicative purpose	Persuasive
Authentic task type	Analysis
Level 5 up	
Aim: To raise awareness of density of language.	

Preparation: Select a television/radio advertisement with strong language element.
- Play advertisement as listening/viewing comprehension to allow learners to catch all the language.
- Learners analyse how language used to persuasive effect, e.g.
- 'Weighted', emotive, evocative, connotative lexis
- Use of phonological features e.g. onomatopoeia, rhyme, alliteration, repetition.
- Word-play; ambiguity (lexical/syntactical).
- Language register; e.g. colloquial, formal, literary.
- Use of different discourse types (e.g. dialogue, song, voice-over)
- In mono-cultural groups if possible, learners do double-translation of text of advertisement, i.e. (a) translate text from English into learners' L1 using types of linguistic strategies they have observed in the English text. (b) Re-translate back from L1 into English for learners from other cultures, explaining changes (from original text) that emerge.

Task 2

Discourse type	Advertisements with high language content
Communicative purpose	Persuasive
Authentic task type	Analysis
Level 5 up	
Aim: To explore linguistic structure and function.	

Preparation: Collect assortment of advertisements from various media (e.g. television, radio, newspapers, magazines), and identify within them a number of salient language structures e.g. imperative, interrogative, *will* future.
- Before showing the advertisements, ask learners to work in groups. Give each group ONE of the structures you've identified and ask them to discuss and note its functions from their own knowledge.
- Groups then:
- Sift through/view/hear advertisements and select a few that contain 'their' structure.
- Analyse function of their structure within the texts and compare/contrast with their prior assumptions about it.
- Share findings with class.

Task 3

Discourse type	Advertisements with low language content
Communicative purpose	Persuasive
Authentic task type	Inferencing
Level 2 up	
Aim: To analyse use of non-linguistic elements; music, sound, images (and editing of them) for persuasive/affective impact in advertisements.	

Preparation: Select television advertisement/s with low linguistic-content and in which music/sound/images are strategically used.
- Before viewing, discuss use of non-linguistic elements of advertisements; music/sound, images, cultural cues/images.
- Brainstorm how such elements can be used for impact in advertisements e.g. by association with other familiar genres e.g. films (film genres e.g. action movie, romance and associated film scores), songs, computer games, cartoons.
- Show advertisement and assess (a) which (of above) elements are used (b) their effectiveness (c) whether the advertisement has trans-cultural appeal and if not (d) what changes might be made for each culture? (e) discuss and make necessary changes, in mono-cultural groups if possible.

Task 4

Discourse type	Advertisements with TC content
Communicative purpose	Persuasive

Authentic task type	Inferencing
Level 5 up	
Aim: To infer societal values implicit in advertisement/s.	

Preparation: Compile a selection of advertisements for cross-section of products e.g. health/beauty, foods, soft drinks, beer, cars, consumer goods (e.g. mobile phone, sports goods), DIY.
- Pre-viewing: brainstorm characteristics valued by different societies and which advertisements play on e.g. beauty, youth, health, hygiene, wealth, family, consumerism, image, self-esteem, tradition, heritage etc.
-Show selected advertisements a number of times as necessary.
- Ask learners to identify the implicit value appealed to in the advertisements e.g. *L'Oreal* shampoo - slogan *Because you're worth it*; beauty, self-esteem.
- If a large enough cross-section of advertisements shown, *rate* the importance of valued characteristics e.g. (1) beauty (2) image ...
- Learners compare these to values (and their prioritisation) in their own cultures.

Task 5

Discourse type	Advertisement with TC content
Communicative purpose	Persuasive
Authentic task type	Inferencing
Level 2 up	
Aim: To identify culture-specific indicators (of TC).	

Preparation: Find an advertisement incorporating cultural indicators e.g. use of slang, setting, music, behaviours (e.g. gender-specific roles), rituals (e.g. mealtimes, tea-drinking, pub), foods (this can be used with Levels 2 or 3 if cultural indicators are limited to visual elements shown e.g. eating certain foods, behaviours/rituals).
- Show advertisements asking learners to
- Identify culture-specific indicators of TC.
- Discuss and make notes on:
- How these differ from their own culture/s.
- In what ways they may seem alien to their own culture/s.
- Which indicator/s from their own cultures might have equivalent effect/s in the advertisement.
Suggested advertisements (by product): beer, soft drinks, foods, tea/coffee, consumer goods e.g. mobile phones, sports shoes, cars.

Task 6

Discourse type	Advertisements featuring foreigners
Communicative purpose	Persuasive
Authentic task type	Inferencing
Level 5 up	

Aim: To infer attitudes to/stereotypes of other cultures.

Preparation: Select advertisements figuring people from other cultures, if possible, a culture represented in the class.
-Learners watch advertisement and infer:
-Function of foreigner/s (to endorse the product, for ridicule, for sex appeal, for contrast with native etc.)
-Whether stereotyped, if so in which way/s? (e.g. as a lover, a gourmet, a perfectionist, a chauvinist)
- Comment on accuracy/basis for stereotype.
Suggested advertisements (by product): some beers, coffees, 'foreign' foods e.g. pizza, pasta.

Task 7

Discourse type	Advertisements with defined gender roles
Communicative purpose	Persuasive
Authentic task type	Inferencing
Level 4 up	
Aim: To infer TC attitudes to gender roles.	

Preparation: Select advertisements which depict gender-role stereotyping (or reversal of this)
- Show advertisement/s and analyse implied gender roles.
- Learners compare to own cultures.
- If relevant, learners work in mono-cultural groups (if possible) to rework advertisement (images/language) to reflect cultural variances.
- Present reworked version of advertisement to class.
Suggested advertisements (by product): luxury foods, convenience foods, beers, household cleaning products (e.g. washing powders), beauty products, cars, DIY (shops, products).

Task 8

Discourse type	Advertisements with high information content
Communicative purpose	Persuasive
Authentic task type	Extraction
Levels 2 - 4	
Aim: To extract factual information from advertisements.	

Preparation: Record a collection of television/radio advertisements which give factual information e.g. price, food ingredients, date of an event, shop opening times, 'unique' features/selling point of product, advantages over competitors etc. A table for noting the information available from the advertisements with headings *price, ingredients* etc.

- Show/play the advertisement once; ask learners to work individually to complete as much as possible of the information required in the table.
- Repeat showing/playing as necessary, but do as few times as possible.
- Learners cross-check information in pairs/groups.
Suggested advertisements (by product): supermarkets, foods, electrical goods, services (e.g. gas, electricity, banking)

Task 9

Discourse type	Enigmatic advertisement
Communicative purpose	Provocative
Authentic task type	Inferencing
Level 2 up	
Aim: To speculate on/infer product being advertised.	

Preparation: Select advertisement (television/radio) in which product being promoted is not obvious until the end.
-Show/play advertisement section-by-section; in pauses, learners speculate on the product being advertised, justifying their guesses. Note suggestions on the board.
- Reveal product - re-assess previous guesses.
- Discuss how/whether suspense contributes to promotion of product.
- Discuss applicability of this style of advertising to other cultures.

Task 10

Discourse type	Food/drink advertisement
Communicative purpose	Provocative
Authentic task type	Analysis
Level 4 up	
Aim: To raise awareness of sensory reaction/s to food/drink advertisements; craving, thirst etc.	

Preparation: Make a collection of radio/television food/drink advertisements which attempt to stimulate appetite/thirst. Prepare a (6) column table for elements of the advertisements with headings *language, images, music, sounds, dialogue, cultural evocations* etc.
- Play each advertisement and ask learners to say how it makes them feel e.g. hungry, thirsty etc.
- Ask learners to identify the elements - language, images, etc. each advertisement uses to stimulate these responses and note in the table.
Suggested products: luxury foods (chocolate, desserts), breakfast cereals, convenience foods, milk, soft/alcoholic drinks.

Task 11

Discourse type	Promotional literature
Communicative purpose	Persuasive
Authentic task type	Extraction
Level 5 up	
Aim: To extract and evaluate factual information.	

Preparation: Compile a selection of promotional literature from comparable institutions (e.g. from companies producing similar product, hotels/holidays in same area, colleges offering similar courses etc.). Compile these into sets. Draw up a role for each group in the class, e.g. to compare holiday brochures; *'You are a parent of 2 children under four, looking for 1-week holiday including children's activities for up to 1000 euros etc. Which holiday would you choose?'* Give each group their set of relevant brochures.
- Groups look at their set of brochures and draw up comparisons on a table, indicating pros and cons of each choice.
- Groups identify the best choice for their role.
- Report back to other groups/the whole class and justify their choices.

Task 12

Discourse type	Classified advertisements
Communicative purpose	Soliciting
Authentic task type	Reaction
Level 6 up	
Aim: Decoding of abbreviations; inferring 'unwritten' information; practising negotiating skills.	

Preparation: 1). For each pair of learners, a different set of pictures or inventory of contents of a flat/house with different essential items missing (e.g. cooker, beds). 2) A few pages of newspaper/magazine classified advertisements (e.g. from local newspaper).
- Working in pairs, learners (a) identify the items missing from 'their' flat/house (b) settle on budget (or budget set by teacher) (c) find at least one classified advertisement with requisite item/s and infer 'unwritten' information from the advertisement ('in need of repair' =old!) (d) Prepare questions for seller of the item/s (e) One partner volunteers to try to 'buy' the item/s.
- Learners switch pairs.
- Each learner indicates to new partner which small ad or advertisements s/he is interested in.
- New partner takes on the role of the seller: interprets the small advertisement and adds the omitted or implied details e.g. colours, history.
- S/he also decides on intentions (e.g. '100 euros ono' = 'I'll accept 90 euros' etc.).
- Pairs simulate phone *or* e-mail negotiation.
- Students return to original partner and report on success of the transaction.

Notes

1   *The Sunday Times* Culture section, 12 March 2000: 22.

2   The last four examples drawn from Fraser (1999) online at
    http://www.adslogans.co.uk/ans/index.html accessed 6 June 2003.

3   A comprehensive resource of advertising slogans and on using advertising for teaching and
    learning can be found on http://www.adslogans.co.uk/general/students.html accessed 6 June
    2003.

4   Slogan used in 2000 advertising campaign for Cadbury's snack bars.

5   1990s Esat Digifone magazine advertisement.

6   Slogan used in 1990s British Rail advertising campaign.

7   In a coursebook chosen at random, it is stated only that the imperative is used 'to tell people very
    directly to do certain things' (Sinclair 1995: 78 in the coursebook *Activate your English*) and the
    imperative is practised only in the context of giving directions (*ibid.*: 46-8).

8   Television advertisement for Macdonald's 2003.

9   As at time of writing (summer 2003) the Irish government is planning to ban alcohol advertising.

10 All from advertising campaigns run on Ireland's RTE television 2001-3.

11 A 2002 British Tourist Board advertisement campaign run in Ireland, for example, chose to
    revert to archetypal British images, Westminister Abbey, Trafalgar Square, cups of tea, bowler
    hats and suits of armour. One wonders whether this merely showed a lack of imagination on the
    part of the copywriters or whether it was, in fact, a sort of snide 'up yours' to the Irish whose
    attitudes to their former governors still tends to be ambivalent.

Chapter Nine:
Song and Music

Song and music are truly universal - they cross cultures and even species - not only birds, but whales and apes all produce a kind of music. Music is an essential part of the human experience. It is part of the most important public events in life - weddings, funerals, religious services, and the most intimate ones - the bedtime lullaby sung to a baby, singing in the bath or shower, and it follows us through the routines of our daily lives - in the lift, in the supermarket, in the restaurant. But our connection with music and song begins well before birth; hearing is the first sense to develop in a growing foetus (the development of hearing is perfected around the twelfth week), so music constitutes some of our first communications from the outside world as we grow inside our mother's womb. As babies, songs are among our first encounters with language, through lullabies and nursery rhymes, and a child's first babblings are more musical, in their repetitiveness ('da-da-da' 'ma-ma-ma') than 'linguistic'. Since song, it has been claimed, predated and possibly evolved into speech (Murphey 1992: 6), it could be said that our L1 development in a sense traces that of our forebears.

The link of music and song to L1 development has an obvious corollary in L2 learning, which is why, of all the products of the TC, music and song are consistently well represented in the language classroom. In the ELT context, the international span of the British/American music industry means that many learners are familiar with and enjoy English language songs. This, of course, makes learners more receptive to their use for learning, playing into the hands (as it were) of the language teacher. Furthermore, for many overseas learners, the perception that song is a 'way into' English culture is a self-fulfilling prophecy. The first focus of this chapter is, then, to look at the ways in which song can be exploited in language-and-culture learning.

9.1 Song and Culture

As with those other 'artistic' products of the TC, literature and film, the cultural element in song is three-dimensional - a song is at the same time a product of its culture, a representation of it, and can even influence it. Certain styles of song spring from particular cultures - the Portuguese *Fado*, for example, or the Irish *Sianos*. These are typical products of their cultures but do not necessarily *represent* them in that they do not necessarily embody the values, behaviours and preoccupations of the contemporary culture. Song represents its culture, defined in this way, when it functions as a force for social expression and even change, as did, for example, the American protest songs of the 1960s. A more recent example might be the punk rock movement, so symptomatic of the disaffected youth of Old-Labour Britain, and a movement that arguably helped dispel the innocence from pop music from thence on. Song can be both an instrument for social change, and a *gauge* of social change, it can be used to trace socio-cultural movements, changes in behavioural norms of society, and so on.

To take Irish music as an example, the effective marginalisation - in the modern affluent state that is Ireland today - of its traditional folk songs, which portray the country's poor, unhappy past, reflects the radical changes in this society over the past few decades. Today's Ireland is a culture seemingly more comfortable with an image reflected in its young prettily-packaged bands, Boyzone, Westlife and The Corrs. This adoption of a brash young image in music as elsewhere, may also be seen as indicative of how comfortably Ireland is assuming the values of the consumer-led cultures of its fellow English-speaking societies.

Songs, then, are very much 'of their time', both in musical style and content. Songs of different eras (the 50s, say, or the 60s) are distinctive and instantly recognisable. Because of all these factors, songs can be considered cultural artefacts, they are revelatory of their culture both in depth and in breadth. Single songs can be analysed, or samples from a thematic thread can be examined, tracing societal trends, preoccupations, phenomena, or, if done on a broad enough scale, social change. One obvious theme might be the American anti-war feeling expressed in songs of the 1960s and 70s - traced through such songs as *Where have all the flowers gone* (Pete Seeger) and *Alice's restaurant* (Arlo Guthrie). Another is that theme close to the hearts of teenage learners, the dysfunctional side of education, represented in such songs as *Another brick in the Wall* (Pink Floyd) and *I don't like Mondays* (the Boomtown rats)[1]. Such themes as these also illustrate how songs may constitute unifying as well as distinguishing factors between cultures (see Task 9). Today, because the borders between cultures are dissolving, particularly in a medium such as pop music, so accessible to international audiences via the mass media and the Internet, it can be argued that songs are tending to lose their cultural identity: 'The world is evolving a common culture and pop songs are its backbone' (Griffee 1992: 6). If this is the case, learning a foreign language song might be said to hold the (added) attraction of participation in this new 'world culture' (*ibid.*).

9.2 Song and Currency

Songs have a unique currency, one which has not only to do with up-to-dateness of language, but more to do with the ever-fresh and immediate quality born of the way they blend words and music to engage our emotions. In this section, we will examine this aspect of currency first of all, turning to look at the specific area of language in the second part of the section.

9.2.1 Song and affect

Hearing is the sense which arguably has the most impact on affect. As has been noted earlier, hearing is the first sense to develop (which is why an infant's attachment to its mother's voice pre-dates birth) and the developing baby hears and reacts to music in its mother's womb:

'We are born with the sense of hearing which has been almost perfected at the twelfth week after conception and which works during the whole of pregnancy. In fact at birth

a child recognises those melodies or rhythms which it has known in a passive way in the mother's uterus' (Menuhin 1998[2]).

The primacy of our sense of hearing and with it our sensitivity to music, suggest that music and song have a closer appeal to our 'language acquisition device' than spoken language (Murphey 1992: 7). This theory has been given greater plausibility by the evidence that musical and language processing occur in the same area of the brain[3] (Maess *et al.*, 2001). This suggests that our brains recognise the constituents of musical and linguistic sequences in the same way (*ibid.*). This might explain some of the extraordinary attributes of songs, the rapidity with which they can be unconsciously and unwittingly memorised (the 'I can't get that song out of my head'-syndrome), and the tenacity of the melody-lyrics link that enables songs to be recalled in their entirety even after years of absence from the 'conscious' memory.

The repetitiveness of songs - they are repetitive in themselves, and they lend themselves to being sung over and over - also makes them a vehicle for acquiring language. The effortless way in which children learn and retain songs in their first language even before they are able to understand the words, suggests that something in the combination of repetition, music and rhythm promotes learning and retention. The way in which opera singers learn and sing whole operas in languages they do not know is further evidence of the tenacity of song in the memory - indeed, as Murphey points out, it seems to be easier to *sing* language than to *speak* it (Murphey 1992: 6-7). It can be argued, of course, that these examples are a sort of parrot-learning and omit the knowledge of language use that is crucial to acquisition - indeed, giving us the sort of comic childhood mistakes as 'Gladly the *cross-eyed bear*' ('Gladly the cross I'd bear') and 'blessed art thou *a monk swimming*' ('blessed art thou amongst women'). Such errors notwithstanding, the line between 'parrot-learning' and automaticity - fluency in language involving both knowing what to say (knowledge of language use) and producing language rapidly without pauses, and which is a valid aspect of language learning (see, for example, Ellis 1994: 389-91) - is evidently subtly crossed at some point, in L1 acquisition at least.

The importance of music to us even at the pre-natal stage, means that throughout our lives, music and song reach us at an elemental level and are able to elicit emotional responses from deep within us. Much of the rationale for using them in language learning turns on this factor, whether this is seen to work because of learners' emotional involvement in the songs which 'lowers the affective filter', to use Krashen's concept, or because music relaxes the mind, thereby maximising retention of the language, the precept on which the techniques of Suggestopedia are based (see Chapter 1 Section 1.1.3 for an outline of this approach). The primacy of the affective factor in songs suggests that, as with that other emotive cultural product covered in this book, film (see Chapter 10), songs can most fruitfully be exploited for language learning not as mere language *input* (although this is one element in their use, see the following section), but via what Murphey calls 'insearch'. This entails using the feelings, experiences and thoughts stimulated by the music/songs as the primary materials for learning and teaching (Murphey 1992: 15).

An essential point that will also be elaborated below, is that the power of song arises from the interdependency of lyrics and melody. However, with the possible exception of genres such as protest songs where the medium is exploited partly as a means of reaching broader audiences, the melody is generally the stronger element because of its direct appeal to our emotions. This is why people can 'sing along' to a song without knowing the words, singing 'la la la' with as much enjoyment and involvement as if they were singing the actual lyrics. It is also why, while songs are always fodder for instrumental versions, the lyrics of a song devoid of its melody appear strangely arid.

This suggests that it can be fruitful to approach a song via its music (rather than vice versa, as is the most conventional approach, see Section 9.2.2 below). This can be done in songs that have an introductory instrumental section or instrumental interlude, or ones that have an instrumental version. Hearing the music alone, unimpeded by linguistic 'interference', learners are free to imbibe the mood and feeling of the song, visualise images and so on. Apart from the language that this activity can produce, this liberates learners temporarily from the stress of straining to understand the foreign language, making them more suggestible to language acquisition (according to the principles of Suggestopedia, see Chapter 1 Section 1.1.3 and above). After hearing the music, learners might note down feelings, images and thoughts that the music produces in them and then express these as prose, poetry or sketches (see Task 1). Alternatively, learners might write as the music is playing, what Murphey calls 'stream of consciousness writing' (1992: 42-3). At some proficiency levels, this can be done in the L1 in order to make association as free from conscious language processing as possible. The task of translating notes into the TL can in itself become a productive language exercise (see Task 2). These types of activities serve as good 'warm-ups' for listening to the whole song, preparing the learners for it by setting the mood, predicting its images or language, and by generally whetting their appetites for it.

An activity that is very authentic and also trades on the emotional effect of songs is simply to elicit 'gut reactions' to a song played in class. This can be done by asking learners such things as whether they like the song, whether they would bother to listen to it attentively in a non-classroom situation, whether they would actually switch it off given the chance and so on[4] (see Task 4). The evocative power of music and song can also be exploited in the context of its association with two other cultural products, films and advertisements. Learners might listen to an excerpt from an evocative song or piece of music and suggest film genres, or advertisements it might accompany. This might even be extended into creating advertisements using the music or song as a 'jingle'[5] (see Task 6).

Finally, the most authentic activity of all with a song, and the one that can work the most strongly on affect is - as football fans have long demonstrated - singing along in a group. While this is easier with younger learners who have fewer inhibitions (see Section 9.3 'The challenge of song' below), adult learners are also often disposed to sing along (although this is partly a factor of socio-cultural conditioning - in Vietnamese society, to take one example, learners are perfectly comfortable with singing in class, as singing is a common part of their culture, Huy Lê 1999: 5). Where necessary, singing along is greatly encouraged if it is instigated by the teacher, who may even choose to present the song by singing it 'live' rather than use a recording[6]. Joining in with another person jars less that joining in with a recording, and once the choral effect takes hold, singing together can have therapeutic as well as language learning effects.

9.2.2 Teaching the language of song

A widespread attitude in language teaching is to treat TL songs merely as authentic examples of grammatical structures[7]. In this approach, the standard battery of language learning activities - comprehension and analysis questions, clozes, text reconstruction and so on, is reiterated. One coursebook example, for instance, asks learners to predict the words omitted from the printed text of the Don McLean song *American pie*. They are told that the missing words rhyme with the last word of the line before - e.g. to rhyme with *chance*, they might predict *dance*, and so on (*English File*, Oxenden and Latham-Koenig 2001: 111). Yet certain of these activities, such as comprehension and analysis questions, actually interfere with listener/learners' appreciation of the song because they inevitably guide, and thus skew, interpretation of a song. This blinkered approach forfeits the capacity song has for arousing feeling and the language production potential that this offers.

One obvious way to avoid wasting this emotive potential where a language focus desired, is to use songs that the learners like - in fact, to use the learners' choice of songs as much as possible (Murphey 1992:14). Such songs will have some significance for the learners and will therefore prove more productive in terms of discussion, analysis and so on, than songs that reflect the teacher's (or resource book writer's!) tastes. This principle can be applied most directly by giving learners the opportunity to 'teach' a song they are familiar with, either through presentation, or interactively, by setting their peers tasks (see Task 3). The teacher can discreetly guide the focus where necessary, curbing overlong discussions, or elucidating language points. Handing over to the learner in this way is an acknowledgement that the learner's interpretation of a song is as valid as anyone else's, including the teacher's. This boosts self-confidence which is such an important factor of motivation. Another way in which song can be used as a stimulus for language output is to ask learners to express the song as a story - in writing, or orally. The songs selected for this must of course, tell a story - teachers/learners will have their own favourites, but suggestions might include ballads e.g. *Clementine*, *The Band Played Waltzing Mathilda*, or well-known pop/rock songs such as *I don't like Mondays* (the Boomtown Rats) or Bruce Springsteen's *The River*. This activity is made more communicative and authentic if learners listen to different songs (in groups) and then 'tell' them to learners from different groups or 'swap' the stories they have written about them (see Task 10).

Another motive for extending the view of songs as mere listening comprehension material, is the strength of the relationship between the language and the melody, which has already been alluded to above. The tenacity of the association between the two elements, once made, is well illustrated in the round of one classic BBC radio panel game, where contestants are asked to sing a set of song lyrics to the tune of another song. The results are, not unexpectedly, hilarious and completely incongruous because they rupture what we have come to perceive as entities (the songs) by mismatching their constituent parts. The relationship between the melody and the lyrics can, therefore, be one useful starting point for devising learning activities. While this 'singing one song to the tune of another' exercise is unusual, there is a long tradition of something similar; putting invented lyrics to well-known tunes. This is a practice beloved of football fans 'One ..., there's only one ...' to the tune of *Guantanamera*[8]) and of children ('Oh dear what can the matter be, three old ladies stuck in the lavatory' to replace 'Oh dear what can the matter be, Johnny's so long at the fair'). This type of activity can be enjoyable and useful for language learners, the lyrics of the original song acting as a 'structural template' for their versions, making the activity effectively into a latter-day substitution drill. Level wise, this can be as simple ('Old Macdonald had a cup - glass - jug') or as complex as the teacher wishes (see Task 7).

All this having been said, learners are, of course, often keen to know the words of songs that appeal to them through their melodies. Since this is also true of native speakers, listening to songs for their lyrics is an authentic 'real-life' activity; the challenge in the classroom is to make it one that stimulates the learning of language beyond the confines of the lyrics of the song. Being the treatment of songs invariably used by coursebooks (see the example of *American Pie*, given above), the cloze or gap-fill would seem too obviously pedagogical a format for this task. Yet the gap-fill format can be authentic if the gaps left are words/expressions that are ones that are difficult for even the native speaker to catch or are ones that are commonly misheard[9]. This is quite appropriate for pop/rock songs, genres whose lyrics can often be difficult to make out. Another authentic gapping system is to give the learners a preview of the lyrics *before* listening to the song but omitting words that can be fairly easily estimated from syntactic or semantic clues. For example, the chorus of the Irish ballad *Sonny* (Mary Black), goes like this:

Sonny don't go away,
I'm here all alone,
Your Daddy's a sailor,
Never comes home.
Nights are so long
Silence goes on.
I'm feeling so tired
And not all that strong.

Gapped as follows:

Sonny don't __ ____,

I'm here all ____,
Your Daddy's a ____,
Never ____ ____.
Nights are so ____
Silence ____ ____.
I'm feeling so ____
And not all that ____.

The stanza retains enough of its meaning to elicit words like *leave* in the first line, *day/night* in the second, *soldier, salesman* in the third, *returns, around* in the fourth, *dark, lonely* in the fifth, *deepens* in the sixth, *lonely, old* in the seventh and *happy, good* in the last (as well as some correct guesses)[10].

In songs that are culture-specific, pre-listening gaps can be used to check the expectations set up by the cultural as well as the linguistic context. Here is the first stanza of the song *Flight of Earls* originally sung by the Dublin City Ramblers:

I can hear the bells of Dublin
In this lonely waiting room
And the paperboys are singing in the rain.
Not too long before they take us
To the airport and the noise
To get on board a transatlantic plane.

This can be gapped as follows:
I can hear the ____ of Dublin
In this lonely ____
And the paperboys are singing in the ____.
Not too long before they take us
To the ____ and the noise
To get on board a transatlantic ____.

The words *noise, birds* and even *guns* would all be syntactically and semantically acceptable in line 1, but suggesting the last would give the song a particular setting (and arguably say as much about the learner's cultural background as that of the song!). Most learners (at levels suitable for an appreciation of this particular song, intermediate and up) will insert the word *rain* in line 3, reflecting their background knowledge of the target culture, i.e. of the allusion to the classic film/song *Singin' in the rain*. This type of exercise can be simplified for lower level learners by offering a set of (syntactically correct) choices for each gap (the first gap in the above song might offer *noise, bells, guns* for instance), and the cultural and other significance of the learner's choices might be discussed.

As even these two samples of contemporary song illustrate, the language of songs can be at the same time very accessible, yet richly varied. Compared to a similar cultural product, such as poetry, the language of songs has a high degree of redundancy, achieved through allusion (as in the example above), borrowings (from other songs, rhymes[11] etc.), idiom, cliché, as well, of course, as the use of simple repetition (Griffee 1992: 3-4). Yet at the same time, the language of songs ranges across a surprising spectrum of genres and registers (Murphey 1992: 84), or along the 'cline of literariness', to use Brumfit and Carter's 1991 terminology (see 'Literature', Section 5.1). Illustrations of this include:

The archaic e.g. 'A spaceman came travelling on his ship from afar' (from *Spaceman*, Chris de Burgh, 1975).

The poetic e.g. 'All I do is kiss you through the bars of a rhyme' (from *Romeo and Juliet*, Dire Straits, 1980)

The colloquial e.g. 'I said, how about breakfast at Tiffany's?' (from *Breakfast at Tiffany's*, Deep Blue Something, 1995)

The idiomatic e.g. *Don't think twice, it's all right* (Bob Dylan, 1963)

Slang/non-standard e.g. *Can't get no satisfaction* (The Rolling Stones, 1965).

Indeed, songs can provide a very valuable component of colloquial and non-standard language use that is often missing from coursebooks (see Chapter 3 Section 3.2 'Currency'), providing easy-to-remember contexts for such language. Songs such as *It ain't me Babe* (Dylan), *He ain't heavy, he's my brother* (The Hollies) and *Ain't Misbehavin* (Fats Waller, from the show of the same name) for example, might be used to draw learners' attention to a 'non-standard' form that has at this stage attained respectability. This also goes for the introduction of idiomatic language which is often given heavy-handed treatment in coursebooks in the form of lists of idioms and their glosses, and which is thus often lost on the learner. For instance, the fact that many learners are aware of the idiomatic (and culture-specific) identification, in English, of the colour blue with sadness and depression, tends to come out of their knowledge of the musical genre 'The Blues' and of songs using idioms such as ('Don't be blue' etc.) rather than from any coursebook.

As well as using colloquial language, songs demonstrate the 'natural' pronunciation of the spoken language; while this is, of course, available from other authentic media such as film, it is far more memorable in songs for reasons detailed above. Among the most common phonological features are reductions such as the ubiquitous *gonna (You're gonna lose that girl)* and *wanna (I wanna hold your hand)* and the reduction of -ing to /n/[12]. Word-final/word-initial assimilation, such as the word final *t* + word-intial *y* to /ch/ ('Don't you step on my blue suede shoes') are another common feature.

These days, the accessibility of song lyrics on the Internet can be a great boon for the teacher wishing to focus on the lyrics of a particular song. At the same time, it can also serve to free the teacher from the role of supplying them in tasks where they do not. Suggesting that learners go to Internet sources if they want to see the lyrics, can signal to the learner that the language is not the only (or the most crucial) aspect of a song as well, of course, as fostering autonomy[13].

9.3 The Challenge of Song

A point made earlier in this chapter is that unlike other media (with the exception of some advertisements), songs do not necessarily require knowledge of the language in which they are sung for enjoyment and/or participation. Witness foreign language hits in Britain such as *Nessun dorma*, the popularity of English language songs abroad, and the earlier example of opera singers singing operas in languages they do not know. Acceptance of non-comprehension in this particular genre begins from early childhood. As has been noted above, a child's innate feeling for music, stimulated by songs and rhymes sung to it in the early months at the dawning of language awareness, 'carries' the child naturally into language development. With children's rhymes and songs, it is evidently not the meaning of the language that engages the child. The language of such songs is notoriously antiquated and often nonsensical, as Cook points out with reference to rhymes such as *Pease porridge hot* (2000: 24-5). Nor - fortunately, perhaps, given this factor - is this language usually the language which the child starts to use meaningfully. Rather, it is the music, the rhythm and the rhyme (as well as the interaction with the adult singer that accompanies it) that appeals to the child and awakens the development of language.

This connection of songs to language acquisition in the L1 context has a clear corollary in early learning of the foreign language. The same characteristics that promote the learning of the first language - linguistic patterns of rhythm, rhyme and repetition, the supportive combination of language and melody and the direct appeal of melody to affect - make it the perfect introduction to the foreign language for beginners or elementary learners. Indeed, many learners may have their first encounters with the foreign language through song (in the form of pop songs or children's songs) and may even still recall these songs decades later[14]. There is also the far-reaching advantage of the motivational value of providing an accessible and enjoyable introduction to the target language - an introduction that may make the difference between pursuing the learning of the language or abandoning efforts in the early stages.

Because of their saliency in learning the L1 and in the primary school classroom, songs are a natural choice for young L2 learners and indeed, these are probably the easiest learners to use songs with. Young children are uninhibited, suggestible and throw themselves into singing with great gusto. Any of the huge selection of songs that exist for NS children are as suitable for foreign youngsters since, as has been noted above, children have a high tolerance of non-comprehension and with children's songs the essential elements are the tune, the accompanying actions or sounds, the repetition and, ultimately, the sheer participation, rather than the meaning. The techniques of repetition and substitution have traditionally been used in children's songs to practise vocabulary, numbers, the alphabet etc, as represented in such classics as *Old MacDonald had a Farm*, *Ten Green Bottles*

Hanging On the Wall, This old Man, he played one, and so on. Other such songs include actions - *Head and shoulders, knees and toes, I'm a little teapot, Ring-a-ring-o'roses*[15]. Into this category fall 'Campfire' songs such as *If you're happy and you know it, Rock my soul* which can be suitable for older learners too[16]. What is notable is that all these involve some sort of interaction in the form of actions, sounds, numerical progression or lexical substitution. Actively participating in the song, not just by singing it, but also by reinforcing the meanings of the words with actions, sounds or cognitive engagement, promotes learning (see Task 7).

This observation is, of course, the basis for the language learning approach Total Physical Response (TPR) developed in the 60s (Asher 1965) which recognises the interplay of the senses in learning - and in particular the importance of the link between words and actions (see the outline of TPR in Chapter 1). The precepts of TPR, as well as those of Neuro-Linguistic Programming (NLP, see Chapter 1), hold that the learner's kinaesthetic, visual, and tactile as well as auditory modalities should be activated in learning. This is fulfilled in singing songs, through clapping, dancing, acting out or instrument playing. Furthermore, the 'silent period' in language learning, when learners understand language but are not yet ready to produce it, is respected in the TPR approach. With songs, learners are asked only to move, to do actions, mime or touch along with the song, and not necessarily to vocalise until they feel ready to do so. The TPR approach to songs is as valid for older as well as young learners although older learners may be more inhibited in following TPR procedures.

The same might be said about one of the most popular applications of song in language learning, Jazz Chants. As their name suggests, Jazz Chants are chants or poems that use jazz rhythms to illustrate the stress and intonation patterns of conversational English. The chants or poems are basically repetitive but new words are progressively substituted to teach new vocabulary or structures. For example, the 'Valentine Jazz chant' practises the simple past tense and goes:

I sent a valentine to Sue.
She sent a valentine to you.
You sent a valentine to Lee.
But you didn't send one to me.

I bought a valentine for Bill.
She bought a valentine for Jill.
You bought a valentine for Sue.
But she didn't buy one for you[17].

And so on.

Chanting is done all together, the class might be divided into groups, or individuals might be asked to offer the substitution, and the chanting is usually accompanied by clapping, or if appropriate, actions. Their creator, Carolyn Graham, has to date produced four books for children and four for adults and young adults[18].

This section has, more than the others, concentrated on exploiting the kinaesthetic appeal of song, singing along and doing actions. Other kinaesthetic tasks can extend to joining in with an improvised 'orchestra' (clapping, tapping fingers/pencils/rulers on tables, clashing cups together etc.) as well as creative actions such as drawing. 'Drawing the song'[19] can be an activity appealing to youngsters and to the more kinaesthetically-inclined adult (see Task 11). This activity can also be done 'in reverse', with learners asked to identify a series of cartoons in order (e.g. they might be given a set of drawings representing the animals on Old MacDonald's farm), holding them up at the correct point in the song (see Task 7)

9.4 Songs for Language Learning: Summary and Principles

To sum up, the approach to using song here basically starts from the L1 perspective, using song for participation, (inter)action or introspection, as well as, of course, for enjoyment. This approach eschews the reductivist attitude too often taken in the language classroom, of reducing the song to its lyrics and its lyrics to mere language exercises. It emphasises a view of songs as an interweaving of music and language, and suggests that much of their language learning value comes from the language production elicited as a result of exploiting this interdependency. Easing the typically unrelenting focus on linguistic input is also a way of reducing pressure on the learner and lowering the 'affective filter'. Through movement and active participation, songs can be used in the classroom to implicate modalities other than the merely auditory - the kinaesthetic, the visual, and the tactile, senses that are neglected in the use of many other media but which are essential to some learners, and especially to children. Turning from the participant-oriented aspect of song to the performance-oriented (a distinction made in Huy Lê 1999: 2), the main point made in the first Section 'Song and culture', is that a song is a cultural artefact and can be invaluable as a sample of its culture, embodying its values and even sometimes helping to change it. As much as any other cultural product (such as films, newspapers, literature), songs chart the social history of their culture and reveal the attitudes, preoccupations and behaviours of its members.

Principles for the use of songs for language learning
- Exploit songs as cultural artefacts.
- Exploit the innate predisposition for linking music, rhythm and language.
- Exploit the power of the auditory over other senses.
- Exploit the emotive strength of songs.
- Exploit the mutually supportive melody-lyrics relationship.
- Use songs not only as language input but as stimuli for language output.
- Use the learners' songs, not the teacher's.
- Apply TPR and NLP principles - enlist learner participation through activity and interaction.

Further reading
Murphey, T., 1992. *Music and Song*. Oxford: Oxford University Press.

Griffee, D., 1992. *Songs in Action*. New York: Prentice-Hall.

Grenough, M., 1976. *Sing it! Learn English through Song* (series of 6 books). McGraw-Hill Companies.

9.5 The Tasks

Task 1

Discourse type	Song - general
Communicative purpose	Engaging
Authentic task typology	Response
Level 3 up	
Aim: To connect with a song via its melody. To recreate song lyrics.	

Preparation: Select a song with an instrumental introduction or interlude, or instrumental version if available.
- Play instrumental part of the song a few times as necessary.
- Ask learners to:
    - Respond to the mood/feeling the music evokes or the atmosphere it creates, by drafting a short prose poem (or song) to go with the music *or* visualising and drawing scene/s.
    - Share their texts/pictures with others if wish.
    - Speculate on sentiments, ideas the song expresses.
    - Speculate on the culture the song belongs to.
- Listen to *whole song* and confirm/revise ideas above, then discuss:
- How the addition of voice contributes to the feeling in the song.
- Similarity to their own prose poem/song /drawing.
Note: The task may conclude at this point if the lyrics are judged too difficult for the learner level.
- In groups, learners pool words/phrases they have caught so far.
- Add words from same semantic groups in preparation for more detailed listening (e.g. if they have heard the word *love* semantic associations might be *heart, break*).
- Suggest some rhymes for ends of the phrases (for example, they might suggest *you* to rhyme with *do* in the lines from the Beatles song 'Love, love me do, you know I love you'[20]).
- Replay song as necessary for learners to recreate song as closely as possible.
- Discuss cultural-specificity *or* universality of song's theme.

Task 2

Discourse type	Song - general
Communicative purpose	Engaging
Authentic task typology	Response
Level 3 up	
Aim: To engage with a song via its melody and/or as 'warm-up'.	

Preparation: Select a song with an instrumental introduction or interlude, or instrumental version if available.
- Play instrumental part of a song
- Learners write their feelings/responses *as the music is playing* (for lower levels, use L1 if preferred).
- In pairs discuss/compare what they've written[21].
- If L1 has been used, learners first translate their notes into the TL for their partner.
- Elicit any common responses/ideas from whole class and note on board.

Task 3

Discourse type	Song - general
Communicative purpose	Engaging
Authentic task typology	Transference
Level 4 up	
Aim: To exploit personal involvement with a song by asking learners to make a presentation on it.	

Preparation: Ask learners to prepare the following outside of class time, individually or in pairs:
- Choose a favourite song, find a recording of it (or learn to sing it) and prepare to talk about it.
- Each learner/pair then presents the song to the class either (a) as a presentation or (b) via tasks.
- If (a), learner/s play/sing the song to the class, giving key phrases (e.g. the chorus)*, saying why they have chosen this song, explaining the story it tells, its background, style etc.
- Replay the song as required.
- Elicit questions/comments from the class.
- If (b) learner/s give tasks e.g. worksheet with questions* and activities, ask the class to sing along, and so on.
(*Difficult expressions/vocabulary may be dealt with in either of these stages.)
These presentations may be done, one per lesson, as a 'series' over a period of time.[22]

Task 4

Discourse type	Songs- general
Communicative purpose	Engaging
Authentic task typology	Reaction/response
Level 4 up	
Aim: To elicit 'gut reactions' to a song	

Preparation: compile a small selection of different style songs e.g. rock, pop, jazz, 'easy listening'. Draw up a 6 columned table with headings e.g.:
Do you like the song? Would you like to hear it again? Would you accept it as background music? Would you switch it off? What sort of person would like this style of song? Emotions evoked?
- Learners listen to the selection once and complete the table.
- Compare responses in pairs/groups.
- Try to agree on ONE song to hear again[23] (the teacher may opt to use this song with some of the other tasks suggested here).

Task 5

Discourse type	Song - evocative
Communicative purpose	Engaging
Authentic task typology	Extension
Level 5 up	
Aim: To encourage visualisation of aural input.	

Use a song that is descriptive, evocative and/or describes event/s.
- Play the whole song and suggest that learners 'listen for enjoyment' focusing on the music and the feelings it evokes rather than the lyrics. Suggest that learners close their eyes while listening.
- Ask learners to jot down the feelings evoked by the song e.g. sadness, nostalgia.
- From these feelings alone, ask learners to speculate what the song may be about (whether or not the words understood).
- Replay the song several times, asking learners to focus on visualising the description/s given in the lyrics combined with the feelings from the music.
- Ask learners to compose a picture or series of pictures (cartoons) depicting descriptions or events in the song. Learners may to work together using group input or making a group composition.
- Show compositions to other groups if desired.
Suggestions: songs by Bruce Springsteen, Mark Knopfler, Chris de Burgh.

Task 6

Discourse type	Song/music - evocative
Communicative purpose	Engaging
Authentic task typology	Transference
Level 4 up	
Aim: To apply music/song to another genre/cultural product.	

Preparation: Find an evocative piece of music or song.
- Learners listen and note ideas for *advertisements* (for which products?) that the music might accompany.

- In groups, learners create an advertisement using the music or song as a 'jingle', adapting the lyrics if necessary.
- Groups present/act out their advertisement to the musical accompaniment[24].
Suggestions: Mike Oldfield, Enya, Mark Knopfler, South American music.

Task 7

Discourse type	Song - children's/ballad
Communicative purpose	Provocative
Authentic task typology	Reaction
Level 2 up (especially suitable for young learners).	
Aim: Kinaesthetic engagement with song.	

Preparation: choose a song that tells a story or uses substitution (see suggestions below). Prepare and copy a series of cartoons or pictures or find objects to illustrate the story/ substitutions.
- Play the song and ask learners to hold up the appropriate picture/object at the correct points in the song.
Suggested songs: *Old MacDonald* (use plastic farm animals), *This Old Man* (pictures and numbers), *Clementine* (pictures), *Michael Row the Boat Ashore* (pictures).

Task 8

Discourse type	Song - traditional
Communicative purpose	Engaging
Authentic task typology	Inferencing
Level 3 up	
Aim: To extrapolate socio-cultural/historical information from song.	

Preparation: use a traditional TC song or a song with a particular socio-cultural/historical background.
- After playing the whole song the first time ask learners to do the following (if wished, prepare these prompts on a transparency or handout);
- Describe the mood/feeling of the song using a few adjectives (e.g. nostalgic, regretful, bitter, celebratory)
- Note any place names or names of people.
- Jot down what they remember of the chorus of the song (if there is one) or any repeated lines.
- Speculate on the historical era that the song recollects/is from.
Play the song again, asking learners to (in addition to above):
- Note what socio-cultural/historical phenomenon is represented in the song e.g. emigration, revolution, war.
- Note the development or illustrate the story told in the song.
- Note any striking linguistic expressions.
- Pool ideas in groups or as a class.

Give learners the words of the song and play again. Ask learners to
- Complete any above tasks they haven't completed.
- Underline any words/expressions that reveal the cultural base of the song and brainstorm their meaning /significance in groups.
- Via the Internet, investigate the origins of the song and any culture-specific references, and report back on their findings in a subsequent lesson.
Suggestions (Irish): Level 3 up; *Molly Malone, Galway Bay. It's a long way to Tipperary*, Level 5 up; *Sonny, The Wild Rover* Level 6 up; *Flight of Earls, Fairy tale of New York* (The Pogues).

Task 9

Discourse type	Songs - themed
Communicative purpose	Engaging
Authentic task typology	Inferencing
Level 5 up	
Aim: To explore TC or universal theme through songs.	

Preparation: Select a few songs on a specific theme (culture-specific or universal) (see suggestions below).
- Play the songs and ask learners to identify the *theme* only (e.g. loneliness, poverty, war)
- Replay songs and ask learners to perceive the *attitude* expressed by the singer/song to the theme (e.g. defiance, pride, anti-war).
- Divide class into groups, assigning one song to each group.
Each group:
- Researches 'their' song on the Internet or via other resources, looking for (a) writer (b) date when first released (c) the lyrics.
- Analyses lyrics for expressions applying to the identified theme and other striking language.
- Prepares a short presentation on their song.
- Presents their song to the class.
- As whole class, pull together treatment of the theme in the culture in general and compare to own cultures if applicable.
Suggested songs/themes: American anti-war feeling - *Where have all the flowers gone, A hard rain's gonna fall* (Bob Dylan), *Alice's restaurant*.
The under-privileged - *In the Ghetto* (Presley), *Eleanor Rigby* and *Lady Madonna* (the Beatles), *The Streets of London* (Ralph McTell) *The Boxer* (Simon and Garfunkel), Abuse - e.g. *My name is Luka* (Susanne Vega),
Education - *Another brick in the Wall* (Pink Floyd), *Schools Out* (The Donnas), *I don't like Mondays* (the Boomtown rats)
Misunderstood youth - *She's leaving home* (the Beatles)[25].

Task 10

Discourse type	Songs with a storyline

Communicative purpose	Engaging
Authentic task typology	Transference
Level 4 up	
Aim: Detailed listening and genre transfer.	

Preparation: Choose a selection of songs that tell a story (see suggestions below). Put each on different audio-tapes.
- Divide learners into groups and give each a tape and tape-recorder. Groups then:
- Work in separate areas of the room or different rooms if available.
- Listen to song in detail to understand the story being told.
- Rewrite the song as a story.
- Mix with different groups and 'swap' stories. Play each other the songs if interested.
Suggested songs: Ballads e.g. *Clementine, The Band Played Waltzing Mathilda.* Rock e.g. *I don't like Mondays* (the Boomtown Rats) or Bruce Springsteen songs such as *The River*.

Task 11

Discourse type	Music
Communicative purpose	Engaging
Authentic task typology	Reaction
Level 3 up	
Aim: Creative reaction to musical input	

Preparation: Find a short piece of evocative music.
- Play a few times as necessary.
- Learners write a reactive piece (prose/poem) to go with the music or draw scene/s it evokes.
- Share and explain their pieces.
Suggested music: film soundtracks, classical music.

Task 12

Discourse type	Sound effects
Communicative purpose	Provocative
Authentic task typology	Reaction
Level 4 up	
Aim: Interpreting non-linguistic prompts.	

Preparation: Record a series of sound effects on tape, making a different tape for each group in the class[26]. Give a tape and a tape recorder to each group.
- Each group composes a story/play around the sound effects.
- Groups read/perform their story integrating the sound effects.

Task 13

Discourse type	Pop music video
Communicative purpose	Engaging
Authentic task typology	Analysis
Level 4 up	
Aim: To compare impact of visual and aural input.	

Preparation: Choose a rock video and record the song onto audio-tape (or use the tape/CD of the song).
- Learners work in 2 groups in separate rooms if possible. Group 1 watches the video of the song without the sound.
Group 2 listens to the audio-tape.
- Based on the visuals alone, Group 1 guesses at:
- What the song is about
- Who is singing (man/woman, group)
- The mood of the song (sad, lively, defiant etc.)
- Any words/phrases they may catch (by lip-reading).
- Group 1 then prepare sketches of key images (images that recur or are representative of) the video.
- Based on the audio alone, Group 2 listens for gist and notes:
- The theme of the song.
- Any recurring words, expressions or the chorus.
- Who is singing - male/female/group, naming these if possible.
- The mood of the song (sad, lively, defiant etc.)
- Group 2 then imagine what sort of video images would appear in a video of this song and prepare some sketches ('story-boards') of their suggested video.
- The two groups then 'jigsaw' their findings, confirming or correcting the speculations of the other group. (This can be done by members of each group pairing off). Finally, show original video to class to allow them to confirm their ideas.

Notes

1   The comtemporary thematic categories listed in Murphey 1992: 136-8 were the inspiration for this idea.

2   From Yehudi Menuhin's Keynote address to ATEE Conference Mary Immaculate College, Limerick, Ireland, August 1998.

3   In the area known as *Broca's area*.

4   Based on Murphey 1992: 40-1.

5   This draws on Murphey 1992: 43-5.

6   This is suggested in Griffee 1992: 88.

7 This is the approach taken in Grenough (1997) which has a taxonomy of popular songs and the grammatical points they illustrate. For example, she suggests that Stevie Wonder's song I just called to say I love you gives practice in direct and indirect quotations, When the Saints go marching in practices the present tense, and so on.

8 'Guantanamera' - based on a poem by Jose Marti, lyric adaptation by Julian Orbon, original music by Jose Fernandez Diaz, music adaptation by Pete Seeger and Julian Orbon.

9 For example, for years I heard the lyrics of the chorus of the Dire Straits song 'Money for Nothing' (1988) as 'Money for nothing and your chips for free'. The actual line being: 'Money for nothing and your chicks for free'.

10 Based on responses elicited during my own use of this task in classes.

11 A classic example of a borrowing from a children's rhyme can be found in The Donna's song 'Schools Out': 'No more pencils, no more books, no more teacher's dirty looks'.

12 This is so pervasive that teachers/learners will easily find their own examples of this from songs they like; the Rolling Stones' 'Jumpin' Jack Flash' and the chorus from Creedance Clearwater Revival's 'Proud Mary' ('Rollin', rollin' down the river') are just two examples of reduction of the verb form -ing. The folk song 'Clementine' with its repetitive chorus 'Oh my darlin'...' illustrates that the reduction occurs in nouns as well as verb endings.

13 A comprehensive source of song lyrics can be found on http://www.lyrics.com/

14 An example of this comes from my own experience of learning French as an eight-year-old, and being able to effortlessly recall all the words of one of the children's songs learned, *Il etait un petit navire*, nearly forty years later.

15 The Web site http://www.theteachersguide.com/ChildrensSongs.htm is an excellent source of children's songs. (accessed 27 November, 2002).

16 The Web site http://www3.sympatico.ca/cottagecountry/dir-cam.htm has a large selection of campfire songs (accessed 27 November 2002). A huge international collection of folksongs can be found on: http://ingeb.org/ accessed 27 November 2002).

17 From OUP-USA Web page, http://www.oup-usa.org/esl/isbn/s0194349276.html accessed 27 November 2002.

18 E.g. *Jazz Chants Fairy Tales* and *Holiday Jazz Chants* both published by Oxford University Press, USA in 1988 and 1999 respectively.

19 This is suggested by Griffee 1992: 18-19.

20 'Love Me Do' is from the Beatles album *Please Please Me* (1963).

21 Based on Murphey 1992: 42-3.

22 Activity suggested by Chandler and Stone 1999: 24.

23 Based on Murphey 1992: 40-1.

24 This draws on Murphey 1992: 43-5.

25 The contemporary thematic categories listed in Murphey 1992: 136-8 were the inspiration for this idea.

26 Sound effects available from http://www.a1freesoundeffects.com/

Chapter Ten:
Film

Any teacher who has used a film with learners will have felt the thrill of excitement in the class, the learners' anticipation of entertainment and enjoyment at the sight of the VCR. Of all the cultural products discussed here, film is the one that is designed to appeal most directly and fully to our emotions. It is also the one most clearly entrenched in learners' minds as a medium of entertainment. This means that the key issues relevant to the use of film for language learning all have to do with affect. How, first of all, can the affective responses to film be harnessed for language learning? Secondly, how do we move from entertainment to learning without 'killing the magic', as Stempleski and Tomalin (2001: 9) put it? As will be discussed below, using film for language learning requires practitioners to walk a fine line between getting learners to become involved in the film on the one hand, while exploiting its language learning potential on the other. It also requires an attitudinal shift on the part of the practitioner, from treating films as merely extensive stretches of language input for comprehension, to approaching them as cultural artefacts via content- and task-based frameworks. Because with film the teaching approach taken is so vital, this is the main focus here - the challenge that using film in the classroom poses to the teacher.

10.1 The Challenge of Film

Film is probably the most challenging of all the cultural products discussed here to use productively for language learning. There is, firstly, the potential disadvantage shared with its small-screen counterpart, the identification of film-viewing with passivity, a disadvantage that has to be balanced against the positive aspects of watching a film, enjoyment and emotional involvement. Secondly, comes the challenge that the length and richness of the medium poses to the teacher designing tasks to accompany films. Finally, of course, there is the challenge this complex cultural product poses to the learner trying to comprehend it. This section suggests ways the teacher can address these difficulties, via a number of differently angled approaches.

10.1.1 Balancing learning and enjoyment

Some of the principles for avoiding the first problem, the degeneration of enjoyment and relaxation into passivity, have already been discussed in relation to television in Chapter 6. These basically turn on appropriate preparation of the *tasks* to accompany the text on the one hand, and of *the learners* themselves on the other. Learners need to be made aware of the rationale for using the medium in general, as well as that of using a particular film. Without over-preparing for a film or spoiling the suspense and sense of discovery, it may be necessary to check learners' knowledge of vocabulary and/or of culture-specific concepts, customs etc. that are essential to an understanding of the film (e.g. funeral rites in Ireland for the film *Waking Ned Devine*). An overemphasis on pre-teaching vocabulary, should, however, be avoided. After all, the audio-visual medium is in many cases the clearest medium for illustrating the meaning of new vocabulary items. Pointing out certain vocabulary items at the start can also induce learners to listen out for them, which can interfere with their comprehension of the whole. In moderation, preparation helps focus the learners on the film as a learning as well as an entertaining experience and, if carefully done, can actually heighten the anticipation of the film (Summerfield 1993: 28) much as a film trailer does. Tasks or activities associated with the film should, for the first viewing at least, be kept simple and unobtrusive so that they do not intrude on the learner's appreciation of the film. These might consist of a set of 'authentic' questions, i.e. 'intuitive' questions that viewers might naturally ask themselves as the film or film excerpt progresses e.g. 'why is he so nervous?' 'why won't she agree to marry him?'[1], the responses to which will fuel class/group discussions after the viewing. Asking learners to keep track of/note down certain language or actions, however, particularly on the first showing, might cause them to miss things and thus interfere with their comprehension. In general, a good gauge of how well you are maintaining the balance between learning and enjoyment - encouraging the first without spoiling the second - is the reaction of the students. It can sometimes be more profitable in the long term to 'waste' an opportunity for learning so as not to forfeit one's audience to tedium.

One crucial element in the enjoyment of a film is the viewing environment. The difference in the impact of a film when seen on the big screen as compared to a television monitor, is not only due to the size of the screen, but on the setting, the lighting and, most crucially, the audience. As Summerfield points out, the experience of watching a film with other people is very different from watching it alone because 'as a member of an audience one is aware of - and affected by - the reactions of others' (1993: 30). The film audience in a sense forms a sort of bond, as people do with other types of shared experiences (*ibid*.). This shared emotion can be channelled into learning if the showing of the film is immediately followed up by group discussion or by reaction/response tasks.

One way of garnering immediate response to the film is via some form of an 'image-sound skim' (Lacey 1972). In this technique, learners are simply encouraged to mention images or sounds from the film that particularly struck them and what feelings these evoked. The rational for this is to allow the film to 'continue working', to elicit response while it is still 'warm', before the viewer has had time to analyse what s/he has seen. Slightly more detailed follow-up - simple reaction prompts such as 'what (in the film) pleased you? ' 'what surprised you?' 'what upset you?' - can then follow (Lacey 1972, Stempleski and Tomalin 2001: 41-2) (see Task 2).

The image-sound skim technique is authentic in that it is a way of recreating and to an extent externalising in the pedagogical environment, the sort of gut reaction to a film that is heard in the remarks of an audience leaving a cinema. It is respectful of the learners' emotions, giving them time to come to terms with the feelings the film has elicited and not marring the 'afterglow' of the film by forcing them to distance themselves from it and analysis it immediately. Once the emotional effect has worn off, it is time for some of the more detailed, analytical and language work suggested in the following sections.

10.1.2 The content-based approach

A commonly cited impediment to the use of film in the language learning classroom is length. This is not so much because the time required to show a film is too long - many films would fit into two 45-minute lessons - but because much current practice in the use of video in language learning still tends to equate exploitation of video material to extension of it in terms of time, hence the classic 'three-minute snippet' guideline. The irony that abbreviating discourse can actually make it *more* difficult to understand because of the loss of context has often been pointed out: 'If listeners are presented with little bits of words on tape and asked to identify the consonants and vowels that these bits are composed of, they cannot do it. They perceive an acoustic blur without sufficient structure to enable them to recognise what they have been listening to' (Underwood 1994: 10-11). Re-listening to short segments of dialogue encourages learners to use the seriously flawed listening strategy of bottom-up processing. This reduces phonological segments to acoustic signals which have no significance in isolation, that is, outside the context of the complete word, sentence or utterance (see also Brown 1993: 150-1) and explains why the snatches of dialogue in film trailers can be hard for even native speakers to make sense of. At the root of the practice of segmenting authentic texts that are relatively long is, of course, the attitude that treats all input as 'language comprehension'. Yet the traditional comprehension-focused repertoire - comprehension questions, clozes, vocabulary lists etc. - appears all the more artificial in the case of a medium so familiar to learners in a 'lay' context. It also neglects the potential of the 'multi-media' and multi-sensory aspect of film:

> 'One-track activities, such as listening-comprehension-only strategies, fail to exploit the multi-modal potential of video movies. Not only should activities achieve a balance of target modes - including picture, movement, language, sound and captions - but they should include techniques that actively involve students in building an awareness of the interplay and various relationships that exist between the different modes.' (Wood 1995[2])

This suggests that what is more beneficial than the short-term aim of focusing on comprehension of a single film/excerpt, is the long-term goal of honing a critical awareness and appreciation of film as an art form and as a technical accomplishment, with language being acquired through and as part of this process. This swaps a comprehension-based approach for one that is content-based, one where film is seen as a 'complete communication process' and where language acquisition arises through response to it as such. A content-based approach, in other words, exploits the input (the film) not to *teach* language but to *release* it (Tomalin 2000). A key aspect of this approach is that it retains the authentic purpose of film, its calculated appeal to affect. Among its basic precepts are a focus on the holistic emotional response to a film as a multi-sensory event, and the maintaining of sensitivity to and respect for this response.

The content-based approach underpins the treatment of film suggested in this section and divides into four basic types of activities. The first is the most 'natural' one, watching and responding to a whole film, viewed either in one go, as in the cinema, or with 'breaks' as on commercial television. The second activity type is making comparisons, either between film remakes and their originals or comparing book-based films to the book they were adapted from. The third, also using book-based films, is using the two media to 'support' each other for comprehension. The fourth - in films where 'personality' is the salient element - is focusing on characters in the film. The last three activity types might involve watching whole film/s or just excerpts from it/them.

In stressing activities in which film is seen as a vehicle for language learning rather than as extended language input, a content-based approach is not intended to preclude language focus work where the requirement emerges. Like any audience, learners miss fragments of dialogues, hear language used in ways that are new to them, or simply take a liking to particular modes of expression, any of which will merit time spent on them after the showing of the film/excerpt is over.

A stretch of film dialogue, might also serve to 'flesh out' language structures or lexical items learners have already encountered, illustrating them in authentic communicative situations (Massi and Merino 1996: 20). Learning phrasal verbs, for instance, is too often a fairly soulless exercise in coursebooks, since these are mainly used in the spoken language, and are only really brought to life in dialogue. A conversation rich in phrasal verbs - such as one occurring in the film about American college kids, *Clueless* in which two girls are talking about one of their boyfriends' possessiveness (he is always 'calling her up' and so on), learners witness the verbs 'in action', strengthening their understanding of their meaning and use as well as important phonological features, such as where the stress falls in phrasal verbs.

Depending on the level of interest in the class, the language focus activities might be brief or extended and might be undertaken as a whole class or in groups. More extended work, if desired, might draw on a variety of resources, ranging from the script of the film (most conveniently, from the Web[3]) to on- and off-line grammatical resources and practice exercises.

10.1.3 The whole film

The prospect of watching a whole film in a foreign language can be daunting to many learners. It is important therefore that the film is initially approached in a way that diminishes this apprehension. One of the simplest and most authentic ways to do this is to 'milk' the opening sequence over which the credits appear. More and more often, in modern films, the opening sequence has some significance - it may be an action scene, or it may give some important background to the key character/s. Since the opening sequence is intended to whet the curiosity and appetites of the audience, it is natural and authentic to exploit this in the language classroom. This can be done by pausing the film after these opening shots and speculating where the scene is taking place, what can be inferred about the character or characters figuring in it, and more generally, what the film is going to be about, what is its genre (comedy, thriller, romance etc.) and so on. If there is dialogue in the opening sequence, the sound can even be turned down in order to get the students to make inferences from the images alone and to speculate on the dialogue that takes place. Learners will probably eventually be able to produce an approximation of the dialogue and this assists comprehension once the actual conversation is heard, as well as building confidence. This type of approach is particularly appropriate with low level learners for whom watching a TL film is a big hurdle (see Task 8).

Perhaps the most authentic activity with film entails having learners watch and react to a film inside the classroom as they do outside it. The most natural reaction to seeing a film is, of course, to talk about it after viewing it (see the idea of an 'image-sound skim' above). More analytical discussion might follow this, focusing on any aspect of the film; the characters and the actors who play them; the plot; the script; the cinematography; or particular elements of the film (the music, the settings, the costumes etc.). More analytical still, but a useful activity in that it gives learners an additional textual dimension, is comparing a film review or summary, with the film itself. The review/summary can be read before the film (as is usually done in 'real-life') and can thus act as a preparation activity for the film, introducing the main theme, setting and characters. Re-read after seeing the film, the reviewer's interpretation of it might prove controversial and supply food for debate or written work. A further dimension can be added to this activity by comparing different reviews of the same film, and assessing which review is the most 'accurate' in the learners' opinions (see Task 5).

If watching a film in its entirety is difficult for logistical reasons, an alternative is to use the authentic chunking system of the commercial break - approximately 15 minutes of viewing followed by a four-minute interval for the type of reaction and discussion described above. Another natural cut-off point might be the soap opera tactic of breaking off the story at a critical moment, thus creating suspense and promoting speculation. This lends itself to the prediction of events from the cut-off point, and might involve writing passages of dialogue and/or preparing storyboards. The break-off strategy should, however, be used with caution as such interruptions can be irritating and frustrating for the learner (as they are for native speaker viewers when a television film is interrupted by a commercial break at a particularly gripping moment) and may thus prove counter-productive. As with the use of all cultural products, in other words, the practitioner has to juggle pedagogical expediency and emotional appropriacy.

10.1.4 Comparison: film remakes
One of the most fruitful areas for content-based work with film is comparison,

exploiting the long-established movie traditions of re-making films and of adapting films from books. Examples of remakes that could be used with language learners include *Romeo and Juliet* (Zeffirelli, 1968 and Luhrmann 1997), *Sabrina Fair* made in 1954 by Billy Wilder and the 1995 remake *Sabrina*, by Sidney Pollack; *The Thomas Crown Affair* (1968 and 1999) and *The King and I* (Lang, 1956) remade as *Anna and the King* (directed by Tennant) in 1999 and, if this particular genre is to the taste of one's students, *Psycho* (1960, Hitchcock, and 1998, Gus van Sant). Comparison of remakes is probably most practical in the language learning context when done on a micro-level, comparing treatment of a particular scene in the film and its remake, possibly according to specific criteria (e.g. the settings, characters, plot and mood of the two versions and so on[4] (see Task 18). As such activities do not rely too heavily on comprehension of the language alone, they can be used with learners of varying proficiency levels (Tomalin 2000). Once learners are familiar with the concept and practice of the remake, they may even be set the task of 'designing' remakes of films they are familiar with (either ones viewed in class or elsewhere). This could involve suggesting alternative historical/cultural settings, contemporary actors and theme music, and even an updated title[5] (see Task 19).

10.1.5 Comparison: the film of the book

To turn to the phenomenon of the film of the book, the more obvious comparison tasks apart (see below) an important issue to be addressed with a class proficient enough to read a novel and to watch a film in its entirety, is the whole controversial issue of 'film of the book' adaptations. This might be done directly, through the media of a formal debate (see Task 16) or informal discussion, research, learner journals or other written assignments or may be implicit in the comparison task. The key issues of the debate that might be highlighted to learners, are *interpretation* and *popularisation*. On the one hand, it can be argued that the film of the book is always a compromise. The amount of editing, alteration, and interpreting required in transferring written discourse to the audio-visual medium make it merely one of a multiplicity of possible interpretations of the written text. Especially if the original is a so-called 'classic', to transfer it to film is to popularise it, a case, perhaps of the 'canonisation of the junior branch' in reverse (see Chapter 5 'Literature' Section 5.1), effectively *de*-canonising the work and dragging it back to a parochial level.

The opposing viewpoint is that written text can be seen as being open to interpretation the moment it is released from the writer's pen. As reader-response theory sees it (see Chapter 5 Section 5.1), response to literature is personal and wholly internal, with the reader in a sense creating his/her own version of the work. If reading is a constant act of personal, internal interpretation, then the film of the book may be conceived as a public, externalised one.

As for popularisation, film versions and adaptations may be said to make literature, with its depth of historical/cultural background, more accessible to language learners and NSs alike, potentially rousing interest in reading the work in the original. Film versions can make some of the more 'difficult', inaccessible classics come alive for modern audiences (films of Shakespeare's plays being a good example of this). Perpetuating classic and universal stories through the medium of film, therefore, may be a way of introducing them to a young, screen-oriented generation.

The most satisfactory way out of the 'novel versus film' controversy is probably to acknowledge that the two media are at the same time distinctive and yet complementary. They may each be evaluated on their own terms as samples of their medium or genre, yet as a complementary unit, each is supplemented by the other (Pulverness 2000).

From the teaching point of view, the phenomenon of 'the film of the book' is a decidedly welcome one. First of all, to a learner audience raised on the visual media, the film of the book will have greater immediacy than the written text. The multi-media aspect of the text-film unit can be exploited for learning in many ways for comparison, contrast, introduction, support and explanation. All such activities are authentic in that they arise naturally from the relationship between the two forms of the story and are for that reason 'native speaker-like'. Secondly, the TL film may stimulate an interest in its cultural setting and/or encourage the learner to go to the original text itself.

Book to film adaptations, of course, proliferate. Adapting the novel to the big screen has been a challenge to the film industry almost since its inception. *Oliver Twist*, for instance, was first filmed as early as 1922[6], when the cinema was still in the silent era. Among the many other classics reaped for the big screen are works by Joyce, *A Portrait of the Artist as a Young Man*, *The Dead* and even *Ulysses* (in production at time of writing); works by the Bröntes, *Wuthering Heights*, *Jane Eyre*; and a spate of Jane Austen adaptations dating from the 1990s - *Sense and Sensibility, Pride and Prejudice, Emma*. Contemporary literature adapted for the big screen includes *The English Patient* (Minghella 1996), *Bridget Jones Diary* (Maguire 2001), *The Shipping News* (Hallström 2002) and useful with younger learners - the *Harry Potter* books (films released in 2001 and 2002). In the Irish cultural context, there has been *Angela's Ashes* (Parker 1998) (a rather stereotypically daunting depiction of 1950s Ireland) and those portrayals of life in modern-day inner-city Dublin that are equally daunting in their way, *The Commitments* (Parker 1991), *The Snapper* (Frears 1993) and *The Van* (Frears 1996)[7] (for more on cultural stereotyping, see the 'Film and Culture', Section 10.2 below).

As has been suggested in the outline of the 'book-to-film controversy' above, the transition from one-dimensional text to multi-dimensional film is always contentious because the film is a subjective interpretation of the former. Objective comparison is impossible as one 'side', the film version, is relatively more constant than the other (the written one, which is open to personal interpretation). A lot of language learning 'mileage' can be gained from this dilemma as learners argue their case for and against the closeness of the film version to their conception of the text version. Comparison activities may range from the micro-level, comparing the transfer of a single scene to film according to criteria such as adherence to, or changes in, historical and cultural backdrop, setting, characters and dialogue, to macro levels of overall treatment in the book-to-film transfer, alterations to the plot, character set and so on. Learners might, finally, assess the effect of the additional media in the film version - the visual aspect, the soundtrack, the spoken dialogue - discussing whether this adds to the impact of the original text or whether it spoils imaginative interaction with the text by giving it a definitive interpretation (see Task 17). Selection of works for such comparison activities might range from 'faithful' renditions of novels (such as the 1987 John Houston film of Joyce's *The Dead*, the Frears film of Roddy Doyle's *The Snapper*) to ones in which only the plot is retained, as in the films *10 Things I Hate About You* (Junger, 1999) and *The Lion King* (Disney 1994) based on the plots of *The Taming of the Shrew* and *Hamlet* respectively.

Many of the classics have more than one screen adaptation, Shakespeare's plays being the most common, and this allows for a sort of multi-dimensional comparison, between different film versions as well as with the original. For example, as well as the three versions of *Hamlet* that use Shakespeare's prose (by Laurence Olivier, 1948, Franco Zeffirelli, 1990, and Kenneth Brannagh, 1996), in the Disney cartoon version, *The Lion King* (1994) mentioned above, the story is played out in the animal kingdom. *Richard III* has been filmed set in its original period (in Bushell and Olivier's 1955 version), in a 1930s fascist state (Loncraine, 1996) and adapted to the present day in Al Pacino's version, *Looking For Richard* (1996). Versions of *Romeo and Juliet* have included the musical set in 1950s American gangland, *West Side Story* (Robbins and Wise, 1961) (see Task 18).

Many modern stage-plays have been turned into successful films and while the stage-play as a genre can be a demanding one for language learners because the centrality of dialogue means that the dialogue has to carry the plot, the film is generally more accessible. Shaw's *Pygmalion*, for example, became the musical *My Fair Lady* (Cukor 1968), and was subsequently the inspiration for the film *Educating Rita* (Gilbert 1983). As with any musical adaptation of a 'straight' play or a novel, there is great scope for analysing how far the seriousness of the issue/s arising in the original (in the case of *Pygmalion*, self-identity) is/are diluted or trivialised in the musical version. *The Field* (Sheridan 1990) and *Dancing at Lughnasa* (O'Connor 1998) are two successful stage-to-film adaptations offering portraits of life in 1950s Ireland which may, however, be a little too stereotypical for the tastes of the teacher wishing students to learn about modern-day Ireland (see Section 10.2 'Film and culture' below).

10.1.6 Film as a visual aid

While most of the discussion above has focused on the comparison activities which book to film adaptations so naturally lend themselves to, film can also be used in language learning contexts to support a text. The film version of a literary work, or extracts from it, can be used, in effect, as a 'visual aid' (Bouman 1996: 29). This is particularly valuable as a way of introducing lower level learners to literature that might otherwise be beyond them. Depending on the type of task, scenes can be viewed before, during or after reading the narrative. On a micro-level, the film version can make explicit scenes that may be textually complex, such as passages describing actions, or descriptive passages (an example is the description of the Christmas dinner in *The Dead* rather pedantic in its detail on paper, but mouth-watering on screen). Or the film may simply liven up what might look, on the page, like 'flat' dialogue, rendering it more comprehensible by its visual clues. For example, in films like *The Portrait of a Lady* (Campion 1996) and *Washington Square* (Holland 1997), Henry James' quiet and understated prose and dialogue is very powerful transferred to the big screen where it is interpreted by facial expression and gesture as well as through language.

10.1.7 Focus on character

The fourth activity type categorised at the start of this section, focusing on characters in a film, is applicable to films which have a set of personalities and where these, rather than the action, are salient. One type of task that is possible here builds on the authentic phenomenon experienced while - or just after - seeing a film, and in which we find ourselves unconsciously identifying with one of the characters. Learners can choose to 'be' one of the characters in the film to empathize with him/her and to draw up a character sketch, to intuit reasons for his/her words and actions and so on. This is most useful (and, usually, practical) if a number of learners choose to 'be' each of the characters in the film, as this encourages greater interaction, discussion and analysis. If the film is viewed in sections, the character sketches might be composed on an on-going basis, and this gives even greater scope for discussion as learners revise interpretations of their characters according to words or actions in the latest section. Films that lend themselves well to this type of work are, first of all, ones with characters that are to an extent stylised, since they are more 'black and white', with traits that are more clearly recognizable. The people of Cavan in *The Butcher Boy* (Neil Jordan 1998) might be included here, or the characters in Woody Allen's *The Purple Rose of Cairo* (1985) which gives the added dimension that the same actor plays the double role of two very different personalities, as a film actor and as the character he interprets. Less obvious, but attractive especially for younger learners to identify with, are the characters in Peter Weir's *Dead Poets Society* (1989) which focuses on a group of schoolboys and their unconventional new teacher. Another peer group portrayed in a film for younger audiences is the one in the *Harry Potter* films (based on the novels by J. K. Rowling), which has very stylised characters, the wonderfully idiosyncratic teachers of Hogwarts school and, of course, Harry Potter's stepfamily, the unsavoury Dursleys (see Task 3).

One of the fundamentals to remember when using films for language learning, is that a film can be enjoyed and understood even without language, as the films of the Silent era demonstrated. It has been estimated that as much as 80% of our communication is non-verbal (Stempleski and Tomalin 1990: 4) and - as far as today's films are concerned - only about 10% of the vocabulary of any film is said to be communicatively essential (Wood 1995). All this suggests that learners of all proficiency levels can follow a film in the TL, particularly, of course, if the plot turns on actions more than on dialogue. Exposure to *extensive* stretches of language input in films can be a novel experience to the language learner habituated to the short excerpts used in the typical intensive language comprehension exercise, but can provide valuable training in tolerating uncertainty and guessing in context.

Few of the activities suggested in the above sections depend on 100% comprehension of the dialogue in the film. Furthermore, it may be recalled that the precepts of the content-based approach are that language learning and practice should not consist of reiterating language heard in the film but of *reacting* to it, with language use arising 'naturally' from the viewing of the film. For lower level learners in particular, the language produced by these means might be captured by getting learners to build up an ongoing database of 'the language of film' under such categories as 'stars', 'production', 'distribution', 'publicity' and so on[8]. Like some great literature, some great film moments involve quite simple language which can convey deep meaning or emotion, as in the famous and often misquoted line from *Casablanca*[9] 'play it, Sam'. Indeed, it is their simplicity which makes many of the most well-loved movie lines so enduring ('ET phone home'[10]/ 'I'll be back!'[11]). Famous movie lines such as these might be used as a simple but effective introductory activity to the subject of film in general[12] (see Task 1). The discussion (and disagreement!) that the activity tends to promote is an excellent springboard for introducing film in the classroom as well, of course, as valuable language use in itself.

10.2 Film and Culture

Film is the archetypal 'universal' audio-visual medium, predating its successor, television, by many decades. One aspect of this universality is that film can form 'a common frame of reference' for NNSs (Stempleski and Tomalin 2001: 1). Classic films such as *Casablanca* and more recent box-office successes such as that utterly British comedy, *Four Weddings and a Funeral* (Newell, 1994) are familiar to audiences around the world, thus making them instantly accessible to the language teacher's (possibly) multi-cultural audience of students. *Four Weddings* is, unfortunately, the exception rather than the rule, however, and in general, the more introspective and culturally revealing films are less well known outside their culture. The advantage of familiarity, in other words, has usually to be balanced out against the value of the cultural information imparted by the film.

This cultural information extends from the implicit - values and ideals, to the observable - how people speak, move, behave and relate to each other (Pulverness 1999a: 10). In films, learners can witness 'at first hand', linguistic features ranging from articulation of speech sounds to contextualisation of language register (i.e. linguistic choices) as well as paralinguistic features - culture-specific gestures and facial expressions. A well-crafted film about contemporary society can yield huge amounts of cultural information from trivia - What do people eat and drink, where and with whom? - How do people spend their free time? - Where do they shop, what do they wear, what are their grooming habits? - to their basic value-systems, attitudes to birth, death, religion, the family, foreigners and so on. The North American 'interiors' presented in the films of Woody Allen (e.g. *Manhattan,* 1979), the working-class British and Irish ones depicted by Mike Leigh (e.g. *Secrets and Lies,* 1996) and Stephen Frears (*The Snapper*) respectively, have high cultural content, showing on one level, the trivia of day-to-day life (the kitchen, the pub, the local store) while on another, implying more widespread societal attitudes (e.g. to the theme common to *Secrets and Lies* and *The Snapper,* illegitimacy). Ironically, the greatest risk when using the TC film for learning, is that its cultural and linguistic density can prove overwhelming and tempt the teacher (or students) to milk it too far thereby undermining its effectiveness. It may be more effective for the teacher to opt to focus on and develop a few specific themes. In the two films mentioned above, for example, the attitude of the TC to illegitimacy, the family relationships and support network offered to the mothers-to-be, and/or on the 'trivial' level, the interiors and exteriors, the 'two up two down' houses, grey urban settings and the omnipresent pub.

One issue facing the language teacher wishing to illustrate the TC via film, is the phenomenon of what can be termed the 'self-conscious culture', a striking case history of which can be found in my own present cultural context, Ireland. For decades the image of Ireland was based on external perceptions of the culture as depicted by the nostalgic Irish-American school of film-making, stretching from Ford's *The Quiet Man* (1952) to *Far and Away* (Howard 1992), which painted Ireland as a 'pastoral idyll'. Only quite recently has the newly burgeoning Irish film industry been able to counter the Hollywood myth, projecting a more accurate image of Irish society 'from the inside out'. Films such as *The Commitments, The Snapper, The Butcher Boy* (Jordan 1997) and *The Magdelene Sisters* (Mullan, 2002) expose changing attitudes to the institutions once central to Irish life (the Church, the family, Republicanism), revealing an Ireland where the dominance of the Church has been swept away in what McCarthy calls 'the Irish equivalent of the collapse of communism'[13] (2002: 6). Contemporary Ireland, in short, is totally at odds with its traditional Hollywood image. Cultural self-consciousness can provide a fruitful focus in the language classroom, with contrasts being drawn between, say, the Irish myth and the Irish reality; the rural idyll of *The Quiet Man* juxtaposed against the urban squalor of the setting of a film such as *The Commitments.* Issues of authenticity and subjectivity might also arise here. Which Ireland is being projected and by whom, yet, on the other hand, how realistic and authentic can we expect, or wish, any fictionalised version to be?

Such issues can also be referred to the culture of the learner group, with the teacher using a TL film in which the learners' culture is represented in scenes or characters, through the eyes of the target language speaker[14]. Learners might be asked to analyse this portrayal, pointing out stereotyping, idealisations, datedness or other inaccuracies if they occur[15] (see Task 13). A more complex linguistic counterpart to this activity is to use a subtitled film, either a TC film translated into the learners L1 or vice versa, and ask learners to 'check' translations and suggest reasons for the changes observed (changes might reflect differing forms of address, cultural attitudes to taboos, taboo words, or simply practical expediency - length of the utterance or mouth synchronization) (see Tasks 14 and 15).

Rich font of cultural information though it is, however, cultural-specificity can be counter-productive as well as productive in the language classroom. Learners might perceive a film as representing too narrow a sector of the English-speaking world (e.g. working class London in Leigh's *Secrets and Lies*), one from which they themselves are too culturally distant. A way to 'force' involvement in films otherwise too remote for learners might be to analyse the film's *lack* of appeal to their culture/s, pointing out cultural 'gaps' or areas of potential misunderstanding. In order to give them more meaning, scenes might be re-situated, and possibly acted out, in the native cultural context (see Tasks 6 and 11).

10.3 Film for Language Learning: Summary and Principles

Film, in conclusion, is a medium with enormous potential for exploitation in language and culture learning contexts, and the fact that it has been hitherto rather under-exploited may be partly due to the forbidding breadth of scope that it offers. Another possible reason for teachers' hesitancy to address film, it has been suggested, is the tendency to conceive of film in comprehension-based terms, and thus as a prohibitively long comprehension exercise. If film is handled via a content-based approach, however, it becomes far more accessible, with elements of affective engagement, response and cultural analysis taking precedence over comprehension of the language input. Working with film, the language learnt is not just the language that occurs within it but also the language 'released' by it in classroom interactions (Tomalin 2000). Film today is a genre that is linked, perhaps more than any other, to another genre, the novel (in 'film of the book' adaptations), and these links can be exploited in comparative analyses in the language classroom. There is also great potential for cross-cultural comparisons when using films, as they can offer painstakingly accurate and rich representations of a culture. The patterns of behaviour, lifestyle and modes of non-verbal communication that film can portray can be as valuable to the learner as the language input it provides. As with other cultural products, finally, film can give historical, sociological and attitudinal insights into a culture, revealing (depending on the directorial viewpoint) how it sees itself or how others see it.

Principles for the use of film for language learning

- Prioritise the affective impact of film.
- Balance learning and enjoyment.
- Adjust from a comprehension-based focus to a content-based one.
- Exploit the input (the film) not to *teach* language but to *release* it.
- The 'difficulty' of the dialogue alone is not a barrier to using a film with learners of a particular language level.
- Exploit comparison opportunities offered by film remakes and book-to-film adaptations.
- Exploit all the elements of a film, visuals, music, as well as language.

• Exploit TC films for their portrayal of all aspects of the target culture from the trivial to the profound.

Further reading

Baddock, B. 1996. *Using Films in the English Class*. Hemel Hempstead, Phoenix ELT.

Stempleski, S. and B. Tomalin 2001. *Film*, Oxford: Oxford University Press.

Summerfield, E. 1993. *Crossing Culture through Film*, Maine: Intercultural Press Inc.

10.4 The Tasks

Task 1

Discourse type	Lines from film dialogue
Communicative purpose	Engaging
Authentic task type	Extension
Level 4 up	
Aim: Introduction to use of film in the language classroom.	

Preparation: Without telling learners the purpose of the activity, get them to write down any famous movie lines they remember, the movie it is from, the circumstances in which it is said, and who said them (character and/or actor).
- Collect learners' notes and list the lines only on the first column of 5-column table on board/transparency *or*
- Produce your own list of favourite movie lines and list these on the first column of 5-column table on board/transparency.
- Head the next columns 'film' 'scene', 'actor/character' 'other info' (e.g. year, director).
- Learners copy and complete table, in pairs/groups if wished.
- Discuss ideas as whole class[16].
- Resolve any disagreements by checking on Internet or other resources (e.g. *Halliwell's Film & Video Guide*[17]).

Task 2

Discourse type	Whole film
Communicative purpose	Engaging
Authentic task type	Response/reaction
Level 4 up	
Aim: To express spontaneous reaction to a film.	

Preparation: Choose a provocative/emotive film plus prepare the prompts as below.

- Learners watch the whole film *or* a scene from it.
- After viewing whole film, ask learners to mention *images* or *sounds* from the film that immediately come to mind and note these on the board.
- ask what *feelings* these images and sounds elicited. Note on board.
- Use simple reaction prompts e.g. 'what/who did you like in the film/scene?' 'what/who didn't you like in the film/scene?' 'what surprised you?' 'what upset you?' 'what struck you most?'[18]
Note: This technique can be a prelude to other tasks.

Task 3

Discourse type	Whole film
Communicative purpose	Engaging
Authentic task type	Extension
Level 5 up	
Aim: Engagement with a film through identification with its characters.	

Preparation: Choose a film which centres round a set of characters (see suggestions below).
- Over a number of sessions, watch the film section by section.
- Learners adopt roles of characters in the film (a number of learners might have to 'adopt' each character):
- Once they are familiar with 'their' character, learners outline character sketches.
- After a few more scenes, learners use their imaginations to develop their characters to account for their personality and behaviour: imagine their background e.g. family and relationships? likes/dislikes?
- Learners get together with other 'character/s' to write invented episodes involving their characters.
- Enact the dialogues to the class.
Suggested films: *Dead Poets Society, Circle of Friends, Harry Potter* films.

Task 4

Discourse type	Whole film
Communicative purpose	Engaging
Authentic task type	Analysis
Level 5 up	
Aim: To analyse and interpret an allegorical film.	

Preparation: Choose a film which may be interpreted as allegorical or metaphoric e.g. *The Purple Rose of Cairo, Edward Scissorhands, The Phantom of the Opera, Frankenstein, Animal Farm.*
- View film in its entirety or in sections (possibly using other tasks).
- Learners suggest possible allegories e.g. Edward Scissorhands, Phantom of the

Opera, Frankenstein's monster all as Christ-like figures, *Animal Farm* as allegory of communism etc.
- Learners 'test' their theories by summarising the story told in the films and checking analyses on the Internet or on other resources.
- Check their theories using other resources e.g. film reviews and analyses on the Web.

Task 5

Discourse type	Whole film
Communicative purpose	Engaging
Authentic task type	Analysis
Level 6 up	
Aim: To view a film critically.	

Preparation: Choose a film of interest to your learners and which had contrasting reviews (find reviews in newspapers/magazines or on the Web). Make copies of the reviews. Also make copies of a 'sample' review of *another* film to give learners a film review 'model'.
- Tell learners they are to view and respond to a film as 'film critics'.
- Brainstorm aspects of a film that a film review addresses, e.g. the
- Genre (thriller, comedy etc.)
- Characters, and the actors' depiction of them
- Screenplay and the language
- Plot
- Explicitness of violence/sex
- Cinematography (e.g. settings, music, costumes)
- Emotive impact of the film
- Learners then look at the sample review to confirm their ideas and for aspects they have missed, also checking for useful new film-related vocabulary/terminology.
- Learners (or groups of learners) choose one aspect of the film they would like to cover
- View the whole film in class over a number of lessons if necessary, or ask learners to watch the film on video/DVD out of class. Then they:
- Discuss their reactions and write on their chosen aspect/s of the film (working in their groups if wished).
- Look at the sample review for the order in which the aspects might appear.
- The class assembles the review in agreed order, on word-processor/Web page if available, or by cutting and pasting on one sheet.
- Finally, compare with real reviews of the film.

Task 6

Discourse type	Whole TC film
Communicative purpose	Engaging

Authentic task type	Inferencing
Level 6 up	
Aim: To rate the cultural specificity of a film.	

Preparation: Choose a film set in, and representative of the TC and whose screenplay is available on the Web.
- Brainstorm what sort of assumptions in a film (or other cultural product) make it culturally specific e.g. implicit attitudes to:
social, gender, racial distinctions and roles, values and ethics (crime, wealth, parenthood, the family unit, medicine, sexual behaviour etc.), institutions e.g. family, government, education.
- View the whole film in class over a number of lessons if necessary, or ask learners to watch the film on video/DVD out of class.
- In mono-cultural groups if possible, rate the film's suitability for/appeal to viewers from own culture, giving reasons based on its implicit attitudes (as previously identified);
- Identify particular scene/s or aspects of the film that would be unsuitable for certain cultures and explain why.
-Access the film's screenplay on the Web, find one of above-identified scenes, then re-script to suit own culture audiences.
- Enact to other groups/the whole class.
Suggested films (Irish culture): *The Snapper*, *The Commitments*, *The Butcher Boy*, *Angela's Ashes*, *The Field*; (British culture): *Four Weddings and a Funeral*, *Secrets and Lies*, *The Full Monty*, *Little Voice*, *Local Hero*.

Task 7

Discourse type	Whole TC film
Communicative purpose	Engaging
Authentic task type	Transference
Level 6 up	
Aim: To analyse and transfer from one medium to another.	

Preparation: choose a film of interest to your learner group.
- Brainstorm in class to characterise publicity materials associated with a film, trailer, advertisement, video/DVD cover blurb, newspaper review.
- Learners search for, or teacher may bring, samples of each for reference.
- Learners choose which they wish to produce, and form groups according to choices.
- Groups analyse the sample of their chosen type of publicity material and produce a 'template'.
- View the whole film in class over a number of lessons if necessary, or ask learners to watch the film on video/DVD out of class.
- Learners extrapolate required information and prepare their publicity material.
- The group producing the trailer might select key scenes from the film for it, and extract these scenes from the film's screenplay on the Web.

- Groups circulate their publicity materials (the group producing the trailer may wish to enact it) and exchange feed-back.

Task 8

Discourse type	Whole film - opening sequence
Communicative purpose	Engaging
Authentic task type	Inferencing
Level 3 up	
Aim: To introduce a film and to whet interest.	

Preparation: Choose a film whose opening sequence is significant (e.g. shows important event/action, gives important background to key character/s).
- If there is dialogue in this opening sequence, *turn down sound*.
- Show the sequence and ask learners to speculate:
- Where the scene is taking place
- What they infer about the character/s figuring in it
- What the film is going to be about and its genre (comedy, thriller, romance etc.)
- (If played *with* sound)
    How/what the music adds to these impressions.
- (If played *without* sound)
    What is being said, then produce a feasible dialogue.
- Play the sequence *with* sound and compare learners' dialogues with actual one.
- Assess how the music adds to the impact of the scene.

Task 9

Discourse type	Dramatic film scene
Communicative purpose	Engaging
Authentic task	Extension
Level 4 up	
Aim: To predict behaviour/events.	

Preparation: Choose a scene from a film which culminates in a dramatic event (sudden departure, violent act, accident etc.)
- Show the scene and PAUSE before the dramatic event.
- In groups, learners
- Characterise the protagonists, assess the situation and predict the event.
- Write dialogue/screenplay to show how event ensued.
- Record or video their scenes (if possible) and show to class *or* act out their prepared scenes.
- Watch event as it happens in the film - compare own versions!

Task 10

Discourse type	'Social' film scene
Communicative purpose	Engaging
Authentic task	Analysis
Level 4 up	
Aim: To empathise with a film character.	

Preparation: Select a film scene which a number of characters interact (e.g. dinner party, restaurant, visit, meeting, social event).
- Outline the scene to the learners, briefly putting the characters in context.
- Give each learner/group of learners ONE character and ask them to think about the feelings of this one character as they watch the scene.
- Watch the scene.
- Ask each learner/group to discuss their feelings about what happened in the scene from the viewpoint of 'their' character.
- Form a group or groups representing the group in the film and discuss their reactions 'in character' (using first person pronoun!).[19]

Task 11

Discourse type	Culture-specific scene
Communicative purpose	Engaging
Authentic task	Transference
Level 6 up	
Aim: To raise awareness of cultural differences.	

Preparation: Select a film scene that is highly culture-specific (TC or another culture).
-View the scene and ask learners to analyse in which ways the scene is culture-specific, e.g. settings, behaviours, traditions, characters, values, attitudes etc. that are typical of the culture.
-Working in mono-cultural groups if possible, groups re-situate the scene in their own cultural context by making appropriate changes to setting, behaviours etc and re-scripting as necessary.
- Learners may wish to access the film's screenplay on the Web to find the exact scene and lines.
- Groups read/enact their adapted scenes.
- Feedback and class discussion re: changes each group has made.

Task 12

Discourse type	Short dialogue
Communicative purpose	Engaging
Authentic task	Reaction
Level 5 up	

Aim: To recall and reformulate dialogue.

Preparation: Find a section of film dialogue about 5 minutes in length. The dialogue should be intelligible, fairly free-standing and interesting. Mark short sections of the dialogue that you think the learners may be able to recall from memory.
- Play the whole dialogue and then ask the learners to recall as much as they can about the situation: who/where the speakers were, what they talked about and if they said anything striking.
- Re-play the dialogue stopping *before* the first short section you have assigned for recall.
- Ask the learners to recall as accurately as they can, the words *following* the pause.
- Encourage correct reformulation as well as accurate recall and write the closest suggestions on the board.
- Continue playing dialogue until the next assigned stopping point and repeat.
- Repeat once or twice as necessary.
Once learners have adequately recalled specified sections, replay the whole dialogue to help learners consolidate their comprehension of it.[20]

Task 13

Discourse type	TC Film - scene featuring foreigners
Communicative purpose	Engaging
Authentic task	Analysis
Level 5 up	
Aim: To explore cultural stereotyping.	

Preparation: Select a scene from a TC film which features a person/people from one of cultures of the learner group.
- Learners watch the scene and notice how the foreigner/s is/are portrayed, e.g.:
-Implict attitudes of film-makers or characters in the film to the foreigner.
-Stereotyping
-Idealisation
-How up-to-date?
-How accurate/inaccurate do learners think the portrayal is?[21]
- Learners discuss their perceptions, which will vary depending on their cultures.
- Suggest how the foreign character might *really* act in this situation.

Task 14

Discourse type	Scene from foreign film subtitled in English
Communicative purpose	Engaging
Authentic task	Analysis
Level 5 up	
Aim: To analyse the effect of film subtitles on the film's emotive impact.	

Preparation: Find a foreign film with English subtitles (*not* in one of the learners' first languages). Select an emotional or shocking scene that is as context-free as possible (e.g. an argument, fight, crime etc.).

- Play the whole scene with the sound turned down. Repeat if learners need more time to read and comprehend subtitles (but do not pause video during scene).
- Learners discuss their reactions to:
- The emotional impact (sad, shocking, depressing etc.) of the scene.
- The effect of being able to understand the dialogue without the sound.
- The contribution of body language and facial expression to the impact.
- Speculate on whether the scene will have *more* impact with the sound; which elements might contribute to this? (E.g. voices, music, sound effects).
- Play the whole scene with the sound up.
- Compare the emotional impact with the sound-less version:
- What contributes most to the (enhanced) emotional impact of the sound version? (Voices, music, sound effects etc.?)
- Discuss the effect of voice, when heard speaking an unknown foreign language (sounds more dramatic, serious, ridiculous etc.)
- Re-watch the scene with the sound, and speculate on the accuracy of the translation. (comparing the lengths of the utterances with the subtitles etc.).
- Debate constraints/advantages of subtitling versus dubbing.

Task 15

Discourse type	Scene from film from learner's L1 subtitled in English or English film subtitled into learner's L1 (see Note)
Communicative purpose	Engaging
Authentic task	Analysis
Level 4 up	
Aim: Analysis of translation.	

Preparation: Choose an interesting, fairly free-standing scene from film in learner's L1 subtitled into English *or* an English film subtitled into learner's L1 (Note: this activity for use with mono-cultural learner groups only).

- Play the scene twice to get students familiar with it.
- Replay enough times for learners to copy down the *spoken* dialogue on one column of a 2-column table.
- Replay again, asking learners to copy the subtitles which accompany the dialogue into the second column.
- Learners 'check' translations.
- Learner's note any changes observed and suggest reasons for these (e.g. omission of taboo words, different form of address, constraints of length).
- Debate constraints/advantages of subtitling versus dubbing.

Task 16

Discourse type	Film of book - entire or scene
Communicative purpose	Engaging
Authentic task	Extension
Level 5 up	
Aim: To debate ethics of making films of classic novels.	

Preparation: Find film adaptations (one successful and one not) of two classic novels (see suggestions below) and obtain copies of the novels (or find on the Web).
- If necessary, inform the class of *the debate* as a genre.[22]
- Divide class into two for a debate on making films of classic novels. Establish the motion e.g. 'this side believes it is unethical to reduce canonical literature to film'.
- The class works in two groups to establish support or opposition to this motion. Elicit and establish the bases for the two positions e.g. (proposing the motion) *popularisation*, *reducing* of the canon to popular fodder, versus (opposing the motion) *openness of text to interpretation, accessibility and familiarity* with the canon of literature.
- In their own time, learners view the films and read the books (or parts of them).
- The two groups reinforce their positions using any additional points arising from their viewing and reading.
- Initiate the debate, giving representatives from each side a fixed time limit (e.g. 3 minutes) to put forward their arguments in turn.
- Once all the arguments have been heard, the class acts as the audience for the debate and votes on the motion.
Suggestions: *A Passage to India*, E. M. Forster, film adaptation 1985, (directed by David Lean), *Great Expectations,* Charles Dickens, latest film adaptation 1997 (starring Gwyneth Paltrow, directed by Alfonso Cuaron).

Task 17

Discourse type	Scene from film of book
Communicative purpose	Engaging
Authentic task	Extension
Level 4 up	
Aim: To visualise and engage with a literary text.	

Preparation: Choose a film based on a book. Find a scene which occurs in both the film and the book. Make copies of the scene from the book.
- Read the scene in class.
- In groups, learners discuss, describe and note how they imagine the characters, settings, accompanying musical score, and any *changes* that might occur in transition to film.
- Prepare storyboards for the scene.
- Enact/describe to the other groups.

- Watch film version of the scene.

Compare to how imagined:
- Appearance and depiction of characters (including behaviour, voice, manner)
- Settings
- Atmosphere
- Effect (cheery, amusing, depressing, scary etc)
- Any omissions/additions etc.
- Learners discuss how close the film comes to their visualisation of it.
- Infer the rationale for any changes made.

Suggested film- book adaptations: *The End of the Affair*; *Circle of Friends*; *The Dead*; *A Portrait of the Artist as a Young Man*; *The Snapper*; *The Remains of the Day*; Cartoon version of *Animal Farm*. Films of Jane Austen novels, *Pride and Prejudice*, *Sense and Sensibility*, *Emma*.

Task 18

Discourse type	Scenes from film remake
Communicative purpose	Engaging
Authentic task	Inferencing
Level 5 up	
Aim: To compare film interpretations and infer reasons for differences.	

Preparation: Get the new and original versions of a film that has been re-made (see suggestions below). Select the same (interesting, fairly free-standing) scene from the two films. Prepare and copy a 3-columned table headed *criteria for comparison*, *original* and *remake*. In the Column 1 list comparison criteria: *setting (time, place, situation), characters (sex, age, other) plot, emotions, music, other...*
- Tell learners they are going to watch the same scene from two versions of the same film.
- Give learners the table and ask them to compare the two scenes from the two films according to the given criteria.
- Learners get into groups and compare the differences they have noted.
- Ask them to infer the possible reasons for changes, including how the changes reflect the era in which the film is made[23].

Suggestions: *Sabrina Fair (1954)* vs. *Sabrina (1995)*, *Pygmalion (1938)* vs. *My Fair Lady* (1968), *The Thomas Crown Affair* (1968 and 1999), *Psycho* (1960 and 1998), many Shakespeare films e.g. *Romeo and Juliet* (1968 and 1997), *Hamlet* (1948, 1990 and 1996).

Task 19

Discourse type	Classic film
Communicative purpose	Engaging
Authentic task	Extension
Level 5 up	
Aim: To design a remake of a classic film.	

Preparation: Brainstorm in class for a classic film all or most of the learners have seen. Get a copy of the film.
- Tell learners they are to design a remake of the film.
- Show a representative/famous clip from the film to refresh learners' memories.
- In groups, learners suggest:
- Alternative historical/cultural settings
- Contemporary actors for the major roles
- Modernisation of dialogue - modern slang, idiom, register, references.
- Updated concepts (if necessary), theme music and title[24].
- Groups compare their suggestions.
(Suggested films *Casablanca*, *Gone with the Wind*).
Note: it may be useful to do Task 18 prior to this one.

Task 20

Discourse type	Film trailers
* Communicative purpose	Provocative
Authentic task	Inferencing
Level 5 up	
Aim: To infer information about a film and make reasoned choices.	

Preparation: Get a video of a film that has a number of trailers preceding it. Copy the trailers onto one or more tapes (if a large class).
- Divide the class into groups. Give each learner group a tape and ask them to:
- Watch the trailers and note the titles of the different films being advertised
- Decide on the genre of each film (comedy, thriller etc.)
- Note any actors they recognise
- Infer a general idea as to what each film is about
- Note any constraints they perceive as far as their own tastes and language levels are concerned e.g.
- The rating it received from the censor
- The amount of violence or sex in the film
- The language (accents, colloquial language, speed of delivery etc.)
- Decide (on the basis of the above and of their own interests)
- *Which film* they would most like to see, reaching a democratic decision and giving reasons for their choice.
- Each group then announces their choice, with reasons, and the class tries to reach a unanimous decision on which film they would like to see, the basis of this discussion.[25]
- If acceptable, the teachers may opt to use chosen film for further tasks.

Notes

1   Questions from my task sheet for the proposal scene from the television adaptation of *Pride and Prejudice*, BBC 1996.

2   Originally accessed as: Film communication in TEFL. *Video Rising: Newsletter of the Japan*

Association for Language Teaching. 1995, 7(1) on
http://members.tripod.com/~jalt_video/vr_Wood1.htm (Accessed 28 January 2000).

3   Film scripts available from http://www.script-o-rama.com/table.shtml

4   This activity is suggested by Stempleski and Tomalin 2001: 107-8.

5   Activity suggested by Stempleski and Tomalin 2001: 60-2.

6   This version directed by Frank Lloyd.

7   Films based on the three novels constituting Roddy Doyle's *Barrytown Trilogy* (1995).

8   This activity is suggested by Stempleski and Tomalin 2001: 18-19.

9   Directed by Curtiz, 1942.

10 From the film *ET*, directed by Steven Spielberg 1982.

11 First uttered by Arnold Schwarzenegger in the 1984 film *Terminator* (directed by James Cameron).

12 Activity suggested by Stempleski and Tomalin 2001: 14-16.

13 McCarthy repeats an anecdote from the director of the film *The Magdelene Sisters*, Peter Mullan, in which Mullan asked a woman what Ireland was really like in the 1950s. Her reply was 'Think KGB' (McCarthy 2002: 6-7).

14 This activity may not be applicable to a multi-cultural group.

15 This activity is suggested by Stempleski and Tomalin 2001: 96-7.

16 This activity draws on Stempleski and Tomalin 2001: 14-16.

17 2003 edition edited by J. Walker, published by HarperCollins Entertainment.

18 Based on 'image-sound skim' technique, Lacey 1972, Stempleski and Tomalin 2001: 41-2.

19 From Tomalin 2000.

20 From Duff and Maley 1991: 147-8.

21 This activity is based on Stempleski and Tomalin 2001: 96-7.

22 See debating society rules e.g. http://www.lancs.ac.uk/socs/luds/rules.htm (accessed 14 July 2003).

23 From Tomalin 2000.

24 This activity is based on Stempleski and Tomalin 2001: 60-2.

25 Adapted from Chandler and Stone 1999: 81.

Chapter Eleven:
ICT

11.1 Introduction

The various language professionals have begun to take strides of varying length with respect to different Internet situations, the field of foreign language teaching taking the first and longest ones [...] it is in relation to foreign language pedagogy that the most searching discussions have taken place along with some innovative and effective practices relating to both teaching and learning (Crystal 2001: 232).

ICT has provoked an unprecedented excitement among the language teaching community, inspiring a daunting body of literature (both electronic and print-based) in a relatively short time span. This proliferation both reflects, and is an attempt to keep pace with, the rapidly changing ICT landscape. It also represents an endeavour to ground the use of these technologies in pedagogical theory and research, to prevent, in effect, the technology from 'leading' the pedagogy. It is perhaps surprising that 20-odd years on in the communications revolution, a recently published report concludes that the jury is still out on the language pedagogies associated with the new technology; 'although increasing use is being made of ICT for content research and immediate communication needs in foreign languages, at present, not enough attention is being devoted to questions of how the new media can systematically aid language acquisition and learning' (International Certificate Conference (ICC) Report, 2003: 5[1]).

The radical effect that technology has had on language pedagogy is unquestionable, however, stimulating a reassessment of the learner-teacher relationship and an overt shifting of responsibility for learning from the teacher to the learner, and thereby reaffirming the long association between technology and autonomy (Benson 2001: 136) (see Chapter 1 Section 1.1.3 and Chapter 2 Section 2.7 for more on learner autonomy). The technology has also added a new repertoire of skills. These are known as 'electronic literacy' - the ability to find, select, organise and make use of information, as well as to read and write in the new medium (Shetzer and Warschauer, 2000: 173), or simply 'the new literacies' - the interplay of technical, critical, linguistic and cultural skills required for use of the Internet (ICC report: 2003: 4,14). The transferability of these skills and their reciprocity with language learning gives the use of the new technologies the motivational edge on other media. For it is not only a case of using ICT for language learning, but of learning the language and skills needed to make effective use of ICT. Learners feel that they are acquiring not only 'knowledge', but skills to operate technologies which emancipate them from the traditional teacher-to-learner (or expert-to-non-expert) knowledge transfer paradigms.

Against this background of a paradigm shift in language pedagogy - and bearing in mind that writing about the Web in language teaching is 'rather like writing about 'the book' in language teaching' as Vogel points out (2001: 134) - the scope of this chapter is to focus on authenticity-centred applications of ICT. It looks at the pedagogies associated with the three technologies most used for language learning (see below), and looks at what the technologies can offer in the way of authentic texts and activities. The rapid pace of change also means that the most state-of-the-art information will probably be that found in the online journals and Web pages given in the further reading list, with the printed volumes covering the more established practices and the pedagogical theory and research.

The information and communication technologies most commonly used for language pedagogy are the Internet, i.e. the Web and electronic mail (e-mail), and corpora, and these are the three covered here. The use of synchronous communication in 'chat rooms' for language learning is less established and the type of language it contains arguably too unformed to be of real value for language learning (Crystal refers to the 'linguistic confusion and incoherence' that characterises chat room discourse 2001: 169).

This chapter has a slightly different structure from those covering the other cultural products. Each technology is covered in a separate section, and because of their relative newness, each starts with a short section introducing the pedagogical practices emerging for it. For each technology, it is then illustrated how the advantages of using authentic texts in language learning - their cultural content, currency and challenge - are particularly salient in this ICT context. The currency sections also reassess the concept of authenticity in the light of the effect of the technologies on language, and discuss the usefulness of the new, language varieties evolving within them, for language learning.

11.2 The Web

11.2.1 Using the Web for language learning

In discussing the use of the Web for language learning a useful starting point is the distinction between exploiting it as a *resource* and as a *medium* (see Conacher and Royall 1998: 38). As a *resource*, the Web offers sites which contain material produced for native speakers and these sites fall roughly into three categories. The first is material not written for the Internet, which has been transferred to it either directly or in abridged form. Poetry, song lyrics, books, film scripts and some journal articles all fall into this category. The second category is material not written originally for the Internet but adapted for it. This includes newspapers and journals, many of which publish adapted online versions in conjunction with their hard copy versions. The third category is material written specifically for the Internet, such as the material found on personal, institutional, commercial and informative sites e.g. government sites, medical, financial and tourist information, and so on. The thousands of sites written specifically for language learning, offering language practice via interactive exercises and activities, constitute the Web's function as a *medium*. However, it is the *resource* aspect of the Web that has been the most generative in terms of language learning methodologies and techniques, and we will look at this first.

As far as the teacher is concerned, this resource aspect has revolutionised language learning materials' preparation. Teachers no longer need to hunt out authentic texts from libraries and bookstores but can download texts and write materials based on them on their own PCs. Texts for many of the tasks suggested in this book for using literature, newspapers and songs can be sourced on the Web (see Web sites listed in the Culture section below (Section 11.2.3) and Eastment (2000) in the 'further reading' section). Tasks can be set for learners to work with the chosen text/s off-line, i.e. using texts and materials printed out by the teacher, or, alternatively, online.

Working online raises a number of issues unprecedented in any other medium used for learning. The first is connected to the degree of learner autonomy that working on the Web bestows. The linking capabilities of the Web are its defining feature and interaction via these links is the authentic *modus operandi* of working on it. While learners can, technically, be confined to a single site specified for a given task by downloading it onto the class PCs or a network, this severs its external links and in effect de-authenticates it as a Web task. On the other hand, the learner suddenly let loose in this new medium can be a bit like a child in a toy shop, surfing the Web indiscriminately and dallying with sites that s/he happens upon, and this is unlikely to promote much real language learning. If they are to work effectively on the medium, learners need as a basis, an awareness of the principles of learning autonomously and of their role and responsibility in this (see Chapter 1 Section 1.1.3). Without this, the technological cart is once more before the pedagogical horse, and, to pursue the metaphor, learners the hapless passengers. Among the responsibilities most pertinent to the use of the Web is that of critically reflecting on choices and decisions (see Little's definition of learner autonomy, 1991: 4). This requirement can be seen, in fact, to coincide with what is needed for electronic literacy, especially learning to be *selective*, i.e. how to evaluate the quality and relevance of information found on the Web and to exclude the 'dross'. As Volger points out, selectivity is not a skill learners need in the traditional classroom where input is generally selected by the teacher (2001: 137).

As has been pointed out in Chapter 1 (Section 1.1.3), learner autonomy does not, of course, imply a simple relinquishing of teacher control, but rather a readiness on the part of the teacher to 'take a back seat' as guide and facilitator of his/her students' learning. Teacher control is still very much in evidence via the *task*, which has to be all the more detailed and specific in order to direct and contain learners' use of the medium. This is particularly important in that clear direction will help learners steer a path through the barrage of text from the Web that can be quite daunting at first, especially to lower level learners.

One type of task that involves clearly directed use of the Web is the 'cybertrail', an electronic treasure hunt in which users follow a series of links from site to site, solving clues in order to find the next site. These can be set up by the individual teacher (or even by other learners), plus there are a number of Web sites with 'ready-made' cybertrails (see for example http://www.well.ac.uk/wellproj /workshp1/treasure.htm). Cybertrails emulate genuine browsing or surfing, but are more focused and help to eliminate the aimless nature of surfing (Atkinson 1998: 29-30). A suggestion for a simplified version of a cybertrail is given in Task 15. 'Virtual shopping' and job hunting are other genuine activities involving search and evaluation skills that can be undertaken. Learners may be asked to search for and 'buy' items on a shopping list, using commercial sites on the Web (see Task 6), or to search for a job to fit a given curriculum vitae in the appointments pages of online newspapers (such as *The Times Higher Educational Supplement, The Guardian*) or in the many sector-specific discussion lists containing sections on job vacancies. The use of the Web by tourists to research the town, region or country they plan to visit prior to a trip suggests the use with learners of 'tourism tasks'. These can be very motivating, particularly if learners are researching places they intend either to actually visit in the future, or places in the target language country which have been discussed in class. Because it is primarily a linguistic activity, searching is an excellent if challenging language exercise (see 'Challenge' below). It is also a wholly authentic task, honing electronic literacy skills, and having a genuine goal or incentive, the eliciting of 'hits' containing relevant information.

Another aspect of the Web that offers great possibilities for language learning is its function as a news medium. Most national and private broadcasting companies now broadcast the news and other programmes online. The Internet is, Tripathi puts it, 'a great resource for harnessing the teachable moment' (Tripathi 1998). Learners can be asked to compare breaking news incoming from online audio/audio-visual news, with the news in print-based newspapers. Learners might also perform journalistic tasks, transferring live audio-visual input into print, or reworking written news reports from online newspapers, news agencies or the BBC online, for presentation via a different medium, such as their own audio or visual recording (Atkinson 1998: 25). Evaluating and comparing news from different sources (see, for example, Windeatt *et al.* 2000: 36-7), possibly including learners' native language news sites, is another useful, authentic activity which hones analytical skills. Some of the larger news sites, such as CNN and the BBC, even have education pages with worksheets, activities and related links which might be integrated into tasks.

These types of activities demonstrate how the well-designed Web task can undercut the tendency to use the Web passively, by building in creativity. The most demanding creative task for learners is actually setting up a Web page, the hundreds of thousands of personal, class and school Web pages found on the Internet being evidence of the popularity of this type of activity[2] (although there are as yet, few samples of Web page design by adult language learners, see Mishan 2004). Among the motivational and language learning benefits from this activity is that it gives learners a real audience for their work, a NS audience who may even give them feedback in the target language.

To turn from using the Web as a *resource* to its function as a *medium*, this implies the possibility of online interaction, i.e. a two-way process (Conacher and Royall 1998: 38). In the context of language learning, and the English language in particular, the main source of interactive material is the proliferation of interactive sites designed specifically for learners. While these can be a gentler introduction to using the Web in the TL, especially for lower levels, the quantity and quality of these Web sites mean that these too have to be approached with caution. Eastment (2000) noted that at time of writing, there were 4,500 ELT sites listed on the *Internet TESL Journal* site[3] alone. Yet as far as their quality and the extent to which they exploit their medium are concerned, ELT sites have so far been a source of grave disappointment to practitioners:

> 'A good educational Web site satisfies two sets of criteria: a winning formula would be one which combined excellent use of the medium with excellent content. In fact we find different configurations: enthusiastic use of the medium but poor pedagogical quality, sound pedagogy making little use of the potential of the medium, and varia-tions along the way.' (Lamy 1997: 27)

This leads to the conclusion that material written for the Web too often replicates what is done by its non-digital predecessors; 'at the time of writing [...] a shelf of EFL workbooks and coursebooks would offer far more in terms of exercises, activities and ideas than the whole of the World Wide Web' (Eastment 1999: 23-4).

Although the synchronicity of form and content has improved since these dismal assessments were made, for as long as the Web remains an unregulated medium (effectively unmediated by editorial control), it is the *resource* aspect of the Web - and for language learners this means online dictionaries and usage guides as well as authentic texts - which offers greater prospects for combining the learning of language and electronic literacy skills. The function of language learning Web sites might be seen as a useful back up resource of ready-made interactive exercises for learners and teachers to avail themselves of. The biggest metasites (e.g. Dave Sperling's Internet café[4] and TESL-J[5]) are 'safe' yet extensive places to leave learners to navigate exercises and activities of their own choosing (see Task 1).

11.2.2 Currency and the Web

The currency of the Web quite simply outranks that of any other medium. The up-to-date-ness of the information it carries and of the language it uses, its capacity to cater minutely to personal needs and interests thanks to powerful search capabilities, and not least, the transferable electronic literacy skills required to use it, all give the Web an immediacy and relevance that galvanises students using it in their language learning.

Its fluid, ever-changing nature is one of the most motivating aspects of the Web to exploit for language learning. The example has already been given above of online newspapers which carry breaking news stories more up-to-the-minute than any other news media except, perhaps, TV networks such as Sky News. Language learners can have the satisfaction not only of doing real-world tasks such as re-drafting incoming news information as written or oral news reports (see above), but of knowing that they may actually be beating their real-life equivalents to it.

Most airlines and travel companies now have a Web presence and it is more and more common to get last-minute deals in flights and holidays online than through a travel agency. Tasks such as competing to find the cheapest flight to a given destination on a given date, are thus both authentic and fun (see Task 7).

Another attraction of the Web relevant to language learning is its eclecticism. As the most extensive resource of the written word on the planet[6], individual and group interests can be minutely catered to. Material on subjects of interest can be found either by searching, or by joining one of the 90,000 plus discussion lists on subjects ranging from everything from art history to zoology[7]. One way to focus and 'pull together' group interests is to set a class project such as writing a newspaper or setting up a Web page[8] with contributions from individuals or groups on the topics of their choice. In this way, a learner interested in, say, the comparative size of the military forces in the world and one enamoured of musicals[9] will both be equally engrossed in their task.

For learners of the English language in particular, there has always been a sort of circular motivation for using the Web: 'It is not only a matter of using the Internet to learn English but also of learning English to be able to function well on the Internet' (Warschauer and Whittaker 1997), or, as expressed by a little boy quoted by Crystal, the need to learn English is 'because the computer speaks English' (2001: 216). This is a perception based on the original dominance of the English language on the Web, which although steadily falling[10], remains strong enough at time of writing to give it the motivational edge on many other media for learners of English. The above quote from Warschauer and Whittaker indicates that another of the motivational aspects of using the Web for language learning is the acquiring of electronic literacy skills. Especially for learners from countries whose languages have little Web presence (e.g. those from Turkey or Ukraine[11]), English is the default language through which to do this.

Let us turn lastly to the most problematic aspect of currency and the Web, Web language as a new language variety (or set of varieties), to assess the demands we are making of learners using this medium.

Web Language And Authenticity

It is commonplace to acclaim the Web as a portal to authentic texts (see, for example, ICC report 2003: 21, Crystal 2001: 235, Vogel 2001: 140). Yet what sort of 'authenticity' are we talking about? As has been noted in Chapter 1, the concept of authenticity has to be reassessed in order to take account of what the technologies have done to language.

The Web is 'graphically more eclectic than any domain of written language in the real world' (Crystal 2001:197), and this eclecticism is accentuated by the fact that the Web is an open, unedited forum for anyone, regardless of age, education and first language background. But these 'real world' varieties (academic, business, journalistic, literary and so on) rub shoulder to shoulder with a new and evolving genre, one that has many of the characteristics of advertising and tabloid journalism. That 'first stop' for visitors - the Web home page - has evolved its own generic characteristics. The main rationale for these are the need for 'scannability' and impact within the constraints of the computer screen on which the language appears. The page is treated as a physical space (Amitay 2000: 31) in which the number of 'functional areas', and hence words, are restricted, and so information has to be presented in clearly marked, self-contained, easy-to-process chunks (Eayrs 1999). The language, and the graphic form in which it appears, are thus part of a whole, as in advertising and journalism. Linguistically, this need for clarity and simplicity makes for such features as the preponderance of the present tense and avoidance of complex linguistic structures (Amitay 2000: 31); features, too, of advertising copy.

One factor that problematises authenticity is the dimensionality of text on the Web. The time-honoured conceptualisation of text in a linear, sequential model has been transformed, on the Web, to one with a non-linear structure. This structure is manifest both *within* the Web page - 'the eye moves about the page in a manner dictated only by the user's interests and the designer's skill' (Crystal 2001: 196) - and, more significantly, *between* Web sites. The technical capacity to link from one text to another effectively wrests the text from the author's control, making the reader an active participant in the creative process (Shetzer and Warschauer 2000: 175). The actual 'text' that gets read is ephemeral and varies from reader to reader, depending on the links accessed (see also Henriquez 2000). Authenticity, it can be said 'becomes conflated with authorship' (Kramsch *et al.* 2000: 96). In the context of language learning, all this can be very empowering, since endowing learners with 'authorship' and 'agency' ('the power to take meaningful action and to see the results of our decisions and choices', Murray 1997: 149[12]), puts them on a par with native speakers.

11.2.3 Culture on the Web

The Web is a repository of a huge range of cultural products in electronic form, and as such is an invaluable resource of authentic texts for teachers and learners. Samples of all the cultural products covered in this book can be found online:

Literature	http://www.bibliomania.com/
The broadcast media	http://www.bbc.co.uk/
	http://www.rte.ie/
	http://www.cnn.com/
Newspapers	http://www.newsd.com/
Advertising	http://www.adslogans.co.uk/
Songs	http://www.lyrics.com/
Film (film scripts and clips)	http://www.script-o-rama.com/table.shtml

The Web offers students 'the opportunity for virtual travelling without having to pay for a ticket', as Vogel puts it (2001:135). The many 'self-conscious' culture sites with 'tourist level' cultural information (heritage, folk lore, folk songs, recipes, etc) aimed at potential visitors and, (often in the case of Irish sites), at the Irish diaspora (e.g. Irelandseye.com) offer this type of armchair travelling and can be very useful for language learners (see Task 5).

Naturally, there has to be a downside to all this instant cultural gratification. While the Web is a medium that increases access to cultural products, the niggling question remains as to whether it is really providing access to the authentic target culture. One might argue that channelling cultural products through this medium omits the crucial perspective of the *status* of the cultural product within the TC. Works of art and literature have no intrinsic value, they have only the value that society places on them by virtue of the regard in which they are held, and of their status as cultural artefacts. Freely available from the Web at the click of a mouse and stripped of this cultural 'interface', the value attributed by a society to a work of literature or art is not apparent. The Web projects a play by Shakespeare, an article from a newspaper and the home page of a seventeen year old rock fan all through the same medium, on the same screen and with the same or similar typological features. The Internet, in other words, is a great *leveller*: it absorbs materials and works from different media and re-projects them indiscriminately through the same medium, one that may not, in fact, always be suitable to the material. Many of the great novels of the English language are now available online with a hypertext interface[13]. This means that the user can go to chapters at will by clicking the hypertext, a facility which undermines the convention of reading a novel from start to finish. The hypertext medium encourages movement, surfing, skimming and scanning, not in-depth reading. The fact that the Internet has spawned a new genre, the Internet novel, which exploits the hypertext medium and is interactive[14], suggests that the medium is not really suitable for the novel in its traditional form. Furthermore, rather like the commercialisation of paintings such as the 'Mona Lisa', seen on everything from matchboxes to T-shirts, or the use of Puccini's *Nessun Dorma* as a football hymn, over-accessibility and over-exposure to change, cultural products can devalue and reduce them. In the final analysis, then, it can be argued that the Web *reproduces* cultural products but forfeits their cultural status in the process.

One solution to this dilemma in the context of language learning is to emphasise the importance of teacher mediation in availing of these resources. The teacher can act as 'cultural guide' raising awareness of the significance of works of literature, the status of different newspapers and so on, thus adding an essential dimension to the cultural experience, rather than leaving learners to encounter these cultural products 'cold'.

The issue of the access it gives to world cultures is further complicated by the fact that the Web has by now its own cultural attributes. The Web is transnational, and with its spread, a sort of international culture seems to be developing, one whose formative force is the technology and one which transcends the cultures of individual languages. The strongest influence on the internationalisation of the Internet is, of course, its original domination by the English language, and while this dominance is diminishing (see above, and Crystal 2001: 218-23) English is still the language of - and the culture influencing - global communication. This has led to a sort of 'Coca-colarisation' of the Internet, as American (or at least English-speaking) culture permeates cyberspace. This effect touches everything from the technical level of Web site design, to broader issues such as the way language is used on the Web and the cultural models of communication which it assumes.

At the technical level, Web site design templates, hypertext protocols etc., which dictate and delimit what will go onto the Web site and where, remain in English or are translations from English, which means the parameters universally operate within a schema imposed by English. As regards content, the influence of the English language can be seen in the language registers being adopted for the Internet in languages other than English. The flatter hierarchies and informality of American and, more and more, British and other English-speaking countries, are beginning to permeate other languages (see, for example, Fouser *et al.*'s study of Japanese and Korean features of CMC, 2000: 52-62). This can be seen in the dropping of titles, and the adoption and frequency of such features as the familiar *you* forms, the first person pronoun, oral forms of salutation, and of generally more informal language registers (see Daly 1996[15], Gimenez 2000, Amitay 2000 and Section 11.3.2 on e-mail language below).

The transfer to the Internet of other constituent elements of culture, such as commerce, service industries, information services, entertainment and leisure, all using similar trans-lingual, global interfaces must also inevitably have a levelling influence. There is then, the risk that all this is the 'slippery slope' to intercultural conformity, to a dilution and eventual eradication of the differences between cultures. More insidious still, is the potential 'coca-colarising' effect at deeper levels of culture, as the Internet spreads the values and behaviours of the consumer society that conceived it, into homes and institutions throughout the world. Particularly in the context of culture, then, we should perhaps take on board the warning that 'every technology has two sides to its consequences; on the one hand for every technology we develop in an attempt to improve life, we believe we also will, on the other hand, find life impoverished in some way' (Jones 1997: 1).

11.2.4 The Challenge of the Web
Ironically, it is this very internationalism that makes the Web probably the most familiar medium to use with language learners these days. The types of discourse and conventions - the Web page format, search procedures, hyperlink interactivity - are all by now universal (apart from distinctions due to graphology or writing systems), much as are those associated with television and newspapers. This means that as a medium it is less intimidating than other products of the TC might be, it also allows learners to 'take refuge in' native language materials, dictionaries, grammars, even translations, all on the same platform.

On the other hand, because of its extensiveness, diversity and intrinsic 'wordiness', using the Web *effectively* is a challenge to even native speakers. While the challenge is even greater for language learners, the sense of achievement at successfully navigating the Web in a foreign language is proportionally higher. It is up to the teacher, therefore, to design do-able Web tasks to harness this kind of motivation force.

Despite its size, and despite many of the derogatory comparisons with disordered libraries and so on which dogged the Web in the early years, the Web has an intrinsic organisational schema which makes information far more easily accessible, and in far greater quantities, than in the library it is so often contrasted with. Helping learners hone their searching skills, then, is a job that can be done through 'search and sift' tasks set at all proficiency levels. The most common way of searching is 'keyword' searching, that is, typing a search term - a name, term, expression and so on, into a search engine (the largest and most popular search engine at time of writing is *Google*[16]). This is fairly straightforward if searching for proper names and people, but where the search term is more abstract (e.g. finding the numbers of languages available on the Web) this invokes the use of synonyms or a broadening of the search concept. On the most basic level, correct spelling is vital (and the differences between British and American English spelling can be significant). A good, illustrative starting exercise with learners is to exploit such variations to see what different results are thrown up by different spellings or phrasing[17]. Search tasks geared to learners' interests, where they are searching for information on a favourite pop or sports star etc. are also do-able at all levels and learners can evaluate and compare the usefulness of the various sites thrown up (see tasks in Windeatt *et al.* 2000: 26-31). A core enabling skill for searching the Web is *evaluation* of sites thrown up by a search engine and it is in part the transferability of evaluation skills that motivates learners to practise them (see Task 1).

11.3 E-Mail

11.3.1 Using e-mail for language learning
E-mail is the oldest and best-established form of electronic communication, dating back to its first incarnation in 1981 as BITNET[18]. It is today the largest communication system in the world, with an estimated 605.6 million users worldwide.[19] It is the only computer technology to consist of human-to-human, rather than human-to-machine communication (Warschauer 1996b). It is also the most stable and easy to use, and requires the least amount of hardware, software and memory. As such, it is often the first, and sometimes the only, form of ICT that some people encounter. For all these reasons, it is hardly surprising that its potential for language learning was quickly spotted by practitioners.

The by now standard pedagogy for using e-mail for language learning is *tandem learning*, whereby two learners with different L1s work together in order to learn about each other's language, culture, character and possibly personal and professional life. The core principles of tandem learning are reciprocity, autonomy and bilingualism (Little and Brammerts 1996: 10-11). Each partner should benefit equally from the relationship, by providing models of the native language, cultural information, and corrective feedback. The principle of autonomy means that tandem learners are responsible for their own and their partners' learning. Tandem learning involves both receptive and productive skills, with production being, as appropriate, in the native language to offer NS models, and in the target language for TL practice (hence the principle of bilingualism). The teacher's part in the tandem learning set-up is to provide advice and support for the learner on such things as providing effective feedback, potential cross-cultural misunderstandings and so on. As for the practical aspects, networks such as the *International E-Mail Tandem Network*[20] with 36 institutions in 18 countries, and the American network *Intercultural e-mail classroom connections* (IECC[21]), with over 7650 subscribers in 82 countries[22], facilitate the finding of TL partners (see Tasks 8 and 9).

Tandem learning can also take place within the framework of a partnership between institutions. Among the numerous successful reported *institutional partnerships* are such major ones as the English-German project reported in Little and Ushioda 1998. Many other smaller-scale projects are reported in Warschauer's *Virtual Connections* (1995), which although somewhat dated now, is still the largest collected volume of reports on e-mail projects of which I am currently aware, and illustrates the potential for using the keypal partnership creatively in a great variety of ways.

Participation in *discussion lists* is another e-mail interaction that has been used successfully for language learning. A *discussion list* is a membership-based forum devoted to a specific subject. Its members have access to messages submitted to the list and they can also contribute input via e-mail. For learners, the advantage of writing to a discussion list, rather than corresponding with an individual, avoids some of the problems inherent to one-to-one exchanges, such as one partner losing interest and 'dropping out' of the partnership. There are at present over 90,000 online discussion lists covering a huge range of topics (Liszt 2000), some of which have been set up specifically for students of English. *English-l*, for instance is a list dedicated to English language learners, while *SL-Lists (International EFL/ESL E-mail Student Discussion Lists)* is a set of ten special-interest lists (e.g. on sports, current events, science and technology).

Discussion lists that are 'closed' can be set up as part of collaborative partnerships between two or more colleges (see, for example, Gousseva 1998, Woodlin 1997). E-mail messages are posted by the students to a listserv (distribution list) set up by the institution/s involved, to be distributed only to its own subscribers. Gousseva's project involved 50 students from institutions in at least 8 countries and was designed to investigate the potential of cross-cultural, computer-mediated communication for writing classes. Woodlin's consisted of collaboration between a British and a Spanish university; the learners communicated on a one-to-one basis with tandem partners as well as with the group via a specially set up discussion forum.

Another option for a closed discussion forum is a shared workspace on the Internet. (Free) workspace is available from search engines such as *Yahoo!* (from http://groups.yahoo.com/) and software companies such as http://bscw.gmd.de/. Workspaces function as a cross between a Web page bulletin board and an e-mail discussion list; documents, photographs as well as messages can all be posted on them. Although 'closed', some of them can also be opened to the 'public' on the Web. Many of the tasks below, e.g. Tasks 8 to 14, suggest using workspaces.

11.3.2   Currency and e-mail

The obvious currency of e-mail is at the same time hugely attractive to language learners yet fraught with linguistic dangers as the following description of e-mail language will illustrate. A new variety of language, by now classified as a genre in its own right (see books on writing in the medium, such as Hale and Scanlon 1999), e-mail is often described as a 'hybrid', combining features of written and oral discourse. Some e-mail messages can be as formal as business letters or academic treatises, with the linguistic and discourse characteristics of these genres. More common, and more often encountered and sent by language learners, are messages with features from the oral end of the spectrum, whose 'written' credentials are limited to their physical manifestation and to the header ('sender', 'recipient', 'subject' etc.) imposed by the e-mail system. It is this orality within a written framework that is the unique and distinguishing feature of e-mail language. Particular features of register and discourse, including syntactic, stylistic, lexical as well as graphic elements, are used in an attempt to simulate the rhythms, informality and paralinguistic features of oral interchange (Fouser *et al.* 2000, Daly 1996, Yates and Orlikowski 1993). Register is kept at an informal, conversational level through the use of oral forms of greetings and closings ('Hi', 'Hello', 'Cheers') and other conversational features such as omission of pronoun subjects and auxiliaries ('Forgot to mention that John e-mailed me'[23] 'Been too busy'). Abbreviation and short sentences often make for a 'telegram' style: 'The demo was great. A million people of all kinds. We travelled at approx 1 mph! It was brill. Never made it to Hyde Park. After 3+ hours we were so cold...' This informality extends to the eschewing of rules of spelling, grammar, and punctuation (especially capital letter for the first-person pronoun) in order to give the appearance of fluency and spontaneity; 'Your card was great i can't understand how you remember, and spot on the day.' 'thanks for telling us your coming, don't know yet what i'm doing over christmas. hope you are having a bit of the very nice good weather. how is peter and mike and work.'

Another oral feature of e-mail language is an 'apparent interactiveness' (Gains 1999: 93) which mimics conversational 'turn-taking'. This is enabled in part by the technical capabilities of e-mail which allows for a response to incorporate the original text of the message being answered. Even without availing of this facility, a message written in response to another will often adopt some of the discourse features or lexis of the original message 'as if [...] conducting a conversation with an absent interlocutor' (Gains 1999: 93). Thus, phatic responses to the 'interlocutor's' questions are typical ('No: 'the' race is this Sunday (gulp!)!') Questions interwoven with the text are often effectively 'rhetorical' in that the writer does not expect an immediate response, or indeed, one at all ('Have I commented on your wedding pictures yet?' 'Snow, huh?'). Another e-mail phenomenon is responding to imagined questions or exclamations of the absent interlocutor (Gains 1999: 93), as in the sample; 'Dear x, Hallo [*sic*] again! I know, I know... I have been searching for that reference ever since!' (see also 'Challenge' below, for the value of e-mail turn-taking for language learning). Some of the features making for this sort of self-conscious casualness are by now 'prescribed' by e-mail-writing guides (e.g. Flynn and Flynn 1998, Hale and Scanlon 1999) which advocate the use of contractions, and dispense with many of the traditional 'constraints' of written grammar, freeing users to start sentences with conjunctions, end them with prepositions and so on (Crystal 2001: 108) (see also Task 18 on the characteristics of junk/spam mail).

E-mail has, finally, evolved two new and unique graphological features. The first is the use of *acronyms*, abbreviations of commonly used phrases. These have already become fairly standardised with comprehensive lists available on the Web. The most frequently used are things like ATB ('all the best'), BTW ('by the way'), LOL ('laughing out loud') and IMHO ('In My Humble Opinion'). One sign of this standardisation is that such acronyms are being adopted in text-messaging as well. The second feature unique to the e-mail genre, is the typographic representations of paralinguistic features. Some of these consist of the word describing the feature itself, but enclosed by visually representative symbols, such as *grin* and [hug]. Another group consist of standardised compositions (e.g. 'smilies'). that use keyboard characters. These symbols are known as 'emotes' or 'emoticons' (emotive icons) and are a kind of emotional shorthand. Most emoticons are designed to be interpreted with the reader's head tilted over to the left. A smiley, for example is keyboarded as :-)a sad face as :-(a wink by ;) something said tongue-in-cheek by :-J and so on. Even such an overtly vocal cue as shouting can be transmitted, in e-mail convention, by typing in capital letters. Examining and analysing all these features can, of course, be a fascinating exercise for learners (see Task 16).

E-mail technology, can, all in all, be seen to have brought into being an evolving and generative variety of language. Yet, quirky graphological features apart, if the defining characteristics of the language of e-mail are the flouting of established linguistic convention at the levels of lexis and graphology and (as a consequence) often register, where does this leave the language learner? The problem for learners trying to emulate the genre is that such a disregard for convention has to come from a position of command over the language: 'The bending and breaking of rules, which is a hallmark of lucid linguistic behaviour, always presents a problem to those who have not yet developed a confident command of the rules per se', observes Crystal (2001: 236-7).

In reconciling such drawbacks with the evidence that e-mail *is* useful for language learning (see 'Challenge' below), it would seem that when composing e-mails in the TL, learners tend to ignore the convention that online writing is more informal and conversational than off-line writing (Biesenbach-Lucas and Weasenforth 1998) and their e-mails are closer in genre to informal letters. In their degree of syntactic and linguistic complexity learner e-mail messages contrast with their oral interactions (Warschauer 1996c). It would seem that learners of the language naturally aspire to 'correct' forms of the language before taking liberties with it, and are more wary of the misspellings, carefree punctuation etc. (deliberate or not), typical of the native speaker e-mailer. One might also look to factors other than the linguistic which make e-mail so valuable for language learning. There is, for instance, the motivational impact of corresponding with a native speaker about real, personal, cultural issues, and the advantage to affect of not being under time pressure to reply and produce the TL, factors which will be examined in more detail in the following two sections.

11.3.3 E-mail and culture

With its idiosyncratic conventions of 'written orality' and concretisation of paralinguistic features, the e-mail medium has in a sense created a culture of its own, one with flattened hierarchies and a classless structure. This sense of a shared culture eases communication between 'real' cultures as e-mail users 'bend' their own (native) cultural conventions towards those of the medium. The anonymity of the e-mail transaction, with the electronic interface masking national, racial, gender, age and class features, can help dispel prejudices and preconceptions, as personal relationships develop with people from societies and backgrounds hitherto un-encountered (Belisle 1996, Gousseva 1998, Warschauer 1996c and 1997). A student in one e-mail project is quoted as saying 'I've learned that once we take away our colours, accents and anything else that would separate us in a physical world everyone is really similar' (Gousseva 1998). E-mail is thus a great equaliser, one that neutralises not only cultural and social context cues, but also non-verbal cues, and the advantages that come with the ability to think fast, speak loudly and otherwise over-ride others in face-to-face discussion (Warschauer 1997). Learners from traditionally reticent cultures, such as the Japanese, have revealed large improvements in participation in discussions when these were via e-mail[24].

At the simplest level, e-mail, in tandem learning partnerships, can function as an invaluable medium of exchange of cultural information. The cultural information gained via e-mail correspondence is far more personalised than is possible via other media (such as a course-book) and also more stimulating, since its interchange format allows for questions, clarifications, reactions etc. Discussions of culture with foreign keypals raises cultural awareness in general and even deepens learners' knowledge of their own cultures, since the need to analyse and describe elements of one's own culture that are normally taken for granted, helps us 'to see ourselves as others see us' (see Tasks 8 and 9).

11.3.4 The challenge of e-mail

E-mail is in many ways the least challenging of the ICT applications discussed here as regards difficulty of the language *per se*, because it is learner-led in terms of the language level used, the subject matter discussed and the pace of the interaction.

In tandem learning partnerships, learners quickly recognise the proficiency level of their partner and gear their responses accordingly.

Its relative simplicity in this respect does not, however, undermine the usefulness of e-mail for language learning, which is attested to in a growing body of empirical evidence (see, for example, Little and Ushioda 1998: 100, Warschauer 1995, 1996c and 1998). Many of its advantages stem from its unique combination of features of oral and written discourse, discussed above. The concretisation of typically oral features in written form, for instance, makes for what Warschauer calls 'the benefit of noticing' (Warschauer 1998b). Words or expressions that can be lost in the stream of conversation are salient on screen. Frequently heard idiomatic or colloquial expressions which are hard to decipher aurally, become clear if their written form is seen in an e-mail message. The potential for learning is increased still further because this relative permanency gives the opportunity for reflection and retention, whereas 'the linguistic substance of oral communication remains only fleetingly in our short-term memory' (Little and Ushioda 1998: 97).

A second 'oral' characteristics of e-mail discourse that is helpful to the learner is its emulation of conversational 'turn-taking' mentioned in Section 11.3.2 above. Like oral interchange, e-mail discourse tends to be responsive in that it draws on previous discourse, in the same way that dialogues do: 'We respond directly to each others' messages, but, even more pervasively, choose our words from previously heard talk. Utterances thus reflect and create one another' (Baym 1995: 40). The fact that with e-mail, the interchanges are written, makes it easy for students to exploit this reflective feature, borrowing from native-speaker partners and thus activating new language features. The written format also means that errors can be corrected and meanings verified without interrupting the 'speaker's' flow as would be the case in conversation. In other words, there is the same negotiation of meaning so characteristic of authentic oral exchanges (e.g. requests for clarification, reformulations or self-corrections and comprehension checks), but with the added benefits of the dialogue being 'recorded' in writing and having extended time in which to process it (and this applies to both input and output modes):

> 'Because students have more time to process language in [networked communication] than in oral conversations, and because they can view their language as they produce it, they are more likely to 'monitor' and edit their messages, all of which can result in even more 'quality' interlanguage than there would be in a non-electronic environment.' (Pellettieri 1996: n.p.)

Finally, learners are often more readily disposed to experiment with newly-learned forms in a forum which is private (bearing in mind that even the teacher's presence can be an inhibiting influence), and where feedback is delayed, than in 'live' conversation (in or outside the classroom). For this reason, e-mail is a particularly suitable medium for metalinguistic discussion, in which learners discuss questions about the TL with their correspondents (see Task 8).

11.4 Corpora and Concordancing

11.4.1 Using corpora and concordancing for language learning

The corpus - a computer database storing a collection of texts, and the concordancer - the program which manipulates it, are probably the ICT systems least exploited for language learning (Rézeau 2001: 147). Yet a TL corpus provides the largest single resource of authentic language available to the language learner, and the concordancer constitutes a flexible, user-directed and user-friendly tool for exploring it. The reasons why teachers (and learners) are so circumspect about using corpora and concordancing - and the arguments in favour of their use - will become apparent below.

Corpora are electronic databases containing texts which have been either downloaded from other electronic sources (the Internet, CD ROM etc.), scanned from paper into electronic form, or transcribed from audiotapes of the spoken language. Corpora are 'tagged' morphosyntactically - that is, there is a code which gives the *part of speech* of each word - using tagging systems such as the mark-up language SGML (Standard Generalised Markup Language). The largest corpora contain millions of words: the Cambridge International Corpus (CIC) contains over 600 million words at time of writing; the COBUILD Bank of English, runs to 450 million words; the British National Corpus (BNC) consists of 100 million words. More modest corpora can be built by teachers or learners themselves using such programs as WordSmith Tools[25] or MonoConc[26]. The concordancing software used to handle these huge quantities of data have the capacity to sort and present it in a number of ways. For instance, they can generate statistically sorted word lists (showing, for instance, the 100 most frequently occurring words in a given text/corpus). The most useful facility as far as language learning is concerned, is the capacity to search for *key words* - a single word (such as *cup*) or a word string (e.g. *cup of tea*) - for which they can generate *collocation lists* (the words most commonly used with the key word/string), or 'key word in context' (KWIC) conconcordances. A KWIC concordance lists a series of (separate and unrelated) lines from a corpus, each of which displays an occurrence of the key word (or word-string) within this one-line context. The occurrence of the key word in the lines is aligned vertically, thus appearing as a column on screen (or on the page when printed). This mode of presentation makes the key word stand out and its collocations and syntactic restrictions can be examined by looking at its context - the phrases to the left or the right side of the column (see Fig 1)

Figure 1

half the caffeine of an average	cup of tea.	[h] ASSAM [/h] [p] A black tea from
now, and decided to have a	cup of tea.	[p] Not far from the bridge he
then sit down to read it with a	cup of tea.	[p] Perhaps the daftest idea of
off with a good old-fashioned	cup of tea.	[p] It's sort of a tradition with
Now that's not everybody's	cup of tea.	[p] Tetley's, we hear, is lining
lucky to get a sandwich and a	cup of tea	after a race, let alone a cheque.
doesn't offer me a drink or a	cup of tea,	and without asking me to sit down,
a dinosaur book. Bjork makes a	cup of tea,	and we begin. [p] [h] LONDON
reluctant customers over a	cup of tea	and adds the golden rule: 'Never the
owner sat me down with a	cup of tea	and broke the news [p] Garage owner

[The first 10 lines of a concordance for the string *cup of tea* generated using the online *COBUILD Concordance Sampler* from the Collins COBUILD Web site on http://www.cobuild.collins.co.uk/ accessed 8 April 2003.]

Some concordancers have lateral movement, enabling more of the sentence in which the key word/s occurs to be seen, and most have a feature allowing the user to view the broader context surrounding the key word (e.g. a full sentence, paragraph or section). The software also specifies the number of times the key word occurs within the corpus. Collocates of the key word can be identified and sorted alphabetically to the left or to the right.

Its dense, one-dimensional appearance belies the wide range of information about the language contained within the KWIC concordance. This ranges from the semantic - the meaning/s ascribed to the key word/s, to the syntactic - word order and tense restrictions, to the cultural (see below). Most notably, of course, the concordance reveals collocates (words frequently found 'in the company of' the key word/s), common 'clumps' in which the key word occurs; idioms, fixed phrases, and so on, as well as the relative frequency of the key word and of these patterns.

Corpora were originally used for such things as sociolinguistic studies (such as Schonell *et al.* 1956, *The Oral Vocabulary of Adults*) and analysis of child language acquisition (for example Beier, Starkweather and Miller 1967). Corpora gradually acquired a wider range of uses including the development of speech recognition technology, forensics and, most obviously, lexicography (the COBUILD corpus, the source for the Collins COBUILD dictionaries, was begun in 1980), but their potential for language pedagogy did not begin to be exploited until the early 1990s. The chief methodology to be associated with corpora and concordancing is known as Data Driven Learning (DDL): 'The language-learner is [...] essentially, a research worker whose learning needs to be driven by access to linguistic data - hence the term 'data-driven learning' (DDL)' writes the pioneer of the approach, Tim Johns (1991a: 2). For teachers and learners new to the approach, this research and discovery-learning aspect is just one of the radical features of DDL, for pedagogy conventionally presents *rules* rather than the *evidence* for them. Teachers and learners will also need to recognise and accept that discovery learning is 'divergent learning' in the sense that findings and outcomes of different learners will not always concur. Another unfamiliar feature of the approach is the atypical appearance of the 'raw data' (the KWIC concordance) with which the 'researchers' are to work. The presentation of text in this unmediated block format can be bewildering at first encounter, and the most essential point to emphasise to learners is that each concordance line is separate and unconnected from the next and is (probably) sourced from a different original text.

DDL can be teacher- or learner-led to varying degrees, depending on the facilities available (whether computers are available to the learners, or only to the teacher), and on whether the teacher wishes to control the 'raw data', that is, the concordances consulted by the learners (as he or she may do in the case of lower level learners). Teacher-led tasks might use print-offs of concordances accompanied by a task, e.g. asking learners to infer the meanings of phrasal verbs or the differences between varieties of English (see Tasks 24 and 23), or (an enjoyable creative exercise) to make the concordance lines into complete sentences (adding beginnings and/or endings as necessary). Alternatively, the concordances might be edited in some way. The key word might be deleted, for instance, as in a cloze test (this can be done by the concordancing software or failing that, using correction fluid on the print-out) and learners can be asked to infer it from the context (Figure 2).

Figure 2

Wearing long dresses of fine cloth, and white and gold, they strolled
[p] Wearing a blue suit with a and white tie, Juppe was playing at
t he drawbridge that leads to the -brick, crenellated building has 'No
trudge off after receiving the card against Leicester, and
haemoglobin derived from out of date cells, or from animal sources, and
wine, but concentrates principally on . Consequently, Cabernet Franc is the
lives Another charity, the British Cross, says it has already sent ten
in this vast blue, white, and facility are steam rooms, Swedish/
woman from whom he had bought the flowers in his coat, the agent from
Henry Wallbank's face turned . He shifted from foot to foot made
salmonella bacteria: poultry, meat, or pork? [p] A: Poultry is
cloves 120ml dry white wine 125g pepper 400g risotto rice 1 bay leaf
of garnets they can be cruel with -rimmed eyes. Simon Wilson of the
a low-scoring series, with the winning Sox making a total of only 12 runs.

[Selected lines from a concordance for the key word *red*, generated using the online *COBUILD Concordance Sampler* from the Collins COBUILD Web site on http://www.cobuild.collins.co.uk/ accessed 8 April 2003]

Concordance lines might also be redrafted into exercises (fill-the-gap exercises etc.). This has the advantage (especially if teaching lower level learners) of omitting overly complicated or non-representative occurrences if desired.

At the more learner-led end of the spectrum, learners might use corpora which they or their teachers have built (see above). Alternatively, they can access online corpora and their concordancers. Currently, the most useful of these are the

COBUILD Bank of English (see URL above), the BNC[27], and the Hong Kong Virtual Language Centre.[28]

Search engines such as *Google* can also be used to search for structures, patterns or lexis, by using the 'Advanced search' option and typing the query into the 'Find results with the exact phrase' box.

A sample of DDL tasks is summarised here, with cross-referencing to a detailed task description where available:

• Deducing meaning from context (this is particularly useful for phrasal verbs and idioms) (see Tasks 24 and 22).

• Distinguishing meanings and usages of inflected forms of the same word (e.g. *magic* versus *magical*) or of different structures used with a word e.g. *like to* versus *like -ing*[29] or *stop -ing* versus *stop to -* .

• Inferring marked-ness of an item. Words such as *terribly, awful, awfully*, for example, tend to be learned in the marked meanings they carry in written English, but can be seen to be fairly un-marked in the spoken language (see Tasks 20 and 21).

• Inferring gender preferences for a word e.g. the application of the noun *blond/blonde* exclusively to women[30] and of the adjective *taciturn* to men (Fox 1998: 31) (see Task 25).

• Inferring the *pragmatics* of words/phrases, i.e. the meaning and effect of the use of language in a particular situation and which may be at odds with its semantic uses (Fox 1998: 36), e.g. words such as *right*[31] and *actually* (*ibid.*: 37) (e.g. *I don't actually have the papers to prove...*).

• Exploring differences between international varieties of English (see Task 23). Many corpora incorporate sub-corpora of different varieties; the COBUILD Bank of English contains 3 sub-corpora 'British transcribed speech', 'written British' and 'written American' which are separable when searching. The Hong Kong Virtual Language Centre site mentioned above contains 12 corpora including the classic Brown and LOB corpora (of American and British English respectively) and a 1.2 million-word corpus of the English language newspaper, *The South China Morning Post.*

• Researching and writing a dictionary definition (of a word of the learner's or teacher's choosing (see Task 28).

• Checking grammar rules, either ones given in a grammar or coursebook or a hypothesis that the learner has drawn up him/herself (see Task 26).

• Practice in refining queries for the concordancer.

One of the best sources of ready-made DDL tasks and ideas for these is still the Web page of the originator of the methodology, Tim Johns (http://web.bham.ac.uk/johnstf /timconc.htm).

11.4.2 Currency and the corpus

As far as the study of the contemporary language is concerned, corpora, particularly those of the spoken language, are an incomparable resource[32]. The often startling findings about the spoken language coming from such corpora are beginning to inform pedagogical works, as was mentioned in Chapter 3. For the learner, the opportunity of actually going to 'the horse's mouth' (so to speak) helps dispel the myth propagated in the traditional prescriptive approach, that language use is derived from rules. It reveals how, on the contrary, language use actually *makes* the rules (Rézeau 2001: 150). The corpus offers the wherewithal to check the prescriptive grammar rules drawn up for us by 'armchair linguists' and 'perpetuated from one generation to another of dictionaries, grammars and coursebooks' (Johns 1994: 30), rules that have, moreover, traditionally been based mainly on written paradigms (e.g. Carter *et al.* 1998: 67). All of this has made for the development of rules that are incomplete because of the requirement to simplify them (think, for example, of the logical but vastly oversimplified rules we give to learners for the uses of *some* and *any*). Such prescription can even be seen as a form of censorship which places the learner at an even greater disadvantage to the native speaker in terms of potential for language competency (see Carter 1998 on this issue).

Accounts of practitioners reporting on their experiences with using DDL suggest that the use of the corpus in language pedagogy emancipates learners as never before. They show learners turning to the corpus (rather than to the teacher or the grammar book!) for confirmation of their own hypotheses, or of prescriptive rules they have gleaned from books or from the teachers themselves (see, for example, Stevens 1995, Owen 1996, Hadley 1998, Tyrwhitt-Drake 1999, Gavioli and Aston 2001). Many such writers do point out that the use of the DDL methodology can have uncomfortable consequences, questioning not only the 'received wisdom' of reference books, but, even more awkward for the teacher, his/her own NS intuitions (e.g. Owen 1996, Stevens 1995). This highlights DDL not merely as a methodology for language learning but as an approach in which learner-teacher roles are radically adjusted, with the learner assuming greater autonomy and control.

One perceived advantage of the corpus is that it is 'pure' language, unencumbered by contextual features, or by the 'distractions' of its original mode and medium. As such, it is ripe for linguistic analysis by the learner (as well as by the linguist). However, this does presuppose a particular learning style, and this is discussed below in 'The challenge of the corpus'. This perception of the corpus as pure, 'naked' language is likewise not without its issues as Section 11.4.4, 'Culture and the corpus', will show.

11.4.3 The challenge of the corpus

Of the ICT systems discussed here, the corpus - and particularly, the way in which corpus data is presented - constitutes the greatest challenge and the greatest potential impediment to its use by language learners. This is due to its limitations in two areas, the proficiency levels of the learners with whom it can be used, and the modes of learning (learning styles) that it imposes.

Learners of all levels, let alone those of lower proficiency levels, can be put off by the dense wordiness of concordances, finding it hard to see the 'trees' for the 'wood' (to reverse the metaphor). False-beginners in one study (Hadley 1998) were initially 'overwhelmed' by the concordance's form - according to some students the sentences were 'incomplete' and therefore 'incoherent'. Nevertheless, the key to making concordances accessible to learners is, as always, via the *task*, and with this in mind, DDL can be used successfully at lower levels: 'working with the same concordance, a beginner may be able to draw relatively low-level conclusions [...] a more advanced learner will be able to make more subtle high-level inferences' (Johns 1986: 159). Control of the task might involve paring down and/or selecting lines from the concordance, as has been suggested in Section 11.4.1 above. Concordance sample workbooks in which this has been done are now in fact available, see Goodale's books on tenses and phrasal verbs, 1995.[33] Finally, the corpus may be controlled for proficiency level 'at source', building a corpus or sub-corpus exclusively of suitably 'simple' texts.[34]

Whatever the task or corpus, once learners have been guided to distinguish the trees within the wood (to pursue our reverse-metaphor), they often find that the sort of lexical focus that concordances lend themselves to, make for straightforward yet fascinating tasks. This is not, it should be noted, at the expense of the study of grammar and syntax. The primacy of lexis over syntax, the way in which lexis 'attracts' (or 'is primed') for collocation with certain other lexis, in certain grammatical functions, in certain discourse types and so on, is the basis of a new linguistic theory, 'Lexical Priming', Hoey 2003), which reacts against the domination by syntax dating from Chomsky (*Syntactic Structures* 1957) and before. The basic tool of research into lexical priming is, of course, the concordance, which operates at the level of lexis, and whose defining feature is the exposure of collocation. Concordances thus allow learners - and especially elementary and post-elementary learners -to start their study of the language 'naturally', at the lexical level, to see which lexical items tend to link to which, to observe typical, recurring language clusters, and thus to build up a 'web' of lexical interrelationships.

Let us now look at the second limitation of data-driven learning suggested above, the learning style the methodology caters to, and the analytical processes it requires. The defining characteristic of DDL is its stringently linguistic focus. This involves two types of processes; *inductive* learning and *deductive* reasoning. *Inductive* learning works by perceiving patterns and forming generalisations and hypotheses (Murison-Bowie 1996: 190, Johns, 1991b: 30). In the context of DDL, corpus evidence of the language point being studied is examined for salient features, then generalisations are made and finally rules are formulated (Murison-Bowie 1996: 192-3).

Deductive reasoning, on the other hand, is a process of hypothesis testing, i.e. hypothesis-experiment-conclusion (the 'classic method of scientific enquiry', Murison-Bowie 1993: 41-2). In deductive reasoning, learners might be asked to put forward a hypothesis as to the rules they expect to emerge for a particular feature, *before* the process begins (this might be their own hypothesis, or they may be testing a prescriptive rule they have been taught). This might be done by looking at samples from the corpus, and, in the final stage, modifying or reformulating the rule as necessary in accordance with the evidence (*ibid.*).

Such analytical ways of studying language are mainly suitable to the introverted, analytic-type learner who tends naturally to use hypothetical-deductive reasoning and problem-solving strategies (see, for example, Oxford's 1993 analysis of learning styles). A concordance can be very intimidating to the more intuitive, instinctive-type learner, who sees language suddenly reduced to a dense list of disconnected phrases. Not all learners possess, or are trained in, the inductive and deductive reasoning skills required to interpret corpus data, nor will they necessarily learn the language in that way. Some learners need initial guidance in the processes required to elicit general rules of use from examples of particular instances.

The DDL approach as a whole will inevitably lead learners to re-evaluate their perceptions of grammar, as they see its prescriptive edicts questioned or contradicted by observation (see Section 11.4.2, 'Currency and the corpus', above), and this can be a particularly alien experience to learners from certain cultures. Weaning such learners off dependency on the authority of their dictionaries/grammars can be extremely hard. Zimbabwean students, for example, are described as regarding the textbook as a 'monolithic authority' (Stevens 1995) having modes of study which are therefore 'rarely analytical, and frequently unreflective' (*ibid.*). Hadley (1998) found his group of Japanese students well-disposed towards the study of grammar but described how they defaulted to dictionaries when faced with the unfamiliar format of the concordance: 'At first the students were terrified at seeing pages full of English words. Many scrambled furtively for their dictionaries' (Hadley 1998). The Japanese education system is not one that rewards effort, as Hadley points out (*ibid.*), so there is little incentive in expending the effort involved in extrapolating grammar rules through DDL tasks rather than simply consulting the course- or grammar-book. Resistance may also come from entrenched cultural attitudes, an example of which is the Japanese belief that native English speakers are ignorant of the grammar of their own language (Hadley 1998). In Asia in general, adherence to the Grammar Translation approach is built into coursebooks and entrance examinations, so a learning methodology which threatens to destabilize this is likely to be resisted.

11.4.4 Culture and the corpus

The two technologies discussed so far in this chapter have both been seen to have broadened the concept of culture from that of the culture associated with a language and society, to that associated with a system of communication and the new variety of language it has generated. In the context of this last technology, the corpus, the concept of culture has to be re-assessed yet again. The fact that the corpus - a database of authentic texts - is rich in cultural content ought to be incontestable. And certainly, corpora are mines of culture-specific usages of language, such as pragmatic uses mentioned in Section 11.4.1 above, idioms and collocations (see Tasks 22 and 24).

Its relationship with culture becomes problematic when we examine the issue of context. The corpus, it can be argued, is made up of 'transplanted' language, language that has been deracinated from the original circumstances of its production and thus from its original socio-cultural context. Information about its situational context, its intended audience, its communicative intent and its communicative impact are all lost in the transition from source to electronic corpus. Corpora, in other words 'contain information about production but not about reception' (Cook 1998: 58), they give an effectively one-dimensional representation of the language. What is more, extricating language from its cultural context effectively ruptures the language-culture bond, which, as was argued in Chapter 3, is fundamental to the existence of both elements. The language corpus consists, then, metaphorically speaking, of 'naked' language. Cultural interpretations have to depend on examining this naked language, inferring, and in effect endeavouring to restore, cultural elements, in order to re-establish the language-culture balance. The language has, in other words, to be recontextualised, to 'recreate' the contextual conditions in which it occurred. So while corpus data are certainly attested instances of language use, the cultural information remains elusive, still dependent on the same subjective strategies of inference and human intuition that were supposedly made redundant with the advent of electronic corpora (see 'Currency' above). To give a perhaps simplistic example, the cultural connotations of 'a nice cup of tea' (in British/Irish culture) can scarcely be inferred 'cold' from a concordance, and will probably require native speaker interpretation and elaboration.

Bearing in mind, then, the importance of NS intervention (possibly reassuring to those teachers who are still worried they may be 'replaced' by computers) corpora can be excellent sources of such cultural information. This includes culturally determined collocations (such as 'beer and skittles'), pragmatics (see Currency above), and collocations of superordinates e.g. colours, animals, parts of the body, to form idioms. A good, learner-led starting point (especially useful as a gentle initiation for lower level learners) is to brainstorm culture-specific concepts (for Britain and Ireland, learners might come up with such things as *pub, rain, tea* and *chips*), for which learners can generate concordances. They might use these to look at such things as pub names, collocations with *rain*, 'culture-specific' food combinations[35] and so on. At more advanced levels, idioms based on colours, metals, animals, foods, parts of the body etc. can all be researched (see Task 22).

Advanced level learners might also look at issues of gender and language - the ways in which certain words collocate with certain genders (*bully*, and *taciturn* with men, *blond* with women and so on), an interest which might lead them to explore the whole thorny issue of the political-correcting of the English language.

11.5 Conclusion

This chapter has attempted to give some idea of the opportunities ICT offers for new ways of teaching and learning languages. Underlying the methodologies described for using the Web, e-mail and corpora for language learning lies a radical role-shift in which the teacher moves from the centre of the class stage and the learner has direct access to the pathways to knowledge. Learner-emancipation is only one of the advantages of using ICT over using other media for language learning. Other crucial ones implicit in the methodologies described here, are that the technologies require and hone transferable electronic literacy skills and that this forms an unassailable attraction and motivation for language learners. This chapter has also placed some emphasis on the new varieties of language evolving in the IC technologies, the language of the Web and e-mail, suggesting that these pose a challenge not only to the language learner but also to the very concept of authenticity.

Further reading

Atkinson, T., 1998. *WWW - The Internet*. London: CILT (Centre for Information on Language Teaching and Research).

Dave Sperling's ESL café http://www.eslcafe.com.

Eastment, D., 2000. Non-ELT Web sites ... and how to find them, *Modern English Teacher* (April 2000).

Felix. U., ed. 2003. Language learning online: towards best practice, Lisse: Swets and Zeitlinger.

ICT for Language Learning: http://www.ict4lt.org

Internet TESL Journal and linkshttp://www.aitech.ac.jp/~iteslj/links

Johns, T. homepage: http://web.bham.ac.uk/johnstf/timconc.htm.

Language Learning and Technology (LLT) Journal: http://llt.msu.edu/

Townshend, K., 1997. *E-mail: Using Electronic Communications in Foreign Language Teaching*. London: CILT (Centre for Information on Language Teaching and Research).

Warschauer, M. homepage: http://www.gse.uci.edu/markw/

Warschauer, M., ed., 1995. *Virtual Connections - Online Activities and Projects for Networking Language Learners*. Hawai'i: University of Hawai'i Press.

Windeatt, S., D. Hardisty and D. Eastment, 2000. *The Internet*. Oxford: Oxford University Press.

11.6 The Tasks

11.6.1 The Web

Task 1

Discourse type	Language Learning Web sites
Communicative purpose	Interactive
Authentic task typology	Response
Level 4 up	
Aim: To search the Web, try out and evaluate language learning Web sites.	

Preparation: (a) List *Criteria for site evaluation* in Column 1 of a multi-columned table. Criteria might include:
• User-friendliness: speed of site download, attractiveness and navigability of the interface etc.
Interactivity: how well the material exploits the medium.
• Reliability: accuracy and reliability of information.
• Authenticity of language samples.
• Source/authority: the URL discloses the site's geographical origin (e.g. uk, ie for Ireland, jp for Japan) and/or whether it is commercial (.com, .co from the UK) organisational (.org) or educational (.edu if from the US and .ac from the UK).
• Currency: when was the site last updated?
The other columns in the table can be labelled *URL 1, URL 2, URL 3* etc.
(b) List of language learning Web sites (optional).
- Learners work individually or in pairs to seek and evaluate sites with different types of materials: online grammars and dictionaries, interactive learning activities (e.g. gap-fill exercises, hangman), 'fun' pages (e.g. jokes, cartoons), cultural information.
- Use the list of criteria in the table to comment on each site examined.
- To conclude the task, learners discuss their findings, try out the suggestions of others and possibly draw together their recommended sites as a reference list (on class Web page or group workspace if available).
Note: Free group workspace is available, for example, from the search engine *Yahoo!* (groups.yahoo.com), and the software company BSCW http://bscw.gmd.de/) and is easy to set up.

Task 2

Discourse type	Online literature

Communicative purpose	Informative
Authentic task typology	Extraction
Level 5 up	
Aim: To search the Web; to carry out research on literary works.	

This type of activity follows encounter with any literary text via tasks such as ones given in Chapter 5, 'Literature'.

Preparation: Choose and download an (extract from) a novel, short story or poem that has already been used in class. Set up a group workspace (see Note in Task 1) and post the text.

- Learners work individually or in pairs to search the Web for more information on the text e.g. the full text (if a novel or short story), a review of the text, biographical information on the author, other works by the same author, other works on the same topic etc.
- Learners compile their findings on a word-processed document, producing a summary and a list of live links (if possible) to additional texts associated with the original by theme/author.
- Learners then disseminate their documents on the class Web page, group workspace or e-mail, as available.
- One learner/group may compile all the class documents into one list of links and post it on the Web page/workspace or distribute via e-mail, as available.

Task 3

Discourse type	Online literature
Communicative purpose	Informative
Authentic task typology	Extraction
Level 5 up	
Aim: To use the Web to extend familiarity with poets' works.	

This type of activity follows work on poetry, via tasks such as those suggested within Chapter 5, 'Literature'.

- Learners work in pairs to search the Web for other poems by a poet whose work they have read in class.
- Each pair chooses *one poem* that appeals to them.
- Learners write (type) a short review of their chosen poem, giving the name of the poet, personal reactions, summarising its theme, mood etc. but omitting the title.
- Reviews are printed off, and two pairs swap reviews.
- Each pair reads the reviews written by the other and works from the reviews to identify and find the poems on the Web.
- After reading the poems, pairs regroup, check their findings and discuss their agreement with the reviews.

Task 4

Discourse type	Online screenplays
Communicative purpose	Informative
Authentic task typology	Transference
Level 5 up	
Aim: To animate text (screenplay).	

This type of activity follows encounter with film scenes via activities such as those suggested in Chapter 10, 'Film'.
- Working in groups, learners access the screenplay of a film, an extract of which they have already used in a class activity.
- Each group selects a scene from the film screenplay (NOT the scene already viewed).
- Groups fill out this scene for transfer to screen; decide how this scene would be played, the setting and props, the costumes worn and the music.
- Groups assign roles and present their scenes in class, describing necessary details as above *or* video and present scenes if possible.
- Other groups guess which film the scene comes from and comment on the interpretation.

Task 5

Discourse type	Online TC information
Communicative purpose	Informative
Authentic task typology	Transference
Level 4 up	
Aim: To use the Web to investigate TC traditions.	

This type of activity might come out of a learner enquiry e.g. about traditions associated with TC festivals (e.g. Christmas, St. Patrick's day).
- Learners search the Web identifying different aspects of the traditions e.g. significance of the traditions, food and drink etc. associated with it.
- Each learner selects ONE aspect which interests him/her, researches this and writes (types) a short summary or compilation of material on this aspect.
- Teacher or learners produce a class document on the chosen tradition by compiling learners' findings and printing these out or by putting up on the class Web page or workspace if available.

Task 6

Discourse type	Online commerce
Communicative purpose	Persuasive
Authentic task typology	Extraction
Level 4 up	

Aim: To practise searching the Web.

Preparation: Draw up a Web shopping list: without telling learners why they are doing this, ask them to write on the top of a sheet of paper their *favourite book*, or a book they would like to read, then to fold down and hide what they've written. Learners pass the sheet on to their neighbour. Ask learners to then write *the name of a place* they would like to visit and repeat the procedure with a *music CD*, *a computer game*, a favourite *food*, an *occasion* they need to mark (birthday, wedding, holiday) etc., and finally, their approximate *monthly income* (real or imagined). Once the list is finished, each learner opens up the sheet s/he is holding. Tell the students that this is their Web shopping list - the figure at the bottom is their budget!
- Learners then draw up a 3-columned table (on MS Word), with their shopping items in the left column, the second for recording the site where it can be purchased and the third for the price.
- Learners search the Web and find the required items, entering the required information into the table.
- This may be competitive, with the 'winner' being the first person to find all the items and stay within the budget (the holiday may stretch the budget, and may need to be calculated on the basis of the yearly income).

Task 7

Discourse type	Online commerce
Communicative purpose	Persuasive
Authentic task typology	Extraction
Level 4 up	
Aim: To practise searching the Web.	

Preparation: Choose a popular holiday destination (Majorca, Gran Canaria etc.) and before setting the task in class, check availability and price-variability of flights/holidays to the destination by looking on a search engine such as *Google*, using appropriate key words e.g. *flights Majorca*. Check also if there are particular days on which flights usually go out.
- Tell the learners this is a competition to find the cheapest *return flight* to (destination) on (dates). Tell them they must check that there are seats actually available on the flights. Alternatively, they could search for a *package holiday* (set the requirements - self-catering, half-board etc.). Set a time limit.
- Working individually or in pairs, learners search for the cheapest flight/holiday they can find and note the relevant sites.
- Stop on the time limit and go round the class to see who has found the lowest fare. The winner must show the class the Web site where the fare was found!

11.6.2 E-mail

Task 8

Discourse type	E-mail - external
Communicative purpose	Interactive
Authentic task typology	Reaction
Level 4 up	
Aim: To foster autonomy and teamwork in a tandem learning context.	

Preparation: Set up a group workspace on the Web for the class (e.g. on groups.yahoo.com) (a free service) *or* an e-mail distribution list consisting of the class members and the teacher.

-Learners set up e-mail tandem partnerships via the *International E-Mail Tandem Network* on the Web at http://www.slf.ruhr-uni-bochum.de/, where they click the link to the Tandem Partners and follow instructions, *or* via the *IECC (Intercultural E-Mail Classroom Connections)* at http://www.iecc.org/.

- Discuss the nature of tandem partnerships, *viz.*, that they are based on mutual collaboration (reciprocity) in the study of the target language and culture, and that they are independent of the teacher, whose role is that of advisor or guide if required.

- Brainstorm in class re. the potential and responsibilities of having a NS correspondent, e.g. 'keypals' should:

- Assist each other in learning their target languages via corrections, suggestions, responding to queries etc.

- Ask and respond to queries about social and cultural information.

- Find mutual interests and establish a relationship.

- If learners wish, draft the structure of an introductory message.

- Brainstorm the areas of culture which learners might ask keypals about e.g. traditions, foods, leisure activities, music, literature, sport etc.

- Each learner chooses ONE of above areas to try to cover with his/her keypal.

- Learners use the group workspace/class Web page or e-mail distribution list to distribute any information covering the agreed *cultural areas* that they receive from their keypals (at their discretion), plus any information covering *language points* relevant to class work, that they receive from their keypals (at their discretion).

Task 9

Discourse type	E-mail - external
Communicative purpose	Interactive
Authentic task typology	Transference
Level 4 up	
Aim: To solicit and present information on the target language culture.	

Preparation: Set up a group workspace on the Web for the class (e.g. on groups.yahoo.com) (a free service) *or* an e-mail distribution list consisting of the class members and the teacher.

-Learners set up e-mail tandem partnerships via the *International E-Mail Tandem Network* on the Web at http://www.slf.ruhr-uni-bochum.de/, where they click the link to the Tandem Partners and follow instructions, *or* via the *IECC (Intercultural E-Mail Classroom Connections)* at http://www.iecc.org/

Discuss the nature of tandem partnerships, *viz.*, that they are based on mutual collaboration (reciprocity) in the study of the target language and culture, and that they are independent of the teacher, whose role is that of advisor or guide if required.

- Brainstorm in class re. the potential and responsibilities of having a NS correspondent, e.g. the 'keypals' should:

- Assist each other in learning their target languages via corrections, suggestions, responding to queries etc.

- Ask and respond to queries about social and cultural information.

- Find mutual interests and establish a relationship.

- This activity can only be done once learners have established their e-mail partnerships.

- Brainstorm the areas of culture which learners might wish to ask keypals about e.g. traditions, foods, leisure activities, music, clothes, meeting people, family life, working life etc.

- One group is assigned to draft a large questionnaire containing these elements, with spaces for information to be entered (e.g. on a table in MS Word or a database).

This is then distributed to the other learners (on paper or via the group workspace/e-mail distribution list) for revision/feedback and a final version agreed.

- Learners choose one or two areas to ask their keypal about.

- Draw attention to the need for politeness, sensitivity and subtlety in asking about some of these elements.

- Depending on level, learners may wish to draft questions for the teacher to monitor before sending off to keypals.

- As learners receive their replies, they enter relevant information on the questionnaire.

- Learners may wish to check incoming information from other partnerships with their own keypals; this may require more checking or expanding the information in that section.

- Once the questionnaire is completed, it can be posted on the class workspace/Web page as available.

Task 10

Discourse type	E-mail - internal
Communicative purpose	Interactive
Authentic task typology	Reaction
Level 3 up	
Aim: To solicit and provide peer assistance in creative writing.	

Preparation: Set up a group workspace on the Web for the class (e.g. on groups.yahoo.com) (a free service) *or* an e-mail distribution list consisting of the class members and the teacher.

- Discuss the concept of collaborative learning; people learn from having to correct and explain to others, concept of mutual assistance, independence from the teacher etc.
- This activity is one method for doing creative writing and may be used in conjunction with other suitable creative writing activities or projects.
- Brainstorm a set of subjects for creative writing - these may connected to a work of literature or other cultural products used in class.
- Each learner chooses a subject and writes a short text (less than 400 words).
- They then send their texts to the class workspace/e-mail distribution list, with queries or notes appended if they wish.
- Peers respond with reactions, suggestions, language corrections etc.
- Learners revise their texts accordingly and re-post/re-distribute.
- Feedback loop continues until everyone is satisfied with their text.
- Final drafts of texts can be posted on the class workspace/Web page as available.
- Teacher may be interested in eliciting feedback from the learners on this method of working.

Task 11

Discourse type	E-mail - internal
Communicative purpose	Interactive
Authentic task typology	Reaction
Level 3 up	
Aim: To extend discussion on classroom topics and develop class relationships.	

Preparation: Set up a group workspace on the Web for the class (e.g. on groups.yahoo.com) (a free service) *or* an e-mail distribution list consisting of the class members and the teacher.
Note: This is not a stand-alone activity but parallels the normal work of the class. This class workspace/e-mail distribution list could be set up at the beginning of the course and may be particularly useful for lower levels whose face-to-face communication is slow.
- Tell learners the workspace/list is to be used to pursue and develop discussions, subjects or language points that have arisen in class. Learners may wish to post anything arising from these e.g. comments, questions, additional information, reactions etc. Remind the learners that these comments etc. are not aimed at the teacher but at the other students; the teacher is just another group member.
- If the students are reticent at the beginning, the teacher may need to initiate the first discussion on a topic arising in class.

Task 12

Discourse type	E-mail - internal

Communicative purpose	Soliciting
Authentic task typology	Reaction
Level 4 up	
Aim: To work collaboratively in creative writing with a focus on coherence.	

Preparation: Set up a group workspace on the Web for the class (e.g. on groups.yahoo.com) (a free service) *or* an e-mail distribution list consisting of the class members and the teacher.

This activity is a way of practising cohesive markers (adverbs or adverbial conjunctions).

- Learners need to be aware of the concept of cohesive markers and be able to use some of them. They should have access to resources for cohesive devices such as the sections on Conjunctions and Coherence and Transitions found in a 'guide to grammar and writing' on the Web at http://webster.commnet.edu/HP/pages/darling/grammar.htm.

- One learner (or the teacher) writes the first sentence or two of a story, which must end at a cohesive marker e.g. 'Angelika was rich and beautiful, yet...'

-This is posted to the workspace/distributed on e-mail list and any learner or a number of learners may continue the story, adding a sentence or two but always ending with a cohesive marker e.g. 'Angelika was rich and beautiful, yet she was not very happy. Her husband was a successful businessman whose work often took him away for long periods. Unfortunately,...'

- This will result in a number of different stories being created simultaneously. Learners may abandon unsuccessful ones en route.

- When all the stories are finished, learners may say which they think is/are the most successful, and why. This may raise the issue of 'overdoing' cohesion and it may be necessary to emphasise that the story-writing was intended mainly to raise awareness and practise cohesive devices.

Task 13

Discourse type	E-mail - internal
Communicative purpose	Soliciting
Authentic task typology	Reaction
Level 4 up	
Aim: To practise coherence.	

Preparation: Set up a group workspace on the Web for the class (e.g. on groups.yahoo.com) (a free service) *or* an e-mail distribution list consisting of the class members and the teacher.

Note: This activity has to be preceded by Task 12. Like Task 12, it requires some knowledge of cohesive markers, and learners may be referred to resources referred to in Task 12 if necessary.

- The teacher (or a designated learner) *deconstructs* one of the stories written in Task 12, by removing the cohesive markers, jumbling the sentences and phrases and putting each on a separate line.

- This text is then posted on the workspace/distributed to the e-mail list.
- The learners work individually or in pairs to construct a story by cutting, pasting and linking the sentences/phrases with suitable cohesive markers. NB. Learners are not to reconstruct the original story but create a new one.
- Learners are told to work as quickly as possible; the first feasible story posted, wins!

Task 14

Discourse type	E-mail - internal
Communicative purpose	Soliciting
Authentic task typology	Reaction
Level 3 up	
Aim: To work collaboratively on creative writing.	

Preparation: Set up a group workspace on the Web for the class (e.g. on groups.yahoo.com) (a free service) *or* an e-mail distribution list consisting of the class members and the teacher.
This activity should follow work on poetry or song that has raised awareness of rhyme, rhythm and of poems with specific structures (e.g. the limerick, the sonnet, the haiku).
- One learner (or the teacher) writes the first line of a poem of a particular type and posts it on the workspace/distributes it on the list. The type of poem e.g. limerick, sonnet, should be stated if it is not obvious. An easier alternative for lower level learners is to let the learners themselves develop a rhyme scheme.
- Another learner/other learners writes/write a second line and post/s it/distributes it, and so on.
- In this way, a number of different poems are created simultaneously.
- When all the poems are finished, learners may vote on which they think is/are the most successful, saying why.
This method may be used for the creation of other literary genres: short stories, plays, screenplays.

Task 15

Discourse type	E-mail - internal
Communicative purpose	Informative
Authentic task typology	Extraction
Level 3 up	
Aim: To scan for specific information within e-mail messages.	

Preparation: This is an e-mail 'treasure hunt'; it involves learners finding partial clues to an answer (which may be a sentence, a poem, a number, a place, a famous person etc.) from within a series of e-mails sent to them by the teacher. To prepare the 'treasure' (the answer), compile a series of informative/junk e-mails (from university/college listservs, discussion lists or commercial mailings). At the top of each, give one clue to the answer e.g. 'the first clue: the date of the U2 concert in the University of Limerick concert hall' - 'the second clue: add the number of the lecture theatre where the talk on sports medicine is taking place (...and so on). The *total number* has special significance; what is it? Send the number and your answer to teacher@classroom' etc.

Set up an e-mail distribution list for the class.

- Send these e-mails to learners at regular intervals; tell them not to send you the answers to each separate clue but only when they have found the complete answer.

- After experience with these, learners may wish to create their own treasure hunts (they will need to set up a class distribution list).

Task 16

Discourse type	E-mail - internal
Communicative purpose	Informative
Authentic task typology	Analysis
Level 5 up	

Aim: To identify and interpret e-mail-specific features (abbreviations, acronyms, paralinguistic features, emoticons).

Preparation: Compile a set of e-mails from personal/business/discussion lists. Teacher and learners set up an e-mail distribution list for the class. Circulate the file to the learners.

Brainstorm in class for existing knowledge of e-mail-specific features e.g. abbreviations ('ATB' = all the best), acronyms, paralinguistic features ([hug]), emoticons (- :).

- Working individually or in pairs, learners first identify what they consider to be any e-mail-specific features within the messages.

- Learner/pairs then compile a list of examples of the features by category (acronym, emoticon etc.), together with their meanings, and circulates it to the others for comparison.

- Learners may then be referred to a Web site listing such features e.g. the 'acronyms, emoticons and smilies page' on http://www.muller-godschalk.com/emoticon.html

Task 17

Discourse type	E-mail - internal
Communicative purpose	Informative
Authentic task typology	Analysis
Level 6 up	

Aim: To compare linguistic and discourse features of e-mail messages with those of letters, within a specific register, and to infer e-mail conventions.

Preparation: Choose a genre that is of interest to the learner group; personal, business, commercial message, academic discussion etc. This activity presupposes some familiarity with the chosen genre in letter-writing. Compile a set of e-mails within the selected genre (learners might contribute messages). Collect and photocopy a set of 'snail-mail' letters from the same genre.

Teacher and learners set up an e-mail distribution list for the class.

- Brainstorm in class for existing knowledge of types of differences between the two media e.g. attention to grammar, spelling, level of formality, openings and closings, use of e-mail specific features etc (e.g. emoticons Task 16), layout, length.
- Working individually or in pairs, learners compare their e-mail and letter samples, identify differences and deduce e-mail conventions e.g. use of the subject header, salutation, looser grammar and spelling, brevity.
- Each learner/pair compiles a set of e-mail conventions, giving examples, and circulates it to the others for comparison.

Task 18

Discourse type	E-mail - junk/spam mail
Communicative purpose	Persuasive
Authentic task typology	Analysis
Level 6 up	

Aim: To identify linguistic functions associated with (e-mail) promotion e.g. intriguing, persuading, appealing.

Preparation: Teacher and learners set up an e-mail distribution list for the class. Teacher compiles a set of 'spam' e-mails on one file and circulates to the learners. Brainstorm some linguistic functions and forms associated with commercial promotion and list on board/slide as 2-column table e.g. function: *intriguing.* form: *'Have you confirmed your interest?'*; function: *persuading.* form: *'Don't let this slip by you!'* function: *tempting.* form: *'Limited availability!'* etc.

- Circulate the 'spam' mail file to all learners.
- Working individually or in pairs, learners analyse the mail for the identified functions and forms, adding any others they might find. Ask them to list their findings on 2 - column table as before, under *function* and *form.*
- At the end of the task, learners circulate their tables via the class e-mail list to cross-check their findings.

Task 19

Discourse type	E-mail - internal
Communicative purpose	Informative
Authentic task typology	Transference
Level 5 up	

Aim: To switch genre (business e-mail to business letter). This task might follow Task 18).

Preparation: Find a business/work-related e-mail suitable for re-writing as a business letter and circulate it to the class.

Teacher and learners set up an e-mail distribution list for the class.

- Working individually or in pairs, learners re-write the message as a business letter as a word-processed document, adding phrases etc. where necessary.
- Learner/pairs circulate their letters via the list and give mutual feedback.

11.6.3 Corpora and concordancing

Task 20

Discourse type	Concordances
Communicative purpose	Informative
Authentic task typology	Extraction
Level 5 up	
Aim: To raise awareness of culture-specific significance and collocation of apparently unmarked lexis.	

Preparation: Select an apparently unmarked lexis or word-string with specific cultural significance/collocation e.g. (for English) *drink, tea, - and chips*

- Give learners links to an online spoken corpus e.g. on Collins COBUILD Web site http://www.cobuild.collins.co.uk/, or the BNC online http://www.natcorp.ox.ac.uk
- Working in mono-cultural pairs/small groups if possible, learners;
- Generate a concordance for the target item.
- Note collocations, infer socio-cultural implications.
- Find own cultural equivalence (not necessarily a translation) of collocations/phrases containing target item.
- Regroup into multi-cultural groups and discuss cross-cultural similarities and differences their work has revealed.

Task 21

Discourse type	Concordances
Communicative purpose	Informative
Authentic task typology	Analysis
Level 6 up	
Aim: To 'test' marked-ness of apparently marked lexis.	

Preparation: Suggest (or ask learners to suggest) an apparently marked lexical item e.g. *terribly, awfully, perfectly.*

- Learners brainstorm their ideas on connotations, meaning, collocations of selected item.
- Using suitable corpus (in case of above examples, spoken English) teacher generates and prints, or learners generate, concordances for target item.
- Working in pairs/groups, learners code concordance lines 'positive' 'negative' or other appropriate coding.

- Learners test their findings against their original ideas and revise hypotheses as to marked-ness and collocations of item.

Task 22

Discourse type	Concordances
Communicative purpose	Informative
Authentic task typology	Extraction
Level 6 up	
Aim: To explore idiom.	

Preparation: Choose a superordinate whose hyponyms are idiom-prone e.g. *colours, animals, parts of the body*.
- Learners work in pairs. Give each pair a hyponym of the superordinate - a colour / an animal etc. or allow them to choose.
- Using a suitable corpus (e.g. British spoken) pairs generate concordances for their selected colour/animal etc.
- Learners go through the concordance, separating idiomatic from literal usages.
- Learners list idioms and idiomatic usages that have emerged, and interpret their meanings.
- Learners swap partners and exchange findings.
- Pool all findings in class, or ask a group of learners do so and compile a handout for the rest of the class and/or post on class Web page/workspace if available.
- This activity can be repeated at intervals with different superordinates so that a series of handouts might be produced or the Web page/workspace entry extended.

Task 23

Discourse type	Concordances
Communicative purpose	Informative
Authentic task typology	Analysis
Level 6 up	
Aim: To raise awareness of structural or lexical differences in different varieties of English.	

- Use 2 or more corpora or sub-corpora of different varieties of English (e.g. for American versus British English, LOB versus Brown corpora, online at Hong Kong Virtual Language Centre web site at http://vlc.polyu.edu.hk/default.htm, or American and British sub-corpora of COBUILD corpus at http://www.cobuild.collins.co.uk/).
- Select one or more structural differences e.g. *speak to/with* in British /American varieties.
- *Either* learners generate concordances experimenting with strings *speak to* and *speak with* within the two corpora and deduce which collocation is most common in which variety.

- *Or* Preparation: teacher generates and prints *speak + to, speak + with*, and learners work in pairs to deduce which variety is which.
- Learners swap partners and consolidate findings.

Task 24

Discourse type	Concordances
Communicative purpose	Informative
Authentic task typology	Analysis
Level 5 up	
Aim: Familiarisation with phrasal verbs.	

Preparation: Teacher selects (or learners request) a lexical verb that combines with several prepositions/particles to form phrasal verbs e.g. *get*. Generate and print a series of concordances for different phrasal verbs formed with *get* e.g. *get on, get through, get by* (one phrasal verb for each class group). Blank out the preposition/particle following the lexical verb in each concordance. Copy each concordance to provide one for each group member.
- Learners work in groups. Each group is given one concordance (i.e. one phrasal verb) to work on.
- Group tasks are (a) to identify their phrasal verb by identifying the missing particle (b) to extract the different meanings and collocations (including idiomatic) of each phrasal verb (this might include the addition of another particle to make another phrasal verb). The group with *get on*, for example, might find; *get on = continue, get on with someone* (another phrasal verb) *get on someone's nerves* (c) in the concordance, mark representative examples of each meaning.
- Learners swap groups and exchange findings, explaining the meanings using the examples marked.
- Findings may be compiled on class workspace or Web page if available.

Task 25

Discourse type	Concordances
Communicative purpose	Informative
Authentic task typology	Analysis
Level 6 up	
Aim: Raise awareness of gender-specific collocations in language.	

Preparation: Select or let learners identify words suspected as having gender-specific collocation or application e.g. *blond, handsome, bully*. Learner-groups choose one item each.
Learners generate concordances for each target item.
- Working in pairs/groups, learners confirm or refute their hypothesis on gender-specificity of their item and expand it to include other frequent collocations.

- Learners generate more concordances to confirm their hypotheses re. other collocations if required.
- Learners regroup and exchange findings.

Task 26

Discourse type	Concordances
Communicative purpose	Informative
Authentic task typology	Analysis
Level 4 up	
Aim: To address grammar problems.	

Preparation: Choose/ask learners to select an item requiring clarification/analysis e.g. *say/tell* distinctions, uses of *some/any*, reported speech. This might be an item the learners have noticed whose real and/or spoken use clashes with the grammar rules prescribed for it.
- Learners brainstorm their current understanding of the syntax and rules associated with the item/s e.g. *say something, tell someone something*; *any* used in questions and negative sentences, *some* in positive sentences.
- Teacher or learners generate concordance/s of selected item/s.
- Working in pairs/groups, learners identify various uses of / structures used with target item/s.
- Learners regroup, consolidate findings, revise their hypotheses and add to/correct the grammar rules.

Task 27

Discourse type	Concordances
Communicative purpose	Informative
Authentic task typology	Analysis
Level 4 up	
Aim: To identify collocations typical of a specific genre.	

This activity might be part of genre-specific study e.g. on journalism, song etc.
Preparation: Identify a number of words which appear to recur in the genre with particular collocations e.g. in journalism, the items *hotly* + words associated with conflict (*hotly* + *deny, debate, contest* etc.) *sweeping*[36] is associated with change (*new measures, changes*). Generate and print concordances of the selected items. Blank out the target items and write as a list above each concordance.
- Working in pairs/groups, learners;
- Identify the missing item in each concordance, choosing from this list.
- Note any other collocations of the target words.

Task 28

Discourse type	Concordances
Communicative purpose	Informative
Authentic task typology	Transference
Level 6 up	
Aim: To deduce and formulate dictionary definitions.	

Preparation: Tell learners they are being asked to produce a properly formulated dictionary definition.
- Each learner:
- Identifies a word they have encountered whose meaning/s and collocations they would like to explore.
- Accesses and downloads a definition (of a random word) from an online dictionary e.g. the *Merriam-Webster* on http://www.m-w.com./netdict.htm, to act as a template *or* uses a text-based dictionary for this.
- Generates and examines concordances, deduces meanings and formulates definitions in dictionary format according to their template. The definition should include authentic samples from the concordance/s.
- Writes their definition.
- On completion, assesses the accuracy of the definition by comparing with a dictionary definition.
- Exchanges definitions with other learners.

Notes

1   Published online, March 2003, accessed on http://www.icc-europe.com March 29 2003.

2   The American School Directory (ASD) (online) listed approximately 104,000 K-12 school Web sites as of 14 April 2003.

3   http://www.aitech.ac.jp/~iteslj/links

4   Found at http://www.eslcafe.com

5   Found at http://iteslj.org/links/

6   The December 2002 Netcraft Web Server survey received responses from 35,543,105 Web sites (figures as of 1 April 2003, from http://www.netcraft.com/Survey/index-200212.html)

7   Statistics as of 1 April 2003 from *Topica*, an online directory of discussion lists found on http://www.liszt.com

8   See Mishan 2004 for a task-based approach to learner Web authoring.

9   Based on subjects covered in the author's class newspaper project, Spring 1998.

10 In 1998, the total number of newly created non-English sites exceeded that of newly created English sites (Crystal 2001:218).

11 See statistics on numbers of people online in different world languages on http://www.glreach.com/globstats/index.php3, accessed 14 April 2003.

12 'Language and society in cyberspace.' Article adapted from plenary presented at TESOL Convention, Orlando, Florida, 1997. Originally accessed 7 December 1998 on http://www.tesol.org/pubs/articles/

13 The Web site Bibliomania offers over 60 novels, a broad selection from *The Oxford Book of English Verse* as well as the collected works of poets such as William Blake and Oscar Wilde, the works of Shakespeare plus works of non-fiction and reference books.

14 e.g. *The Seed* (online) 'an organic, forever growing book' telling the history of a fictional world called Erinn. *The Seed* is a series of interlinked short stories, to which anyone can contribute, available at http://freepages.pavilion.net/users/wrench/welcome.htm

15 Electronic mail: Strangely familiar texts. Originally accessed 9 January 1999 on http://cougar.vut.edu.au/~dalbj/email.htm

16 http://www.google.com

17 A simple example in the author's teaching context is the very different results gained by using the search terms 'Limerick' and 'limericks'. The first throws up hits relating to the city and the second, hits containing collections of limericks, the comic 5-line poems with a set rhyme scheme.

18 BITNET was the original communications network of academic sites that predated the Internet, and was phased out by 1996.

19 Estimated figure as of September 2002. Source: Nua Internet Surveys, http://www.nua.com/surveys/ accessed 15 April 2003.

20 http://www.slf.ruhr-uni-bochum.de/email/infeng01.html

21 http://www.iecc.org/

22 Statistics from http://www.iecc.org 15 April 2003.

23 This and all following e-mail extracts in this section are from the author's private e-mail correspondence.

24 In a study by Warschauer comparing face-to-face participation with that in e-mail, it was shown that 'the four quietest members of the class in face-to-face discussion (all Japanese), increased their participation almost ten-fold (from only 1.8% of comments to a 17.3% of comments) and thus went from almost total silence to relatively equal participation' (Warschauer 1996c).

25 Written by Mike Smith available from Oxford University Press, http://www.oup.com/elt

26 MonoConc and MonoConc Pro available from Athelstan, http://www.athel.com

27 Online at http://www.natcorp.ox.ac.uk

28 Online at http://vlc.polyu.edu.hk/default.htm

29 These first two examples draw on samples of DDL materials produced by participants in a workshop in Usti nad Labem (North Bohemia) March 2000 found on Tim Johns DDL page: http://web.bham.ac.uk/johnstf/timconc.htm accessed 8 April 2003.

30 Author's class task, summer 1997.

31 Analysis of one corpus (The software company Abacus Communications' corpus of telephone dialogues) revealed 4 distinct uses of the item *right*, only 10% of which were with the meaning of *correct*, which is the first dictionary meaning (e.g. COBUILD Student's Dictionary 1997: 550) and usually the main meaning known to learners.

32 The most important spoken corpora in the context of British English are the sub-corpora of the COBUILD Bank of English, and the British National Corpus (BNC), each of which contain 10 million words and the 6 million word CANCODE corpus of spoken English in Britain and Ireland. There are, however, many smaller works with data on different varieties of English which are relevant for learners in the cultural contexts using these varieties. The L-CIE, for example, is a corpus of Irish English being built by the University of Limerick, Mary Immaculate College, Limerick and the University of Nottingham.

33 *Concordance Samplers 2: Phrasal Verbs* and *Concordance Samplers 3: Tenses*, both published by Collins Cobuild.

34 As has been done for a unique project on teaching literacy at primary school level at Key Stage 2; *An investigation into corpus-based learning about language in the primary school*, being carried out by Sealey and Thompson (SLALS, University of Reading) and Scott (University of Liverpool), see http://www.rdg.ac.uk/slals/sst.htm for details.

35 For instance, the string *and chips* concordanced on a 3.5 million word corpus of *The Times Newspaper* January 1995 (downloaded from the HKVLC site on 2 June 1999) produced 21 hits, over 50% of which collocated with *fish* either directly or with one of its hyponyms (e.g. cod, haddock). Over 80% of the results generated from the 10-million word corpus of spoken English in the COBUILD Bank of English collocated directly with fish.

36 Items taken from activity on collocation in Chandler and Stone 1999:15.

Appendix One

Chapter Three: Coursebooks reviewed

Clare A. and J. Wilson, 2002. *Language to Go, Upper Intermediate*. Harlow: Pearson Education Ltd.

Crace A. and R. Wileman, 2002. *Language to Go, Intermediate*. Harlow: Pearson Education Ltd.

Cunningham, G. and S. Mohamed, 2002 *Language to Go, Pre-Intermediate*. Harlow: Pearson Education Ltd.

Cunningham, S. and P. Moore, 1998. *Cutting Edge, Intermediate*. Harlow: Longman.

Doff A. and C. Jones, 1997. *Language in Use, Upper Intermediate*. Cambridge: Cambridge University Press.

Evans, V. and J. Dooley, 1998. *Enterprise*. Swansea: Express publishing.

Forsyth W., 2000. *Clockwise, Intermediate*. Oxford: Oxford University Press.

Gairns, R. and S. Redman, 1998. *True to Life, Upper Intermediate*. Cambridge: Cambridge University Press.

Haines, S. and B. Stewart, 2000. *Landmark, Upper Intermediate*. Oxford: Oxford University Press.

Le Maistre, S. and C. Lewis, 2002. *Language to Go, Elementary*. Harlow: Pearson Education Ltd.

O'Dell, F., 1997. *English Panorama, Advanced*. Cambridge: Cambridge University Press.

Hutchinson, T., 1997. *Lifelines, Intermediate*. Oxford: Oxford University Press.

Oxenden C. and C. Latham-Koenig, 2001. *English File*. Oxford: Oxford University Press.

Taylor, L., 1997. *International Express, Pre-Intermediate*. Oxford: Oxford University Press.

Taylor, L., 1997. *International Express, Intermediate*. Oxford: Oxford University. Press.

Walton, R. and M. Bartram, 2000. *Initiative*. Cambridge: Cambridge University Press.

Appendix Two

The English-Speaking Union Framework

Carroll, B. and R. West, 1989. *The ESU Framework: Performance Scales for English Language Examinations.* London: Longman.

9
Has a full command of the language, with consistent accuracy, fluency, appropriate usage, organization and comprehension. An exceptional level of mastery, not always reached by native speakers, even quite educated ones.

8
Uses a full range of language with proficiency approaching that in the learner's own mother tongue. Copes well even with demanding and complex language situations. Makes occasional minor lapses in accuracy, fluency, appropriacy and organization which do not affect communication. Only rare uncertainties in conveying or comprehending the context of the message.

7
Uses the language fully effectively and confidently in most situations. A few lapses in accuracy, fluency, appropriacy and organization, but communication is effective and consistent, with only a few uncertainties in conveying or comprehending the content of the message.

6
Uses the language with confidence in all but the most demanding situations. Noticeable lapses in accuracy, fluency, appropriacy and organization, but communication and comprehension are effective on most occasions, and are easily restored when difficulties arise.

5
Uses the language independently and effectively in all familiar situations. Rather frequent lapses in accuracy, fluency, appropriacy and organization, but usually succeeds in communicating and comprehending general message.

4
Uses a basic range of language, sufficient for familiar and non-pressuring situations. Many lapses in accuracy, fluency, appropriacy and organization, restricting continual communication and comprehension, so frequent efforts are needed to ensure communicative intention is achieved.

3

Uses a limited range of language, sufficient for simple practical needs. In more exacting situations, there are frequent problems in accuracy, fluency, appropriacy and organization, so that normal communication and comprehension frequently break down or are difficult to keep going.

2

Uses a narrow range of language, adequate for basic needs and simple situations. Does not really have sufficient language to cope with normal day-to-day, real-life communication, but basic communication is possible with adequate opportunities for assistance. Uses short, often inaccurate and inappropriately worded messages, with constant lapses in fluency.

1

Uses a few words or phrases such as common greetings, and recognizes some public notices or signs. At the lowest level recognizes which language is being used.

Bibliography

Alderson, J. and A. Urquhart, eds. *Reading in a Foreign Language*. London: Longman.

Allan, M., 1985. *Teaching English with Video*. Harlow: Longman.

Allen, R., 2002. *Soap Opera*. Museum of Broadcast Communications Web site. Retrieved 17 December 2002 from http://www.museum.tv/index.shtml

Allwright, R., 1979. 'Language learning through communicative practice', in: C. Brumfit and K. Johnson, eds. *The Communicative Approach to Language Teaching*. Oxford: Oxford University Press, 167-82.

Alptekin, C., 1993. Target-language culture in EFL materials. *ELT Journal*, 47, 2, 136-43.

Amitay, E., 2000. 'Anchors in context: a corpus analysis of authoring conventions for Web pages', in: L. Pemberton and S. Shurville, eds. *Words on the Web: Computer-Mediated Communication*. Exeter: Intellect Books, 25-35.

Arnold, E., 1991. Authenticity revisited: How real is real? *English for Specific Purposes*, 10, 3, 237- 44.

Arnold, J. and H. Douglas Brown, 1999. 'A map of the terrain,' in: J. Arnold, ed. *Affect in Language Learning*. Cambridge: Cambridge University Press, 1-27.

Arnold, J., ed., 1999. *Affect in Language Learning*. Cambridge: Cambridge University Press.

Asher, J., 1977. *Learning Another Language Through Actions: The complete teacher's guide book*. Los Gatos: Sky Oaks Production.

Atkinson, T., 1998. *WWW - The Internet*. London: CILT (Centre for Information on Language Teaching and Research).

Bachman, L., 1990. *Fundamental Considerations in Language Testing*. Oxford: Oxford University Press.

Bacon, S. and M. Finnemann, 1990. A study of the attitudes, motives, and strategies of university foreign language students and their disposition to authentic oral and written input. *The Modern Languages Journal*, 74, 4, 459-70.

Baddock, B., 1991. Film, authenticity and language teaching. *Language Learning Journal*, 3, 16-19.

Baddock, B., 1996. *Using Films in the English Class*. Hemel Hempstead: Phoenix ELT.

Bandler, R. and J. Grinder, 1975. *The Structure of Magic: volume 1: A book about language and therapy*. Palo Alto: Science and Behavior Books.

Bassnet, S., and P. Grundy, 1993. *Language through Literature*. Harlow: Longman.

Baym, N., 1995. 'From practice to culture on Usenet', in: S. Star, ed. *The Cultures of Computing*. Oxford: Blackwell, 29-52.

Beckett, S., 1965. *Waiting for Godot: A tragicomedy in two acts*. 2nd ed. London: Faber and Faber.

Beier, E., J. Starkweather and D. Miller, 1967. Analysis of word frequencies in spoken language of children. *Language and Speech*, 10: 217-27.

Bell, J. and R. Gower, 1991. *Intermediate Matters*. Harlow: Longman.

Bell, J. and R. Gower, 1998. 'Writing materials for the world: A great compromise', in: B. Tomlinson, ed. *Materials Development in Language Teaching*. Cambridge: Cambridge University Press, 116-29.

Belisle, R., 1996. E-mail Activities in the ESL Writing Class. The Internet TESL Journal. 1996, 2(12). Retrieved 10 January 1999 from http://www.aitech.ac.jp//~iteslj

Benson, P., 2001. *Teaching and Researching Autonomy in Language Learning*. Harlow:Longman.

Benson, P., 1997. 'The philosophy and politics of learner autonomy', in: P. Benson and P. Voller, eds. *Autonomy and Independence in Language Learning*. London: Longman, 18-34.

Benson, P., and P. Voller, eds., 1997. *Autonomy and Independence in Language Learning*. London: Longman.

Bhatia, V., 1993. *Analysing Genre: Language use in professional settings*. Harlow: Longman Group UK Ltd.

Biber, D., 1988. *Variation across Speech and Writing*. Cambridge: Cambridge University Press.

Biber, D., S. Johansson, G. Leech, S. Conrad and E. Finegan, 1999. *Longman Grammar of Spoken and Written English*. Longman Publications Group.

Biesenbach-Lucas, S. and D. Weasenforth, 1998. *The Appropriateness of e-mail in composition instruction*. Retrieved 29 July 2003 from http://www.insa-lyon.fr/Departements/CDRL/appropriateness.html

Boud, D., 1981. 'Towards student responsibility for learning', in: D. Boud, ed. *Developing Student Autonomy in Learning*. London: Kogan Page, 21-37.

Boud, D., ed., 1981. *Developing Student Autonomy in Learning*. London: Kogan Page.

Bouman, L., 1995. Video, an extra dimension to the study of literature. *Language Learning Journal*, 12, 29-31.

Breen, M., 1987. Learner contributions to task design, in: C. Candlin and D. Murphy, eds. *Language Learning Tasks*. Englewood Cliffs, NJ: Prentice-Hall.

Breen. M. 1985. Authenticity in the language classroom. *Applied Linguistics*, 6, 1, 60-70.

Broady, E. and M. Kenning, 1996. *Promoting Learner Autonomy in University Language Learning*. London: CILT (Centre for Information on Language Teaching and Research).

Brown, D. 1986. 'Learning a second culture', in: J. Valdes, ed., *Culture Bound: Bridging the Gap*. Cambridge: Cambridge University Press, 33-48.

Brown, G., 1993. *Listening to Spoken English*. Harlow: Longman Group UK Ltd.

Brown, G. and G. Yule, 1983. *Discourse Analysis*. London: Longman.

Brumfit, C. and K. Johnson, eds., 1979. *The Communicative Approach to Language Teaching*. Oxford: Oxford University Press.

Bryson, B., 1994. *Made in America*. London: Martin Secker and Warburg.

Butler, I., 1999. Integrating language and literature. *Folio, Journal of the Materials Development Association MATSDA*, 5, 2, 33-40.

Buttjes, D. and M. Byram, eds., 1991. *Mediating Languages and Cultures*. Clevedon and Philadelphia: Multilingual Matters.

Bygate, M., P. Skehan and M. Swain eds., 2001. *Researching Pedagogic Tasks: Second Language Learning, Teaching and Testing*. Harlow: Pearson Education Ltd.

Byram, M. 1989. *Cultural Studies in Foreign Language Education*. Clevedon: Multilingual Matters.

Byram, M., 1991. 'Teaching culture and language: Towards an integrated model', in: D. Buttjes and M. Byram, eds. *Mediating Languages and Cultures*. Clevedon and Philadelphia: Multilingual Matters, 17-32.

Byram, M., V. Esarte-Sarries, S. Taylor and P. Allatt, 1991. 'Young people's perceptions of other cultures: The role of foreign language teaching', in: D. Buttjes and M. Byram, eds. *Mediating Languages and Cultures*. Clevedon and Philadelphia: Multilingual Matters, 103-19.

Byram, M., C. Morgan and colleagues, 1994. *Teaching-and-learning Language-and-Culture*. Clevedon and Philadelphia: Multilingual Matters.

Byrd, P., ed., 1995. *Materials Writer's Guide*. Boston: Heinle and Heinle Publishers.

Byrne, D., 1986. *Teaching Oral English*. Harlow: Longman.

Candlin, C., 2001. 'Taking the curriculum to task', in: M. Bygate, P. Skehan and M. Swain, eds. *Researching Pedagogic Tasks: Second Language Learning, Teaching and Testing*. Harlow: Pearson Education Ltd., 229-43.

Carrell, P. and J. Eisterhold, 1988. 'Schema theory and ESL reading pedagogy', in: P. Carrell, J. Devine and D. Eskey, eds. *Interactive Approaches to Second Language Reading*. Cambridge: Cambridge University Press, 73-92.

Carter, R., 1991. 'Linguistic models, language and literariness: Study strategies in the teaching literature to foreign students', in: C. Brumfit and R. Carter, eds. *Literature and Language Teaching*. Oxford: Oxford University Press, 110-32.

Carter, R., 1997. *Investigating English Discourse*. London: Routledge.

Carter, R., 1998. Orders of reality: CANCODE, communication, and culture. *ELT Journal*, 52, 1, 43-56.

Carter, R. and J. McRae, 1996. *Language, Literature and the Learner*. Harlow: Addison Wesley Longman Ltd.

Carter, R., R. Hughes and M. McCarthy, 1998. 'Telling tails: Grammar, the spoken language and materials development', in: B. Tomlinson, ed. *Materials Development in Language Teaching*. Cambridge: Cambridge University Press, 67-86.

Carter, R., and M. McCarthy, 2000. New issues in using language corpora in ELT. Paper presented at *IATEFL conference*, Dublin, March 2000.

Chandler, J. and M. Stone, 1999. *The Resourceful English Teacher*. London: First Person Publishing Ltd. and Surrey: DELTA Publishing.

Chambers, A. and G. Davies, 2001. *ICT and Language Learning: a European Perspective*. Lisse: Swets and Zeitlinger.

Chomsky, N., 1957. *Syntactic Structures.* The Hague: Mouton.

Chomsky, N., 1965. *Aspects of the Theory of Syntax.* Cambridge, Massachusetts: Massachusetts Institute of Technology (MIT) Press.

Chomsky, N., 1988. *Language and Problems of Knowledge.* Cambridge, Massachusetts: Massachusetts Institute of Technology (MIT) Press.

Clare A. and J. Wilson, 2002. *Language to Go, Upper Intermediate.* Harlow: Pearson Education Ltd.

Clarke, D., 1989. Communicative theory and its influence on materials production. *Language Teaching,* 22, 2, 73-86.

Collie, J. and S. Slater, 1987. *Literature in the Language Classroom.* Cambridge: Cambridge University Press.

Collins COBUILD Student's Dictionary. 1997. London: HarperCollins Publishers.

Collins, A. and M. Quillian, 1972. 'How to make a language user', in: E. Tulving and W. Donaldson, eds. *Organisation of Memory.* New York: Academic Press, 310-15.

Comenius, J., 1658. *Orbis Sensualium Pictus.*

Conacher, J. E. and F. Royall, 1998. An evaluation of the use of the Internet for the purposes of foreign language learning. *Language Learning Journal,* 18, 37-41.

Cook, G., 1990. 'Adverts, Songs, Jokes and Graffiti: Approaching literary through 'sub-literary' writing' in: D. Hill and S. Holden. *Effective Teaching and Learning.* Modern English Publications in association with the British Council, 128-33.

Cook, G., 1992. *The Discourse of Advertising.* London: Routledge.

Cook, G., 1995. 'Theoretical issues: Transcribing the untranscribable', in: G. Leech, G. Myers and J. Thomas, eds. *Spoken English on Computer.* New York: Longman, 35-53.

Cook, G., 1996. 'Making the subtle difference: Literature and non-literature in the classroom', in: R. Carter and J. McRae, eds. *Language, Literature and the Learner.* Harlow: Addison Wesley Longman Ltd, 166-84.

Cook, G. 1998. The uses of reality: A reply to Ronald Carter. *ELT Journal,* 52, 1, 57-63.

Cook, G., 2000. *Language Play, Language Learning.* Oxford: Oxford University Press.

Cook, G., 2001. 'The philosopher pulled the lower jaw of the hen.' Ludicrous invented sentences in language teaching. *Applied Linguistics*, 22, 3, 366-87.

Cooper, R., M. Lavery and M. Rinvolucri, 1991. *Video*. Oxford: Oxford University Press.

Corder, P., 1974. 'The significance of learners' errors', in: J. Richards, ed. *Error Analysis: Perspectives in Second Language Acquisition*. London: Longman, 19-30. First published in *IRAL*, 1967, 5, 161-70.

Cotton, C. 1877. *The Essays of Montaigne* (Translation) Edited by W. Hazlitt.

Crace A. and R. Wileman, 2002. *Language to Go, Intermediate*. Harlow: Pearson Education Ltd.

Crandall, J., 1995. 'The why, what and how of ESL Reading Instruction: some guidelines for writers of ESL reading textbooks', in: P. Byrd, ed., *Materials Writer's Guide*. Boston: Heinle and Heinle Publishers, 79-94.

Crystal, D., 2001. *Language and the Internet*. Cambridge: Cambridge University Press.

Crystal, D., 1997. Watching world English grow. *IATEFL newsletter*, 135, 10-11.

Cummings, e. e., 1960. 'ygUDuh', in: *Selected poems 1923 - 1958*. London: Faber and Faber Ltd.

Cunningham, G. and S. Mohamed, 2002. *Language to Go, Pre-Intermediate*. Harlow: Pearson Education Ltd.

Cunningham, S. and P. Moore 1998. *Cutting Edge, Intermediate*. Harlow: Longman.

Dahl, R., 1982. *Roald Dahl's Revolting Rhymes*. Jonathan Cape Ltd.

Davies, A., 1984. 'Simple, simplified and simplification: What is authentic?' in: J. Alderson and A. Urquhart, eds. *Reading in a Foreign Language*. London: Longman, 181-98.

De Andrés, V. 1999. 'Self-esteem in the classroom or the metamorphosis of butterflies', in: J. Arnold, ed. *Affect in Language Learning*. Cambridge: Cambridge University Press, 87-102.

Defoe, D., 1965. *Robinson Crusoe*. Harmondsworth: Penguin. (1st edition published 1719).

Dendrinos, B., 1992. *The EFL Textbook and Ideology*. Athens: N.C. Grivas.

De Villiers, J. and P. de Villiers, 1978. *Language Acquisition*. Cambridge, Massachusetts: Harvard University Press.

Devitt, S., 1997a. Interacting with authentic texts: multilayered processes. *Modern Languages Journal*, 81, 4, 459-69.

Devitt, S., 1997b. Generating and exploiting multiple authentic text from an authentic base text. Paper presented at the *ELT Authors' Conference*, Dublin, June 1997.

Devitt, S., 2002. Content (including Literature) in Language Learning. Paper presented at the *IRAAL/CLT conference*, University of Limerick, November 2002.

Dingle, J., 1999. Why are ELT books always so anodyne? The publisher's perspective. Paper presented at the *MATSDA conference*, Dublin, January 1999.

Doff A. and C. Jones, 1997. *Language in Use, Upper Intermediate*. Cambridge: Cambridge University Press.

Dörnyei, Z., 1994a. Motivation and motivating in the foreign language classroom. *Modern Languages Journal*, 78, 3, 273-84.

Dörnyei, Z., 1994b. Understanding L2 Motivation: On with the challenge! *Modern Languages Journal*, 78, 4, 515-23.

Douglas, N., 1917. *South Wind*. North Books.

Doyle, R., 1987. *The Commitments*. Random House Inc.

Doyle, R., 1990. *The Snapper*. London: Martin Secker and Warburg Ltd.

Doyle, R., 1991. *The Van*.

Doyle, R., 1993. *Paddy Clarke Ha Ha Ha*. London: BCA/Martin Secker and Warburg Ltd.

Doyle, R., 1996. *The Woman Who Walked into Doors*. London: Jonathan Cape.

Dubin, F. 1995. 'Issues in the writing and publication of grammar textbooks', in: P. Byrd, ed., *Materials Writer's Guide*. Boston: Heinle and Heinle Publishers, 45-63.

Duda, R. and P. Riley, eds., 1990. Learning Styles. *European Cultural Foundation, proceedings of the first European Seminar*, Nancy, 26-29 April, 1987. Nancy: Presses Universitaires de Nancy.

Duff, A. and A. Maley, 1990. *Literature*. Oxford: Oxford University Press.

Durant, M., 1996. 'Designing groupwork activities: A case study', in: R. Carter and J. McRae, eds. *Language, Literature and the Learner*. Harlow: Addison Wesley Longman Ltd, 67-88.

Eastment, D., 1999. *The Internet and ELT*. Summertown: The British Council.

Eastment, D., 2000. Non-ELT Web sites ... and how to find them. *Modern English Teacher*, April 2000.

Eayrs, M., 1999. English teachers on-line - accessing e-mail and Internet resources for ELT. Paper presented at the *MATSDA conference*, Dublin, January 1999.

Eckstut, S. and Lubelska, D., 1989. *Widely Read*. Harlow: Longman.

Edmonson, W., 1997. The role of literature in foreign language learning and teaching: Some valid assumptions and invalid arguments. *AILA Review*, 12, 42-55.

Eliot, T.S., 1948. *Notes towards the Definition of Culture*. London: Faber and Faber.

Ellis, R., 1985. *Understanding Second Language Acquisition*. Oxford: Oxford University Press.

Ellis, R., 1993. Second language acquisition research: How does it help teachers? *ELT Journal*, 47, 1, 3-11.

Ellis, R., 1994. *The Study of Second Language Acquisition*. Oxford: Oxford University Press.

Ellis, R., 1997. *SLA Research and Language Teaching*. Oxford: Oxford University Press.

Esch, E. 1997. 'Learner training for autonomous language learning', in: P. Benson and P. Voller, eds. *Autonomy and Independence in Language Learning*. London: Longman, 164-76.

Evans, V. and J. Dooley, 1998. *Enterprise*. Swansea: Express publishing.

Falla, T., 1993. *Headway Elementary Video Activity Book*. Oxford: Oxford University Press.

Felix, U., ed., 2003. *Language Learning Online: Towards best practice*. Lisse: Swets and Zeitlinger.

Fernández-Toro, M. and F. Jones, 1996. 'Going Solo: Learners' experiences of self-instruction and self-instruction training', in: E. Broady and M. Kenning, eds. *Promoting Learner Autonomy in University Language Learning*. London: AFLS

(Association for French Language Studies) /CILT (Centre for Information on Language Teaching and Research), 185-214.

Flynn, N., and T. Flynn, 1998. *Writing effective e-mail.* Menlo Park, CA: Crisp Publications.

Fielding, H., 1996. *Bridget Jones's Diary.* Viking.

Finocchiaro, M. and C. Brumfit, 1983. *The Functional-Notional Approach: from theory to practice.* Oxford: Oxford University Press.

Fletcher, S., 1996. *E-mail: A Love Story.* London: Headline Book Publishing.

Forster, E. M., 1924. *A Passage to India.* 1978 edition, London: Edward Arnold.

Forsyth, W., 2000. *Clockwise, Intermediate.* Oxford: Oxford University Press

Fouser, R., N. Inoue and C. Lee, 2000. 'The pragmatics of orality in English, Japanese and Korean computer-mediated communication', in: L. Pemberton and S. Shurville, eds. *Words on the Web: Computer-Mediated Communication.* Exeter: Intellect Books, 52-62.

Fox, G., 1998. 'Using corpus data in the classroom', in: B. Tomlinson, ed. *Materials Development in Language Teaching.* Cambridge: Cambridge University Press, 25-43.

Fraser, R. 1999. *The Art and Science of the Advertising Slogan.* Retrieved 6 June 2003 from http://www.adslogans.co.uk/ans/index.html

Freebairn, I., 2000. The coursebook: future continuous or past? *English Teaching Professional*, 15, 3-5.

Freeman, C., 1999. Literature in the language classroom: A case study. *Folio, Journal of the Materials Development Association MATSDA*, 5, 2, 29-32.

Gains, J., 1999. Electronic mail - A new style of communication or just a new medium? An investigation into the text features of e-mail. *English for Specific Purposes*, 18, 1, 81-101.

Gairns, R. and S. Redman, 1998. *True to life, Upper Intermediate.* Cambridge: Cambridge University Press.

Gardner, R., 1985. *Social Psychology and Second Language Learning: the Role of Attitudes and Motivation.* London: Edward Arnold.

Gardner, R. and W. Lambert, 1972. *Attitudes and Motivation in Second Language Learning.* Rowley, Massachusetts: Newbury House.

Garrett, N., 1986. The problem with grammar: what kind can the language learner use? *Modern Languages Journal*, 70, 2, 133-47.

Gathercole, I., ed., 1990. *Autonomy in Language Learning*. London: CILT (Centre for Information on Language Teaching and Research).

Gattegno, C., 1972. *Teaching Foreign Languages in Schools: The Silent Way*. New York City: Educational Solutions.

Gavioli, L and G. Aston 2001. Enriching reality: language corpora and language pedagogy. *ELT Journal*, 55, 3, 238-46.

Geddes, M., 1981. 'Listening', in: K. Johnson and K. Morrow, eds. *Communication in the Classroom*. London: Longman.

Gilroy, M. and B. Parkinson, 1997. Teaching literature in a foreign language. *Language Teaching*, 29, 213-25.

Gimenez, J., 2000. Business e-mail communication: Some emerging tendencies in register. *English for Specific Purposes*, 19, 237-51.

Goddard, A., 1998. *The Language of Advertising*. London: Routledge.

Golding, W., 1958. *The Lord of the Flies*. London: Faber and Faber.

Gonzalez, A., 1994. 'The cultural content in English as an international auxiliary language: Problems and issues', in: M. Tickoo, ed. *Language and Culture in Multilingual Societies*. Singapore: SEAMEO Regional Language Centre, 54-63.

Goodale, M., 1995. *Concordance Samplers 2: Phrasal Verbs*. Collins Cobuild.

Goodale, M., 1995. *Concordance Samplers 3: Tenses*. Collins Cobuild.

Gousseva, J., 1998. Crossing cultural and spatial boundaries: A cybercomposition experience. *The Internet TESL Journal*, 4, 11. Retrieved 29 July 2003 from: http://iteslj.org/Articles/Gousseva-CyberComp.html

Graddol, D., 1997. *The Future of English?* London: British Council.

Graham, C., 1988. *Jazz Chants Fairy Tales*. New York, NY: Oxford University Press.

Graham, C., 1999. *Holiday Jazz Chants*. New York, NY: Oxford University Press.

Grauberg, W., 1997. *The Elements of Foreign Language Teaching*. Clevedon: Multilingual Matters.

Gray, J., 2000. The ELT coursebook as a cultural artefact: how teachers censor and adapt. *ELT Journal*, 54, 3, 274-81.

Grellet, F., 1981. *Developing Reading Skills*. Cambridge: Cambridge University Press.

Grenough, M. 1976. *Sing it! Learn English through Song* (series of 6 books). McGraw-Hill Companies.

Griffee, D., 1992. *Songs in Action*. New York: Prentice-Hall.

Grundy, P., 1993. *Newspapers*. Cambridge: Cambridge University Press.

Guariento W. and Morley, J., 2001. Text and task authenticity in the EFL classroom. *ELT Journal,* 55, 4, 347-53.

Guillot, M., 1996. 'Resource-based language learning: Pedagogical strategies for le Monde sur CD-ROM', in: E. Broady and M. Kenning, eds. *Promoting Learner Autonomy in University Language Teaching*. London: CILT (Centre for Information on Language Teaching and Research), 139-58.

Guiora, A., B. Beit-Hallahmi, R. Brannon, C. Dull and T. Scovell, 1972. The effects of experimentally induced changes in ego states on pronunciation ability in a second language: An exploratory study. *Comprehensive Psychiatry*, 13, 421-8.

Hadley, G., 1998. *Sensing the Winds of Change: an Introduction to Data-driven Learning*. Retrieved 29 July 2003 from http://web.bham.ac.uk/johnstf/winds.htm

Haines, S. and B. Stewart, 2000. *Landmark, Upper Intermediate*. Oxford: Oxford University Press.

Hale, C. and J. Scanlon, 1999. *Wired style: Principles of English usage in the digital age*. New York: Broadway Books.

Harben, P., 1999. An exercise in applying pedagogical principles to multimedia CALL materials design. *ReCALL*, 11, 3, 25-33.

Harmer, J., 1996. Is PPP dead? *Modern English Teacher*, 5, 2, 7-14.

Hartley, L., 1953. *The Go-Between.*

Heaney, S., 1966. 'Mid-term Break', in: *Death of a Naturalist*. London: Faber and Faber.

Hemingway, E., 1952. *The Old Man and the Sea*. New York: Scribner; London: Cape.

Henriquez, J. 2000. 'One-way doors, teleportation and writing without prepositions: an analysis of WWW hypertext links', in: L. Pemberton and S. Shurville, eds., *Words on the Web: Computer-Mediated Communication*. Exeter: Intellect Books, 4-12.

Hoey, M. 2003. 'Lexical Priming'. Lecture given at *Applied Linguistics Colloquium*, University of Limerick, January 2003.

Holliday, A., 1994. *Appropriate Methodology and Social Context*. Cambridge: Cambridge University Press.

Hong Kong SAR Government Target Oriented Curriculum (TOC) Framework 1999, 45.

Hooper Hansen, G., 1998. 'Lozanov and the teaching text', in: B. Tomlinson, ed. *Materials Development in Language Teaching*. Cambridge: Cambridge University Press, 311-19.

Hopkins, D. and M. Nettle, 1994. Second language acquisition research: a response to Rod Ellis. *ELT Journal*, 48, 2, 157-61.

Howatt, A. P. R., 1984. *A History of English Language Teaching*. Oxford: Oxford University Press.

Hughes, G., 1981. *A Handbook of Classroom English*. Oxford: Oxford University Press.

Hutchinson, T., 1997. *Lifelines, Intermediate*. Oxford: Oxford University Press.

Hutchinson, T. and A. Waters, 1987. *English for Specific Purposes: A learning-centred approach*. Cambridge: Cambridge University Press.

Huy Lê, M., 1999. The Role of Music in Second Language Learning: A Vietnamese Perspective. Presented at *Combined 1999 Conference of the Australian Association for Research in Education* and *the New Zealand Association for Research in Education*. Retrieved 30 July 2003 from http://www.aare.edu.au/99pap/le99034.htm

Hymes, D., 1971. *On Communicative Competence*. Philadelphia: University of Pennsylvania Press.

Hymes, D., 1979. On communicative competence (extracts), in: C. Brumfit and K. Johnson, eds. *The Communicative Approach to Language Teaching*. Oxford: Oxford University Press, 1-26.

Iser, W., 1980. *The Act of Reading*. Baltimore: The John Hopkins University Press.

Johns, A., 1988. What's real? Some thoughts on authenticity in the classroom. *The ORTESOL Journal*, 9, 1-12.

Johns, T., 1986. Micro-concord: A language learner's research tool. *System*, 14, 2, 151-62.

Johns, T., 1991a. 'Should you be persuaded: Two examples of data-driven learning', in: T. Johns, and P. King, eds. *Classroom Concordancing, ELR Journal*, 4, 1-16.

Johns, T., 1991b. 'From printout to handout: Grammar and vocabulary teaching in the context of data-driven learning', in: T. Johns, and P. King, eds. *Classroom concordancing, ELR Journal*, 4, 27-45.

Johns, T. and P. King, eds.1991. *Classroom concordancing, ELR Journal*, 4.

Johnson, K., 1979. 'Communicative approaches and Communicative processes', in: C. Brumfit and K. Johnson, eds. *The Communicative Approach to Language Teaching*. Oxford: Oxford University Press, 192-205.

Johnson, K., and K. Morrow, eds. 1981. *Communication in the Classroom*. London: Longman.

Jolly, D. and R. Bolitho, 1998. 'A framework for materials writing', in: B. Tomlinson, ed. *Materials Development in Language Teaching*. Cambridge: Cambridge University Press, 90-115.

Jones, S., 1997. Introduction to *Virtual Culture*, in: S. Jones, ed. *Virtual Culture*. London: SAGE publications Ltd., 1-6.

Joyce, J., 1916. *A Portrait of the Artist as a Young Man*. London: The Egoist Ltd.

Joyce, J., 1939. *Finnegans Wake*. London: Faber and Faber. Corrected Ed. NY: Viking, 1959.

Keane, J. B., 1991. *The Field*. Cork: The Mercier Press.

Kelly, L., 1969. *25 Centuries of Language Teaching*. Rowley, Massachusetts: Newbury House.

Kelly-Holmes, H. 2004 forthcoming. *Advertising as multilingual communication*. Basingstoke: Palgrave Macmillan.

Kershaw, G. and G. Kershaw, 2000. Think you could write readers? This is what you need to know. *EL Gazette*, 242, 10.

Kramsch, C., 1985. Literary texts in the classroom: A discourse. *Modern Languages Journal*, 69, 4, 356-65.

Kramsch, C., 1993. *Context and Culture in Language Teaching.* Oxford: Oxford University Press.

Kramsch, C., 1998. *Language and Culture.* Oxford: Oxford University Press.

Kramsch, C. and S. McConnell-Ginet, eds., 1992. *Text and Context: Cross-Disciplinary Perspectives on Language Study.* Massachusetts: D.C. Heath and Company.

Kramsch, C, F. A'Ness and W. Lam, 2000. Authenticity and authorship in the computer-mediated acquisition of L2 literacy. *Language Learning and Technology, 4. 2,* 78-104.

Krashen, S., 1981. *Second Language Acquisition and Second Language Learning.* New York: Pergamon.

Krashen, S., 1989. *Language Acquisition and Language Education.* Hemel Hempstead: Prentice Hall International.

Kress, G. and T. Threadgold, 1988. Towards a social theory of genre. *Southern Review*, 21, 3, 126-41.

Labov, W. 1997. *Language in the Inner City: Studies in the Black English Vernacular.* Oxford: Blackwell.

Lacey, R. 1972. *Seeing with Feeling: Film in the classroom.* Philadelphia: W.B. Saunders Co.

Lamy, M-N., 1997. The Web for French grammar: A tool, a resource or a waste of time? *ReCALL*, 9, 2, 26-32.

Larsen-Freeman, D. and M. Long, 1991. *An Introduction to Second Language Acquisition Research.* London: Longman.

Lazar, G., 1990. Using novels in the language-learning classroom. *EFL Journal*, 44, 3, 204-14.

Lazar, G., 1993. *Literature and Language Teaching.* Cambridge: Cambridge University Press.

Lazar, G., 1994. Using literature at lower levels. *ELT Journal*, 48, 2, 115-24.

Le Maistre, S. and C. Lewis, 2002. *Language to Go, Elementary.* Harlow: Pearson Education Ltd.

Leckie-Tarry, H., 1995. *Language and Context.* London: Pinter Publishers.

Lee, W. Y., 1995. Authenticity revisited: Text authenticity and learner authenticity. *ELT Journal*, 49, 4, 323-28.

LeLoup, J. and R. Ponterio, 1995. 'Addressing the need for electronic communication in foreign language teaching', in: R. Steinfeldt, ed. *Educational Technologies*. Monograph of the New York State Council of Educational Associations, 39-54. Retrieved 30 July 2003 from: http://www.cortland.edu/www/flteach/articles/nyscea.html

Leow, R., 1993. To simplify or not to simplify: A look at intake. *SSLA*, 15, 333-55.

Lightbown, P., 1985. Great expectations: Second language acquisition research and classroom teaching. *Applied Linguistics*, 6, 173-89.

Lightbown, P., 2000. Classroom SLA Research and Second Language teaching. *Applied Linguistics*, 21, 4, 431-62.

Lightbown, P. and N. Spada, 1993. *How Languages are Learned*. Oxford: Oxford University Press.

Little, D., 1990. 'Autonomy in language learning. Some theoretical and practical considerations', in: I. Gathercole, ed. *Autonomy in Language Learning*. London: CILT (Centre for Information on Language Teaching and Research), 7-15.

Little, D., 1991. *Learner Autonomy 1: Definitions, Issues and Problems*. Dublin: Authentik Language Learning Resources Ltd.

Little, D., 1997. Responding authentically to authentic texts: a problem for self-access learning? In: P. Benson and P. Voller, eds. *Autonomy and Independence in Language Learning*. London: Longman, 225-36.

Little, D. 1999. 'Learner autonomy is more than a Western cultural construct', in: S. Cotterall and D. Crabbe (eds.) *Learner Autonomy in Language Learning: Defining the Field and Effecting Change*. Frankfurt am Main: Lang, 11-18.

Little, D., S. Devitt and D. Singleton, 1989. *Learning Foreign Languages from Authentic Texts: Theory and Practice*. Dublin: Authentik Language Learning Resources Ltd.

Little, D. and D. Singleton, 1990. 'Cognitive style and learning approach', in: R. Duda and P. Riley, eds. *Learning Styles*. European Cultural Foundation, proceedings of the first European Seminar, Nancy, 26-29 April, 1987. Nancy: Presses Universitaires de Nancy, 11-19.

Little, D., and H. Brammerts, 1996. A guide to language learning in tandem via the Internet. *CLCS Occasional Paper No. 46*. Dublin: Trinity College, Centre for Language and Communication Studies.

Little, D. and E. Ushioda, 1998. Designing, implementing and evaluating a project in tandem learning via e-mail. *ReCALL*, 10, 1, 95-101.

Littlewood, W., 1981. *Communicative Language Teaching.* Cambridge: Cambridge University Press.

Long, M. 1991. 'A feeling for language: The multiple values of teaching literature', in: C. Brumfit and R. Carter, eds. *Literature and Language Teaching*, Oxford: Oxford University Press, 42-59.

Long, M., 1993. Assessment strategies for second language acquisition theories. *Applied Linguistics*, 14, 3, 225-49.

Long, M. and Robinson, P. 1998. 'Focus on form: Theory, research and practice', in: C. Doughty and J. Williams, eds. *Focus on form in classroom language acquisition.* Cambridge: Cambridge University Press.

Longman Dictionary of Contemporary English Third Edition, 2003. Harlow: Longman.

Lozanov, G., 1978. *Suggestology and Outlines of Suggestopedy.* London: Gordon and Breach Science Publishers Inc.

Macrae, L., *Ye canny shove yer granny off a bus - unexpected new poems by Lindsay Macrae.* Puffin.

Maess, B., S. Koelsch, T. C. Gunter, A. D. Friederici, 2001. Musical Syntax is processed in Broca's area: an MEG study. *Nature Neuroscience,* 4, 540-5.

Maley, A., 1993. *Short and Sweet: Short texts and how to use them. Volume 1.* London: Penguin Books.

Maley, A. and S. Moulding, 1985. *Poem into Poem.* Oxford: Oxford University Press.

Massi, M. and A. Merino, 1996. Films and EFL: What's playing in the language classroom? *Forum*, 34, 1, 20. Retrieved 29 July 2003 from http://exchanges.state.gov/forum/vols/vol34/no1/p20.htm

McCarthy, G., 2002. Washing Catholic Ireland's Dirty Laundry. *The Sunday Times Culture Section*, 20 October 2002, 6-7.

McCarthy, M. 1998. *Spoken Language and Applied Linguistics.* Cambridge: Cambridge University Press.

McCarthy, M. and R. Carter, 1994. *Language as Discourse.* Essex: Longman Group UK Ltd.

McCarthy M. and R. Carter, 1997. *Exploring Spoken English*. Cambridge University Press.

McCarthy, M., and F. O'Dell. 2001. *English vocabulary in use, Upper-intermediate*. Cambridge: Cambridge University Press.

McCourt, F., 1996. *Angela's Ashes*. London: HarperCollins Publishers.

McGarry, D., 1995. *Learner Autonomy 4: The Role of Authentic Texts*. Dublin: Authentik Language Learning Resources Ltd.

McGough, R., 1999. *The Way Things Are*. Viking (Penguin).

McGrath, I., 2002. *Materials Evaluation and Design for Language Teaching*. Edinburgh: Edinburgh University Press.

McKay, S., 1991. 'Literature in the ESL classroom', in: C. Brumfit and R. Carter, eds. *Literature and Language Teaching*. Oxford: Oxford University Press, 191-8.

McRae, J., 1996. 'Representational language learning: From language awareness to text awareness', in: R. Carter and J. McRae, eds. *Language, Literature and the Learner*. Harlow: Addison Wesley Longman Ltd, 16-40.

Melles, G., 2003. Using language and culture to construct group work in higher education, *HERDSA* Conference Proceedings, 2003. Retrieved 31 October 2003 from http://surveys.canterbury.ac.nz/herdsa03/pdfsref/Y1128.pdf

Menuhin, Y., 1998. Keynote address presented at *ATEE Conference*, Mary Immaculate College, Limerick, Ireland, August 1998.

Merriam Webster Dictionary Online http://www.m-w.com./netdict.htm

Mills, M., 1998. *The Restraint of Beasts*. London: Flamingo, HarperCollins Publishers.

Mishan, F., 2004. 'A Task-based approach to Web-authoring for Learning Languages', in: A. Chambers, J. E. Conacher and J. Littlemore (eds.), Birmingham: University of Birmingham Press.

Modiano, M., 2001. Linguistic Imperialism, culture integrity and EIL. *ELT Journal*, 55, 4, 339-46.

Morgan, E., 1973. 'The first men on Mercury', in: *From Glasgow to Saturn*. Cheadle: Carcanet Press.

Morgan, J. and M. Rinvolucri, 1983. *Once Upon a Time: Using stories in the Language Classroom*. Cambridge: Cambridge University Press.

Morrow, K., 1977. 'Authentic texts in ESP', in: S. Holden, ed. *English for Specific Purposes*. London: Modern English Publications, 13-15.

Morrison, T., 1970. *The Bluest Eye*. New York: Rinehart and Winston.

Murison-Bowie, S., 1993. *Micro-Concord Manual: An introduction to the practices and principles of concordancing in language teaching*. Oxford: Oxford University Press.

Murison-Bowie, S., 1996. Linguistic corpora and language teaching. *Annual Review of Applied Linguistics*, 16, 182-99.

Murphey, T., 1992. *Music and Song*. Oxford: Oxford University Press.

Murphy, R., 1986. *Culture and Social Anthropology: An Overture*. 2nd ed. Englewood Cliffs, NJ: Prentice Hall.

Murray, D., 1997. Language and Society in Cyberspace. Article adapted from plenary presented at *TESOL Convention*, Orlando, Florida.

Nelson, G., 1995. 'Considering culture: Guidelines for ESL/EFL textbook writers', in: P. Byrd, ed., *Materials Writer's Guide*. Boston: Heinle and Heinle Publishers, 23-44.

Ngugi wa Thiong'o, 1991. 'Literature in schools', in: C. Brumfit and R. Carter, eds. *Literature and Language Teaching*. Oxford: Oxford University Press, 223-9.

Nostrand, H., 1989. Authentic texts and cultural authenticity: An editorial. *The Modern Languages Journal,* 73, 1, 49-52.

Nunan, D., 1988. *The Learner-Centred Curriculum*. Cambridge: Cambridge University Press.

Nunan, D., 1989. *Designing Tasks for the Communicative Classroom*. Cambridge: Cambridge University Press.

Nunan, D., 1990. 'The teacher as researcher', in: C. Brumfit and R. Mitchell, eds. Research in the Language Classroom, *ELT Documents*. Modern English Publications, 133.

Nunan, D., 1991. *Language Teaching Methodology*. Hemel Hempstead: Prentice Hall.

Nunan, D., 1997. 'Designing and adapting materials to encourage learner autonomy', in: P. Benson and P. Voller, eds. *Autonomy and Independence in Language Learning*. London: Longman, 192-203.

O'Dell, F., 1997. *English Panorama, Advanced.* Cambridge: Cambridge University Press.

Orwell, G., 1951. *Animal Farm: A Fairy Story*. Harmondsworth: Penguin Books.

Owen, C., 1996. Do concordances require to be consulted? *ELT Journal*, 50, 3, 219-24.

Oxenden C. and C. Latham-Koenig, 2001. *English File.* Oxford: Oxford University Press.

Oxford Paperback Dictionary, 1983. 2nd Edition. Oxford: Oxford University Press.

Oxford, R., 1993. 'Style Analysis Survey'. University of Alabam. Later published in: J. Reid, ed., 1995. *Language learning styles in the ESL/EFL classroom.* Boston: Heinle and Heinle, 208-15.

Oxford, R and M. Ehrman, 1993. Second language research on individual differences. *Annual Review of Applied Linguistics*, 13, 188-205.

Oxford, R and J. Shearin, 1994. Language learning and motivation: Expanding the theoretical framework. *The Modern Languages Journal*, 78, 1, 12-26.

Patten, B., 1967. 'Little Johnny's Final Letter', in: *Little Johnny's Confession.* London: Allen and Unwin.

Peacock, M., 1997. The effect of authentic materials on the motivation of EFL Learners. *ELT Journal*, 51, 2, 144-53.

Pellettieri, J., 1996. Network-based computer interaction and the negotiation of meaning in the virtual foreign language classroom. Unpublished. University of California at Davis.

Pemberton, L. and S. Shurville, eds., 2000. *Words on the Web: Computer-Mediated Communication*. Exeter: Intellect Books.

Pennycook, A., 1997. 'Cultural alternatives and autonomy', in: P. Benson and P. Voller, eds. *Autonomy and Independence in Language Learning.* London: Longman, 35-53.

Phillipson, R., 1992. *Linguistic Imperialism*. Cambridge: Cambridge University Press.

Picken, J., 1999. State of the ad: The role of advertisements in EFL teaching. *ELT Journal*, 53, 4, 249-55.

Pienemann, M., 1985. 'Learnability and syllabus construction', in: K. Hyltenstam and M. Pienemann, eds. *Modelling and Assessing Second Language Acquisition.* Clevedon, Avon: Multilingual Matters.

Prabhu, N. S., 1987. *Second Language Pedagogy.* Oxford: Oxford University Press.

Prodromou, L., 1988. English as cultural action. *ELT Journal*, 42, 2, 73-82.

Pugh, A., 1996. 'A history of English teaching', in: N. Mercer and J. Swann, eds. *Learning English: Development and Diversity.* Routledge: London, 159-87.

Pulverness, A., 1999a. Context or pretext, cultural content and the coursebook. *Folio, Journal of the Materials Development Association MATSDA*, 5, 2, 5-9.

Pulverness, A., 1999b. Now write about your country: ELT and the ownership of cultural learning. *IATEFL Literature and Cultural Studies SIG Newsletter*, 18.

Pulverness, A., 1999c. Editorial. *Folio, Journal of the Materials Development Association MATSDA*, 5, 2, 2.

Pulverness, A., 2000. Showing and telling: Joyce's 'The Dead' and Huston's 'The Dead'. Paper presented at *IATEFL conference*, Dublin, March 2000.

Pulverness, A., M. Kocanova and D. Hollo, 2000. You've got mail: Cross cultural materials writing. Paper presented at *IATEFL conference*, Dublin, March 2000.

Ramsey, G. 1996. The question of authenticity. *Zielsprache Englisch,* 26, 3, 17-19.

Reah, D., 1998. *The Language of Newspapers.* London: Routledge.

Revell, J. and S. Norman, 1999. *Handing Over: NLP-based Activities for Language Learners.* London: Saffire Press.

Rézeau, J., 2001. 'Concordances in the classroom: the evidence of the data', in: A. Chambers and G. Davies, eds. *ICT and Language Learning: A European perspective*, Lisse: Swets and Zeitlinger, 147-66.

Richards, J., ed., 1974. *Error Analysis: Perspectives in Second Language Acquisition.* London: Longman.

Riley, P., 1990. 'Requirements for the study of intercultural variation in learning styles', in: Duda, R. and P. Riley, eds. *Learning Styles.* European Cultural Foundation, proceedings of the first European Seminar, Nancy, 26-29 April, 1987. Nancy: Presses Universitaires de Nancy, 43-54.

Rinvolucri, M., 1999a. 'The humanistic exercise', in: J. Arnold, ed. *Affect in Language Learning.* Cambridge: Cambridge University Press, 194-210.

Rinvolucri, M., 1999b. The UK, EFLese sub-culture and dialect. *Folio, Journal of the Materials Development Association MATSDA*, 5, 2, 12-14.

Ronaldson, A., 1996. *Rebecca*. Simplified edition of Daphne Du Maurier's *Rebecca*. Harlow: Addison Wesley Longman Ltd.

Rossner, R., 1988. Materials for communicative language teaching and learning. *Annual Review of Applied Linguistics*, 8, 140-63.

Roxburgh, J., 1997. Procedures for the evaluation of in-house EAP textbooks. *Folio, Journal of the Materials Development Association MATSDA*, 1, 4, 15-18.

Sanderson, P., 1999. *Using Newspapers in the Classroom*. Cambridge: Cambridge University Press.

Sapir, E., 1929. 'The Status of Linguistics as a Science', in: D. G. Mandelbaum, ed., 1958. *Culture, Language and Personality*. Berkeley, CA: University of California Press.

Schonell, F., I. Meddleton, B. Shaw, M. Routh, D. Popham, G. Gill, G. Mackrell, C. Stephens, 1956. *A Study of the Oral Vocabulary of Adults*. Brisbane and London: University of Queensland Press/University of London Press.

Selinker, L., 1972. Interlanguage. *International Review of Applied Linguistics*, 10, 209-31.

Shanahan, D., 1997. Articulating the relationship between language, literature and culture: Towards a new agenda for foreign language teaching and research. *The Modern Language Journal*, 81, 2, 164-74.

Sharwood Smith, M., 1994. *Second Language Learning: Theoretical Foundations*. London: Longman.

Shetzer, H. and M. Warschauer, 2000. 'An electronic literacy approach to network-based language teaching', in: M. Warschauer and R. Kern, eds. *Network-Based Language Teaching: Concepts and Practice*. New York: Cambridge University Press, 171-185.

Sihui, M., 1996. 'Interfacing language and literature: With special reference to the teaching of British cultural studies', in: R. Carter and J. McRae, eds. *Language, Literature and the Learner*. Harlow: Addison Wesley Longman Ltd., 166-84.

Shilts, R., 1993. *And the Band Played on*. USA: St Martin's Press.

Short, M. and C. Candlin, 1991. 'Teaching study skills for English literature', in: C. Brumfit and R. Carter, eds. *Literature and Language Teaching*. Oxford: Oxford University Press, 89-109.

Sinclair B., and P. Prowse, 1996. *Activate your English Intermediate*. Cambridge: Cambridge University Press.

Sinclair, J., 1991. *Corpus, Concordance, Collocation*. Oxford: Oxford University Press.

Skehan, P., 1996. A framework for the implementation of task-based instruction. *Applied Linguistics*, 17, 1, 38-62.

Skehan, P., 1989. *Individual Differences in Second-Language Learning*. London: Edward Arnold.

Steffensen, M. and C. Joag-Dev, 1984. 'Cultural Knowledge and Reading', in: J. Alderson and A. Urquhart, eds. *Reading in a Foreign Language*. London: Longman, 48-61.

Steinbeck, J., 1947. *The Pearl*. Viking Press.

Stempleski, S. and B. Tomalin, 2001. *Film*. Oxford: Oxford University Press.

Stevens, V., 1995. Concordancing with language learners: Why? when? what? *CAELL Journal*, 6, 2, 2-10.

Stubbs, M., 2001. Texts, corpora, and problems of interpretation: a response to Widdowson. *Applied Linguistics*, 22, 2, 149-72.

Summerfield, E., 1993. *Crossing Culture through Film*. Maine: Intercultural Press Inc.

Swaffar, J., 1985. Reading authentic texts in a foreign language: A cognitive model. *The Modern Language Journal*, 69, 1, 16-32.

Swales, J., 1990. *Genre Analysis: English in Academic and Research Settings*. Cambridge: University of Cambridge Press.

Swan, M., 1996. *Practical English Usage*. 2nd edition. Oxford: Oxford University Press.

Sweet, H., 1899. *The Practical Study of Languages*. London: J.M. Dent and Co.

Swift, G., 1985. *Learning to Swim and Other Stories*. London: Heinemann.

Taylor, D., 1994. Inauthentic authenticity or authentic inauthenticity? The pseudo-problem of authenticity in the language classroom. *TESL-EJ*, 1, 2, A-1. Retrieved 30 July 2003 from http://www.kyoto-su.ac.jp/information/tesl-ej/ej02/a.1.html

Taylor, L., 1997. *International Express, Pre-Intermediate*. Oxford: Oxford University Press.

Taylor, L., 1997. *International Express, Intermediate*. Oxford: Oxford University Press.

Terrell, T., 1991. The role of grammar instruction in a communicative approach. *Modern Languages Journal*, 75, 1, 52-63.

The Impact of Information and Communications Technologies on the Teaching of Foreign Languages and on the Role of Teachers of Foreign Languages, 2003. Report coordinated by International Certificate Conference (ICC), Frankfurt, commissioned by EC Directorate General of Education and Culture. Retrieved 30 May 2003 from http://www.icc-europe.com/

Thornbury, S., 1999. Window-dressing versus cross-dressing in the EFL sub-culture. *Folio, Journal of the Materials Development Association MATSDA*, 5, 2, 15-17.

Thornbury, S., 2000. McEnglish in Australia. Paper given at the *13th EA Educational Conference* (English in Australia, Australia in English), Fremantle, Western Australia, October 2000.

Thurstun, J. and C. Candlin, 1997. *Exploring Academic English: a workbook for student essay writing*. Sydney: NCELTR.

Titone, R., 1968. *Teaching Foreign Languages: An historical sketch*. Washington D.C.: Georgetown University Press.

Toh, G. and M. Raja, 1997. ELT Materials: Some perceptions on the questions of cultural relevance. *Guidelines*, 5, 19 part 2, 45-72.

Tomalin, B., 1986. *Video, TV and Radio in the English Class: An introductory guide*. London: Macmillan.

Tomalin, B., 2000. Using films in ELT. Paper presented at *IATEFL conference*, Dublin, March 2000.

Tomalin, B. and S. Stempleski, 1990. *Video in Action*. Oxford: Prentice Hall International.

Tomalin, B. and S. Stempleski, 1993. *Cultural Awareness*. Oxford: Oxford University Press.

Tomlinson, B., 1995. *ACELS Materials Development Seminar*. Dublin, 1995.

Tomlinson, B. ed., 1998. *Materials Development in Language Teaching*. Cambridge: Cambridge University Press.

Tomlinson, B., 1999. What do you think? Issues in materials development. *Folio, Journal of the Materials Development Association MATSDA*, 5, 2, 3-4.

Tomlinson, B, 2001. Humanising The Coursebook. *Humanising Language Teaching*, Year 3; Issue 5; September 2001.

Tomlinson, B., B. Dat, H. Masuhara, R. Rubdy, 2001. EFL Courses for adults. *ELT Journal*, 55, 1, 80-101.

Townsend, S., 1999. *Adrian Mole: The Cappuccino Years*. Soho Press, Inc.

Townshend, K., 1997. *E-mail: Using Electronic Communications in Foreign Language Teaching*. London: CILT (Centre for Information on Language Teaching and Research).

Tripathi, A., 1998. *Using the Internet in education*. WELL discussion list. Retrieved 27 April 1998 from well@mailbase.ac.uk

Trudgill, P., 1993. The world is our oyster. *The Sunday Times* Wordpower supplement. Part 3: The global language, 9-15.

Tudor, I., 1996. *Learner-centredness as Language Education*. Cambridge: Cambridge University Press.

Tulving, E. and W. Donaldson, eds. *Organisation of Memory*. New York: Academic Press.

Tyrwhitt-Drake, H. 1999. Responding to grammar questions on the Internet: providing correction through the corpus. *ELT Journal*, 53, 4, 281-7.

Underwood, M., 1994. *Teaching Listening*. Harlow: Longman Group UK Ltd.

Valdes, J., 1986a. 'Culture in literature', in: J. Valdes, ed. *Culture Bound: Bridging the Gap*. Cambridge: Cambridge University Press, 137-47.

Valdes, J., ed., 1986b. *Culture Bound: Bridging the Gap*. Cambridge: Cambridge University Press.

Van Lier, L., 1996. *Interaction in the Language Curriculum: Awareness, Autonomy and Authenticity*. Essex: Longman.

Vanpatten, B. and T. Cadierno, 1993. Input processing and second language acquisition: A role for instruction. *Modern Languages Journal*, 77, 1, 46-56.

Vincent, M., and R. Carter, 1991. 'Simple text and reading text', in: C. Brumfit and R. Carter, eds. *Literature and Language Teaching*. Oxford: Oxford University Press, 208-22.

Vogel, T., 2001. 'Learning out of control: some thoughts on the World Wide Web in learning and teaching foreign languages', in: A. Chambers and G. Davies, eds. *ICT and Language Learning: A European perspective*. Lisse: Swets and Zeitlinger, 133-46.

Vogely, A., 1995. Perceived strategy use during performance on three authentic listening comprehension tasks. *The Modern Languages Journal*, 79, 1, 41-56.

Wajnryb, R., 1996. Death, taxes and jeopardy: Systematic omissions in EFL texts, or life was never meant to be an adjacency pair. *9th Educational Conference, Sydney. ELICOS Association*.

Walker, J., ed., 2003. *Halliwell's Film & Video Guide* 2003 edition. HarperCollins Entertainment.

Walton, R. and M. Bartram, 2000. *Initiative.* Cambridge: Cambridge University Press.

Warschauer, M., ed., 1995. *Virtual Connections - Online Activities and Projects for Networking Language Learners*. Hawai'i: University of Hawai'i Press.

Warschauer, M., 1996a. 'Motivational aspects of using computers for writing and communication', in: M. Warschauer, ed. *Telecollaboration in Foreign Language Learning*. Honolulu, HI: Second Language Teaching and Curriculum Center: University of Hawai'i Press, 29-46.

Warschauer, M., 1996b. 'Computer-assisted language learning: An introduction', in: S. Fotos, ed. *Multimedia language teaching*. Tokyo: Logos International, 3-20. Retrieved 30 July 2003 from http://www.gse.uci.edu/markw/call.html

Warschauer, M., 1996c. Comparing face-to-face and electronic discussion in the second language classroom. *CALICO Journal*, 13, 2, 7-26.

Warschauer, M., 1997. Computer-mediated collaborative learning: Theory and practice. *Modern Language Journal*, 81, 4, 470-81. Retrieved 30 July 2003 from http://www.gse.uci.edu/markw/cmcl.html

Warschauer, M., 1998a. Online learning in sociocultural context. *Anthropology and Education Quarterly*, 29, 1, 68-88. Retrieved 30 July 2003 from http://www.gse.uci.edu/markw/online.html

Warschauer, M., 1998b. 'Interaction, negotiation, and computer-mediated learning', in: M. Clay, ed. *Practical Applications of Educational Technology in*

Language Learning. Lyon, France: National Institute of Applied Sciences. Retrieved 30 July 2003 from http://www.insa-lyon.fr/Departements/CDRL/interaction.html

Warschauer, M., 1999. *Electronic Literacies: Language, Culture, and Power in Online Education*. Mahwah, NJ: Lawrence Erlbaum Associates.

Warschauer M., 2000a. 'On-line learning in second language classrooms: an ethnographic study', in: M. Warschauer and R. Kern, eds. *Network-based Language Teaching: Concepts and Practice*. New York: Cambridge University Press, 41-58.

Warschauer, M. and P. Whittaker, 1997. The Internet for English teaching: Guidelines for teachers. *TESL Reporter* 30, 1, 27 -33. Retrieved 30 July 2003 fromhttp://iteslj.org/Articles/Warschauer-Internet.html

Warschauer, M. and D. Healey, 1998. Computers and language learning: An overview. *Language Teaching*, 31, 57-71. Retrieved 30 July 2003 from http://www.gse.uci.edu/markw/overview.html

Warschauer M., and R. Kern, eds., 2000. *Network-based language teaching: Concepts and practice*. New York: Cambridge University Press.

Webb, C., 1963. *The Graduate*. US: World Publishing.

Welsh, I., 1993. *Trainspotting*. London: Martin Secker and Warburg Ltd.

Wessels, C., 1987. *Drama*. Oxford:Oxford University Press.

White, L., 1984. Against comprehensible input: The input hypothesis and the development of second language competence. *Applied Linguistics*, 8, 95-110.

Widdowson, H. G., 1978. *Teaching Language as Communication*. Oxford: Oxford University Press.

Widdowson H. G., 1979a. 'The authenticity of language data', in: H. G. Widdowson, ed. *Explorations in Applied Linguistics*. Oxford: Oxford University Press.

Widdowson, H. G., ed., 1979b. *Explorations in Applied Linguistics*. Oxford: Oxford University Press.

Widdowson, H. G., 1983. *Learning Purpose and Language Use*. Oxford: Oxford University Press.

Widdowson, H. G., 1984. Authentic versus purposeful activities. Address to *Joint Council of Languages Association Conference*, n.p.

Widdowson, H. G., 1998. Context, community and authentic language. *TESOL Quarterly*, 32, 4, 705-16.

Widdowson, H. G., 1990. *Aspects Of Language Teaching*. Oxford: Oxford University Press.

Widdowson, H. G., 2000. On the limitations of linguistics applied. *Applied Linguistics*, 21, 1, 3-25.

Widdowson, H. G., 2001. Interpretations and correlations: A reply to Stubbs. *Applied Linguistics*, 22, 4, 531-38.

Wilkins, D., 1976. *Notional Syllabuses*. Oxford: Oxford University Press.

Willing, K., 1988. *Learning Styles in Adult Migrant Education.* Adelaide: National Curriculum Resource Centre.

Willis, D., 1994. 'A Lexical Approach', in: M. Bygate, A. Tonkyn and E. Williams, eds. *Grammar and The Language Teacher.* Hemel Hempstead: Prentice Hall.

Willis, J., 1996. *A Framework for Task-Based Learning.* Harlow: Addison Wesley Longman Ltd.

Willis, J., 1998. 'Concordances in the classroom without a computer: Assembling and exploiting concordances on common words', in: B. Tomlinson, ed. *Materials Development in Language Teaching.* Cambridge: Cambridge University Press, 44-66.

Wilson, D., 1997. Accessible authenticity: Using Internet resources with school foreign language learners in difficulty. Paper presented at *FLEAT III*, University of Victoria, Victoria, British Columbia, Canada, August 1997.

Winchester, S., 1998. *The Surgeon of Crowthorne*. London: Penguin books.

Windeatt, S., D.Hardisty and D. Eastment, 2000. *The Internet.* Oxford: Oxford University Press.

Wood, D., 1995. Film communication in TEFL. *Video Rising: Newsletter of the Japan Association for Language Teaching.* 1995, 7(1).

Woodlin, J., 1997. Email tandem learning and the communicative curriculum. *ReCALL*, 9, 1, 22-33.

Wright, T. 1987. *Roles of Teachers and Learners.* Oxford: Oxford University Press.

Yano Y., M. Long and S. Ross, 1994. The effects of simplified and elaborated texts on foreign language reading comprehension. *Language Learning*, 44, 2, 198-219.

Yates, J. and Orlikowski, W., 1993. Knee-jerk Anti-LOOPism and other E-mail Phenomena: Oral, Written, and Electronic Patterns in Computer-Mediated Communication. *MIT Sloan School Working Paper #3578-93, Center for Coordination Science Technical Report #150*. Retrieved 29 July 2003 from: http://ccs.mit.edu/papers/CCSWP150.html

Young, D., 1999. Linguistic simplification of SL reading material: Effective instructional practice? *The Modern Languages Journal*, 83, 3, 350-66.

Zeyand, A., 1997. Improving the quality of English language teaching in the state of Kuwait with special reference to the speaking and listening of final year students in secondary education. Ph.D. Thesis, University of Hull, UK.

Index

10 Things I Hate About You 223

ABBA 50
acculturation, newspapers and 161
acronyms, e-mail and 253
acting, as group 111
activities, film and 219
activity, definition xii
actors 50
Adrian Mole: The Cappuccino Years
    101
Adult Migration Education Service 30-
    31
advertisements 63 *see also* advertising
    advertising 182-95
    affect and 184-5
    alcohol 186
    in America 186
    in Britain 186
    classified ads, classroom task 194
    colloquial language 183-4
    culture and 185-8
    currency and 182-5
    European attitudes and 187
    featuring foreigners, classroom
        tasks 191-2
    gender roles 186-7, 192
    high information content,
        classroom task 192-3
    high language content classroom
        tasks 189-90
    internationalism 187-8
    linguistic density 182-3
    literature and 184
    low language content classroom
        task 190
    music and 184-5
    in newspapers 155
    principles for language learning
        188-9
    sex and 187
    TC content classroom tasks 190-91
    on websites 247

affect
    and advertising 184-5
    and language learning 25-9
    and newspapers 160-62
affective filter 27-8
affective responses to literature 105-6
agony column, classroom tasks 175-7
airlines 246
alcohol 56, 186
Alfred, King 3, 10
Allan, M. 132, 135
Allen, R. 136
Allen, Woody 224, 226
Allwright, R. 3
Alptekin, C. 53
American advertising 186
American culture 49
American music 196, 197
Amis, Martin 101
Amitay, E. 247, 249
analytical learners 30, 31, 38
Angela's Ashes 101, 105, 129, 222, 231
Anglo-Saxon 3
Animal Farm 111, 118, 120, 229, 230,
    237
Anna and the King 221
Apollinaire 104
appropriacy of tasks 80-81
armed forces 20
Arnold, J. 16, 27, 40, 55, 61, 73
Ascham, Roger 4, 10
Asher, J. 6, 205
Atkinson, T. 244
attitude, as affective filter 28-9
Auden, W. H. 94, 120
audio tapes 111-12
audiolingual methods of language
    teaching ix, 5
audio-visual media 62, 133
Austen, Jane 111, 222
authentic materials x-xi, 3-6 *see also*
    authenticity, of texts
authentic tasks *see* tasks
authenticity
    approach ix, x-xi
    debate x
    definition 1, 10-11, 18-19

and electronic data 13-14
factors of 18-19
historical background 1-9
language use 15-18
learner autonomy, and 10-11
and pedagogical rationale 44-64
and SLA 21-42
of tasks 62-3, 70-83
of texts 11-15, 17, 18, 41-2, 56, 64, 70
of web language 246-7
authority-oriented learners 31
autonomous learning 7-11, 35-7 ,241, 143, 250-51

background knowledge, as learning resource 63
Bacon, S. 26, 28, 29, 34
Bandler, Richard 7
Bangalore project 83-5
Barnes, Julian 101
Barry's Tea 186
Bartram, M. 51
Bassnet, S. 64, 106, 109
Baym, N. 255
BBC 139, 244
Beatles, The 100, 207, 211
Beckett, Samuel 24, 64, 105, 114
Beier, E. 257
Belisle 254
Bell, J. x, 51, 55
Benson, P. 7, 8, 9, 36, 70, 241
Bhatia, V. 76
Biber, D. 58, 77
Biber model of dimensions 77
Biesenbach-Lucas, S. 253
Bild-Zeitung 155
Bisto 186
Black, Mary 201-2
Bloody Sunday 56
Bluest Eye, The 111
BNC (British National Corpus) 256, 259
Bolitho, R. x, 54
books, and film versions 221-24
Boomtown Rats, The 197, 211
Borges, Jorge Luis 121, 127

bottom up processing 39-41
Bouman, L. 105, 223
Boyzone 197
brain 6, 40-41, 42
Brammerts, H. 250
Brannagh, Kenneth 223
Brazil 49
Breen, M. 11, 16, 74
Bridget Jones Diary 101, 222
British colonies 102-3
British National Corpus (BNC) 256, 259
broadcast media 247 see also radio: television
broadcasting companies 135
Brontë sisters 222
Brown, D. 27, 40, 55, 61, 76, 218
Brown corpus 259
Brumfit, C. 3, 76, 83, 98, 203
Bryson, B. 186
Budweiser 184
Bulmers cider 185
Butcher Boy, The 224, 226, 231
Butler, I. 99
Buttjes, D. 46, 73
Bygate, M. 68
Byram, M. 46, 48, 74
Byrd, P. x

Cadbury 187
Cadierno, T. 32, 35, 40
Cambridge International Corpus 256
campfire songs 205
Campion 224
Candlin, C. 58, 74, 98, 108
canonical literature 24
Carlsberg 183
Carrell, P. 47, 48
Carroll, Lewis 125, 129
Carter, R. 5, 23, 38, 57, 98, 99, 100, 105, 108, 203, 260
Casablanca 225, 238
censorship 54
challenge
corpora and 261-2
definition 95
e-mail and 254-5

film and 216-25
and language learning 44-5, 61-4
literature and 109-12
newspapers and 162-3
subject matter and 61
television, and 137-8
web and 249-50
chanting 205-6
character, film and 224-5
Chaucer, Geoffrey 99
children
literature 24
music, and 197-8
song and 204, 210
television, and 138
China 49, 53, 74
Chomsky, N. 2, 3, 55, 261
choral reading 111
Cicero 4
Circle of Friends 120, 229, 237
Clarke, D. 17, 18, 71, 80
classroom tasks
advertisements featuring
foreigners 191-2
advertisements with gender roles
192
advertisements with high
information content 192-3
advertisements with high language
content 189-90
advertisements with low language
content 190
advertisements with TC content
190-91
agony column 175-7
children's songs 210
classic film 237-8
classified ads 194
concordances 276-80
culture-specific film scene 233
documentaries 144-6
dramatic film 232
enigmatic advertising 192-3
events, news items 167-68
evocative songs 209-10
external e-mail 270-76
film adaptations 119-20

film of book 236-7
film dialogue 228, 233-4
film, opening sequence 232
film remake 237
film with subtitles 234-5
film trailers 238
food or drink advertising 193
gender roles in novels 117
general songs 207-9
human interest news items 168-70
internal e-mail 270-76
language learning web sites 265
letters to editor 173-5
music 212
music video 213
names of newspapers 164-5
news bulletins 140-43
news interviews 144
news item opinions 171-2
news items 143-4, 167-72
newspaper features 173
newspaper headlines 165-6
newspapers multiple reporting
172-3
newspaper photos 166-7
online commerce 267-8
online literature 265-6
online newspapers 165-6, 179
online screenplays 267
online TC information 267
poems 120-29
promotional literature 194
radio current affairs 150
radio phone in 150-51
radio programme scheduling
152
radio station surfing 151-2
radio trailers 151
reports 170-71
sections of novels 113-17
sections of stories 113-17
social film 233
song 207-12
songs with storyline 211-12
sound effects 212-13
spam e-mail 275
star interviews 148-9

subtitled film 234-5
TC film scene with foreigners 234
TC news item 143-4, 172
television fiction 146-8
television programme scheduling 152
television station surfing 151-2
themed songs 211
traditional songs 210-11
weather forecasts 149-50
whole film 228-32
whole newspapers 177-9
whole novels 118-19
whole TC film 230-32
classroom, as learning environment 16-18
closure oriented learners 30
CLT (Communicative Language Teaching) 1, 11, 13 *see also* communicative approach
Clueless 219
CNN 244
COBUILD 58, 256, 257, 259
Coca-Cola 183
coca-colarisation 249
coda 159
collectivist cultures 53, 74
Collie, J. 98, 107, 109
Collins COBUILD 58, 256, 257, 259
colloquial language 57, 58, 99, 104-5, 183-4, 203
Comenius 6
Commitments, The 99, 120, 222, 226, 231
communication, and literature 108
communications revolution 241
communicative approaches, to language learning 1-3, 53-5, 69-70, 74, 83, 88-9
Communicative Language Teaching (CLT) 1, 11, 13
communicative learners 31
communicative purpose 75-80
comprehensibility 22-4, 60
comprehension, and poetry 106
computers 132 *see also* e-mail; Internet; Web

Conacher, J. E. 242, 244
concordances
    accessibility 261-2
    classroom tasks 276-80
    corpora and 256-64
    language learning and 256-60
concrete-sequential learning 30, 31
consciousness raising approaches 37-8
content of learning 36
content-based approach to film 218-19
context 63
Cook, G. x, 68, 98, 99, 104, 108, 182, 184, 204, 263
copywriting 183, 184
Corder, S. Pit 25
corpora
    challenge and 261-2
    concordancing and 256-64
    culture 263-4
    currency and 260
    definition 256
    language learning and 256-60
    uses of 257-8
corpus *see* corpora
corpus linguistics 57
Corrs, The 197
coursebook, ELT as genre 44-5, 51-4, 55-6, 59-60
coursebooks 12, 70, 201 *see also* coursebook, ELT as genre
Crandall, J. 63
crossheads, of newspapers 159-60
Crystal, David 14, 49, 56, 242, 246, 247, 248, 253
Cukor 223
cultural awareness 46
cultural products xii, 247
culture
    advertising and 185-8
    corpora and 263-4
    definition 95-6
    e-mail and 254
    film and 225-7
    and language learning 44-54, 82
    literature and 100-104
    newspapers and 154-6
    song and 196-7

television, and 135-6
web and 247-9
cummings, e.e. 99, 104, 126
Cunningham, G. 51
currency
    advertising and 182-5
    corpora and 260
    definition 95-6
    e-mail and 252-4
    and language learning 44-5, 55-60
    and literature 104-9
    newspapers and 156-62
    song and 197-204
    television, and 136-7
    web and 245-7
cybertrail 243-4

Dahl, Roald 110, 128, 129
Daily Mirror 160
Daly 249, 252
Dancing at Lughnasa 223
Data Driven Learning (DDL) 17-18,
    257, 258, 259, 260, 261-2
Davies, A. 70
DDL (Data Driven Learning) 17-18,
    257, 258, 259, 260, 261-2
de Andrés, V. 61
de Burgh, Chris 203, 209
de Montaigne, Michel 2, 10, 19
de Villiers, J. 38
Dead, The 120, 222, 223, 224
Dead Poets Society 106, 224, 229
de-authentication 13
deductive reasoning, DDL and 261-2
Deep Blue Something 203
Defoe, Daniel 102
Dendrinos, B. 51
Devitt S. 25, 63
Dewey, John 35
dialogue
    classroom tasks 228
    of film 218-19
diaspora 186, 248
Dickens, Charles 99, 100
Dire Straits 203
direct method 5
discourse type, definition xii

discovery learning 35
discussion lists 251
Disney, Walt 223
documentaries, classroom tasks on
    144-6
Dolmio Pasta 187
Donnas, The 211
Dörnyei, Z. 26
double translation method 4
Douglas, Norman 185
Doyle, Roddy 48, 56, 99, 101, 105, 111,
    113, 114, 116, 118, 222, 223
du Maurier, Daphne 107-8, 115
Dublin City Ramblers 202
Duff, A. 75, 76, 77, 98, 106
Duffy, Carol Ann 121, 127
durability of learning 35
Durant, M. 111
Dylan, Bob 203, 211

Eastment, D. 243, 245
Eayrs, M. 247
Eckstut, S. 71
Edmonson, W. 47
Educating Rita 223
Edward Scissorhands 229
e.e. cummings 99, 104, 110
Egg Marketing Board 183
EGI (Explicit Grammar Instruction)
    32-5
Egyptian empire 2
Ehrman, M. 32
Eisterhold, J. 47, 48
electronic data, and authenticity 13-14
electronic literacy 241
electronic mail *see* e-mail
Eliot, T. S. 45
Ellis, R. 21, 22, 25-6, 27, 28, 32, 33, 34,
    35, 37-8, 55, 59, 60, 68, 198
ELT (English Language Teaching) x,
    xi, xii, 3, 5
ELT coursebooks, as genre 44-5, 51-4,
    55-6, 59-60
e-mail
    acronyms 253
    authenticity of material 14, 18, 73
    challenge 254-5

culture 254
currency and 56, 252-4
external, classroom tasks 269-70
graphological features 253
interactiveness 252-3, 255
internal, classroom tasks 270-76
intercultural 251
language learning and 242, 250-52
learner autonomy and 250-51
motivation 254
orality 252, 255
register 252
E-mail: a love story 99
Emma 222, 237
emotions 77
empathy 28, 46
enabling skills 92
End of the Affair, The 120, 237
engagement 28, 80-81
English
    as international language 49-51
    as second language 49
English for Specific Purposes (ESP)
    13
English language, and web 248-9
English language culture, diagram 50
English Language Teaching x, xi, xii,
    3, 5
English Patient, The 222
English Speaking Union framework
    285-6
English-1 251
enjoyment, and learning 108-9, 216-18
entertainment media, and learning
    132-5
Esch, E. 8
ESP (English for Specific Purposes)
    13
European attitudes advertising and
187
Examiner, The 155
existing knowledge 82
experience, and learning 73
Explicit Grammar Instruction (EGI)
    32-5
extrinsic motivation 26
extroversion, and learning style 30, 31

Eyre, Jane 222

factors of authenticity 18-19
Fado 196
fairy tales 103
Falklands 49
Far and Away 226
Father Christmas 48-9
Fernandez-Toro, M. 9
Fiat 183
Field, The 223
Fielding, Helen 101, 222
film
    activities 219
    of book, classroom tasks 236-7
    books and 221-24
    challenge and 216-25
    character and 224-5
    chunking 220
    classic, classroom tasks 237-8
    classroom tasks on adaptations 119-
    20
    colloquial speech 99
    and comprehension 225
    content-based approach 218-19
    culture and 225-7
    culture specific, classroom tasks
    233
    dialogue 218-19
    dialogue, classroom tasks 233-4
    discussion after viewing 220
    dramatic, classroom tasks 232
    image-sound skim 217, 220
    introducing literature to pupils
        111-12
    as multi-sensory event 218-19
    versus novel 221-23
    opening sequence, classroom tasks
    232
    plays and 223
    principles for language learning
    227
    remake, classroom tasks 236-7
    remakes 220-21
    short 138
    silent 224
    social, classroom tasks 233

subtitled, classroom tasks 234-5
TC, classroom tasks 234
trailers, classroom task 238
universality of 225
viewing environment 217
visual aid, as 223-4
watching whole 219-20
websites 247
whole, classroom tasks 228-32
filter, affective 27-8
Finnegan's Wake 99
Finneman, M. 26, 28, 29, 34
Finocchairo, M. 76
First National Bank of Chicago 182
Fisk, Robert 100
FL, definition xii
Fletcher, S. 99
Flynn, N. 253
Flynn, T. 253
food advertising 186, 193
Ford 226
formal instruction 35, 36
Forster, E. M. 101, 103, 116
Four Weddings and a Funeral 225, 231
Fouser, R. 249, 252
Fox, G. 38
Frankenstein 229
Fraser, R. 184
Frears 222, 226
Freeman, C. 110
Full Monty, The 231

Gains, J. 252, 253
Galtee Bacon 186
Gardner, R. 26
Garfunkel, Art 211
Gattegno, C. 6
Gazzetta dello Sport 155
Geddes, M. 71
gender roles, advertising and 186
genre, definition xii
Germany 251
Gershwin, George 57
get, passive 57-8
Gilbert 223
Gilroy, M. 97, 98
Gimenez, J. 249

gist-listening, and the radio 138-9
global learners 30
global village 50
globalisation, Web and 248-9
Goddard, A. 53, 184, 186, 188
Golding, William 111, 118
Gone with the Wind 238
Gonzalez, A. 54
Goodale, M. 261
Google 250, 259
Gousseva, J. 251, 254
Gower, R. x, 51, 55
Graddol, D. 49
grading tasks 62-4
Graduate, The 113
grammar 32-5, 59-60, 262
grammar instruction 32-5
graphological features, e-mail and 253
Gray, J. 52
Great Expectations 236
Greek 6
Greene, Graham 101, 115, 116
Grellet, F. 13, 62, 71, 73, 75, 80
Griffee, D. 197, 203
Grinder, John 7
group acting 111
group singing 199-200
Grundy, P. 62, 64, 106, 109, 156, 161
Guardian, The 155, 244
Guarientio, W. 62, 63, 70, 71, 72, 74
Guillot, M. 10
Guinness 184, 188
Guiora, A. 28
Guthrie, Arlo 197

Häagen-Dazs 187
Hadley, G. 260, 261, 262
Haig Scotch 182
Haiku 104
Hale, C. 252, 253
Halliwell's Film & TV Guide 228
Hallström 222
Hamlet 223, 237
Hamlet cigars 185
Harben, P. 39
Harmer, J. 28
Harrods 52

Harry Potter books and films 222, 224, 229
Hartely, J. P. 101
headlines, of newspapers 157-8, 163, 165-6
Heaney, Seamus 106, 124, 127
hearing 197-8
Heineken 183
Hemingway, Ernest 24, 64
Henriquez, J. 247
Hitchcock, Alfred 221
Hoey, M. 261
Holliday, A. 54
Hollies, The 203
home pages on Web 247
Honda 52
Hong Kong 49
Hong Kong Virtual Language Centre 259
Hopkins, D. 25
Hopkins, G. M. 124, 130
horse-racing, newspapers and 155
Howard 226
Howatt, A.P.R. 3, 4, 5
Hughes, G. x, 16, 19
humanistic approaches, to language learning 6-10, 40
Hutchinson, T. 13, 51
Huy Lê, M. 200, 206
Hymes, D. 3
hypertext medium 248

$i+1$ formula 22, 24, 25, 35, 60
ICT (Information and Communications Technology) ix, xiii,1, 10, 11, 19, 241-2
image-sound skim, film and 217, 220
imperialist attitudes 102-3
India 49, 50, 102, 103
Indian culture 49
Indonesia 49
inductive reasoning, DDL and 261-2
Information and Communications Technology (ICT) ix, xiii, 1, 10, 11, 19, 241-2
information gap 133
input 22-5, 38-41, 70, 198-9

instructed SLA 32-5
instruction, definition 32
instrumental motivation 26
intake 22
integrative motivation 26, 55
intention 71
interactional function of language 76, 77
interactional modifications 23-4
interactivity, e-mail and 252-3, 255
intercultural e-mail, classroom connections 251
interest 27
interlanguage 33, 34
International Certificate Conference 241, 246
International E-Mail Tandem Network 251
International Express series of coursebooks 52
internationalism, advertising and 187-8
Internet *see also* Web
    coursebooks and 57, 58
    language teaching and 57, 58, 242, 246-7
    news and 156
    song and 203-4
    text authenticity and 14, 17, 18, 56, 64, 70
Internet TESL Journal 245
interviews 134, 136-7
intrinsic motivation 26, 55
introversion, and learning style 30, 31
intuitive-random learning 30
Ireland 186, 226
Irish culture, in film 226
Irish Field, The 155
Irish language learning 31
Irish literature 101
Irish Lotto 183
Irish music 197
Irish Times, The 155
Iser, Wolfgang 97
Ishiguro, Kazuo 115

Jaffa Cakes 187

Jaguar 182, 187
James, Henry 224
Japan 31, 48-9, 53, 74, 262
jazz chants 205-6
Joag-dev, C. 49, 104
Johns, Tim 257, 260, 261
Johnson, K. 3, 83
Jolly, D. x, 54
Jones, F. 249
Jones, S. 9
Jordan, Neil 224, 226
Joseph, Jenny 121
journalese 157
Joyce, James 99, 100, 111, 113, 222, 223
Junger 223

Keane, John B. 101
Keats, John 104
Kellogg's 184
Kelly, L. 1, 10
Kenco 187
Kerrygold 187
Kershaw, G. 5
Key Word In Context (KWIC) 256, 257, 258
King and I, The 221
Kitkat 182
Knopfler, Mark 209
Korea 53, 74
Kramsch, C. 12, 14, 16, 19, 46, 98, 103, 247
Krashen, S. 21, 22, 23, 24-5, 27-8, 32, 35, 36, 60, 107, 198
Kress, G. 76
Kuwait 53
KWIC (Key Word In Context) 256, 257, 258

L1, definition xiii
L2, definition xiii
Labov, William 159
Lacey, R. 217
Lambert, W. 26
Lamy, M-N. 245
language
  acquisition 25, 37-8

authenticity of use 15-18
corpus 14
and culture 44-54
and currency 56-7
learning *see* language learning
pedagogy, and ICT 241-2
processing 38-41
teaching ix, 200-204
Language for Specific Purposes (LSP) xiii, 72
language learning
  affect 25-9
  as authentic activity ix
  behaviour 17-18
  challenge 44-5, 61-4
  communicative approaches 1-3, 53-5, 69-70, 74, 83, 88-9
  concordances and 256-60
  corpora and 256-60
  culture and 44-54, 82
  humanistic approaches 6-10, 40
  materials focused approaches 3-6
  principles *see* principles for language learning
  process 36
  and task ix, 41
Larsen-Freeman, D. 21, 22, 28, 29, 32, 33, 34, 35
Latham-Koenig, C. 200
Latin 3-4, 6, 10, 19
Lazar, G. 98, 99, 109, 110
Le Carré, John 158
Lear, Edward 129
learner autonomy 7-8, 9-10, 35-7, 241, 243, 250-51
learner centredness 17, 70
learners *see* learning style
learning 36, 73, 108-9, 216-18 *see also* language learning; learning styles; principles of language learning
learning styles 8, 29-32, 54, 111
Leavis, F. R. 97, 100
Lee, W. Y. 12, 16, 17
left brain 6, 40
legends 103
Legenhausen 37
Leigh, Mike 226, 227

Leloup, J. 60
Leow, R. 22, 23
letters to editor, classroom tasks
    173-5
Lightbrown, P. 21, 22, 38
lingua franca 26, 49-50, 52
Lion King, The 223
listening, radio, and 139
Liszt 251
literary language 57, 98, 99, 203
literature
    advertising and 184
    affective responses 105-6
    canonical 24
    children's 24
    challenge and 109-12
    creative responses 108
    culture and 100-104
    and currency 104-9
    definition 97-100
    engagement and 28
    and language learning 97
    principles for language learning
    112-13
    websites 247
Little, D. 8, 9, 10, 12, 25, 26, 27, 28,
    31, 32, 33, 34, 36, 37, 243, 250,
    251, 255
Little Red Riding Hood 103-4, 109
Little Voice 231
Littlewood, W. 83
LOB corpus 259
Local Hero 231
Lodge, David 115
Long, Michael 21, 22, 28, 29, 32, 33,
    34, 35, 60, 107, 108
Longman dictionaries 58, 59
Looking for Richard 223
Lord of the Flies, The 111, 118
Lotto 183
Lozanov, G. 6
LSP (Language for Specific
    Purposes) xiii, 72
Lubelska, D. 72
Luhrmann 221

Macaulay, Lord 102

Macdonald's 185
Macrae, Lindsay 103, 127
macro-skills 92
Maess, B. 198
Magdalene Sisters, The 226
Maguire 222
Maley, A. 47, 52, 75, 76, 77, 86-8, 89-
    90, 98, 106, 124
Mandarin Chinese 49
Manhattan 226
Manley Hopkins, Gerald 123, 124
Merino, A. 219
Mars 184
Massi, M. 219
material, definition xiii
materials design ix-x
materials focused approaches, to
language learning 3-6
Maughan, Somerset 115
Mauritius 49
McCarthy, M. 57, 58, 99, 226
McCourt, Frank 101, 105, 114, 222
McEwan, Ian 101
McGarry, D. 9, 37, 93
McGough, Roger 64, 110, 126
McGrath, I. X, xii, 61, 67, 71
McKay, S. 107
McLean, Don 200, 201
McRae, J. 64, 105, 108, 109
McTell, Ralph 211
media, and learning styles 31-2
medium, definition xiii
Melles, G. 74
melody 199 *see also* song
micro-skills 92
Middle Ages 3-4
Milk Marketing Board 183
Miller, D. 257
Mills, Magnus 105
Milne, A. A. 128
Minghella 222
Mishan, Freda 244
Modiano, M. 50
Mohamed, S. 51
Monde, Le 154
MonoConc 256
Morgan, Edwin 107

Morley, J. 62, 63, 70, 71, 72, 74
Morrison, Toni 111
Morrow, K. 11, 13, 14, 70
motivation 25-7, 55, 161, 254
Müller Rice 187
multi-culturalism 101-2
multiple news reporting, classroom
    tasks 172-3
Murison-Bowie, S. 261, 262
Murphey, T. 196, 198, 199, 200, 203
Murphy's stout 185, 187
Murray 247
music
    advertising and 184-5
    American 196, 197
    classroom tasks 212
    human experience and 196
    industry 196
    Irish 197
    processing in brain 198
    video, classroom tasks 213
musicals 223
Muslim culture 56
My Fair Lady 223, 237

natural grading 63-4
Nelson, G. 53, 74
Nessun Dorma 248
Nettle, M. 25
Neuro-Linguistic Programming
    (NLP) 6, 7, 40, 205
new language 57, 58
New Method, 1950s 5
Newell 225
news 133, 137-8, 244
news bulletins, classroom tasks
    140-43
news interviews, classroom tasks
    144
news items, classroom tasks 143-4,
    167-72, 171-2
news reports, classroom tasks 170-71
newspapers
    advertising 155
    affect and 160-62
    agony column 175-7
    challenge and 162-3

classroom tasks 164-79
collocation 160
crossheads 159-60
culture and 154-6
currency, and 156-62
headlines 157-8, 165-6
horse-racing and 155
language 157-60
layout 155
motivation 161
multiple foci 154
names of, classroom tasks 164-5
online 156-7
personal relevance 161
photos 163, 166-7
principles for language learning
    163-4
sport, and 155
tabloid 155, 156
and task authenticity 62
websites 247
Ngugi wa Thiong'o 102
Nigeria 49
Nike 183
NLP (Neuro-Linguistic
    Programming) 6, 7, 40, 205
NNS, definition xiii
non-comprehension, song and 204-6
non-verbal communication 224
Norman 7
Nostrand, H. 12
novels 111, 113-19, 221-3
NS, definition xiii
Nunan, D. 8, 9, 21, 23, 39, 48, 67, 69,
    70, 71, 73, 75, 93
nursery rhymes 204

O'Connor, 223
O'Dell, F. 51, 58
Old English 3
Old Man and the Sea, The 24, 64, 111
Oliver Twist 222
Olivier, Laurence 223
online commerce, classroom tasks
    267-8
online literature, classroom tasks
    265-6

online news 244
online newspapers 156-7, 165-6, 179
online screenplays classroom tasks 267
online TC information, classroom tasks 267
open learners 30
opera 198, 204
oral method 5
orality, of e-mail 252, 255
Orange 188
original context 13
Orlikowski, W. 252
Orwell, George 111, 118
outcome 68
Owen, C. 260
Oxenden, C. 200
Oxford, R. 25, 27, 29, 30, 32, 61, 262

pace of learning 36
Pacino, Al 223
Paddy Clarke Ha Ha Ha 48, 111, 113, 118
Pakistan 50
Passage to India, A 103, 116, 236
paralinguistic features, e-mail and 253
Parker 222
Parkinson, B. 97, 98
Patten, Brian 110, 127
Peacock, M. 26, 29
pedagogical context, as authentic 16-18
pedagogical rationale, and language learning 44-64
pedagogic tasks, authenticity of 70-71
Pellettieri, J. 255
Pennycook, A. 9
Phantom of the Opera, The 229-30
Philadelphia Cream Cheese 187
Phillipson, R. 49, 102
phone-ins, classroom tasks 150-51
photos, in newspapers 163
physical senses, and learning style 29-30
Picken, J. 182, 185

Pienemann, M. 33, 60
Pink Floyd 197, 211
Pinter, Harold 105, 110
Pitcairn Island 49
plays 110-11, 223
poems 80, 120-29 *see also* poetry
poetry 104, 106, 107, 109-10 *see also* poems
Pollack, Sidney 221
Pontiero, R. 60
pop groups 50
Portrait of a Lady, The 224
Portrait of the Artist as a Young Man, A 111, 113, 222, 237
Prabhu, N. S. 16, 67, 68, 69, 83, 84-5, 88, 89-90
Presentation, Production, Practice 38, 59
Presley, Elvis 211
press *see* newspapers
Pride and Prejudice 111, 120, 222, 237, 238
principles for language learning
    advertising and 188-9
    film 227
    literature 112-13
    newspapers 163-4
    radio 140
    song 206
    television 140
process of language learning 36
Prodromou, L. 51, 53
proficiency, ultimate 35
promotional literature, classroom task 194
pronunciation, song and 203
protest songs 197, 199
Prowse, P. 51
psycholinguistics 48-9
Psycho 221, 237
Puccini 248
Pugh, A. 3
Pulverness, A. x, 4, 51, 52, 105, 222, 225
punk rock 196
Purple Rose of Cairo, The 224, 229
Pygmalion 223, 237

Quiet Man, The 226
Quillian, M. 47

Racing Post 155
radio
    as broadcast medium 132, 138
    current affairs, classroom tasks
    150
    excerpt length 134-5
    fiction, classroom tasks 146-8
    genres of programmes 137, 139
    listening, and 138-9
    phone-ins 139, 150-51
    principles for language learning
    140
    programme scheduling, classroom
    tasks 152
    station surfing, classroom tasks
    151-2
    trailers, classroom tasks 151
Raine, Craig 123, 126
Raja, M. 54
Rebecca 107-8, 115
reader response theory 97
Reah 154, 159, 160
real life tasks 81-2
register, definition xiii
rehearsal approach 72
remakes, film 220-21
Remains of the Day, The 115, 120, 237
repetition in music 198
response 71, 80-81
Revell, J. 7
Rézeau 256, 260
rhythm 104
Richard III 223
right brain 6, 40
Rinvolucri, M. x, 40, 51, 55, 58
risk taking 61, 73
Robinson Crusoe 102
Robbins 223
Rolling Stones, The 203
Roman Empire 2
Romeo and Juliet 221, 223, 237
Ronaldson, A. 108
Rossetti, Christina 124

Rossner, R. 51
Rowling, J. K. 222, 224
Royall 242, 244
RTÉ Radio 1 139

Sabrina 237
Sabrina Fair 221, 237
Sanderson 157, 158, 159
Sapir, E. 45
Sapir-Whorf hypothesis 45-6
Scanlon, J. 252, 253
schema theory 47-9
schemata *see* schema theory
Schonell, F. 257
search engines 250, 259
Second Language Acquisition (SLA)
    xiii, 21-41
Secrets and Lies 226, 227, 231
Seeger, Pete 197
self-access structures 8
Selinker, L. 33
Sense and Sensibility 120, 222, 237
sex, advertising and 187
Seychelles 49
SGML (Standard Generalised
    Markup Language) 256
Shakespeare 99, 100, 222, 223, 248
Shanahan, D. 12, 28, 108
Sharwood Smith, M. 25, 32, 33
Shaw, G. B. 223
Shearin, J. 25, 27
Sheridan 223
Shetzer 241, 247
Shilts, Randy 160
Shipping News, The 222
Short, M. 98, 108
short stories 110-111
Sianos 196
Silent Way, The 6-7
Silk Cut 185
Simon, Paul 211
simplification 23-4
Sinclair, B. 51
Singapore 49
Singleton 31, 32
situational approach 5
Skehan, P. 30, 31, 68, 69

Sky News 245
SLA (Second Language Acquisition)
  xiii, 21-41
Slater, S. 98, 107, 109
SL-Lists 251
slogans 182-3, 188
Smith, Stevie 124
Snapper, The 56, 94, 99, 120, 222, 223,
  226, 231, 237
soap operas 134, 136, 138
socio-cultural context 12-13, 29
song
    campfire songs 205
    challenge and 204-6
    classroom tasks 207-12
    culture and 196-7
    currency, and 197-204
    engagement and 80
    evocative power 199
    gapping system 201-2
    grammatical structure 200
    language of 200-4
    language learning and 204-6
    language teaching, and 200-4
    learning 199
    motivation 200
    non-comprehension and 204-6
    principles for language learning
    206
    pronunciation and 203
    stories in 200
    storyline, classroom tasks 211-12
    themes 197, 211
    traditional, classroom tasks 210-1
    on the Web 247
sound bites 134
sound effects, classroom tasks 212-13
South Africa 49
South China Morning Post, The 259
Spada, N. 38
spam, classroom tasks 275
speaker's competence 2
speaker's performance 3
speech rate 23
Sperling, Dave 245
sport, newspapers and 155
Springsteen, Bruce 209

Sri Lanka 49
St Helena 49
Standard Generalised Markup
Language (SGML) 256
star interviews, classroom tasks 148-9
Starkweather, J. 257
Steffensen, M. 49, 104
Steinbeck, John 71
Stempleski, S. 46, 55, 82, 132, 136,
  216, 217, 224, 225
Stevens 260, 262
Stokes 50
Structural-Oral-Situational method 69
Style Analysis Survey 29
stylistic comfort zone 32
subject matter
    and challenge 61
    of coursebooks 54
Suggestopedia 6, 40, 198
Sumerians 2
Summerfield 217
Sun, The 155, 160
Sunday Sport, The 155
suspense 73
Swaffar, J. 12, 23, 24, 26, 28, 40
Swales, J. 76
Swain, M. 73
Sweet, Henry 4-5, 57, 60, 109, 110
Swift, Graham 105, 110, 114, 115, 116

tabloid press 155-7, 160
tabloidese 157, 158
taboos 55-6
tagging systems 256
Taming of the Shrew, The 223
tandem learning 250-51
task
    analysis of 68-9
    appropriacy 62-3, 80-81
    authentication 71
    authenticity 62-3, 70-83
    and challenge 61
    communicative purposes
    guidelines 75-83
    components of 69-70
    consistency 75-80
    definition xiii, 67-8

grading 62-3
inappropriateness 81
and language learning ix, 41
as model 67-70
pedagogic 70-71
real life 81-2
real world 70-71
stages of 68-9
typologies 67, 83-93
Taylor, D. 11, 16, 18, 19
TC, definition xiii
TC news items, classroom tasks 143-4, 172
teachability 33-4
teacher roles 69-70
teachers, and learner autonomy 7-10
technology, and learner autonomy 241, 243
television
    advertising see advertising
    challenge and 137-8
    children, and 138
    colloquial language 58
    communicative purposes, and 133
    culture, and 135-6
    currency, and 136-7
    documentaries, classroom tasks 144-6
    entertainment 134
    excerpt length 134-5
    fiction, classroom tasks 146-8
    genres 134, 136
    interactivity 133
    as learning medium 132-5
    news 133, 137-8
    principles for language learning 140
    programme scheduling, classroom tasks 152
    station surfing, classroom tasks 151-2
    and texts 62-3
Tennant 221
terminology defined xii-xiii
Terrell, T. 22, 25, 32, 33, 34, 35
Terry's Chocolate Orange 187
text, definition xiii

text driven syllabus 59-60
text messaging 57
texts, authenticity 11-15, 17, 18, 56, 64, 70
themes in songs 197, 211
Thomas Crown Affair, The 221, 237
Thomas, Dylan 127
Thornbury, S. 55
Threadgold, T. 76
Thurstun, J. 58
Times, The 154
Times Higher Educational Supplement 244
Titone, R. 2, 4, 6
TL, definition xiii
Toh, G. 54
Tomalin, B. 46, 55, 82, 132, 136, 138, 216, 217, 218, 221, 224, 225
Tomlinson, B. x, xii, 24, 30, 32, 38, 40, 51, 53, 54, 55, 57, 59, 61, 64, 107, 110, 111
top down processing (TPR) 39-41
Total Physical Response 6, 40, 205
Townsend, Sue 101, 114, 116
Top Down Processing (TPR) 39-41
TPR (Top Down Processing) 39-41
traditional song, classroom tasks 210-1
Trainspotting 99, 101
transactional function of language 76, 77
transculturalism 103-4, 137
Trinity College Dublin 31
Trudgill, P. 49
Trywhitt-Drake, H. 260
Tudor, I. 17, 29, 30, 31, 70
TV see television
typologies, task 83-93

Ulysses 222
Underwood, M. 218
Ushioda 251, 255

Valdes, J. 5
Van Lier, L. 16, 17, 25, 70, 71
van Sant, Gus 221
Van, The 222
Vanpatten, B. 32, 35, 40

Vega, Susanne 211
video 62, 133
Vietnam 200
Vincent, M. 5, 23
vocabulary 37, 216-17
Vogel, A. 40, 241, 246, 247
Volvo 52, 183, 188

Wajnryb, R. 56
Waiting for Godot 24, 64, 110
Waking Ned Devine 216
Waller, Fats 203
Walton, R. 51
Warschauer, M. 61, 241, 246, 247, 250,
    251, 254
Washington Square 224
Waters, A. 13
Weasenforth, D. 253
weather forecasts 64, 133, 137, 149-50
Web *see also* Internet
    authenticity and 14, 18
    challenge 249-50
    culture 247-9
    currency and 245-7
    English language and 248-9
    language and authenticity 246-7
    language learning and 14, 242-5,
    265
    language teaching and 241-2
    as medium 244-5
    as news medium 244
    as resource 242-4
    and texts 64
    transnationalism 248-9
Webb, Charles 113
Webster, Mirriam 57
Weir, Peter 106, 224
Welsh, Irvine 99, 101
West Side Story 223
Western festivals 74
western work culture 53
Westlife 197
white middle class 51
White, L. 22
Whittaker 246
whole brain 6, 40-41, 42
whole film, classroom tasks 228-32

Whorf 45
Widdowson, H. G. x, 10, 13, 14, 15, 19,
    21, 70, 71, 73
Wilde, Oscar 115
Wilder, Billy 221
Wilkins, D. 76, 80
Willing, K. 29, 30-31
Willis, J. 24, 67, 68-9, 70, 74, 85, 88-90
Wilson, D. 17
Winchester, Simon 102
Windeatt, S. 244, 250
Wise 223
Woman who Walking into Doors, The
    101
Wood 218, 224
Woodlin, J. 251
Wordsmith Tools 256
workspaces 251-2
Wright, T. 9
Wuthering Heights 222

Yahoo 252
Yano, Y. M. 23
Yates, J. 252
Yeats, W. B. 125, 127
Young, D. 23, 24

Zeffirelli 221, 223
Zeyand, A. 53, 54